THE STRONG DELUSION

THE STRONG DELUSION

INVASION OF AN OTHERWORLDLY ISLAM

John W. Milor

THE STRONG DELUSION
INVASION OF AN OTHERWORLDLY ISLAM

iUniverse books may be ordered through booksellers or by contacting:

iUniverse
1663 Liberty Drive
Bloomington, IN 47403
www.iuniverse.com
1-800-Authors (1-800-288-4677)

ISBN: 978-1-5320-1444-4 (sc)
ISBN: 978-1-5320-1445-1 (e)

Library of Congress Control Number: 2017901977

Print information available on the last page.

iUniverse rev. date: 09/11/2017

To my great-grandmother Thelma. She planted my first seeds of faith; to that I owe her eternally.

Unknown to her, she also bestowed on me a mantle to reconcile my faith with the existence of extraterrestrial life. In so doing, after twenty years of searching, I believe I have discovered the nature of the *strong delusion* of 2 Thessalonians 2:11

To my great-grandmother Thelma who planted my first seeds of faith that flowered eventually.

Unknown to her, she has bestowed on me a miracle to reconcile my faith with the existence of extraterrestrial life. In so doing, after twenty years of searching, I believe I have discovered the nature of the *strong delusion* of 2 Thessalonians 2:11.

CONTENTS

LIST OF TABLES

INTRODUCTION

The Bible speaks of a deception that will overshadow the world in the last days. This *strong delusion* is spoken of in 2 Thessalonians 2:3–12.

Note: All the Bible verses in this book are from the English Standard Version (ESV), unless otherwise stated. For the sake of brevity, many scripture references are not quoted, so I recommend reading this book along with a Bible translation of your choice for a more in-depth study of the material.[1]

> **2 Thessalonians 2:3–12** [bold emphasis and bracketed comments added]
> Let no one deceive you in any way. For that day will not come, unless the rebellion comes first, and **the man of lawlessness [the Antichrist]** is revealed, the **son of destruction**, opposes and exalts himself against every so-called god or object of worship, so that he takes his seat in the temple of God, proclaiming himself to be God. Do you not remember that when I was still with you I told you these things? And you know what is restraining him now so that he may be revealed in his time. For **the mystery of lawlessness is already at work**. Only he who now restrains it will do so until he is out of the way. And then the lawless one will be revealed, whom the Lord Jesus will kill with the breath of his mouth and bring to nothing by the appearance of his coming. **The coming of**

> **the lawless one is by the activity of Satan with all power and false signs and wonders, and with all wicked deception for those who are perishing, because they refused to love the truth and so be saved**. Therefore God sends them **a strong delusion**, so that they may believe what is false, in order that all may be condemned who did not believe the truth but had pleasure in unrighteousness.

Since my youth, this upcoming deception has both terrified and intrigued me. Jesus stated that it will be so powerful, if it were possible, *it would deceive the very elect* (Matthew 24:24, Mark 13:22).

> **Matthew 24:24**
> For false christs and false prophets will arise and perform great signs and wonders, so as to lead astray, if possible, even the elect.

What deception could have the ability to appeal to every demographic? What deception could draw upon every facet of human wisdom, harmonizing with all the sciences, and simultaneously inspire a sense of spiritual wonder?

Whatever it is, it's big and completely unexpected, and it will force a paradigm shift by all who encounter it. It will court the aspirations of both physicists and theologians, it will unify people from all walks of life, and it will all proceed from a man who will demonstrate the reality of the spiritual realm with such powerful demonstrations that those of divergent faiths will unite and those of no faith will come to believe.

While the world is unprepared for what is coming, at the same time, I venture to speculate that people across the globe can sense we are on the edge of a great precipice. That is most likely why you have picked up this book. Those troublesome echoes in the ether of your mind are calling out to you.

Years ago, not long after I accepted Christ in my early twenties, for reasons I will divulge later in this book, I came to the realization that the strong delusion mentioned above has something to do with extraterrestrial life. To that end, I devoted myself to extensive research for over two decades.

Those familiar with two of my previous books, *Aliens in the Bible* and *Aliens and the Antichrist*, will know that I am a Christian who believes in the existence of extraterrestrial life. I implore you to briefly set aside any conundrum you may have at this point regarding any perceived contradictions in my beliefs. Simply accept the premise that the existence of extraterrestrial life would most likely present the world with an extreme wild tangent that would impose dramatic scientific and spiritual implications on the global community if proven true.

The second element of the strong delusion that I address in this book, which I have never addressed in depth before, involves the religion of the Antichrist. I credit author Joel Richardson's book *The Islamic Antichrist* for opening my eyes to the religion of Islam and inspiring me to write this book. While researching the Qur'an and Hadiths regarding the future return of a Muslim Jesus, I found myself reading about a vision that has haunted my dreams for many years. Everything in this book is the result of that vision.

As a Christian ufologist, I focused almost exclusively on the Bible in the past. In this book, I have expanded my scope to include the book of Enoch, as well as passages from the Qur'an and Hadiths. It turns out that the Qur'an and Hadiths have an inexplicable relationship with the Bible that not only includes a *mirror image* of the End Times prophecy but also discloses a great deal of information about how those End Times events will include extraterrestrial involvement.

The connections that extraterrestrial life and the religion of Islam share with the strong delusion are wide and varied. This book is my best attempt to disclose the information I have discovered regarding the deceptions of the Antichrist and his False Prophet. Recalling the words from 2 Thessalonians on the previous page, where it states,

"Do you not remember that when I was still with you I told you these things?" it is my hope that by illuminating these unbelievable details before they happen, this book will serve the purpose of preserving the elect.

CHAPTER 1

My Great-Grandmother's Encounter

I have been asked many times over the years, "How is it that a person who claims to be a Christian also believes in extraterrestrials?" Those who have read *Aliens in the Bible* might figure it has something to do with my seeing and communicating with a glowing ball of light in the jungle of Panama back in the early 1990s, which I disclose in chapter 1 of that book. However, I actually believed in the existence of extraterrestrials much earlier than that. It all goes back to my great-grandmother.

From my early childhood, I recall the fervent faith of my great-grandparents. From the stories Grandma told and the diary notes she left behind, I learned that when my great-grandfather was born in 1899, his aunt prophesied that he would be a preacher of the word of God. Her prophecy came to pass. He left home with his young bride, and they traveled all over the United States during the Great Depression, spreading the Gospel of Jesus Christ.

My childhood visits to Grandpa and Grandma's house were always accompanied by stories about Daniel in the lion's den, David and Goliath, and other famous biblical accounts. They never missed church; they prayed every day, read their Bible every day, volunteered in various ministries, and dedicated their lives to serving God. If the TV was on, it was an evangelist, and if the radio was playing, it was gospel music. They ate, drank, walked, talked, slept, dreamed, blinked, and breathed Jesus. I have never met anyone in my life so consumed with God as they were.

Grandma had several powerful supernatural encounters in her lifetime, and she had no qualms about sharing these stories with the family. As outlandish as some of her stories were, I still consider her the most reputable source of anyone I know because she was not one to lie.

Her most notable experiences were about the two times Jesus visited her in person. These weren't dreams, or impressions, or some experience in an altered state of consciousness. These visits happened when she was fully conscious, and Jesus literally showed up in bodily form, appearing like a flesh-and-blood human being, except that He was glowing.

The first time she saw Him was when she lived in Oklahoma. She was recovering from a stroke that had nearly killed her. The stroke left her completely paralyzed on the left side of her body. She said she was lying in her hospital bed fully awake during the daytime, and Jesus walked into her room. He was wearing a glowing white robe, and His countenance was brilliant and unspeakably beautiful. He smiled at her, bathing her in a supernatural peace, and instantly she was healed from her paralysis. He then turned and walked out. Later on, the doctors were baffled when she gave her testimony.

While Grandma's stories of Jesus and an angel who saved her life on one occasion were beyond fantastic, in a way, they didn't seem unfitting for those who knew her. As I mentioned, she was utterly consumed with Jesus, so these stories were at least in context with the rest of her life. However, not everything Grandma witnessed in her days fit so nicely within the context of the Christian paradigm most Christians are comfortable with.

Grandma saw a UFO when she was a young girl. Our entire family thought it fascinating to hear such an outlandish story coming from her, of all people. She told this strange story one night at her house when many members of the family were visiting. She was contentedly reading a newspaper article about a wild-goose chase between several police cars and a UFO sighted just outside of the town where we all lived. She spoke up quite suddenly, excited about the article, read it out loud, and then blurted out to everyone's amazement, "When I was a young girl, I saw a UFO."

My interest in UFOs was peaked at the ripe age of five years old when Grandma made this declaration. I didn't know what UFOs were, but whatever they were certainly seemed curious, judging from the dumbfounded looks on everyone's face. It was clear to me that most people thought they did not exist, but if Grandma said she saw one, they had to exist.

Many say UFOs are only a product of this technological age, but I don't consider that a valid fact, knowing my great-grandmother lived in backwoods Kentucky and had never seen an automobile at that time, much less a flying contraption. She said she was very impressed by its polished surface; it was the first thing she ever saw that had a polished alloy surface.

Grandma said it happened one afternoon while she and her sister were walking in the middle of a deserted prairie. They noticed a strange object shaped like a cigar hovering without sound, about twenty feet above the ground. The cylindrical object slowly cruised by, flying right in front of them, less than one hundred yards away. It had a reflective metallic surface like aluminum with a transparent bubble on top. She actually saw a man inside. For those who attribute all UFO activity to top secret government projects, I do not think our military was developing things like this less than twenty years after the Wright brothers made their debut.

There were some bluffs nearby, and when the object reached the bluffs, it went over the cliffs and zipped off at an amazing speed. She said it was gone in the blink of an eye. It made a *zing* sound when it shot like a bullet over the cliffs and out of sight. Grandma even made the sound effect to illustrate her point.

After that, she and her sister rushed home to tell their mother, only to be harshly scolded and sworn to secrecy. Her mother wouldn't hear another word about a man in the sky inside of a shiny thing that flew like a bird.

At least Grandma had her sister to confide in, but unfortunately her sister died when she was very young. Reading that newspaper article must have jolted her memory. She was so enthusiastic when she read the article out loud. It was probably a relief to get that story off her chest after some sixty-plus years of silence.

Nobody in our family ever doubted her. What motive could she have possibly had to commit the sin of lying to her family about something as odd as a UFO sighting?

"I don't care what anybody thinks" she said bluntly, "those things are real!"

Perhaps she found a peculiar familiarity while reading 2 Kings 2:11–12 in her Bible.

> **2 Kings 2:11–12** [bold emphasis added]
> And as they still went on and talked, behold, **chariots of fire and horses of fire** separated the two of them. And **Elijah went up by a whirlwind** into heaven. And Elisha saw it and he cried, "My father, my father! **The chariots of Israel and its horsemen**!" And he saw him no more. Then he took hold of his own clothes and tore them in two pieces.
>
> Note: 1. Elijah was physically taken to heaven in a physical chariot. 2. My two cents: If flying horses were towing a chariot, the chariot would be dangling beneath the horses unless it was capable of defying gravity on its own. Obviously the chariot was capable of defying gravity, and it further applied that antigravity field to pull Elijah up into it (i.e., the whirlwind). This chariot therefore had to have a highly advanced propulsion system and most likely did not have actual horses at all. The author simply knew of no other way a chariot could move, so he attributed the source of power that moved this chariot as being very unusual horses (i.e., horses of fire).

Concerning the transparent bubble on top of the aerial vehicle that my grandma saw, I'm reminded of another passage of scripture that mentions something similar. In the book of Ezekiel, chapters 1 and 10, Ezekiel describes an otherworldly encounter with angels, and what appears to be advanced technology. Below is an excerpt.

> **Ezekiel 1:16–24** [Bold emphasis and bracketed comments added]
> As for the **appearance of the wheels and their construction: their appearance was like the gleaming of beryl**. And the four had the same likeness, their appearance and construction being as it were **a wheel within a wheel**. When they went, **they went in any of their four directions without turning as they went**. And **their rims were tall and awesome**, and **the rims of all four were full of eyes all around**. And **when the living creatures went, the wheels went beside them; and when the living creatures rose from the earth, the wheels rose. Wherever the spirit wanted to go, they went, and the wheels rose along with them, for the spirit of the living creatures was in the wheels**. When those went, these went; and when those stood, these stood; and when those rose from the earth, **the wheels rose along with them, for the spirit of the living creatures was in the wheels. Over the heads of the living creatures there was the likeness of an expanse, shining like awe-inspiring crystal, spread out above their heads**. And under the expanse **their wings were stretched out straight, one toward another** [wings were straight and possibly connected at the ends (one toward the other)]. And each creature had two wings covering its body **[note that two wings on each side, an upper and a lower, connected on the ends, would resemble the panels of a saucer]**.

> And when they went, I heard **the sound of their wings like the sound of many waters**, like the sound of the **Almighty, a sound of tumult like the sound of an army. When they stood still, they let down their wings.**

Most people in Ezekiel's day would sum up such a vision in one word: indescribable. But Ezekiel was an articulate man, as best as he could be with his ancient Hebrew language, and I commend him. This vision may have been completely baffling to Ezekiel, but in this modern age, a number of characteristics are highly indicative of advanced technology.

1. Ezekiel mentions "a wheel within a wheel." Is this not the shape of a flying saucer?
2. Out of all the types of metals that exist, Ezekiel mentions that the wheels had the "gleaming of beryl." Beryllium happens to be commonly used in missile and aircraft construction. It is an exceptionally strong, lightweight metal with many beneficial properties, such as heat and corrosion resistance.
3. How might a man from antiquity describe a device capable of flight, had that person never seen anything fly except for birds? He would likely associate wings with what he thought gave such a device its ability to fly. Here we see four wings joined together, *straight* wings that do not turn (i.e., not fluid, flexible, or flapping). It sounds to me like he could be describing the paneling on the outside of a spacecraft.
4. Does it not appear odd that a living being that flies would have the shape of a wheel? The wheels he describes sound more like transportation devices associated with these angels than they do appendages, such as arms or legs.
5. "And the likeness of the firmament upon the heads of the living creature was as the color of the terrible **crystal**, stretched forth over their heads above." Here Ezekiel states

that there was a crystal over the heads of the four living creatures. Could this be a transparent bubble on top?

Just after Ezekiel witnessed this vision, he reports that he was "lifted up."

Ezekiel 3:12–14 [Bold emphasis and bracketed comments added]
Then the **Spirit lifted me up**, and I heard behind me the voice of a great earthquake: "Blessed be the glory of the Lord from its place!" It was the sound of the wings of the living creatures as they touched one another, and the sound of the wheels beside them, and the sound of a great earthquake. **The Spirit lifted me up and took me away**, and I went in bitterness in the heat of my spirit, the hand of the Lord being strong upon me.

Call it speculation, but I think Ezekiel saw one or more aerial vehicles (probably intergalactic and interdimensional), and the technology was so incomprehensible, he initially referred to the pilots *and* their vehicles as living creatures. However, in Ezekiel 1:21, he distinguishes the living creatures from the wheels by stating that "the spirit of the living creatures was in the wheels." He also states that he was "taken up," further indicating that this was a vehicle and he entered it, just as Elijah entered the chariot of Israel, with its horses of fire.

Many UFOs are described as having a glass-like bubble on top, and that is exactly the case with the UFO my great-grandmother saw. It also appears to be the case with these wheels that Ezekiel saw.

I personally think my great-grandmother encountered an angel, just like Ezekiel's angels, complete with his mode of intergalactic, interdimensional transportation. It leaves me to wonder if my grandma experienced more on that day than she consciously recalled.

While the conclusion I'm drawing from this passage of scripture supports the possibility that angels use technology, it should be noted that angels are limited beings, whereas God is not. The prospect that God, Creator of all things, would need technology for anything is utterly absurd. However, based on what I see in this scripture, it appears that at least some of His angels do use technology.

Taking this scripture into account, and bouncing it off the account in 2 Kings 2:12, which mentions a "chariot of Israel" flown by angels in the sky, and 1 Chronicles 28:18, which mentions a "chariot of the cherubim," as well as other accounts of glory clouds, pillars of fire at night, and a roving Star of Bethlehem, and so forth, I can't help but conclude that angels are physical, interdimensional beings that use technology.

It is not uncommon for Christians to link a UFO/extraterrestrial phenomenon with the realm of the demonic, which is easy to do in light of some horrific alien abduction accounts. Keep in mind, however, that scripture speaks of faithful angels *and* fallen angels. Based on all my research, I think both faithful and fallen angels use technology. It is particularly the association of good angels and technology, which some have mistakenly used to demote God to the status of a created being who relies on technology, that I believe is a powerful contributing factor to the strong delusion.

CHAPTER 2

CHRISTIAN UFOLOGY

While the field of ufology became more defined with the Roswell incident in 1947 and the establishment of Project Blue Book, which immediately followed, the more specialized field of Christian ufology didn't begin to take shape until the 1990s. Even the new term "Christian ufology" may not officially exist. If it doesn't, I hereby pronounce it into existence. It is a specialization in the field of ufology, whereby UFOs and their occupants are defined within the paradigm of a Christian context.

Some ufologists might think Erich von Däniken and Zacharia Sitchin are Christian ufologists. They both have made names for themselves as ancient-astronaut theorists, but one must first be a Christian in order to be a Christian ufologist. Simply quoting from the Bible doesn't make someone a Christian. I will discuss these two ufologists more in depth later in this chapter.

While I'd like to think I am a pioneer in the field of Christian ufology, noted theologian Finis Jennings Dake actually touched upon the subject of extraterrestrial life spanning the cosmos as early as the late 1940s.[1] Following him, there was Dr. Barry Downing in the 1960s, whom I will discuss momentarily, but aside from these scant few authors, the degree of published material by Christians in the field of ufology was minimal. I can personally attest that searches on the internet for "aliens" and "Bible" or similar queries gave few relevant results in the early 1990s. In response to that void, I posted my initial research into the fledgling field of Christian ufology on a free website, in an article titled "My Message to the World." That article formed the basis of my first book, *Aliens in the Bible*.

Just one year after I posted my article, author Chuck Missler produced several audio sermons titled "Return of the Nephilim."[2] I seriously doubt he stumbled across my obscure article, but he was certainly tuned into my channel. I was absolutely floored when I heard Missler on the radio for the first time. Up until that point, I thought I was alone with my otherworldly views of the Bible.

In 1999, I published *Aliens in the Bible*, and in 2006, I published *Aliens and the Antichrist*. During that time, in less than a decade, the field of Christian ufology exploded, as if a prophetic invasion force stormed the beachhead of the church. Regarding all this new literature, I have found that the Christian views of extraterrestrial life tend to fall into four general categories:

1. **Category 1 (ETs Don't Exist):** Christians who attribute the existence of extraterrestrials and their intergalactic spacecraft to natural or manmade phenomenon
2. **Category 2 (ETs Are Evil):** Christians who categorize extraterrestrials and their intergalactic spacecraft as an elaborate satanic deception
3. **Category 3 (ETs Are Good):** Christians who categorize extraterrestrials and their spacecraft, which they define as intergalactic *and* interdimensional, as divine manifestations of God's holy angels from the heavens (the heavens being outer space as one of the definitions).
4. **Category 4 (ETs Are Evil and Good):** Christians who agree with the third category of Christian ufologists in their belief that extraterrestrials are divine manifestations of God's holy angels, but they also agree with Christians in the second category because the Bible documents both good and evil angels. They therefore disagree that *all* extraterrestrials and their spacecraft are divine manifestations of God's holy angels. This is the category in which I fall. I believe that some

extraterrestrials are God's faithful angels, whereas others are fallen angels.

2.1 Christians in Category 1 (ETs Don't Exist)

According to Tariq Malik, staff writer for Space.com, a telephone poll that questioned one thousand Americans revealed that regular churchgoers were less likely to believe in extraterrestrial life (about 46 percent) than nonchurchgoers (about 70 percent).[3] Combining this statistic with the fact that roughly 77 percent of US adult citizens identify themselves as Christians,[4] the conclusion must be drawn that Christian ufologists in the first category appeal to the largest number of active Christians.

Explanations for UFO/extraterrestrial-related phenomena derived from Christian ufologists in this category vary widely, ranging from ball lightning, swamp gas, hallucinations, or hoaxes to meteorites, weather balloons, or experimental military aircraft. An example of a Christian ufologist who doubts the existence of extraterrestrial life and dismisses the bulk of UFO/extraterrestrial phenomena as being misidentified natural or manmade is Kenneth Samples. He is coauthor of *Lights in the Sky and Little Green Men: A Rational Christian Look at UFOs and Extraterrestrials*.[5]

2.2 Christians in Category 2 (ETs Are Evil)

While most active Christians dismiss the majority of UFO/ extraterrestrial-related phenomena as author Samples does (though this statistic is in flux), the largest number of Christian ufologists are more willing to accept that there is definitely a paranormal phenomenon taking place. However, they attribute this phenomenon to a satanic deception rather than actual extraterrestrial beings from other planets. I have narrowed down four primary reasons for this conclusion.

First of all, many propulsion experts agree that the science of propulsion makes the idea of intergalactic space travel seem impossible.[6] Secondly, UFO/extraterrestrial-related phenomena are frequently linked with the realm of the occult.[7] Thirdly, the alien abduction phenomenon as reported by most abductees is not only described as a torturous and horrific experience, but it is also noted that abductions of Christians who call the name of the Lord Jesus Christ for help immediately terminate their abduction.[8] I've interviewed people who have testified to this. And finally, Christian authors in this category sometimes quote scriptures referring to Genesis chapter 6 during the days of Noah, when fallen angels interbred with humanity and produced a race of evil giants known as the Nephilim.

It was the Nephilim that caused God to bring the flood of Noah. Jesus stated that there would be a return to the days of Noah (Matthew 17:26, 24:37). Authors in this category, therefore, hypothesize that the extraterrestrial phenomenon is a return to the intermingling of fallen angels with humanity.

Among the Christian ufologists in this category are Chuck Missler and Dr. Mark Eastman, authors of *Alien Encounters*; Dr. Michael S. Heiser, author of *The Façade*; Dr. L. A. Marzulli, author of *The Nephilim Trilogy*; Dr. I. D. E. Thomas, author of *The Omega Conspiracy*; Cal Thomas, Los Angeles Times Syndicate; Barbara Simpson, author of *The Babe in the Bunker*; Jack Vallee, author of *Messengers of Deception*; Stephen Yulish, retired professor and researcher, and David Flynn, author of *Cydonia: The Secret Chronicles of Mars*.

2.3 Christians in Category 3 (ETs Are Good)

The third category of Christian ufologists, those who believe that most UFO/extraterrestrial related phenomena should be considered as divine manifestations of God and/or His holy angels, is the most controversial category with respect to those of the Christian faith. Part of the reason for this is that some of the most famous ufologists who proposed the ancient-astronaut theory are those who quoted the Bible to support their theories, yet they (namely von Däniken and Sitchin mentioned earlier) were not Christians. Their research demotes the God of the Bible to a created being (i.e., alien, or race of aliens) who seeded life on Earth.[9, 10] This contradicts one of God's immutable attributes as being the one and only Creator of all things as defined in Acts 17:24–26, Colossians 1:14–18, John 1:1–14, and many other scriptures.

> **Colossians 1:14–18** [bold emphasis and bracketed comments added]
> … in whom we have redemption, the forgiveness of sins. He [Jesus] is the image of the invisible God, the firstborn of all creation. For by him [Jesus] **all things were created**, in heaven and on earth, visible and invisible, whether thrones or dominions or rulers or authorities—**all things were created through him and for him**. And he [Jesus] is before all things, and in him all things hold together. And he [Jesus] is the head of the body, the church. He is the beginning, the firstborn from the dead, that in everything he might be preeminent.

Extraterrestrials cannot be substituted for the name of Jesus in the above passage of scripture. Extraterrestrials, angels, and everything else are created beings that *live in the heavens*, which are a multidimensional construct of time/space created by God. Only God is the Creator, and as the Creator of the universe, only He can exist outside of His creation. This distinction is an immutable quality that only God has. Understanding that God is the Creator is a core belief that one *must* hold to in order to be a genuine Christian, much less a Christian ufologist.

Zacharia Sitchin, who quoted more from ancient Sumerian texts than anything else, derived his theory of a race of aliens creating humanity partly from his interpretation of the Old Testament Hebrew word for God, which is *Elohim*. Elohim is a plural word. The wording of God's dialogue in reference to creating humanity is also unique. For the creation of man, God communes with Himself, as if talking to a team in a sort of self-dialogue.

> **Genesis 1:26–27** [bold emphasis added]
> And God said, **Let us** make man in **our image**, after **our likeness**: and let them have dominion over the fish of the sea, and over the fowl of the air, and over the cattle, and over all the earth, and over every creeping thing that creeps upon the earth. So God created man in **his own image, in the image of God created he him**; male and female created he them.

A theologian acquaintance of mine, Michael Heiser, scholar of Hebrew and author of *The Facade*,[11] disagrees with the assertion that Elohim refers to the Trinity in the Old Testament. He contends that this violates some theological interpretational rule, though I am not sure how in spite of his lengthy attempt to explain it to me. The way I see it, if God *is* a Trinity, He has been, currently is, and always will be a Trinity. However, Heiser believes that God's dialogue about the creation of man, such as the phrase "Let us create man in our image," is actually God talking with His high-ranking angels. He argues that God, and only God, does the creating, but His angels are there to witness it.

Theological types have a habit of getting deep into the weeds over semantics like this. I personally don't think this fine point makes much difference if God is indeed the one who created humanity.

Regardless of Heiser's assessment, most Christians I have talked to attribute the plurality of Elohim to the fact that God has a triune nature (Father, Son, and Holy Spirit). Either way, Hebrew scholar or not, God the Father, Son, and Holy Spirit are all specifically defined as God in the New Testament. Whether the wording in the Old Testament is referring to angels or the Trinity alone, it was God in His triune nature who created humanity, not angels, and that's the part that counts.

Sitchin and von Däniken, on the contrary, insist that the plural word for God denotes a race of beings that created humanity, rather than a triune God. What they both fail to convey, however, is that the same Elohim who created the heavens and the earth (Genesis 1:1) and declared "Let there be light" (Genesis 1:3) is also the Elohim who created humanity from the dust of the earth (Genesis 2:7).

> **Genesis 1:1–3** [bracketed comments added]
> In the beginning, God [Elohim] created the heavens and the earth. The earth was without form and void, and darkness was over the face of the deep. And the Spirit of God [Elohim] was hovering over the face of the waters. And God [Elohim] said, "Let there be light," and there was light.

A race of alien beings could not have possibly spoken the universe, and light into existence. Tinkering with DNA is one thing; extraterrestrials can most likely tinker with DNA. Creating the universe and DNA out of nothingness is quite another matter. No created being can do such things.

In summation, Sitchin and von Däniken only pick and choose verses from the Bible that fit their narrative and discard all else as *human error*. Their ultimate conclusion is that ETs created humanity, not God, and that all world religions are nothing more than a misidentification of the extraterrestrial reality.

While there are many ufologists like von Däniken and Sitchin, who quote the Bible as supporting evidence for UFO/extraterrestrial activity, few are Christians, who hold to the biblical worldview that God, the Creator of all things, is also the Creator of humanity. Despite this fact, there are at least two prominent Christian ufologists in this category that I know of.

Barry Downing, author of *The Bible and Flying Saucers*[12] and *UFO Revelation*,[13] made the ancient-astronaut connection with the Bible back in the 1960s, around the same time as Erich von Däniken. Downing received a bachelor's degree in physics from Hartwick College, a bachelor of divinity in theological seminary at Princeton, and a PhD from the University of Edinburgh, where he specialized in the relationship between science and religion. He was also a minister for thirty-four years. Needless to say, Downing is somewhat of a polymath.

In Downing's books, he speaks extensively about flying angelic chariots, the clouds of heaven that transported angels between heaven and the earth, Moses and the burning bush, the parting of the Red Sea, the pillar of cloud and fire that fed and led Israel through the wilderness for forty years, the fact that most angels described in scripture don't have wings, and many other details, all of which establish the idea that UFOs/aliens are God's divine messengers. In today's terminology, they're the same entities as "good guy" extraterrestrials. The Bible is still 100 percent true; Downing simply proposes a new lens through which to view it.

For making this connection, Downing has come under severe attack from some of those in category 2. Guy Malone said he was "downright blasphemous," Gary Bates labeled him "a wolf in sheep's clothing," and Heiser accused him of "hermeneutical rape," whatever that means.[14] I think some of these guys lie awake at night just thinking of these colorful terms. Hermeneutical rape …

In the past, I probably tempted Gary Bates to declare similar things about me, and as I previously mentioned, Heiser and I also corresponded, though on better terms than this. I think these attacks are ridiculous. Whatever happened to civil debates? Downing is a respected minister and a devout Christian; there is no need for this kind of ridiculous hyperbole.

In my correspondence with Downing, we discussed each other's work and also the idea that even Jesus was an extraterrestrial in his preincarnate form, such as when He interacted with Adam and Eve, when Joshua encountered Him as the captain of the Lord's army (Joshua 5:13–15), and when the Israelites witnessed Him and ate dinner with Him on the top of Mount Sinai (Exodus 24:9–18). I totally agree with Downing on this assessment, though with one caveat, which he agrees with.

When Jesus is physically manifest in His multidimensional creation, He can be considered an extraterrestrial *by definition* because He is an intelligent being, not originally from Earth. Jesus even declared that He is a king from another world (John 8:23, 18:36).

> **John 8:23** [bold emphasis added]
> He said to them, "You are from below; I am from above. You are of this world; **I am not of this world** …"
>
> **John 18:36** [bold emphasis added]
> Jesus answered, "**My kingdom is not of this world**. If my kingdom were of this world, my servants would have been fighting, that I might not be delivered over to the Jews. But my kingdom is not from the world."

However, I stress the distinction that Jesus has from all other created beings: He is *not* a created being, and He has the ability to completely exit all dimensions of time/space altogether, including all the dimensions of the heavens. This is something that *no other* extraterrestrial is capable of doing. Jesus is unique, the one and *only begotten Son of God*; there is no other like Him.

Furthermore, if any other claim is made that other people (i.e., religious leaders of other religions) were or are also extraterrestrials, such as Buddha, Muhammad, Confucius, or some modern New Age guru, they have no equal footing with Jesus. Such would also be the case of an otherworldly Jesus who claims to be something other than His biblical definition as the only begotten Son of God, a point I will bring up later.

Simply put, those who claim a divine status that competes with, refutes, or otherwise denies Jesus Christ, as He declared of Himself, are false. The prophets of scripture in both the New and Old Testaments were emphatically clear about this. It's one of the Ten Commandments (Exodus 20:3), and it's also what differentiates Christ from antichrists (1 John 4:1–3; 2 John 1:7).

> **Exodus 20:3**
> "You shall have no other gods before me."
>
> **1 John 4:1–3** [bold emphasis added]
> Beloved, **do not believe every spirit, but test the spirits to see whether they are from God**, for many false prophets have gone out into the world. By this you know the Spirit of God: **every spirit that confesses that Jesus Christ has come in the flesh is from God**, and **every spirit that does not confess Jesus is not from God. This is the spirit of the antichrist**, which you heard was coming and now is in the world already.
>
> **2 John 1:7** [bold emphasis added]
> For many deceivers have gone out into the world, **those who do not confess the coming of Jesus Christ in the flesh**. Such a one is the deceiver and the antichrist.

Downing agrees with me that Jesus is indeed unique. He quoted John 1:1–14 to me, saying that Jesus is the Creator and the incarnate *word of God.* What more of an answer could anyone want? Downing is most certainly a Christian, yet he's also a kind of ancient-astronaut theorist (though not with much of the secular baggage that term often entails).

His emphasis continues to be focused almost exclusively on the so-called good guys, but not so much that he refuses to acknowledge that fallen angels will play their part of the deception in the End Times. He simply believes that it is more important to recognize the true God and His faithful angels, than to recognize the deceivers. After all, the scribes and Pharisees made the mistake of not recognizing Jesus when they accused Him of being demon possessed (Matthew 12:24). To that, Jesus indicated they were toying with an unforgivable sin.

One example of how this might play out in the future is that God's faithful angels will preach the Gospel to people in the End Times (Revelation 6:14). When this happens, how many people might reject this message, not because of its contents but rather because of the possible otherworldly distractions (i.e., intergalactic, interdimensional spacecraft for example) associated with the angel(s)?

> **Revelation 14:6** [bold emphasis added]
> Then **I saw another angel flying directly overhead**, with an eternal **gospel to proclaim to those who dwell on earth**, to every nation and tribe and language and people.

Downing has a good point here, and I agree that we definitely need to be able to discern who the good guys are, regardless of distractions like technology. This will also be a relevant factor for discerning other details involving the good guys, such as the rapture of the church, which might actually be a mass UFO abduction, as well as the arrival and work of the *two witnesses* in Revelation. I will talk more about these guys in successive chapters.

Another noted theologian who focuses almost exclusively on the good guys is Donald P. Coverdell, ThD, author of *The Mystery Clouds*. He doesn't agree that humanity was created by a race of aliens/angels, but he does believe that UFO/extraterrestrial manifestations are primarily divine manifestations of God and His faithful angels.[15]

Like Downing (or perhaps too much like Dr. Downing because his work looks very close to plagiarism), he quotes numerous scriptures referring to the events of the exodus of Israel from Egypt, which included miracles as well as events surrounding a mysterious pillar of fire in the night sky (Exodus 13:21–22, 14:24; Numbers 14:14; Nehemiah 9:12, 14) and a pillar of cloud in the day that rained down a strange bread-like food in the mornings for the Israelites to eat.

Other mysterious clouds associated with God and His faithful angels are mentioned throughout scripture, such as the clouds of heaven (Daniel 7:13, Matthew 24:29–31, 1 Thessalonians 4:13–18,

Revelation 11:12); the clouds of glory present during Moses's meetings with God on Mount Sinai, the tent of meeting, and with Jesus at the mount of transfiguration (Exodus 16:10, 24:16, 40:34–35; Numbers 16:42; 1 Kings 8:11; 2 Chronicles 5:14; Isaiah 4:5; Ezekiel 1:28, 10:4; Matthew 17:5; Mark 9:7; Luke 21:27); and the cloud to which Jesus entered when departing the earth (Acts 1:9).

Coverdell writes about the angelic visitations of Ezekiel, as I have also touched upon, in which the angels were associated with what appeared to be some type of advanced technological mode of transportation referred to as wheels within wheels (Ezekiel 1, 10) and of the angelic *flying chariots of fire* in God's angelic army (2 Kings 6:17), also named the chariot of Israel in a specific encounter with the prophet Elijah (2 Kings 2:11–12).

Coverdell argues that this chariot of Israel was an airborne vehicle piloted by angels; it was used to physically *abduct* Elijah from the ground in a whirlwind and carry him away to heaven. Furthermore, Coverdell points out that before Elijah was taken away to heaven, he may have been routinely abducted by angelic beings as indicated in 1 Kings 18:12 and 2 Kings 2:16.

> **1 Kings 18:12** [bracketed comment and bold emphasis added]
> And as soon as I [Obadiah is speaking] have gone from you, **the Spirit of the Lord will carry you I know not where**. And so, when I come and tell Ahab and he cannot find you, he will kill me, although I your servant have feared the Lord from my youth.

> **2 Kings 2:16** [bracketed comments and bold emphasis added]
> And they said to him [Elisha], "Behold now, there are with your servants fifty strong men. Please let them go and seek your master [Elijah]. **It may be that the Spirit of the Lord has caught him up and cast him**

upon some mountain or into some valley." And he said, "You shall not send."

I agree with all these details that both Downing and Coverdell disclose in their books; nevertheless, I also believe this subject deserves at least an equal degree of attention devoted to understanding the "bad guys." Proposing various interpretations of scripture into both perspectives of this issue (ETs as both good and bad) will hopefully prepare people for any given outcome in the days ahead.

2.4 Christians in Category 4 (ETs Are Good and Evil)

Finally, the last of the four categories of Christian ufologists are those who believe in the existence of extraterrestrial life forms, and they define them as both *good* and *evil*. Downing can be included in this category as far as his beliefs are concerned, but since his research is focused primarily on the good guys, I include him as an example of category 3.

As for me, I fall into category 4, and I have extensively documented my research in *Aliens in the Bible*[16] and *Aliens and the Antichrist*.[17] In *Aliens and the Antichrist*, I devote an equal amount of time and attention to explaining how both perspectives, the biblical roles and identities of good and evil ETs, need to be fully understood in order to comprehend how the strong delusion will unfold. I have a hunch that the reason why the strong delusion will be such a powerful deception is because it will contain so much truth to it.

Christian ufologists in category 4 draw their research primarily from the Bible, just as the researchers from the second and third categories of Christian ufologists do, yet they also reconcile the differences between these seemingly opposing views.

Aside from me, Finis Jennings Dake, theologian and author of *God's Plan for Man*,[18] and another personal friend of mine, Jim Cunningham,[19] Christian UFO researcher and website maintainer for the Strong Delusion website (it was Jim who introduced me to Downing), are among a select few in this last category.

I'm sure there are others in the fourth category because the information I am writing about in this book is finally spreading among Christians. However, this is still relatively new information; most Christian ufology books are less than a decade old. As for the manner in which I address the religion of Islam in this book, and how it will tie into an extraterrestrial reality, I've never seen, heard, or read anything even remotely close to it. That's why I was compelled to write this book.

Like Christian ufologists in the second category, I agree that there is a satanic deception at work within the UFO/extraterrestrial phenomenon, yet at the same time, I also believe the deception contains more truth to it than most Christian ufologists surmise. This makes the deception even more cunning than it would be if there were no truth to it at all.

The truth I refer to concerns the belief that the universe actually *is* populated with life, which is in agreement with Christian ufologists in the third category. However, unlike Christians in the third category, I insist on pointing out that the Bible speaks of *faithful* and *fallen* angels, both of which have mingled in the affairs of humanity since the dawn of history. Both will continue to be involved in the affairs of humanity until the return of God's kingdom of heaven on earth in the future.

During the End Times, the days of Noah will return. This namely consists of public interaction between humans and fallen angels, but I also believe God's faithful angels will be at work in the days to come as well. Revelation 14:6 makes the audacious statement that an angel will proclaim the gospel in the future. Exactly what this will look like when it happens remains a mystery. I will not be surprised if it involves extraterrestrials emerging from their alien spacecraft, similar to what happened with Ezekiel.

In a nutshell, in *Aliens and the Antichrist,* I explain how terms such as *angel* and *host of heaven* are synonymous with extraterrestrial life forms of varying alignments and power (angels are more powerful than nonangelic hosts of heaven). These beings are living on other planets (in the heavens), spanning multiple dimensions. We live on a multidimensional earth, in a multidimensional universe, or rather, a *multiverse*.

I call the idea of Earth being a multidimensional planet, the *onion theory.* In short, hell is in the heart of the earth (Matthew 12:40, Ephesians 4:9), and one of the definitions of heaven includes the sky. The firmament (i.e., sky) is where birds fly (Genesis 2:19, 7:3, 23; Psalm 8:8; Lamentations 4:19). Also, Satan is known as the prince of the power of the *air* (Ephesians 2:2). Moreover, the prophet Daniel gives an account of a prolonged angelic confrontation lasting twenty-one days in answer to his prayers. It is doubtful that angels were battling in God's direct presence in the third heaven, where fallen angels already were cast out. This confrontation could have occurred in the second heaven (outer space); however, the archangel Gabriel's access was specifically blocked from Earth. Therefore, this confrontation likely occurred in the first heaven directly surrounding the earth (Daniel 10:13).

For civilizations to exist in these various places, they must be dimensionally shifted into higher and lower dimensions, beyond our perception. The earth is therefore a multidimensional onion of lithospheres, different dimensions layered on top of each other. Earth is smaller in a lower dimension (where hell is located), and Earth is larger in a higher dimension (where the first heaven is located).[21]

Christian ufologists in the fourth category believe Christian ufologists in the first and second categories will be forced to abandon their premise that there is no such thing as extraterrestrial life in the cosmos, when, in the future, it will become common knowledge as predicted in scripture with the return to the days of Noah.

One means of proof for the existence of extraterrestrial life may be derived when intergalactic travel becomes possible and available to the public, either by means of intergalactic visitors providing that transportation and/or technology to humanity, or with the advent of our own invention of said technology, which NASA may have already completed.[22]

Part of my fixation with the strong delusion is my perception that Christian ufologists in the first and second categories will be more vulnerable to the satanic deception they believe is coming because they will face a paradigm shift they will not be expecting. There *really are* aliens on other planets; they will be able to prove it.

As for those in the third category, they may have a tendency to view *all* UFO/extraterrestrial-related activity as divine manifestations of God and his faithful angels. Because of this, they may be susceptible to misidentifying fallen angels as God's faithful angels. New Age types already are set up for this deception, and many nominal Christians who have fallen for deceptions like the theory of evolution will fall for this as well.

The fourth category of Christian ufology is the most complex because it combines and reconciles information from both the second and third categories. In some cases, it expounds upon topics of the Christian faith, as well as the UFO/extraterrestrial phenomenon, through the cross-referencing of terminology.

For example, in *Aliens and the Antichrist*, I speak of something I define as *the butterfly theory* to explain the origin of angels. This theory suggests that angels did not start out as angels. Instead, they were initially created as various reproductive species spanning the cosmos. They reproduced after their own kind, rather than each being an individual creation. During their reproductive stage, they were not yet angels. Instead, they were like Adam and Eve prior to the fall: perfect, sinless beings, who reproduced after their own kind. Later in their lives, as they spiritually matured, they were eventually *translated*, at which time they became angels. This conclusion was derived by simply pondering the destiny of the human race: those who are saved will be translated (Luke 20:36).

The butterfly theory explains the true identity of Cro-Magnon and Neanderthal, for those who are aware of the flood of Lucifer. Finis Dake was the first I know of to expound upon the flood of Lucifer. This flood destroyed an angelic civilization that once existed on Earth, and the Bible has a lot to say about it. Dake provides an extensive table that documents the differences between the flood of Noah and the flood of Lucifer.[23]

Also in *Aliens and the Antichrist*, I discuss the interesting concept of *cosmic salvation*, concerning other intelligent beings in the universe.[24] All of these details are important in the event that extraterrestrial life becomes a reality because they will defend against the strong delusion, explaining how scripture can harmonize with the existence of extraterrestrial life. In fact, the Bible supports the existence of extraterrestrial life far more than anyone's claim that it refutes it.

I highly recommend reading *Aliens and the Antichrist* as a foundational work to this book. I am offering it as a free download on my website, http://www.aliensandtheantichrist.com. I've been giving away that book and *Aliens in the Bible* as free downloads ever since I published them. If the website is down, contact me at jmilor@yahoo.com, and I will e-mail you a copy.

CHAPTER 3

The Bible I Thought I Knew

Regarding my perspective on extraterrestrial life, my great-grandmother planted the first seeds, but my quest to search for a deeper meaning in scripture didn't come until later. In my early twenties, I encountered Jesus in a dream and woke up a different person. I speak of this encounter in my book *The Eaglestar Prophecy*, which is a free download on my website. There was no church, no sermon, no altar call, none of that; what happened to me was reminiscent of Charles Dickens's famous story *A Christmas Carol*. Most of my friends thought I was joking when I told them God came to me in a dream. I probably sounded something like the Blues Brothers with Dan Aykroyd's famous line, "We're on a mission from God."

I consider this experience, as well as my great-grandmother's encounter with Jesus, a fulfilling of prophecy concerning the last days (Joel 2:28, Acts 2:17–18).

> **Joel 2:28**
> "And it shall come to pass afterward, that I will pour out my Spirit on all flesh; your sons and your daughters shall prophesy, your old men shall dream dreams, and your young men shall see visions."

> **Acts 2:17–18**
> "'And in the last days it shall be, God declares, that I will pour out my Spirit on all flesh, and your sons and your daughters shall prophesy, and your young men shall see visions, and your old men shall dream dreams; even on my male servants and female servants in those days I will pour out my Spirit, and they shall prophesy.'"

On that very day, I started reading the Bible with a sense of clarity I never knew before. Something was different about my perception. Though I had heard the tired phrase of "born again" countless times, it is the most apt description of what I experienced.

Only six chapters into the first book of the Bible, at Genesis 6, I read about beings known as the sons of God, mating with humans, and having children that were genetic freaks of nature. Yep, that's in the Bible. As I read this information, a spark suddenly ignited, as the connection was made between what I was reading and my great-grandmother's testimony from years before.

> **Genesis 6:4** [bold emphasis and bracketed comment added]
> The Nephilim **[giants]** were on the earth in those days, and also afterward, when the sons of God **[angels]** came in to the daughters of man and they bore children to them. These were the mighty men who were of old, the men of renown.

3.1 Does the Bible Speak of Human-Angel Hybrids?

God brought the flood of Noah to save humanity from extinction because an abhorrently evil, violent, and extremely powerful race of human-angel hybrids had taken over the planet. I could hardly believe that something as preposterous as this was in the Bible; it was like reading *Planet of the Apes.* The strange thing is I recalled giants being mentioned in the Bible, such as the story of David and Goliath my grandma used to tell, but it never occurred to me to question where these giants came from. Why did I never ask about them? I asked about everything else.

At this point, I found it difficult to keep reading the Bible from beginning to end without jumping around. My mind raced with questions about these giants and their implications on everything I thought I knew about angels.

The Nephilim (giants) were singled out as unnatural in multiple aspects—almost ten feet tall or more (1 Samuel 17:4), six fingers and six toes (1 Chronicles 20:6), bent entirely on perpetual evil (Genesis 6:5)—they were the inspiration for ancient legends around the world. The heroes of Greek, Norse, Sumerian, Egyptian, and Hindus mythology, among many others, were the Nephilim in the Bible (Genesis 6:4), and their progenitors were not human, but rather fallen angels.

But how could this be? Why would the angels see the daughters of men as attractive (Genesis 6:2)? If sex were completely foreign to what an angel is and does, the entire concept of sexual attraction would also be completely foreign, yet these beings were *attracted* to human women and *wanted* to have sex with them. To me, this meant that they had to be sexual beings at some point in their existence. Scripture does not state this explicitly, but their behavior does not make sense to me if this is not the case. Even if they were capable of shape-shifting, there would still be no point in adopting the form of another species and having sex with it, if that initial attraction or experience with sex or lust never existed to begin with.

This line of questioning led me down a rabbit hole of other questions.

To start with, if there were so many giants on the earth in the past, why haven't their bones been found?

Or have they?

3.2 The Giant Cover-Up

Back when I first conducted research into archaeology about the Nephilim, there wasn't nearly as much information on the internet as there is now. Thanks to pioneer researchers like Glenn Kimball, who inspired the bulk of this section, I was quite surprised to find that the version of prehistoric times I learned in school may have had gaping holes in it.

The giants in scripture are referred to as Nephilim (Genesis 6:4, Numbers 13:33, and many others) and Rephaim (Deuteronomy 2:11, Joshua 12:4, 2 Samuel 21:16, and many others). Simply performing a search for the word *giant* or *giants*, using free e-Sword Bible software with the King James Version including Strong's Enhanced Lexicon, reveals the following definitions for these words:

> **H5303**
> נפל נפיל
> n^{e}phîyl n^{e}phil
> *nef-eel', nef-eel'*
> From H5307; properly, a feller, that is, a bully or tyrant: giant.
>
> **H7497**
> רפה רפא
> râphâ' râphâh
> *raw-faw', raw-faw'*
> From H7495 in the sense of invigorating; a giant: giant, Rapha, Rephaim (-s). See also H1051.

Aside from the canon of scripture, other ancient apocryphal books, such as the books of Enoch, 2 Esdras, Genesis Aprocryphon, Jasher, and Jubilees, also speak of these beings of immense stature.[1]

Robert Wadlow, the tallest man in modern recorded history, was eight feet nine inches. The tallest living man in the world, as of this writing, is Sultan Kosen, who stands eight feet three inches.[2] Both these men reached their heights due to the debilitating disease of gigantism. However, neither Wadlow nor Koson were healthy or robust, and neither would have ever dreamed of outrunning buffalo, much less carrying one (up to two thousand pounds) in one hand, as recounted by the Pawnee Indians in the autobiography of the famous Buffalo Bill.[3]

Stories of these giants are not limited to the Middle East. In fact, over six hundred ancient cultures from around the globe speak of giants, but due to the perceived lack of physical evidence, their existence has long been debated.[4]

The archaeologist in the TV series *The Naked Archeologist* addressed this question of lacking evidence regarding the Nephilim. He devoted an episode to suggesting that these ancient legends of giants are allegorical of the Neanderthal and Cro-Magnon.[5] Whether that's the case or not, simply finding fossils of giant humans would close this debate once and for all, right?

Perhaps not.

I was somewhat disappointed to see that *The Naked Archeologist* only focused on physical bones and completely ignored archaeological archives.

One would think that if giant humanoids were as proliferate as scripture indicates, there would be an abundance of fossil evidence to prove it. The sad fact is, however, that while there are mountains of *documented* evidence of unearthed humanoid skeletons of momentous stature, which were turned over to the Smithsonian Institution on numerous occasions for over one hundred years, most of these findings are nowhere to be found.

The unearthed bones in the Smithsonian archives were not the bones of diseased cripples, but rather of agile, healthy, robust people with average heights of over seven to eight feet tall, and some even ranging between nine and thirteen feet tall.[6–10]

Where are these bones now?

The Smithsonian Institution, easily the largest museum complex in the world, with nineteen museums, nine research centers, and over 140 affiliate museums, has had long-standing problems in the cataloging and location of stored finds due to the changing standards of administrations over the last 150 years.[11, 12] Instead of diffusing knowledge, as Mr. Smithson would have wished, this institution became confused with the problems of sprawling storage. What's worse, the Smithsonian Institution allegedly has deliberately undertaken the task of ensuring that what it has found and continues to find fits in accordance with a version of history it has decided to try to prove ever since 1881.

> The cover-up and alleged suppression of archaeological evidence began in late 1881, when John Wesley Powell, the geologist famous for exploring the Grand Canyon, appointed Cyrus Thomas as the director of the Eastern Mound Division of the Smithsonian Institution's Bureau of Ethnology.
>
> When Thomas came to the Bureau of Ethnology he was a "pronounced believer in the existence of a race of Mound Builders, distinct from the American Indians." However, John Wesley Powell, the director of the Bureau of Ethnology, a very sympathetic man toward the American Indians, had lived with the peaceful Winnebago Indians of Wisconsin as a youth. He felt that American Indians were unfairly thought of as primitive and savage.
>
> The Smithsonian began to promote the idea that Native Americans, who at that time were being exterminated in the Indian Wars, were descended from advanced civilizations and were worthy of respect and protection.
>
> They also began a program of suppressing any archaeological evidence that lent credence to the school of thought known as diffusionism, a school that believes throughout history there has been

widespread dispersion of culture and civilization via contact by ship and major trade routes.

The Smithsonian opted for the opposite school, known as Isolationism. Isolationism holds that most civilizations are isolated from each other and that there has been very little contact between them, especially those that are separated by bodies of water. In this intellectual war that started in the 1880s, it was held that even contact between the civilizations of the Ohio and Mississippi Valleys were rare, and certainly these civilizations did not have any contact with such advanced cultures as the Mayas, Toltecs, or Aztecs in Mexico and Central America.

By Old World standards, this is an extreme and even ridiculous idea, considering that the river system reached to the Gulf of Mexico and these civilizations were as close as the opposite shore of the gulf. It was like saying that cultures in the Black Sea area could not have had contact with the Mediterranean.

When the contents of many ancient mounds and pyramids of the Midwest were examined, it was shown that the history of the Mississippi River Valleys was that of an ancient and sophisticated culture that had been in contact with Europe and other areas. Not only that, the contents of many mounds revealed burials of huge men, sometimes seven or eight feet tall, in full armor with swords and sometimes huge treasures.[13]

The ending scene in the movie *Raiders of the Lost Ark* shows the Ark of the Covenant being boxed up and stashed away in a warehouse that makes the Gaylord Hotel complex in Tennessee look like a backwoods shack in comparison. This is actually not far from the truth. There really are enormous warehouses full of fossils and amazing artifacts that could redefine history as we know it, demanding our history books be rewritten, but they are even more lost in these warehouses than they were when they were buried in the earth.

Going beyond the point of inept record keeping, some of the Smithsonian Institution findings were apparently so controversial that they allegedly were shipped out into the middle of the Atlantic Ocean and thrown overboard.

> In a private conversation with a well-known historical researcher, (who shall remain nameless), I was told that a former employee of the Smithsonian, who was dismissed for defending the view of diffusionism in the Americas (i.e., the heresy that other ancient civilizations may have visited the shores of North and South America during the many millennia before Columbus), alleged that the Smithsonian at one time had actually taken a barge full of unusual artifacts out into the Atlantic and dumped them in the ocean.
>
> Though the idea of the Smithsonian covering up a valuable archaeological find is difficult to accept for some, there is, sadly, a great deal of evidence to suggest that the Smithsonian Institution has knowingly covered up and "lost" important archaeological relics. The Stonewatch Newsletter of the Gungywamp Society in Connecticut, which researches megalithic sites in New England, had a curious story in their Winter 1992 issue about stone coffins discovered in 1892 in Alabama which were sent to the Smithsonian Institution and then "lost."[14]

Sadly, the stone coffins discovered in 1892 that vanished in the hands of the Smithsonian Institution are one example among countless other incidents of fossils, such as giant humanoid skeletons and unusual artifacts, that simply don't *fit* with our current history books. These amazing artifacts simply vanished after being excavated and handed over to the Smithsonian.

Taking a position sympathetic to American Indians back in the 1880s is a fully understandable reason for being biased toward a particular opinion. However, the reason for the Smithsonian Institution's continued insistence on the isolationism school of thought, in the face of thousands of findings of solid evidence to the contrary, is a complete mystery. Even now, the History Channel hosts a program called *Unearthing America*, where the entire theme of the show is dedicated to discoveries proving diffusionism, rather than isolationism; yet time and time again the archaeologist host of the show encounters constant criticism.

I think the Smithsonian Institution has perpetrated a great disservice to the global community by insisting history follow its particular dogma, but this strange obstruction of history is not confined to only the Smithsonian. Archaeologists apparently keep finding more Nephilim, but these findings keep vanishing almost as fast as they're discovered. For anyone interested in this oddity, simply track the websites that speak of them. Try to track down an actual museum and see what happens.

In an article by Glenn Kimball that I read about seven years ago, he stated that he photographed actual giant mummies on display at the Gold Museum in Lima, Peru, which I don't think is affiliated with the Smithsonian Institution.

> Glenn Kimball photographed the mummies of two of these giant men in Lima, Peru, in 1969. These giants are still in the gold museum in Lima, Peru, today and can be seen by anyone who visits. They were mummified, and their golden robes are prominently on display. Their crowns could fit around Glenn's waist. Their golden gloves have fingers ten inches long. Their mummies can be measured with a tape

> and they were both around nine and a half feet tall. There were other personal items fit for a giant king, that wouldn't have been useful to a man of normal size. The actual bodies are there incased in glass for all to see. The news media has never photographed anyone nine and a half feet tall.
>
> These were not mutations. A mutation is something that happens once in a "blue moon." There were two giants in Peru side by side, from successive generations. What makes the story even stranger is that the average height of the Peruvians, both now and historically, is well under six feet high.[15]

In 2009, when I first read about these mummified giants, I hoped to take a trip to Peru and take a detour to the Gold Museum. On its website, the museum used to have a massive human skull of one of the mummies on display inside a glass case; I remember it distinctly. I also recall that I thought it was odd because Glenn Kimball mentioned two complete mummies. Why was only a single skull left?

Unfortunately, my finances fell through at the last minute. About two years after that, I happened to check on this website again because I was updating some research for an article I was writing. I was disappointed to see that the picture of an oversized human skull was no longer on the museum's official website.[16]

I e-mailed the museum and asked about it. Someone from the museum replied, denying that the museum ever had any giant mummies. I insisted that I had read about them from Glenn Kimball's research, that he personally saw and photographed them in 1969, and that I saw a picture of a giant human skull from one of those mummies on display in a glass case, posted on the website just two years prior.

The person who replied to me was adamant and affirmed that whatever I thought I saw was a complete work of fiction, or a different website.

Was it?

I obtained the e-mail address to contact this person from that very same website I documented in my research notes two years before. If that was fiction, it was fiction perpetrated by the museum, and it dates back to 1969, long before the museum's website even existed.

When I first pondered these disappearances, I wondered if there was some eccentric billionaire running around buying all of these bones and paying people to shut up. Then something occurred to me about these Nephilim bones.

The ghosts of the Nephilim are what we now call demons. This is derived from the fact that the same Hebrew word, *Rapha*, is translated as both giants and ghosts. In 1 Chronicles 4:12, 8:2, and 8:37, referenced in Strong's Enhanced Lexicon with H1051, H7497, and H7498, Rapha refers to giants. However, in Proverbs 14:9, Isaiah 9:18, and many others referenced in Strong's Enhanced Lexicon with H7495, Rapha refers to ghosts—that is, demons/devils.

This actually makes perfect sense. The Nephilim of the past were unequivocally evil, and now they're all dead; hence, they are the *ghosts of the Nephilim*. Demons are also unequivocally evil, and their primary activity is seeking a host to possess. They had to be alive at some point in time, so what were they? Simply reading about them should beg the questions, who created them and where did they come from? Answer: demons are the ghosts of the Nephilim.

H1051
בית רפא
bêyth râphâ'
bayth raw-faw'
From H1004 and H7497; house of (the) giant; Beth-Rapha, an Israelite: Beth-rapha.

H7497
רפה רפא
râphâ' râphâh
raw-faw', raw-faw'
From H7495 in the sense of invigorating; a giant: giant, Rapha, Rephaim (-s). See also H1051.

H7498
רפה רפא
râphâ' râphâh
raw-faw', raw-faw'
Probably the same as H7497; giant; Rapha or Raphah, the name of two Israelites: Rapha.

H7496
רפא
râphâ'
raw-faw'
From H7495 in the sense of H7503; properly lax, that is, (figuratively) a ghost (as dead; in plural only): dead, deceased.

In my studies of paranormal phenomenon, I have read how a deceased spirit can sometimes retain a connection, however weak, with its deceased corpse and, in particular, its bones. It is for this reason that graveyards are known as popular hangouts for those who conduct ghost photography. This phenomenon is not even isolated to deceased spirits of lost souls. Take the account of the bones of the Old Testament prophet Elisha for instance. His bones resurrected a dead man (2 Kings 13:21).

2 Kings 13:21 [bold emphasis added]
And it came to pass, as **they were burying a man**, that, behold, they spied a band of men; and they cast the man into the sepulcher of Elisha: and **when the**

man was let down, and touched the bones of Elisha, he revived, and stood up on his feet.

With this in mind, I wonder, what could be the possible side effects of unearthing a Nephilim skeleton and putting it on display in a museum? Maybe that's why the mummies of the Gold Museum were initially discarded except for a single skull. Perhaps there was a slow process whereby the operators of the museum were weighing their business prospects for displaying these Nephilim against the demonic hauntings that were plaguing their museum. They needed the business, but maybe those bones were taking a toll on the museum staff.

Could it be that any museum with Nephilim bones turns into poltergeist central? Maybe that's why the person I talked to so quickly shut me down and didn't want to talk about those mummies.

This thought occurred to me when I was planning my trip to Lima, Peru. I wasn't going to be in the presence of those bones until after fasting for three days. I don't have to concern myself with that now, however. The museum got rid of those bones and doesn't want to talk about them. This could also explain why the Smithsonian went to the extreme of dumping stuff out in the middle of the ocean, far away from any trace of humanity.

All of these details about the Nephilim, their bones, and their current status as demons will play into the strong delusion that is coming our way. Currently, physical proof that the Nephilim once existed eludes us, at least publically, but I predict a day is coming when their bones will finally come to light. The Antichrist might even be the individual to reveal them as I will later discuss.

When the day of disclosure arrives concerning the reality of the Nephilim, it will prove that the angels mentioned in the Bible are physical entities not native to the earth. Most people associate angels with heaven, but the concept of heaven is generally disconnected from *the heavens* (i.e., outer space), despite the fact that most scriptures refer to heaven in the plural and heaven is defined as the abode of the sun, moon, and stars (Genesis 1:14).

Most people also don't think of angels as physical beings capable of reproduction, but finding the bones of their biological children would prove otherwise. Needless to say, proving the existence of the Nephilim will be nearly the same as proving the existence of extraterrestrial life, and it will bring the world much closer to accepting the idea that extraterrestrials are spoken of in the Bible, as well as other ancient literature like the Qur'an and Hadiths.

3.3 More Questions about Angels and the Nephilim

Since I stumbled upon the Nephilim, I was forced to address my understanding of the nature of angels.

When were the angels created and how? Were they each handcrafted as Adam and Eve were, as I had always been led to believe by other Christians, or did they start as Adam and Eve, reproducing after their own kind? Biologically speaking, that made much more sense.

Pondering this, it occurred to me that God is efficient; when He creates things, He usually does not reinvent the wheel. When He created life on Earth, for example, he used the building blocks of DNA to do it. DNA is like biological Legos for life. DNA is efficient.

When God created Eve, He used Adam's rib as a shortcut, so why would He handcraft an entire race of beings that were capable of reproduction? A more likely explanation for the origin of angels is that they did not start out as immortal angels but rather like Adam and Eve, depending on a tree of life in their respective worlds. They most likely reproduced after their own kind until they populated their worlds and reached a level of spiritual maturity whereby God translated them into a higher, completely immortal, nonreproductive *angelic* form.

In summation, when Jesus said we will be like the angels in heaven, which neither marry nor are given in marriage (Luke 20:34–36), He wasn't saying that angels were *not capable of sex*, nor was He saying that angels *never had sex* in their entire existence.

> **Luke 20:34–36** [bold emphasis added]
> And Jesus said to them, "The sons of this age marry and are given in marriage, but those who are considered worthy to attain to that age and to the resurrection from the dead **neither marry nor are given in marriage**, for **they cannot die** anymore, because they are **equal to angels** and are **sons of God**, being sons of the resurrection."

Many if not most Christians seem to think Jesus meant that reproduction is a foreign concept to angels and that they were each handcrafted beings, but I don't believe that is what Jesus said at all. In fact, for Jesus to compare us with the angels, and then say that God's plan is to translate us into a higher form so we will be *like* them, strongly implies to me that they were once a reproductive species just *like* us. The only difference between them and us is that they sinned long after their creation, whereas Adam and Eve sinned very early on, before any humans were ever translated into an angelic, completely immortal form.

This same conclusion is detailed in *Aliens and the Antichrist*, and it boggled my mind when I first considered it. Everything I knew about extraterrestrials and UFOs was making perfect sense from a *biblical* perspective. And the more I read, the more confirmation I found.

Some argue that the sons of God mentioned in Genesis 6 were not angels, but later in the Bible, in the book of Job, the same Hebrew word translated as sons of God, *bene Elohim,* is used to describe Satan and his angelic cohorts (Job 1:5–6, 2:1, 38:7). What's more, the Nephilim represented an entire race of six-fingered, six-toed giants standing nine and a half feet tall or more. How did that happen out of the blue? Genetic flukes with six fingers on each hand and six toes on each foot are incredibly rare, and finding more than one is even rarer, but this was an entire race of six-fingered, six-toed giants.

Some have postulated the argument that the Nephilim may have carried the disease of gigantism, but that disease is also incredibly rare and utterly debilitating. The Nephilim were not hobbling around on crutches, barely able to walk, as those infected with that disease usually are. The Nephilim were robust warriors wearing armor and wielding swords in battle. They were killing machines of unparalleled strength. In my opinion, it is ten times harder to believe that the Nephilim were purely human than to believe that their DNA was tainted with another species of humanoid.

Familiar with von Däniken's research, I realized he was missing something incredibly important that the Bible was making perfectly clear to me. Von Däniken quoted the Bible to support his UFO research, but he was not a Christian. He therefore concluded that aliens had seeded life on Earth, that they are our genetic progenitors—that is, creators. I, however, was coming to grips with another interpretation of his findings.

Since the beings known as the sons of God mentioned in Genesis 6:4 were fallen angels, it would stand to reason that what von Däniken was concluding with his non-Christian perspective was exactly what these beings would want him to conclude. Such an interpretation redefines God, demoting Him to the status of a created species in the universe.

This was the same deception that the Nephilim perpetrated prior to the flood of Noah; they duped humanity into worshipping them as gods. I would like to think that we learned our lesson by now. Unfortunately, we have not because Jesus prophesied that we would see a return to the days of Noah in the future (Matthew 24:27, Luke 17:26–30).

> **Matthew 24:37** [bold emphasis added]
> As were **the days of Noah**, so will be the coming of the Son of Man.

> **Luke 17:26–30** [bold emphasis added]
> Just as it was in **the days of Noah**, so will it be in the days of the Son of Man. They were eating and drinking and **marrying and being given in marriage**, until

> the day when Noah entered the ark, and the flood came and destroyed them all. Likewise, just as it was in **the days of Lot**—they were eating and drinking, buying and selling, planting and building, but on the day when Lot went out from **Sodom**, fire and sulfur rained from heaven and destroyed them all—so will it be on the day when the Son of Man is revealed.

Another time in history that is linked with the days of Noah, in the same context of the End Times, is the time of Sodom and Gomorrah, referenced in the scripture above (Luke 17:28). According to Genesis 19:8–9, the men in Sodom were so consumed with lust and the desire to have sex with the angels who accompanied Lot into his home, they could care less about either of Lot's two virgin daughters. They were literally trying to kick Lot's door in to rape those angels!

> **Genesis 19:8–9** [bold emphasis added]
> "Behold, I have two daughters who have not known any man. Let me bring them out to you, and do to them as you please. Only do nothing to these men, for they have come under the shelter of my roof." But they said, "Stand back!" And they said, "This fellow came to sojourn, and he has become the judge! Now we will deal worse with you than with them." Then they pressed hard against the man Lot, and drew near to **break the door down**.

Interestingly, Jude 1:6–7 starts out describing the angels that left their own habitation; these are obviously fallen angels reserved in everlasting chains. Immediately after the mention of these fallen angels, Sodom and Gomorrah are mentioned, detailing that the people of those cities gave themselves over to fornication, "going after strange flesh."

> **Jude 1:6–7 (ASV)** [bold emphasis added]
> And the **angels which kept not their first estate**, but left their own habitation, he hath reserved in everlasting chains under darkness unto the judgment of the great day. Even as **Sodom and Gomorrah**, and the cities about them in like manner, giving themselves over to fornication, and **going after strange flesh**, are set forth for an example, suffering the vengeance of eternal fire.

Most people think strange flesh is simply a reference to homosexuality, but that's not all. Obviously the people of Sodom practiced homosexuality; that's where the word *sodomy* comes from. However, according to Strong's Enhanced Lexicon, the word *strange* in this passage refers to an "other" or "different" type of flesh. How clear does scripture have to be? These angels were a biological species from the *heavens.*

> **G2087**
>
> ετερος
>
> *heteros*
> *het'-er-os*
> Of uncertain affinity; (an-, the) other or different: altered, else, next (day), one, (an-) other, some, strange.

What strikes me as the most amazing aspect of all of these scriptures is that Jesus singled out the days of Noah, and the events surrounding Sodom and Gomorrah, from all of history to describe what was coming in the End Times. Otherworldly beings having open contact with humanity is what defined these periods in history as different from all other times, and Jesus said we will see this again.

As a born again Christian reading the Bible, I came to the conclusion that in the future Earth will be in open contact with otherworldly beings, as it once was in the days of Noah. Ironically, I didn't believe this as the New Ager I was before, but as a born again Christian who was perfectly open and willing to throw away every New Age book I had ever read.

We are not in the days of open contact yet, but we're being conditioned for it. How on the nose does Hollywood have to be with movies such as *Open Contact*? Every year, more and more movies about otherworldly beings wielding supernatural powers become more prevalent. This is prophecy at work. The bulk of sci-fi and fantasy films are dedicated to otherworldly beings with supernatural powers, and there is no mistaking why. I will not call these films a conscious conspiracy but rather a prophetic wind sweeping through the earth, and even the secular world is on fire with it.

It's going to happen; they're coming. And we as a society sense it deep down inside. Some are afraid, especially the mockers and scoffers, just as Jesus said they would be (Luke 21:26).

The precursor to open contact, returning us to the days of Noah, is exactly what we are seeing with extraterrestrial phenomena today. While not all reported contact with extraterrestrials has been negative, the majority of it is.

Abductees frequently give accounts of being subjected to various reproductive experiments by force. The extraterrestrials conducting these experiments have highly questionable ethics. For entities intelligent enough to organize themselves in collective, industrial, technologically advanced societies, and master science to the point of manipulating gravity, punching wormholes in the cosmos, and traveling between higher and lower dimensions, certainly one would think they would have enough ethics to at least use anesthetics, which they sometimes don't!

I don't buy the *ethnocentrism* dogma about extraterrestrials being amoral, either. I have read about and personally interviewed people who tell about extraterrestrials expressing great satisfaction when inflicting physical and mental rape, torturous pain, horrendous terror, and the list goes on. Beings that are *amoral* do not *enjoy* making people suffer; that is straight-up evil. I am not saying all of them are evil, but some of them most certainly are.

Evil extraterrestrials are also tinkering with our DNA, just as I believe they did in the past, except now they're not creating a race of giants to conquer the world through brute, physical force. So what are they creating?

When Jesus came into this world, the Bible says that His physical appearance was that of an average Joe (Isaiah 53:2). God didn't want people to be distracted by His physical appearance, but rather to be drawn to His message and attracted to His humble, loving heart.

The devil is exactly the opposite. He loves the glory of men, so his goal is genetic superiority, with a primary emphasis on *image*. If Nephilim are spawned today (as some claim within the context of the alien abduction phenomenon), they are no longer extra-large. Instead they stand out for other extraordinary qualities, such as comeliness, intelligence, charisma, wealth, exceptional athletic abilities, or maybe even supernatural power. The *Nephilim 2.0* blend in, yet simultaneously stand out, and dominate society because they are the products of genetic engineering. They are Satan's experiments, working toward genetic perfection.

The Hollywood crowd meets this description. They are masters of the mainstream media, manipulating the geopolitical and social direction of the entire planet, frequently with an ungodly agenda. They have a reputation for their carnality and excessive emphasis on image. It wouldn't surprise me at all if many in Hollywood are Nephilim, though I won't pinpoint any celebrity idols in particular.

Some authors who write about the Nephilim cast the entire idea of their existence into question because the Nephilim tend to fall into a category of *automatically damned* to hell, despite the lack of scriptural support for such a notion. While it's true that the Nephilim in Noah's day were physically wiped out because of their widespread sin and destructive behavior, the issue of the eternal destination of their souls has to do with their actions, not their genetics.

They were all corrupt, and at least some of them became the demons/devils that plague us today, but that's not the same thing as saying they were all damned to hell. The same goes for any modern-day Nephilim that may be among us today.

Scripture tells us that the Nephilim were not part of God's original plan; they exist because angels rebelled and sinned. However, the same could be said of humans, who are the products of rape or sexual immorality/promiscuity. Rape and sexual immorality/promiscuity are sins, but the work of Jesus on the cross has ultimate power over these things. Therefore, children who are products of sinful unions are not automatically damned, but rather they have *free will.* They are judged according to their works and their faith, not their DNA. This applies to all people, and it also applies to the Nephilim of the past, as well as the present if any are among us.

There may be an argument that the Nephilim of the past might have been more susceptible to sin for a number of reasons. For example, the parents of first-generation Nephilim were fallen angels, so they would have been brought up to reject God. Secondly, they were superior in many ways: strength, size, power, and so on. Having superiority at such a young age could have made them proud. This could explain their widespread tendency to fulfill their roles as *gods* and accept the worship of people. While these details don't negate the applicability of free will, they do give insight as to why the Nephilim sunk to the level of depravity that they did.

Pondering the possibility of modern-day Nephilim, why would Satan want his minions to tinker with human DNA in order to create genetically superior people? What is the point of this? When I first conceived this question, Genesis 3:15 immediately popped into my mind.

> **Genesis 3:15** [bold emphasis and bracketed comments added]
> I will put **enmity between you [the serpent] and the woman [Eve]**, and between **your offspring [seed of the serpent, who will be the Antichrist] and her offspring [seed of the woman, who will be Jesus]**; he [Jesus] shall bruise your [the Antichrist's] head, and you [the Antichrist] shall bruise his [Jesus's] heel.

According to this prophecy, given directly after Adam and Eve sinned for the first time, God said He would destroy Satan through the seed of the woman. (Note that the King James Version of the Bible uses the word *seed*, whereas the English Standard Version uses the word *offspring*.)

The New Testament later reveals that Jesus was indeed the product of a literal, biological seed, God's *literal seed* formed in Mary's womb, which crushed the works of the devil. So if Jesus is a literal seed, then the Antichrist must also be a literal, biological seed. Why would one seed be literal and the other symbolic? The principles of hermeneutics teach that biblical interpretations should always be consistent, and the way I see it, this is the most consistent way to interpret this passage of scripture.

I realize that there is a certain degree of symbolism in this passage because Eve was not Jesus's mother but rather His human ancestor. However, the staggering truth is that Jesus literally was genetically part God, part man.

In the same manner, a snake will not be the father of the Antichrist but rather the fallen angel who spoke through the snake. Satan will most likely be the literal father of the Antichrist, and the Antichrist will be a Nephilim—part fallen angel, part man. This explains how he will be able to summon supernatural power, and it will also validate his godlike status as being supernatural in origin.

Consider how awestruck the people of Earth will be when faced with a person who is part human and part something else—something of an otherworldly, wondrous, incredibly powerful race of beings from another planet. Would that not be an unexpected tangent, capable of undermining all of the major religions of the world?

Many will find this outlandish conclusion just that, outlandish. Even many Christians will find this conclusion outlandish. However, at least Christians should realize that Genesis 6 and other scriptures clearly explain that fallen angels of the past were reproducing with humans, and their hybrid children were patently evil. These beings contributed to an extremely significant portion of human history highlighted in the Bible. Because of them, God destroyed the entire planet. In light of this, it should not be such a gigantic stretch for Christians to conclude that these activities will happen again in the future, with Satan himself.

While the fallen angels of the past, conducting their deviant sexual proclivities, were apprehended and chained up (Jude 1:6–7), Satan was most likely not chained up; otherwise, he would not be called the Prince of the Power of the Air (Ephesians 2:2) and the god of this world, reaping a harvest of corruption across the globe (2 Corinthians 4:4). I also don't see how he would have been able to tempt Jesus if he were chained up in Tartarus (Matthew 4:1–11, Luke 4:1–13).

Therefore, while Satan was not among those who were having sex with humans in the past, he was most likely the biggest instigator behind getting the other angels to do it. This is how Satan retains his limited freedom. He deceives others into doing his dirty work. He is like a conniving platoon leader, tricking his troops to go out into the minefield to clear it for him.

God allows Satan this latitude, ultimately to test all of the life in the universe, including angels. Eventually all who choose to follow Satan instead of God will be expunged from the universe.

Satan is in a strange sort of game with God. God's ways are beyond anyone, but Satan thinks he has a handle on the situation. He seems to play by God's rules just enough to be allowed to continue his games, but all the while he believes he is eventually going to get one over on God. The False Prophet and Antichrist spoken of in Revelation are his trump cards.

Satan refrained from sexual relations with humans in the past, but that doesn't mean he plans to permanently avoid partaking of this activity. He just knows that once he does, his time will be short, just as scripture predicts (Revelation 12:12). Therefore, he is taking his time. He wants the Antichrist, as well as the False Prophet, to be the ultimate expression of his handiwork, completing his satanic trinity and his war against God, which he refuses to acknowledge that he already has lost.

While Satan has deceived himself into believing that the rise of his power will result in his ultimate victory, the reality of the matter is that everything he is doing is nothing more than a commander directing his army to mass suicide.

3.4 Does the Bible Speak of Animal-Angel Hybrids?

Based on what I have concluded thus far, much of the alien abduction phenomenon we see today is a recap of the events that occurred during the days of Noah—a genetic interbreeding program between fallen angels and the humans of Earth. This, however, may not be all that is entailed in what the Bible defines as the Nephilim.

In Noah's time, the interbreeding program conducted by angels had no bounds. According to the book of Enoch, and further supported by ancient legends surrounding the globe, angels crossed not only with humans but also with animals, producing a plethora of half-angel, half-animal hybrids (Enoch 7, etc.). The Bible also hints at this activity, stating that *all flesh* had corrupted its way upon the earth.

> **Genesis 6:12** [bold emphasis added]
> And God saw the earth, and behold, it was corrupt, for **all flesh** had corrupted their way on the earth.

With our current understanding of genetics, it isn't possible to directly crossbreed radically different species with each other, yet. However, these beings were angels. Either they used their advanced understanding of genetics to accomplish this goal, or their glorified flesh was far more capable of doing things than our flesh. Either way, evidence of animal-angel hybrids is consistently spoken of in literature from ancient cultures around the world.

While the idea of animal-angel hybrids sounds whacky, scientifically speaking, if genetic experimentation was taking place in the ancient past, would it not also include an exploration into the genetic traits of animals as well? Scientists generally start with simple experiments and work their way up to more complex experiments, right?

Consider the possibility for a moment that creatures such as the Minotaur; centaurs; the dog-headed Set of Egypt; the lustful, conniving goat-man Pan of the Greeks; and the list goes on, may have actually existed. How freakishly bizarre might our world have been in the days of Noah?

Most people these days don't think for a single second that these mutated freaks existed. Nevertheless, for the past few thousand years, demons consistently have been depicted in art of all mediums with humanoid-animal qualities. Why is that?

The typical response to the existence of such entities is that there isn't a shred of physical evidence in existence, but keep in mind what I already discussed concerning that evidence and why it is lacking. It could be that people throughout the ages who have come into contact with the bones of these creatures very much regretted it. If touching the bones of an Old Testament prophet resulted in resurrection, it could be that the bones of these creatures might have resulted in nightmares, corrupt thoughts of murder, suicide, poltergeist activity, diseases, demonic possession, or even death. Such debilitating effects would most certainly have resulted in the disappearance of these cursed bones through the ages. No one in their right mind would want anything to do with them after seeing what happened to people who went near them or touched them.

I find it interesting that while most people, including Christians, will scoff at the idea of angel-animal hybrids, many of these same people are much more likely to believe in the existence of demons. When asked what demons look like, some of these people might even provide descriptions they have heard about from people who have had visions, demonic encounters, or near-death experiences (NDEs). Invariably, many demons are described as having horns. Many demons are described as mutated freaks, bizarre combinations of humanoid-animal hybrids, are they not?

Finally, taking this one step further, could it be that some of these beings still exist in this day and age, in the form of countless mythical creatures that continue to capture the imaginations of cultures around the world, yet mysteriously evade physical capture? Perhaps Bigfoot is part gorilla, part fallen angel, and it has a supernatural transdimensional ability to vanish from this dimension.

Consider the fact that many ancient legends often attribute supernatural abilities to mythological beings. There even may be an entire range of transdimensional beings imbued with supernatural power (i.e., powerful animal-angel Nephilim), and they are the source of many strange phenomena throughout the world. Could it be that many of the legends of lycanthropes, fairies, leprechauns, jinns, and the like, which pervade every culture on Earth, are surviving remnants of the Nephilim of old?

Ironically, the typical Christian response to the existence of paranormal entities is that they are all demonic. In this case, that's my conclusion as well, except I have provided the backstory as to how these beings came into existence.

- It makes sense that demons are commonly described with the physical characteristics of humanoid-animal hybrids.
- It makes sense that there are countless legends of supernatural humanoid-animal beings from ancient times, and those legends still persist with modern-day equivalents.
- It makes sense that beings with supernatural power are exceptionally adept at being intrusive and simultaneously evasive, and pretty much impossible to apprehend.
- It makes sense that there is a lack of physical evidence.
- It further makes sense that the actual existence of such cartoonish myths sounds preposterous to people these days. They want it that way; it makes for a more startling reveal in the future, when the stage is set for the strong delusion.

The days of Noah are returning, just as Jesus said they would, and Satan's strategy is aimed at one primary objective: to create a genetically superior hybrid capable of supernatural feats. The progenitors of the Nephilim have been honing their craft, refining what began as the unbridled experimentation of Noah's day. Some of these early Nephilim freaks are probably still running rampant today, and they have served their purpose in their contribution to the later generations of Nephilim, as well as in the spreading of myth and mayhem since ancient times.

Satan has been busy the past few thousand years, directing his legions to experiment away until they get everything just right. If my interpretation of Genesis 3:15 has any merit, it means his trump card will be his own DNA, combined with a human, in his personal genetic cocktail of the *Nephilim 3.0*. There may be at least two of these Nephilim 3.0s in our future; they will be the Antichrist and the False Prophet.

CHAPTER 4

ANTICHRISTS OF THE PAST

According to author John C. Brunt, the New Testament speaks of the Antichrist as not only a single figure to come in the future but also many people throughout history.[1] Jesus said that false Christs and false messiahs would arise (Mark 13:4–6, Matthew 24:1–2), and it is obvious to anyone who knows a little history that many have.

> **Mark 13:4–6**
> Tell us, when shall these things be, and what shall be the sign when all these things shall be fulfilled? And Jesus answering them began to say, Take heed lest any man deceive you: For many shall come in my name, saying, I am Christ; and shall deceive many.

> **Matthew 24:4–5**
> And Jesus answered and said unto them, Take heed that no man deceive you. For many shall come in my name, saying, I am Christ; and shall deceive many.

Researcher Todd Strandberg listed a number of people on his website who have been considered an Antichrist.[2] Some believe Nero was an Antichrist figure, but Titus probably tops the list, fulfilling Jesus's prophecy about the destruction of the Jewish temple in AD 70. In this instance, Jesus was quoting from the Old Testament prophet Daniel in Daniel 9:27, who I believe was using the *law of double reference*. This prophecy concerned the same event happening more than once in the days to come, by more than one Antichrist.[3]

> **Daniel 9:27** [bracketed comments and bold emphasis added]
> And he [the Antichrist] shall make a strong covenant with many for one week, and for half of the week **he shall put an end to sacrifice and offering**. And **on the wing of abominations shall come one who makes desolate**, until the decreed end is poured out on the desolator.

Prophecies are like that sometimes; they can repeat several times throughout history before a final fulfillment. I'm sure Jesus was well aware of the nefarious Greek emperor Antiochus IV Epiphanes and the role he played in this prophecy.[4] According to the book of 1 Maccabees, Antiochus erected a statue of the Greek god Zeus in the second Jewish temple and sacrificed swine on the altar.

From more recent times, Stalin of the Soviet Union and Chairman Mao of China have certainly shed enough blood to qualify as Antichrist figures. But perhaps the example of an Antichrist most people are familiar with from modern history is Adolph Hitler. His name is practically synonymous with the personification of evil, despite the fact that ten times more blood has been shed in the name of communism under Stalin and Mao.

Most people know about the infamous number of the beast mentioned in Revelation 13:18. Some early interpreters thought individual Roman emperors were being referenced. Irenaeus, for example, as well as many modern interpreters, saw the number 666 as symbolic of all evil.[5] I recall how intrigued I was when I first learned about Hitler's well-known histogram that sums up his name to "666."[6] If A = 100, B = 101, C = 102, and so on, then the following is true:

H = 107
I = 108
T = 119
L = 111
E = 104
R = 117
666

Histograms are interesting, but I don't put much stock in them. After all, Hitler spoke German, and the book of Revelation was written in Greek. For the above histogram to be truly relevant, it would have to equal 666 in one of those languages, not English. But that's beside the point; Hitler is easily identified as an Antichrist for many more reasons than a peculiar histogram.

For starters, Hitler specifically loathed Jews and Christians, and he murdered them relentlessly. The Bible states this to be a primary attribute of the Antichrist, based on his actions. Why else would anyone go out of his or her way to single out a specific group of people to torture, enslave, and slaughter, which the Bible says the Antichrist will do in the future? This is not just war for the sake of greed or power; this is a profound racial hatred that has plagued Jews for thousands of years, no matter where they happen to be.

The pharaoh of Egypt (Exodus 1:5–22); Shalmaneser, the ruler of Assyria (2 Kings 17:5–6); King Nebuchadnezzar of Babylon (2 Kings 24:10–16); Haman of the Medo-Persian empire (Esther 3:9); Antiochus IV Epiphanes, the Greek ruler of Syria (Daniel 8:23–25; 1 Maccabees 1–6); Titus, the Roman emperor who slaughtered over 1.1 million Jews and enslaved more than 97,000 (documented by Jewish historian Flavius Josephus in *The Wars of the Jews*, VI, ix, 3), and Islamic and even corrupt Christian empires since the conversion of Rome under Constantine, all severely persecuted the Jews.[7]

And then there was Hitler, who was consumed with rage over the Jews. In some cases, these bloodthirsty psychopaths even made the specific point of desecrating the Jewish religion. That's like being so filled with hate that torture of all forms, slavery, and murder are not enough. The hatred is so severe that anyone who questions it is added to the list of whom to slaughter next. Why?

Not everyone reading this may agree, but the answer is Satan hates Jews and Christians because he is at war against God. Jesus, God's only begotten Son, came to Earth through the immaculate conception of a Jewish woman in the lineage of King David. Jesus is also the head of the Christian church—that is, the body of Christ (1 Corinthians 12:27). Since both Jews and Christians are directly linked to Jesus (referred to as their Judeo-Christian heritage), they are guilty by association in the low court of Satan, and thus they are Satan's number one targets on the earth. Persecution toward Jews and Christians resonates in this world now, and throughout history, because of Satan's war against God.

It is only because God's protection is on His children that Jews and Christians still exist at all. Now in those times and places where it sometimes seems like God is not protecting His children, such as in the Middle East or any countries where religious persecution is widespread, God has His reasons for allowing things to happen. It all has to do with love, which requires free-will agents and a portion of time-space in order to be expressed. It is a difficult thing to contemplate.

Amazingly, the Christians in most places of persecution understand more than any other people the profound depths of God's heart of love, just as those spoken of in the Bible in Hebrews chapter 11.

> **Hebrews 11:35–40**
> Women received their dead raised to life again: and others were tortured, not accepting deliverance; that they might obtain a better resurrection: And others had trial of cruel mocking and scourging, yes, moreover of bonds and imprisonment: They were stoned, they were sawn asunder, were tempted, were slain with the sword: they wandered about in sheepskins and goatskins; being destitute, afflicted, tormented; (Of whom the world was not worthy:) they wandered in

> deserts, and in mountains, and in dens and caves of the earth. And these all, having obtained a good report through faith, received not the promise: God having provided some better thing for us, that they without us should not be made perfect.

A number of persecuted missionaries have spoken to my pastor directly, and their prayer requests are *never* for the persecution to stop but rather for the saints to endure it. Is that not baffling? It seems so counterintuitive, yet somehow they have come to understand that more people are saved by witnessing their patient and loving endurance of suffering and sacrifice, rather than relief from this turmoil.

As I reflect on American culture, where such persecution does not exist, it has not escaped my attention that American Christians seem to be decreasing in number as well as in faithfulness and obedience, while those in persecuted countries are growing at an exponential rate at the risk of losing their lives. In those places, miracles are not uncommon. The faith of persecuted believers is out of this world.

The persecution of the righteous is a deep mystery to which I can at least say this much: behind all God's actions is a heart of pure love. God's motivation is love, and He is just and merciful. When it seems by the state of affairs in the world that this is not the case, it is because we do not have the mind of God, nor do we have His perception or perspective.

Concerning persecution during the days of Nazi Germany, many Christians risked their lives to save Jews. God put that love in their hearts to do so. Anyone who stood in Hitler's way was marked for death, so the Christians of strong conscience who would not remain silent or inactive regarding Hitler's atrocities were killed. Of the eleven million slaughtered by Hitler, an estimated six million were Jews and at least three million were Christians.[8]

Hitler committed these atrocities, yet strangely he still held mass appeal among the citizens of his country. Did he appeal to every demographic? No, but he certainly appealed to the vast majority of the people of Germany. How?

4.1 How Did Hitler Do It?

Just before World War II, Germany was struggling with extreme poverty, vulnerable to a crippled economy. Seizing on this vulnerability, Hitler picked out a couple of things everyone could agree on. National pride was something that appealed to most Germans. Hitler told the citizens of his country that they should be the rulers of the world because they were better than everyone else. Everything was ripe for their taking if they simply mustered the courage to take it. He made them feel like victims of an oppressive world, that they were the 99 percent (in today's terminology) and that they had to do something about it to turn things around.

Using his twisted logic, Hitler convinced Germany that attacking Poland and stealing everything they had was the right thing to do. Never mind the fact that Poland bore no hostile intentions toward anyone. Propaganda was Hitler's biggest weapon, and he used it expertly. Propaganda can also be used as a tool to achieve wonderful things but certainly not in this case.

Hitler reminded the Germans that they excelled in many things and that Germany had the potential to be one of the most scientifically advanced superpowers of their time. On the surface, his message carried with it a degree of supreme optimism for the average German citizen, but it was at the expense of anyone who was not German, and especially at the expense of the Jews.

Does this boastful and slanderous talk sound familiar?

> **Revelation 13:4–5** [bold emphasis added]
> And they worshipped the dragon which gave power unto the beast: and they worshipped the beast, saying, "Who is like unto the beast? Who is able to make war with him?" And there was given unto him **a mouth speaking great things and blasphemies** ..."

Anti-Semitism was strong in Germany during Hitler's time, so singling out the "undesirables" as a group of people to blame all their problems on harmonized well with Hitler's Arian doctrine of the "master race." A version of this is exactly what the final incarnation of the Antichrist will do in the future, yet his version will be broader in scope. Basically, anyone on his side will be in the *in* group, and anyone not on his side will be in the *out* group. Those in the out group will be dehumanized via propaganda. Once that is successfully accomplished among the masses, all manner of inhuman acts will commence against those in the out group, not unlike what we see among the terrorists of today.

Hitler loved the benefits of science, and he inspired his scientists to throw caution to the wind when it came to ethics. They were free to be "mad scientists." Many of their experiments were horrific, and they justified their actions with scientific ideology. They believed they were merely being consistent, practicing the survival of the fittest, and in fact they were. The theory of evolution, a godless theology taught in the public schools, was the rave back then, providing all the fuel Hitler could ever need or want to support his master race delusion of grandeur.

Unfortunately, the cherished works of Darwin that Hitler so loved and used expertly to his advantage are still in effect, taught in educational institutions around the world. In the minds of the global consciousness, they quietly await for their starring role in the strong delusion.

Actor Ben Stein's documentary, *Expelled: No Intelligence Allowed*, sheds light on the biased, closed-door policy emanating from modern-day academia, requiring the teaching of evolution while simultaneously denying any other alternative.[9] While the documentary was wildly successful, it was also widely criticized as full of "patronizing, poorly structured arguments" and ironically, defined as "dishonest and divisive propaganda."[10]

Regarding the theory of evolution, I believe Charles Darwin was a type of Antichrist. He prepared the way for Adolph Hitler, and I suspect the main Antichrist to come will also tap into his reservoir of deception. In the event that extraterrestrials are proven to exist, advocates of evolution will instantly pounce on the opportunity to announce that they were right all along, and the God of the Bible is a work of *pure fiction.* Christians who are familiar with the research in this book and others like it will be better prepared for that day.

4.2 Did Hitler Have Otherworldly Help?

Hitler was a purveyor of religious artifacts and deeply interested in the occult.[11] He was interested in obtaining religious artifacts rumored to have supernatural power. In fact, he was interested in any power, be it science or the spiritual realm or a combination of both, if it would give him an edge.

While almost everyone knows about the 1947 UFO crash in Roswell, New Mexico, a lesser-known incident is rumored to have occurred about a decade earlier: another UFO crash in the Black Forest of Nazi Germany.[12] The technology gleaned from that crash was so advanced, it crossed the boundary of known science and entered the realm of the supernatural. Since both Hitler and his comrade in arms, Heinrich Himmler, were so obsessed with exotic technology, if such a crash actually occurred, reverse engineering that technology would have been their top priority.

Author Steve Quayle delves deep into the Nazi/UFO connection for anyone who wants to know every sorted detail. I, however, will simply provide enough information here to establish the basics.

In *The Secret History of Extraterrestrials: Advanced Technology and the Coming New Race*, author Len Kasten discloses a plethora of details about Hitler's affiliation with extraterrestrials that goes far beyond the Germans' reverse-engineering ET technology that they were lucky enough to retrieve from a crash.

Dr. Hermann Rauschning, a minor Nazi official, wrote a book shortly following World War II titled *Hitler Speaks*. In it he made the sensational claim that Hitler was in contact with otherworldly beings he referred to as "super humans." These supermen called themselves Aryans; they were purportedly survivors of Atlantis and lived underground in the vicinity of Tibet, among other places. They were tall, blond Caucasians, with an average height of six to seven feet, and were the reported source of inspiration for Hitler's Aryan master race.

Contact with these tall whites was established through the efforts of Karl Haushofer, a former professor of political science at Munich University, who later became deeply entrenched in the occult. As founder of the occult group known as the Vril Society, Karl Haushofer initiated contact with the Aryans through his association with Tibetan monks who were adept at black magic.

Haushofer expressed an early interest in Hitler and visited him during his time in prison, at Landsberg Fortress, in 1924. It was there that he shared his similar occult interests with Hitler and helped him write what became the Nazi bible, *Mein Kampf*, complete with all of its master race propaganda, derived entirely from the Aryans.

Contact was also established with another off-world race of beings from the Aldebaran System within the Taurus Constellation, through a medium by the name of Maria Orsic. Maria was also a member of the Vril Society, and she had much to say about these off-world Aryans. She reportedly channeled their transmissions in the ancient Sumerian language.

Once the Vril Society was able to translate what she was saying, the members learned that these beings claimed to be the founders of the ancient Sumerians. According to ancient Sumerian texts, these Sumerian gods from the stars were referred to as the Annunaki.[13]

I've said it before, and I'll say it again: I think there are far more elements of prophetic truth in sci-fi and fantasy movies these days than people realize. For anyone who has seen the *Captain America* film in which he battles the evil German organization with otherworldly connections, known as Hydra, that was a page right out of Rauschning's book *Hitler Speaks*.

The Annunaki fit the description of the "Watchers" mentioned in the book of Enoch. Both the Hebrews and Sumerians wrote about otherworldly beings inhabiting the same geographic area in the Middle East, at the same time, doing the same things. The only difference between the Sumerian Annunaki and the Hebrew Watchers is that the Hebrews did not consider these otherworldly beings to be gods worthy of worship, whereas the Sumerians did. Like all other ancient legends, the Sumerians spoke of a pantheon of powerful gods from the stars, which they worshipped. The Old Testament prophets, however, described these beings as disobedient fallen angels at war with the one true God.

Concerning *Hitler Speaks*, it is difficult to determine how much of Rauschning's information is true. On the one hand, some of it sounds like the detailed ramblings of a paranoid, basement-dwelling conspiracy theorist. On the other hand, certain facts about Hitler are widely known, such as his deep interest in the occult and his obvious connection with the realm of the demonic to the point of probably being demon possessed.

The Nazis also wielded incredibly advanced technology far ahead of their time. Moreover, the narrative of a powerful otherworldly race of humanoid immortals (angels), many of which are abhorrently corrupt, is consistent with the biblical description of the Watchers. The bad ones would have been right at home striking an arrangement with Hitler.

Whether the rumored UFO crash in Germany really occurred or not, there is considerable evidence that the Nazis had what appears to be otherworldly technology. For anyone who wants to know more about it, consider these resources:

- Book: *Secret Treaty: The United States Government and Extra-terrestrial Entities*[14]
- Book: *The S. S. Brotherhood of the Bell: The Nazis' Incredible Secret Technology* (a.k.a. *The SS Brotherhood of the Bell: Nasa's Nazis, JFK, And Majic-12*)
- Book: *Hitler's Flying Saucers*
- Book: *Man-Made UFOs, 1944-1994: Fifty Years of Suppression*
- TV Show: *Ancient Aliens, Episode 19, Aliens and the Third Reich*

- Steve Quayle's research: Simply search the internet for "Steve Quayle"

The idea that Hitler may have had access to otherworldly technology does pose a slight conundrum. If the Nazis had extraterrestrial allies with technology so advanced that they mastered a propulsion system that could warp the fabric of time-space, why didn't they win the war? There are a number of explanations that address this quandary.

For starters, it could be that the only otherworldly technology the Nazis obtained was limited to the Black Forest crash. Nazi technology was far ahead of its time, yet it was lacking in certain areas. For example, why would the Nazis be able to use antigravity, or possibly even experiment with teleportation or time travel using a bell-shaped device called *Die Glocke*, but not be able to develop an atomic bomb? The answer to this question is reverse engineering. Because reverse engineering is the scientific equivalent of cheating and looking up the answers in the back of the book, without knowing how they were obtained, it can yield sporadic results.

Another reason the Nazis may have been hampered is the simple fact that the Aryans—or Annunaki or whoever they were—might have simply withheld certain technology, determining that the Nazis either didn't need it or shouldn't be trusted with it. Sharing technology to a point is what we see in the world today.

For example, the United States did not give F-16 fighter jets to Israel and Egypt until the F-16 was yesterday's technology. Nations will also get involved in proxy wars, supplying either the governments or rebel factions with various weapons to give them an advantage. This is a sneaky way of choosing sides to obtain a strategic advantage in the country in question, without funding an actual military campaign. The technology that is shared in these international exchanges is never the best of the best. In the case of the Aryans, they would have withheld nuclear power from the Nazis because Hitler would have gone nuts pressing the button and nuking the entire planet into oblivion.

Despite the fact that the claims made about Hitler's otherworldly connections seem too fantastic to believe, I tend to lean in favor of the idea that at least some of these claims are true. The reason I even bring up the extraterrestrial connection with the Nazis is because Hitler was a *type* of Antichrist, and the idea of him obtaining otherworldly satanic help from the *heavens* should be no surprise. The Bible speaks plainly about such things.

Satan is referred to as the "prince of the power of the air" (Ephesians 2:2) and the "god of this world" (2 Corinthians 4:4) because he still holds considerable sway over activities in the upper atmosphere of the earth. Satan most likely instigated the activities of the Watchers, who descended from the sky in the book of Enoch.

Revelation 12:4 refers to Satan casting a third of the "stars of heaven" down to the earth. Obviously these are not literally stars because a single star is larger than the earth. However, the symbols in the book of Revelation actually have literal components. Satan literally deceived members of the host of heaven into joining him in his rebellion against God. Those beings literally did come from among the stars, so referring to them as stars provides a clue as to their origins.

> **Revelation 12:4** [bold emphasis and bracketed comments added]
> **His [the devil's] tail swept down a third of the stars of heaven** and cast them to the earth. And **the dragon** [the devil] stood before the woman who was about to give birth, so that when she bore her child he might devour it.

Scripture is replete with references to intelligent life in the cosmos. Most references to stars place them in the context of celestial spheres in outer space (with the sun, moon, and stars), but a number of scriptures, such as the passage above, also associate stars with powerful beings in the heavens. Job 38:4–7 is yet another clear passage about beings known as the sons of God, who are linked with the morning stars singing together.

> **Job 38:4–7** [bold emphasis added]
> "Where were you **when I laid the foundation of the earth**? Tell me, if you have understanding. Who determined its measurements—surely you know! Or who stretched the line upon it? On what were its bases sunk, or who laid its cornerstone, **when the morning stars sang together** and **all the sons of God shouted for joy**?"

Note that the Hebrew word, *bene Elohim*, referring to the sons of God, is the same Hebrew word referenced in Genesis 6 about the beings who mated with humans and sired the Nephilim. These "angels" (i.e., extraterrestrials) dwell among the stars (outer space).

Concerning the stars (heavens or outer space) and the beings associated with them (host of heaven), God provided the Israelites with a stern warning not to worship them. In today's language, scripture says not to worship beings from outer space.

> **Deuteronomy 4:19** [bold emphasis and bracketed comments added]
> And **beware** lest you **raise your eyes to heaven,** [outer space] and **when you see** the **sun** and the **moon** and the **stars**, all the **host of heaven,** [life in outer space], you be drawn away and **bow down to them** [otherworldly beings] and **serve them**, things that the Lord your God has allotted to all the peoples under the whole heaven.

Certainly one could argue that "host of heaven" means the sun, moon, and stars, and injecting "life in outer space" is a stretch on the interpretation, but if that's the case, then why is there such a clear and strong connection throughout all of ancient history spanning the globe, linking otherworldly beings, aka "gods," with the cosmos? This scripture is simply another example pointing to that same narrative.

Going back to the ancient-astronaut theory, the common thread linking every ancient society on Earth is one civilization after another violating Deuteronomy 4:19. Otherworldly beings came down, infecting societies with a strong delusion, and people worshipped them. One society after another plunged into a quagmire of self-destructive moral decay.

In the days of Noah, shortly after the arrival of the sons of God, "every intention of the thoughts of [people's] hearts was only evil continually" (Genesis 6:5). Following the flood of Noah, the sons of God returned to places like Sodom and Gomorrah, and these two cities now represent the standard of depravity to which all other civilizations are compared (2 Peter 2:6, Jude 1:7). Years later, as Abraham's descendants multiplied into the Israelite nation, they turned against God. What was the result? They ended up burning their children alive, sacrificing them to the so-called god of Moloch (Leviticus 18:21).

Nazi Germany was most likely another example of otherworldly beings exploiting the greatest evil of their day: racism, fueled by a superiority complex inspired by the teachings of evolution. As for today, the evil of racism has mutated. Advocates of the homosexual lifestyle now use the arguments *against* racism to *justify* that lifestyle. By successfully doing this, they have established a precedent that *any* sexual act or behavior—be it incest, bestiality, pedophilia, *anything*—can be justified as a genetically predisposed behavior, and therefore be an acceptable alternative. This is the slippery slope upon which we now stand that the Bible accurately predicted long ago (2 Timothy 3:1–4).

Sexual immorality is the legacy of fallen angels, and cleaning up the mess of that sexual depravity with another abomination is the natural extension of it. That is why over three thousand children are sacrificed on the altar of abortion every day, which I'm sure far exceeds the sacrifices made to Moloch in the past.[15] The vast majority of these sacrifices are cleaning up the mess of sexual immorality.

This is no coincidence. This is the fulfillment of prophecy; this is part of the strong delusion. We have returned to the days of Noah, just as Jesus said we would. Open contact with otherworldly beings is about the only thing that is missing.

4.3 Did Hitler Worship a Strange God?

The warning in Deuteronomy 4:19 still stands today, and it will soon be more relevant than ever. In the future, when the Antichrist rises to power, most of what will make him so powerful will be an otherworldly alliance, which the Bible refers to as a strange or "foreign god."

> **Daniel 11:39** [bold emphasis and bracketed commented added]
> He [the Antichrist] shall deal with the strongest fortresses with the help of a **foreign god**.

Along with the foreign god of the Antichrist will be three lying spirits, referenced in Revelation 16:13–16. These beings will feed the frenzied hype about how wonderful this foreign god is.

A key verse that connects this foreign god of the Antichrist with otherworldly beings in the cosmos is Daniel 8:10–12, which speaks of the Antichrist going into battle against the host of heaven and some of the stars. This is another scripture that directly refers to the stars and associates powerful beings among them.

> **Daniel 8:10–12** [bold emphasis added]
> It grew great, even to the **host of heaven**. And **some of the host** and **some of the stars** it **threw down to the ground and trampled on them**. It became great, even as great as the Prince of the host. And the regular burnt offering was taken away from him, and the place of his sanctuary was overthrown. And a host will be given over to it together with the regular burnt

> offering because of transgression, and it will throw truth to the ground, and it will act and prosper.

Note: The reference to throwing down these heavenly host appears to be talking about Star Wars-type battles in the future, in which the Antichrist will be victorious. It is likely that some of these battles will be warring factions in the enemy's camp. This scripture may very well tie directly to Revelation 12:4 mentioned earlier, which also speaks of Satan casting stars down to the earth.

In summation, scripture speaks of intelligent, powerful beings that have dwelt among the stars since before the creation of the world (Job 38, Nehemiah 9:6, Revelation 12:12). When Lucifer rebelled against God, his kingdom on Earth was destroyed, and his access to the heavens was limited (Ezekiel 28:11–19, Isaiah 14:12–14). Using what remaining freedom he had, Satan deceived humanity not long after God created it (Genesis 3), and through that deception, he obtained greater access and power on the earth, and perhaps even limited access into the heavens once again (Ephesians 2:2; 2 Corinthians 4:4; Job 1:6, 2:1).

Many of Satan's followers tried to take over the world in the days of Noah (Genesis 6), but God put an end to it with the flood of Noah. Following the flood, Satan's followers contaminated the earth yet again in the area around the Tower of Babel (Genesis 11), but God put a stop to what was going on there. Then they contaminated society in the cities of Sodom and Gomorrah, and God destroyed those cities (Genesis 19:24). They then infected the area of ancient Israel (Numbers 13:33, 1 Samuel 17:23, 2 Samuel 21), after which God sent in the Israelites to drive them out and put an end to their evil practices.

While the above infestations of otherworldly beings are documented in the Bible, other infiltrations were going on elsewhere because, as I already mentioned, pretty much *every ancient society in the world* had a great deal to say about otherworldly visitors in times past. When those alien infestations involved fallen angels corrupting society, God countered them. One example of this is

Plato's account of the destruction of Atlantis, which fits this narrative perfectly. Otherworldly beings brought the civilization of Atlantis to unparalleled heights, but their society eventually became abhorrently corrupt and was met with cataclysmic destruction.[16]

Eventually we will come full circle. Otherworldly incursions into this world are increasing every year, and societies around the globe are being conditioned to the idea of extraterrestrial life. When the time is right, just as Jesus prophesied, "the heavens will be shaken" (Matthew 24:29–30, Mark 13:24–26, Luke 21:25–27). I believe this is a direct reference to public disclosure and the initiation of open contact with otherworldly beings.

> **Matthew 24:29–30** [bold emphasis added]
> "Immediately after the tribulation of those days the sun will be darkened, and the moon will not give its light, and **the stars will fall from heaven**, and **the powers of the heavens will be shaken**. Then will appear in heaven the sign of the Son of Man, and then all the tribes of the earth will mourn, and they will see the Son of Man coming on the clouds of heaven with power and great glory.
>
> **Mark 13:24–26** [bold emphasis added]
> "But in those days, after that tribulation, the sun will be darkened, and the moon will not give its light, and **the stars will be falling from heaven**, and **the powers in the heavens will be shaken**. And then they will see the Son of Man coming in clouds with great power and glory.
>
> **Luke 21:25–27** [bold emphasis added]
> "And **there will be signs in sun and moon and stars**, and **on the earth distress of nations in perplexity** because of the roaring of the sea and the waves, **people fainting with fear** and with foreboding of

> **what is coming on the world**. For **the powers of the heavens will be shaken**. And then they will see the Son of Man coming in a cloud with power and great glory.

Returning to the account of Daniel 8:10–12, notice that following the success of the Antichrist against his otherworldly enemies, he claims a deity status. These battles will provide the Antichrist with all the propaganda he could ever want or need. If said battles involve otherworldly invaders, like an *Independence Day* scenario (for those familiar with the movie, which I consider prophetic regarding the strong delusion), just think how popular the Antichrist will be if he appears to save the world. Never mind the fact that the battles in question could simply involve former allies that he has turned on, in order to use them as a propaganda tool. These warring factions in the enemy's camp will be played out before a global audience, as a spectacle of awe and wonder, with the sole purpose of promoting the Antichrist to a godlike status.

> **Daniel 8:10–12** [bold emphasis added]
> It grew great, even to the **host of heaven**. And **some of the host** and **some of the stars** it **threw down to the ground and trampled on them**. It became great, even as great as the Prince of the host. And the regular burnt offering was taken away from him, and the place of his sanctuary was overthrown. And a host will be given over to it together with the regular burnt offering because of transgression, and it will throw truth to the ground, and it will act and prosper.

Hitler fit the mold of an Antichrist in many ways, just as those before him. Aside from having access to advanced technology, Hitler also gave reverence to a *foreign god*. Believe it or not, the symbol of the swastika is the symbol of a foreign god, originating in the Sanskrit language as a symbol of the Hindu god Brahma.[17] The ancient Sanskrit Hindu Vedic writings document yet another example of the "sons of God" mentioned in Genesis 6, up to their wicked ways in ancient India. The Hindus have many artistic renditions of these beings, often much larger than humans, and sometimes having blue skin. For all anyone knows, it could have been Brahma himself who was in contact with Hitler.

Each time the spirit of the Antichrist incarnates in a human being, it comes closer to achieving the goal of world domination. Hitler was, by my assessment, Satan's last greatest attempt, in which he almost pulled off his goal through military might. He failed, as in times past, but he is not done yet. Another deceiver is on the way.

Who will be the next, and how will that next incarnation take the deception further than any before? What do we see in the world today that the Antichrist will have at his disposal? How can the scope of deception be broadened beyond the borders of a single nation?

CHAPTER 5

THE RISE OF ISLAM

Up until this point, I have been discussing various aspects of extraterrestrial life and how they will tie into the strong delusion, and now I will transition into the second element of the strong delusion, which involves the religion of Islam.

When I read Joel Richardson's book *The Islamic Antichrist* in early 2014, I immediately started connecting the dots of his research to my own. The strong delusion will be Satan's masterpiece, and I now believe it will involve not only a return to open contact with otherworldly beings, but it will also involve the religion of Islam, albeit a new, mutated, *otherworldly* flavor of Islam.

To be clear, Richardson speaks of many prophetic things regarding Islam but nothing about extraterrestrial life. I, however, saw an obvious extraterrestrial presence in the Qur'an and Hadiths as I researched them, the same way I saw *Aliens in the Bible*, so my perspective includes Richardson's revelations about Islam, as well as an extraterrestrial presence.

It is obvious to many that the spirit of the Antichrist is moving powerfully today, especially in the Middle East. Just as the shadow of Sauron fell across Middle Earth in *The Lord of the Rings*, so too has the spirit of the Antichrist grown strong in the Middle East—to the extent of public beheadings, torture, mindless violence probably rivaling the days of Noah, and an endless stream of plotting and executing terrorist attacks.

While the issue of racism and hate crimes continues to take center stage in the United States, it's nothing compared to what has been witnessed in the Middle East. No American general in history has ever resorted to cannibalism on the battlefield, but this is not unheard of among Islamic radicals who have a hatred spawn from the very pit of hell.[1] Beheading, slavery, and basic torture are old school; these days jihadists are resorting to crucifixions, organ harvesting, burying and burning people alive, mass rape, cannibalism, and drinking the blood of their victims.[2] They not only partake of these activities; they revel in them, capturing videos of them on their cell phones to post on the internet as victories over the infidels.

Consider the days of Noah, and reflect on the actions of today's jihadists, who think they're actually serving God.

> **Genesis 6:5** [bold emphasis added]
> The Lord saw that the wickedness of man was great in the earth, and that **every intention of the thoughts of his heart was only evil continually.**

5.1 The Christian Perspective of Tolerance and Love

Before I go any further into the topic of Islamic fundamentalism, for those who may have a bone of contention with me for what may appear to be my trashing of the religion of Islam, I hope they will consider reading this book to completion and consider further research into the details I discuss before ascribing to me the propaganda label of "Islamophobe."

As a Christian, I do not believe in forced conversions at the end of a rifle's barrel or at the edge of a machete. That kind of conversion will never be valid in the eyes of God, and it's ridiculous that anyone thinks it would. God wants to win us over with love, not terror.

Does God have the power to destroy the earth at any time, in the blink of an eye, if He so desires it? Of course He does, but He is not doing it because He is the strongest advocate for freedom in the universe. This is common sense. All the cruelty and evil in the world today that people often blame on God is actually the result of God's boundless respect for freedom, the autonomy he has given mankind to self-govern, and His desire for mercy even with the most heinous of people.

God will eventually come and settle things on this planet once and for all, but in this current age, He is giving us time because of His mercy and compassion. We do not always see it this way because we want justice, but justice is a two-way street. *Everyone is guilty of something.* Right now God is giving us time to repent and demonstrate what kind of people we choose to be.

I believe that terror, fear, intimidation, and control are strategies employed by Satan, not God. Whatever relationship people have with God when they go to meet Him after they die is between each person and God. The thoughts and intentions that exist in the hearts and minds of all human beings belong to God, and God alone, to evaluate and judge.

I do not believe that anyone should ever be killed or persecuted because he or she happens to follow a religion that others disagree with. Understandably, however, if a certain religion calls for one particular group of people to conduct heinous crimes of physical violence against another group of people, it's only fair and just to stand up for those who are attacked. That's called self-defense, and this ethical baseline applies to everyone.

For example, if Christian terrorists were acting like ISIS, to say that I would be upset with them is an understatement. What's more, in no way, shape, or form would I make any excuses for them. I would publically denounce them and not declare my affiliation with any aspect of their beliefs because the God I worship is the God of love, and the Bible proves it. Love is not just *an* attribute of God but rather the entire sum of *who He is* (1 John 4:16). Everything God does is motivated by pure love; it is the core of His being.

> **1 John 4:16** [bold emphasis added]
> So we have come to know and to believe the love that God has for us. **God is love**, and whoever abides in love abides in God, and God abides in him.

I honestly believe there are many Muslims who are tolerant, peace-loving people. The problem is not with them but rather with the Qur'an and Hadiths, as I will disclose in this book. Peaceful Muslims either don't know very much about their Islamic doctrine, or they use a variety of ways to excuse the distasteful portions of it.

God speaks with everyone in a unique way. In our innermost beings, God determines whether or not we choose to listen to His voice of love, which transcends religious doctrine, dogma, values, norms, morays, ethics, culture, language … *everything*. God evaluates us for one main thing: love. This is the core of Christianity (1 John 4:16, 5:3; Luke 10:27; 1 Corinthians 13). The more love we have in our hearts, the more receptive we naturally will be to God's voice. Common sense dictates that if this were not the case, how would anyone ever come to know God? Scripture states this point blank in 1 John 4:7–8.

> **1 John 4:7–8** [bold emphasis added]
> Beloved, let us love one another: for love is of God; and **every one that loves is born of God, and knows God**. He that loves not knows not God; for God is love.

The equation of God = love cuts through the religious red tape. This scripture means to me that if a Muslim honestly believes what 1 John 4:7–8 says about love, I would be inclined to consider the *possibility* that the Muslim could be saved by faith in the knowledge of who God actually is: *the incarnation of love*. Having a genuine relationship with God is more than an intellectual body of knowledge; it's more than the syntax and pronunciation of a certain name in a certain language; it's more than semantics. It's love.

Now I can hear Christians rattling off 2 Peter 3:16 and other scriptures, telling me I'm way off base here with my suggestion that Muslims can be saved without converting to Christianity. That's not what I'm saying. Jesus gave us the Great Commission for a reason: to spread the knowledge of Him throughout the earth. That's very important! However, what I'm referring to here is the raw essence of the heart on which God judges people, the stuff He's looking for when He evaluates a soul.

God is looking for love, which is revealed in various ways (selflessness, sacrifice—that isn't suicide bombing, repentance, caring for others, etc.). Those who have love in their hearts respond to the Holy Spirit when He comes knocking.

Those who have not yet accepted Christ but have all the right ingredients in their hearts, I call *pre-Christians*, though most Muslims would reject being called pre-Christians. However, an open face-to-face conversation with Jesus would probably clear things up in short order, which is actually happening all over the Middle East with Muslims right now, and they end up becoming Christians.[3] Seeing Jesus face-to-face can open the eyes of pre-Christians, and ironically, so can seeing the works of the devil.

Consider a Voice of the Martyrs article titled "The Islamic State Drove Me to Christ." In it, Pastor Joseph reports seeing large numbers of Muslim youth in Iraq leaving Islam after learning how the Qur'an inspired ISIS and its slaughter of Christians.[4]

Read 1 John 4:7–8 again. These young Muslims have true love in their hearts; therefore, they are *born of God*, even though all of their lives they were professing Muslims. Seeing the slaughter of fellow human beings has torn into their hearts to such an extent that it opened their eyes to Jesus. Before they could even talk, they were taught by their parents, siblings, relatives, friends, neighbors, town clerics, television—their entire world—to venerate the Qur'an with unyielding, unquestioned adoration. They cannot even say Muhammad's name without the suffix of "peace be upon him." Yet, in the face of all that unrelenting indoctrination, they tossed the Qur'an in the trash when they finally realized that it was not consistent with a heart of love. These people *knew God*, even though they were Muslims.

> **1 John 4:7–8** [bold emphasis added]
> Beloved, let us love one another: for love is of God; and **every one that loves is born of God, and knows God**. He that loves not knows not God; for God is love.

"I was a Muslim, and now I am seeing," one former Muslim told Pastor Joseph after studying the Qur'an in depth. This began when ISIS arrived in his hometown of Mosul. He constantly found himself declaring, "This is not Islam."[5] God gave this man a starting point, but it needed a minor modification. He would have been more accurate to say, "This is not *me*; what you people are doing is *wrong*!"

Realizing his declaration, "This is not Islam," had little substance to back it up, he researched the Qur'an hoping to prove that ISIS was not following *true* Islam. As he studied the Qur'an for hours on end, he eventually discovered that ISIS was, in fact, following true Islam, and it was he who was at odds with it.

Pastor Joseph described yet another man who was shocked at discovering just how precisely the Qur'an had inspired ISIS. Upon this discovery, he became an atheist. This empty state of being did not last very long, however. Days later he happened upon a group of men sitting around a table outside a library. They must have been bold Christians because there were Bibles and Christian literature on the table out in the open, in spite of everything going on in the area with ISIS. When he asked the men for a Bible, they readily gave him one. The following account is what happened next:

> After receiving a New Testament, he returned home and began reading. The story of the woman caught in adultery in John 8 captured his attention, particularly the part in which the crowd asked Jesus, "What should we do with this lady?"

> "Would I stone her?" the man asked himself.
>
> He then read Jesus's response: "He who is without sin among you, let him throw a stone at her first."
>
> "This is God!" the man shouted in his home. "This is the real God we should worship."[6]

I believe this man knew the real God of love before ISIS ever came to town. He was just mixed up about His name. It took the arrival of ISIS to realize that the Allah of the Qur'an was not the type to show love and compassion to defend a guilty, hopeless, humiliated, broken woman, who had no one to turn to and nothing to offer. The real God would do absolutely anything to reach us and teach us about the love He has for us, even if it meant getting nailed to a cross.

If we shut out God's love in our innermost beings, we will eventually listen to other voices. That's when people go beyond the point of basic selfishness and living in the flesh, and into the realm of the demonic.

However, if we hope that God exists and that He is good, that He is loving and forgiving, kind and full of grace, and we seek Him out with that kind of hope in our hearts, it's only a matter of time before we will start hearing His voice. It is this hope, combined with love, that spurs the Holy Spirit to produce faith within us. The key is *what's in our hearts* (Psalm 44:21, 64:6, 139:23–24; Jeremiah 17:10).

So now that that is out of the way, I hope I have left enough room for any Muslims reading this to give me the benefit of the doubt that I *do not hate* Muslims. I think there might even be Muslims who die while being devout Muslims, according to their definition, and they *still* go to heaven because of the genuine truth about love they have in their hearts, which transcends the vocalizations of any given language and will enable them to see Jesus as God when they meet Him.

An example of what I'm talking about might include a sheltered Muslim woman who has a heart of gold, such as Sister Gulshan

Esther, author of *The Torn Veil*. Because of her circumstances, she never heard the Gospel, or at least never accurately, but Jesus heard her desperate prayers, showed up in her bedroom, and miraculously healed her paralysis.[7] She was saved by *faith*, just as the righteous people of Old Testament times were saved by faith (Hebrews 11).

Another example of someone saved by faith might be the South American king known as Nezahualcoyotl (1402–1472). His name meant "Hungry Coyote." Even though he was born into a pagan culture that sacrificed its children, he knew in his innermost being that this was not right. He also knew that there was something inherently wrong with their idolatry, even though he was never exposed to the Gospel.

> As a poet and ruler in Mexico before the arrival of the Europeans, he [King Nezahualcoyotl] wrote, "Truly the gods, which I worship, are idols of stone that do not speak nor feel … Some very powerful, hidden and unknown god is the creator of the universe. He is the only one that can console me in my affliction and help me in such anguish as my heart feels; I want him to be my helper and protection." … During the reign of this king, he built a pyramid to the "God who paints things with beauty," and he banned human sacrifices in his city.[8]

Though this South American king had never heard the Gospel, he nearly quoted the apostle Paul when he gave his sermon on the "unknown God" while in Athens (Acts 17:16–34).

I know Jesus said He is the Way, the Truth, and the Life, and that no one goes to the Father except through Him (John 14:6, Matthew 18:3). And I believe that ultimately there will come a point in everyone's existence when there will be a line drawn for people to accept Jesus. Most people think that line is death, but I personally think it might be a little bit after that. God transcends time, so the concepts of "before" and "after" are somewhat mute when it comes to God. He might have ways of working around what we conceive as unmovable barriers or limits that defy our imaginations.

Certainly not all Christians will agree with me on these theological points, perhaps because they are hearing something that I am not saying, but that's okay. I also suspect that few Muslims would consider the possibility that any Christian (i.e., infidel) will ever make it to heaven either. I just want to be clear; my dialogue in this book about Islam is not intended to *demean* Muslims but rather to highlight aspects of Islamic religious writings that clearly define it as an *Antichrist religion* and, hence, a primary component of the strong delusion.

5.2 Islam in the United States

Islam has been around since Muhammad started writing the Qur'an in AD 609, though throughout my childhood and young adult life, I rarely if ever saw any devout Muslims wearing turbans in the places where I lived. As for the issue of Islamic terrorism in the United States, it was not considered a likely threat back in the early 1980s. This is no longer the case. These days, if there was ever any doubt that radical Islam is spreading across the globe and has reached the United States in force, the events that occurred on 9/11 put that question to rest. Radical Islam is here to stay, and it's not leaving until the return of Jesus.

Even though the Obama administration is on its way out as I write this, it's still worth mentioning that there has been no other president in US history who has promoted the Islamic faith, and devoted as many financial and military resources toward Islamic ambitions, than Barack Obama.

While writing this book, I amassed a great deal of research concerning the extent to which the Obama administration has advanced the cause of radical Islam throughout the world, from supporting Islamic radicals in their elections in other countries and appointing Islamic radicals to high-ranking government positions, to releasing known terrorists from Guantanamo Bay Naval Station

(Gitmo) and releasing billions of dollars to support terrorism. The policy decisions made during the Obama administration will negatively impact the world in incalculable ways for many years to come.[9–18]

The length of this book was getting out of control on this tangent about Obama's role with expanding the influence of Islam in the world, so for the sake of brevity, I stripped most of this research out and reduced it to a bulleted list in the following section. The main point at which all of this research is aimed has to do with the strong delusion. In a nutshell, Obama has been accelerating the arrival of the strong delusion, and there might even be an Islamic prophecy that points him out by name.

5.3 A Possible Islamic Prophecy about Obama

Back in 2008, Forbes published an article about a seventeenth-century Hadith, which speaks of a "promised warrior" who will assist the Shiite Mahdi in conquering the world. This Hadith was originally published on a pro-government Iranian website; the tradition comes from Bahar al-Anvar (translated as "oceans of light") by the mullah known as Majlisi.

The Hadith speaks specifically of a tall black man who will rule in the West, commanding the strongest military force on Earth. He will also carry "a clear sign" from the third imam, whose name was Hussein Ibn Ali. According to the tradition, there will be no doubt among Shiite Muslims that this "promised warrior" will be with them.

Coincidentally, Obama's first and middle name together, Barack Hussein, translates as "the blessing of Hussein," in both Arabic and Persian. Obama's last name, when spelled out in the Persian alphabet, reads as "He is with us."[19] In summation, Obama's full name means "The blessing of Hussein is with us."

Whether or not anyone puts any stock in the above Hadith, I can certainly see a number of other clear signs that Obama fits this Hadith to the letter. Consider his track record:

- Obama's brother is either already on the terrorist watch list for Egypt, or Egypt is strongly considering putting him on it because of his financial ties with the Muslim Brotherhood.[20–21]
- While Obama was still a senator in 2007, he supported Islamic radical Odinga on his campaign trail in Kenya. When Odinga lost the election, there were mass killings.[22]
- Once in office, Obama immediately reopened long-severed relations with Iran in spite of its classification as "a state sponsor of terrorism" for over thirty years (Hamas, Hezbollah, etc.)[23] and their ongoing, rampant human rights violations, including the imprisonment and torture of American citizens for religious and/or political reasons.[24]
- He decided not to address the American prisoners tortured in Iran for years until giving Iran everything it wanted in the nuclear deal.[25–26]
- He has broken long-established US policy to negotiate with terrorists and release terrorists in various prisoner swaps on multiple occasions.[27–29] This activity has incentivized terrorists to take more hostages for future swaps.
- He supported the bloody Muslim Brotherhood revolt known as the "Arab spring."[30]
- He populated high-ranking positions of US government with Islamic radicals who have little respect for democracy and who sympathize with, and have direct ties to, Islamic terrorists.[31]
- He wanted to side with one group of terrorists in Syria who even resorted to cannibalism on the battlefield as a means of dealing with another group of terrorists.[32]
- He allowed ISIS to reclaim Iraq after so many soldiers gave their lives to liberate it.
- As commander in chief, he didn't interfere with the army's ruling that the Fort Hood terrorist attack was an act of *workplace violence*. Because of this, the Fort Hood victims were denied the additional financial compensation and medical assistance paid to soldiers injured or killed in combat-related

or terrorist-attack incidents. Even more preposterous, for over three years, Nidal Malik, who murdered thirteen people and injured thirty-two more while screaming, "Allah Akbar," in the Fort Hood massacre, collected over a quarter million dollars of full-time military salary while awaiting his trial.[33]

- He took the spotlight for eliminating Osama Bin Laden, yet shortly thereafter, every member of Seal Team 6 who was part of that mission was mysteriously killed in a highly suspicious *accident*.[34]
- He swapped and freed an army *deserter*, Robert "Bowe" Bergdahl (who has since been tried and prosecuted by the army), with five top-level terrorists from Gitmo.[35]
- He imported more unvetted Muslims into the United States than any president in US history, while systematically exhibiting a track record of denying Christians who were in far more danger.[36-39]
- He refused to support the American Embassy in Benghazi and allowed four Americans to be murdered, only to shift blame to a YouTube video.[40–41]
- He didn't interfere with the army's decision to discharge decorated soldiers for taking a stand against rampant child abuse and pedophilia taking place on US military installations, instigated by US-trained Afghanis.[42]
- He required US military forces to work with and even train known child molesters in Islamic countries, and dismissed cases of reported child abuse on the grounds of "multiculturalism."[43]
- He quietly released high-threat terrorists from Gitmo, including Osama Bin Laden's bodyguard, Abdul Rahman Shalabi, as well as a 9/11 hacker.[44–45]
- He constantly has advocated for more gun control to disarm Americans as the only response to increased terrorism in the United States.
- And finally, the grand finale, he signed a treaty with Iran, unfreezing $150 billion of economic assets, to pave the way

> for Iran to develop nuclear weapons with advanced delivery capabilities. Government officials openly acknowledge that they *know* some of this money will funnel directly into terrorist groups.[46] In effect, because of Obama, the United States is now quite possibly the *largest* sponsor of Islamic terrorism in the world.

I'm sure I missed many more items that could be added to this list, but it will suffice to prove the point I am making. Never in the history of the United States has a president been such a staunch and active supporter of Islamic ambitions. It is as if Obama has turned his presidency into a résumé of radical Islamic accomplishments, with the clearest sign of all being nuclear weaponry delivered to Iran's doorstep. If signing that treaty was not a clear sign, I don't know what is.

Islamic Sunni theologians don't deny that this Hadith prophecy exists, but they refute Hadith prophecies in general. The appearance of the Mahdi is not mentioned in the Qur'an or the Sunnah (the Prophet's teachings), so many Sunni scholars view it as a Shiite invention.

However, the Mahdi is a central component of Shiite doctrine. Shiites are the minority sect in the Islamic world, but a minority of 1.6 billion people is *a lot*, and with Iran obtaining nuclear power, they are well on their way to becoming a formidable world power. What's more, whether Sunnis want to admit it or not, this Hadith hits the nail on the head when it comes to Obama. Even his name fits with this prophecy.

Author Hal Lindsey devoted a portion of his book *Planet Earth, 2000 A.D.* to the subject of Islamic fundamentalism and its ties to End Times prophecy. I think even Lindsey underestimated the degree of relevance that Islamic fundamentalism will play in the days ahead. It was his assumption in *Planet Earth, 2000 A.D.* that the Antichrist will be a European politician heading up a New Age religion, rather than a Middle Eastern Muslim man.[47]

I agree with him that the Antichrist will eventually command the military might of the ten nations of the revived Roman Empire, but unlike Lindsey, I am leaning in favor of the Antichrist being a Muslim, or at least someone who starts out as a Muslim before he morphs Islam into a new, otherworldly flavor of Islam.

Both Hal Lindsey and John F. Walvoord, author of *Armageddon, Oil, and the Middle East Crisis*,[48] see the Antichrist as a New Age guru of sorts. Neither one of them has peeled away the layers of the Islamic onion the way Joel Richardson or Lisa Haven have.

CHAPTER 6

CHARACTERISTICS OF THE ANTICHRIST

Everything about the Antichrist intimately links him with the religion of Islam, as well as its geographic stronghold.

Islam has its own version of prophetic End Times events, which I will cover in the next chapters of this book. However, without even going into the details of these Islamic prophecies, the religion of Islam alone shares a number of qualities that align with specific character attributes of the Antichrist. Those I will discuss in this chapter are as follows:

- He will speak blasphemy, denying the identity of Jesus (2 Thessalonians 2:4).
- He will exercise extreme violence against those who reject him (Daniel 9:26–27, 1 Thessalonians 5:3, Ezekiel 13:10, Jeremiah 8:11).
- He will favor the execution of his enemies via beheading (Revelation 20:4).
- He will have no regard for the desire of women; he might be a homosexual (Daniel 11:37).
- He will have an exceeding pride (Daniel 8:25, 11:12, 11:36; Revelation 13:5; 2 Thessalonians 2:3–4).
- He will rise to power in the Middle East (Daniel 7–8, Revelation 13, Isaiah 10:20–27, Micah 5:3–15).

I will now cover each of these Antichrist characteristics in detail and show how the religion of Islam aligns perfectly with each one of them.

6.1 The Qur'an Stumbles over Jesus

I mentioned earlier that Islam is as an Antichrist religion. The primary reason I made this assertion is because of what Muhammad wrote about Jesus. There is much beyond this, which I will delve into later, but paramount above all is that Muhammad singled out and directly assaulted the identity and mission of Jesus, contradicting Jesus's words. This specifically defines Islam as *anti-Christ.*

In Muhammad's earlier years, when he lived in Mecca, he started writing the Qur'an and borrowed many of his teachings about ethics and righteousness from the Jews and Christians. A brief look at the Daily Hadith Online website will show surahs about peace, justice, honesty, and the like in a banner on the top of the page.[1] When Muslims claim that Islam is a *religion of peace*, they quote these portions of the Qur'an and ignore the portions Muhammad wrote later on when he lived in Medina.

Muhammad also wrote about Jesus in the Qur'an. By doing so, he created a tripping hazard for his followers. This is what Jesus does to those who try to subvert His message. The Jews stumbled over Him because He fulfilled all of the Old Testament prophecies about Himself, *over 350* of them, to the letter.[2]

The Romans also tripped over Jesus. Neither Pilate nor Herod Antipas, the tetrarch of Galilee, found anything treasonable in Jesus's actions. If anything, they were most likely intrigued with the enigmatic miracle worker who could not be defeated in a verbal spar of theological wit on any count. Pilate didn't want to crucify Him, and Pilate's wife had prophetic dreams; she warned him not to crucify Jesus, but he did so anyway to avoid a revolt.

Muslims also stumble over Jesus, and all of this stumbling is because Jesus is the chief cornerstone and therefore a tripping hazard to those who encounter Him (1 Peter 2:7–8). He is an enigma, not easily explained.

> **1 Peter 2:7–8** [bold emphasis added]
> So the honor is for you who believe, but for those who do not believe, "The stone that the builders rejected has become the cornerstone," and "**A stone of stumbling**, and a rock of offense." They stumble because they disobey the word, as they were destined to do.

Below are four categories of Qur'anic surahs about Jesus, which I believe create a stumbling block for Muslims because they give proof *from the Qur'an* that Jesus is God.

1. Unlike other prophets, Jesus was a miracle, born of the Virgin Mary (Qur'an 3:45–47, 21:91). Because Jesus was immaculately conceived, the implication is that His Father is God. Muslims will not concede to this notion, but how else is Jesus's birth to be understood? Scientifically speaking, because Jesus was a male, He had to inherit this genetic trait, the Y chromosome, from another male.[3] These surahs alone are enough proof that God is the Father of Jesus; He created His seed in Mary through the power of His word. The Qur'an goes further to explain that Jesus, as an infant, had the miraculous ability to speak and defend Himself and Mary from her accusers (Qur'an 19:27–34). This reiterates that Mary did not have sexual relations with any human being; Jesus was supernaturally conceived.

> **Qur'an 3:45–47 (Shakir)** [bold emphasis added]
> When the angels said: O Marium, surely Allah gives you good news with a Word from Him (of one) **whose name is the Messiah**, Isa son of Marium, worthy of

regard in this world and the hereafter and of those who are made near (to Allah). And **he shall speak to the people when in the cradle** and when of old age, and (he shall be) one of the good ones. She said: My Lord! When shall there be a son (born) to I me, and **man has not touched me**? He said: Even so, **Allah creates what He pleases**; when He has decreed a matter, **He only says to it, Be, and it is**.

Qur'an 21:91 (Shakir) [bold emphasis added]
And (remember) her who guarded her chastity: **We breathed into her of Our spirit**, and We made her and her son a sign for all peoples.

Qur'an 19:27–34 (Shakir) [bold emphasis and bracketed comments added]
And she came to her people with him, [Jesus] carrying him (with her). They said: O Marium! Surely you have done a strange thing. O sister of Haroun! Your father was not a bad man, nor, was your mother an unchaste woman. But she [Mary] pointed to him [Jesus]. They said: How should we speak to one who was a child in the cradle? **He [the infant Jesus] said**: Surely I am a servant of Allah; He has given me the Book and made me a prophet; And **He has made me blessed** wherever I may be, and **He has enjoined on me prayer** and poor-rate so long as I live; and dutiful to my mother, and **He has not made me insolent, unblessed**; and **peace on me** on the day I was born, and on the day I die, and on the day I am raised to life. Such is Isa, son of Marium; (this is) the saying of truth about which they dispute.

2. The Qur'an states that Jesus worked many clear signs/miracles (Qur'an 2:87). Some of these miracles are paralleled

in the Bible, while others are found in the Infancy Gospel of Thomas. According to the Qur'an, Jesus spoke as an infant in the cradle (Qur'an 3:46). He created birds out of clay and breathed life into them, healed the blind and lepers, resurrected the dead (Qur'an 3:48–49), and received a table of food from heaven (Qur'an 5:112–114). Jesus also prophesied of His death and resurrection (Qur'an 19:30–33), though Muslims do not believe this to be a reference to His death on the cross.

Qur'an 2:87 (Shakir) [bold emphasis and bracketed comments added]
And most certainly We [Elohim, God the Father, Son, and Holy Spirit] gave Musa the Book and We sent messengers after him one after another; and **We gave Isa, the son of Marium, clear arguments [signs]** and strengthened him with the holy spirit, What! whenever then a messenger came to you with that which your souls did not desire, you were insolent so you called some liars and some you slew.

We gave Moses the Book and followed him up with a succession of messengers; We [Elohim, plural word for God] gave Jesus the son of Mary **Clear (Signs)** and strengthened him with the holy spirit. Is it that whenever there comes to you messenger with what ye yourselves desire not, ye are puffed up with pride? Some ye called impostors, and others ye slay!

Qur'an 3:46 (Shakir) [bold emphasis added]
And **he shall speak to the people when in the cradle** and when of old age, and (he shall be) one of the good ones.

Qur'an 3:48–49 (Shakir) [bold emphasis and bracketed comments added]
And He will teach him the Book and the wisdom and the Tavrat [Law] and the Injeel [Gospel]. And (make him) a messenger to the children of Israel: That I have come to you with a sign [miracle] from your Lord, that I determine for you **out of dust like the form of a bird, then I breathe into it and it becomes a bird** with Allah's permission and I **heal the blind and the leprous**, and **bring the dead to life** with Allah's permission and I inform you of what you should eat and what you should store in your houses; most surely there is a sign in this for you, if you are believers.

Qur'an 5:112–114 (Shakir) [bold emphasis added]
When the disciples said: O Isa son of Marium! will your Lord consent to **send down to us food from heaven?** He said: Be careful of (your duty to) Allah if you are believers. They said: We desire that we should eat of it and that our hearts should be at rest, and that we may know that you have indeed spoken the truth to us and that we may be of the witnesses to it. Isa the son of Marium said: O Allah, our Lord! **Send I down to us food from heaven** which should be to us an ever-recurring happiness, to the first of us and to the last of us, and a sign from Thee, and grant us means of subsistence, and Thou art the best of the Providers.

Qur'an 19:30–33 (Shakir) [bold emphasis and bracketed comments added]
He [the infant Jesus] said: Surely I am a servant of Allah; He has given me the Book and made me a prophet; And He has made me blessed wherever I may be, and He has enjoined on me prayer and poor-rate so long as I live; and dutiful to my mother, and He has

not made me insolent, unblessed; and **peace on me on the day I was born, and on the day I die, and on the day I am raised to life.**

3. The Qur'an states that Jesus went to heaven without physically dying (Qur'an 3:55, 4:157–158), and because of His return in the future, which is prophesied in the Qur'an and Hadiths (Qur'an 43:61, Muslim 41:6924, 6931, 7023), He is still physically alive for over two thousand years. His ability to defy death, create life, and resurrect the dead (Qur'an 3:48–49) are particularly noteworthy in the Qur'an because the Qur'an also declares that *only Allah* has the power to create life and resurrect the dead (Qur'an 16:17, 19–21, 25:3).[4]

    Qur'an 3:55 (Shakir) [bold emphasis added]
    And when Allah said: O Isa, **I am going to terminate the period of your stay (on earth) and cause you to ascend unto Me** and purify you of those who disbelieve and make those who follow you above those who disbelieve to the day of resurrection; then to Me shall be your return, so I will decide between you concerning that in which you differed.

    Qur'an 4:157–158 (Shakir) [bold emphasis added]
    And their saying: Surely we have killed the Messiah, Isa son of Marium, the messenger of Allah; and **they did not kill him nor did they crucify him**, but **it appeared to them so (like Isa)** and most surely those who differ therein are only in a doubt about it; **they have no knowledge respecting it, but only follow a conjecture**, and **they killed him not for sure. Nay! Allah took him up to Himself**; and Allah is Mighty, Wise.

Muslim 41:6924 [bold emphasis added]
Certainly, **the time of prayer shall come** and **then Jesus (peace be upon him) son of Mary would descend and would lead them in prayer**. When the enemy of Allah would see him, it would (disappear) just as the salt dissolves itself in water and if he (Jesus) were not to confront them at all, even then it would dissolve completely, but Allah would kill them by his hand and he would show them their blood on his lance (the lance of Jesus Christ).

Muslim 41:6931 [bold emphasis added]
We are discussing about **the Last Hour**. Thereupon he said: **It will not come until you see ten signs before** and (in this connection) he made a mention of the smoke, Dajjal, the beast, the rising of the sun from the west, **the descent of Jesus son of Mary** (Allah be pleased with him), the Gog and Magog, and land-slidings in three places, one in the east, one in the west and one in Arabia at the end of which fire would burn forth from the Yemen, and would drive people to the place of their assembly.

Muslim 41:7023 [bold emphasis added]
What is this hadith that you narrate that **the Last Hour** would come at such and such time … The Dajjal would appear in my Ummah and he would stay (in the world) for forty—I cannot say whether he meant forty days, forty months or forty years. And **Allah would then send Jesus son of Mary who would resemble 'Urwa b Mas'ud. He (Jesus Christ) would chase him and kill him** …

Qur'an 3:48–49 (Shakir) [bold emphasis and bracketed comments added]
And He will teach him the Book and the wisdom and the Tavrat [Law] and the Injeel [Gospel]. And (make him) a messenger to the children of Israel: That I have come to you with a sign [miracle] from your Lord, that I determine for you **out of dust like the form of a bird, then I breathe into it and it becomes a bird** with Allah's permission and **I heal the blind and the leprous**, and **bring the dead to life** with Allah's permission and I inform you of what you should eat and what you should store in your houses; most surely there is a sign in this for you, if you are believers.

Qur'an 16:17 (Shakir) [bold emphasis added]
Is He then Who creates like him who does not create? Do you not then mind?

Qur'an 16:19–21 (Shakir) [bold emphasis added]
And Allah knows what you conceal and what you do openly. And those whom they call on besides Allah **have not created anything** while they are themselves created; Dead (are they), not living, and they know not when they shall be raised.

Qur'an 25:3 (Shakir) [bold emphasis added]
And they have taken besides Him **gods, who do not create anything** while they are themselves created, and they control not for themselves any harm or profit, and **they control not death nor life, nor raising (the dead) to life.**

4. Lastly, at least three of thc titlcs attributed to Jesus, and Jesus alone, in the Qur'an are titles that can only be attributed to

divinity. These are (1) the Christ or Messiah, (2) the word of God, and (3) the Spirit of God (Qur'an 4:171).

Qur'an 4:171 (Shakir) [bold emphasis added]
O followers of the Book! do not exceed the limits in your religion, and do not speak (lies) against Allah, but (speak) the truth; **the Messiah, Isa son of Marium** is only a messenger of Allah and **His Word** which He communicated to Marium and **a spirit from Him**; believe therefore in Allah and His messengers, and say not, Three. Desist, it is better for you; Allah is only one Allah; far be It from His glory that He should have a son, whatever is in the heavens and whatever is in the earth is His, and Allah is sufficient for a Protector.

Ironically, the three titles of divinity concerning Jesus are found in the exact same Qur'anic surah that says Jesus was no more than an apostle, and it also denies the Trinity. It is as if the source of Muhammad's inspiration became tongue-tied and could not lie about Jesus without contradicting itself.

Taking the above ways that Jesus is declared the Son of God in the Qur'an and supporting Hadiths, Muslims are left with a confusing mishmash of details about Him. He is a supernatural being from birth, born of a virgin, with no mention of who the Father is, yet a vague reference says "**Allah creates what He pleases**; when He has decreed a matter, **He only says to it, Be, and it is**." If Jesus was created by Allah saying "Be," then Jesus was created by God's spoken word. How can that mean anything *but* Jesus being a uniquely created being, different from any other human to ever exist? How can that mean that Jesus is *not* God's Son? The Bible declares exactly the same thing in John 1:1, 14: "In the beginning was the Word, and the Word was with God, and the Word was God … And the Word became flesh and dwelt among us …"

Jesus was able to do many miracles, but Muhammad never performed any miracles. Muhammad is dead. How can Muhammad be a divine prophet even greater than Jesus when Jesus is still alive after two thousand years and clearly holds a place of divinity and power that far exceeds anything attributed to Muhammad? Jesus will even return to the earth in the future, while Muhammad will remain in his grave. I can say this based on the Qur'an and Hadiths, without even quoting the Bible.

Muslims will sometimes say that writing the Qur'an was Muhammad's miracle, but anyone can write a book and say God dictated it to him or her. People have done that a number of times throughout history. Jesus knew people could say or write whatever they wanted, so to distinguish Himself from countless imposters claiming to speak for God, when His authority was questioned, He said, "Which is easier, to say, 'Your sins are forgiven,' or to say, 'Rise and walk'?" After this, Jesus healed a paralyzed man to prove His point (Matthew 9:5–6). What did Muhammad do when people questioned his authority? He killed them. How is that greater than Jesus?

Jesus even wielded power over life and death, which the Qur'an says only God can do. Jesus is further given three unique titles, all of which mean God. Again and again, whenever the Qur'an speaks of Jesus, it declares His divinity, but after all of these declarations, the Qur'an blatantly denies that Jesus is the Son of God (Qur'an 5:17, 9:30, 10:68, 19:88–92). The Qur'an also denies the Trinity, even though the plural word *we* is translated in English to refer to God when speaking of Jesus's conception in Mary's womb (Qur'an 21:91).

> **Qur'an 21:91 (Shakir)** [bold emphasis added]
> And (remember) her who guarded her chastity: **We breathed into her of Our spirit**, and **We made her and her son a sign** for all peoples.

Of course, Muslims have many creative ways to explain away these oddities about Jesus. They say that God created Adam, so

Jesus was no more God's son than Adam was. They also point out the miracles of other Old Testament prophets and suggest that Jesus was no different from them. However, these surahs in the Qur'an and various Hadiths have played a significant part in the conversion of many Muslims to Christianity as many Muslims testify in YouTube videos.[4–6] Even Jesus uses them to reach Muslims, as author Gulshan Esther testified in her book *The Torn Veil*.[7]

In summation, the Qur'an is bipolar, filled with truth but also mixed with contradictions and a bunch of open-ended jihad violence, among other things. It also makes the spread of Islam, with the use of jihad, its main focus as Muhammad did during the latter part of his career. That violence now brings me to the next characteristic of the Antichrist.

6.2. The Violence of the Antichrist

The Antichrist is described as the son of destruction (2 Thessalonians 2:3), and he will do the work of Satan (2 Thessalonians 2:9), waging war with extreme violence (Daniel 11:44, Revelation 12:17).

During his rise to power, the Antichrist will act as if he makes peace, but in the middle of that so-called peace agreement, he will turn toward violence (Daniel 9:26–27, 1 Thessalonians 5:3, Ezekiel 13:10, Jeremiah 8:11). He will then make war with God's saints in nations spanning the globe (Revelation 13:4), and he will prevail against them and murder many of them (Daniel 7:19–21, 25; Revelation 13:7, 17:6). A trademark of a great deal of that murder will involve beheading (Revelation 20:4).

As previously mentioned, Muhammad was emphatically clear about Jesus *not* being the Son of God (Qur'an 4:171, 5:73). Understanding Jesus's identity is central to Christianity and also important for understanding how salvation works. People don't get to heaven through their own effort; otherwise, they would have something to brag about (Ephesians 2:8–9). If it were possible to get to heaven without Jesus's sacrifice, Jesus would not have gone to the cross because He prayed to His Father for a way out of it if there was any other way. There was not (Luke 24:41–42).

Believers in Christ are to pursue holiness and moral perfection (Matthew 5:8; 2 Corinthians 7:1), but when it comes to salvation, all our righteousness is not good enough (Isaiah 64:6, Romans 3:20). Ultimately, it is through our faith in Jesus that we are saved (Psalm 2:7; John 3:16–18, 14:6; Hebrews 5:5–9; Acts 13:32–33; Romans 5:12–15; 1 Corinthians 15:21–22).

> **Matthew 5:8**
> "Blessed are the pure in heart, for they shall see God."
>
> **2 Corinthians 7:1**
> Since we have these promises, beloved, let us cleanse ourselves from every defilement of body and spirit, bringing holiness to completion in the fear of God.
>
> **John 14:6** [bold emphasis added]
> Jesus said to him, **"I am the way, and the truth, and the life. No one comes to the Father except through me.**"
>
> **1 Corinthians 15:21–22** [bold emphasis added]
> **For as by a man came death, by a man has come also the resurrection of the dead.** For as in Adam all die, so also in Christ shall all be made alive.

Rather than seeing Jesus's sacrifice as God's greatest demonstration of love for humanity, Muhammad attacked Jesus's work of salvation on the cross by declaring that Jesus didn't actually die on the cross at all, but someone else was made to look like Him (Qur'an 4:136–176, 4:157–158).

> **Qur'an 4:157–158 (Shakir)** [bold emphasis added]
> And their saying: Surely we have killed the Messiah, Isa son of Marium, the messenger of Allah; and **they did not kill him nor did they crucify him**, but **it appeared to them so (like Isa)** and most surely those who differ therein are only in a doubt about it; **they have no knowledge respecting it, but only follow a conjecture**, and **they killed him not for sure. Nay! Allah took him up to Himself**; and Allah is Mighty, Wise.

In short, Muhammad could not comprehend the humility of Jesus and the extent of His obedience to death, or the degree of mercy and grace that God is capable of. Rather, in Muhammad's mind, if Jesus died on the cross, he saw that as a victory for the Jews, which he could not tolerate.

To spread Christianity, Christians are encouraged to speak the truth boldly (Ephesians 6:19–20, Acts 9:27, 13:46, etc.) and even sacrifice their lives for the sake of the *truth*, which is founded in *love* and *peace*. Those who are killed because of their *message* (not combat) are commended for their faith as martyrs (Hebrews 11). In Christianity, martyrdom is not a requirement for heaven because salvation is a gift (Ephesians 2:8–9); however, Jesus led by example when He died on the cross (John 15:13), and most of His original disciples were martyred as well.

As for the Muslim concept of salvation, Muhammad taught a type of *works righteousness* in the Qur'an, which is lacking in mercy and grace because it does not offer any clear-cut guarantees for those who simply try to live as kind and peaceful Muslims. The only *guarantees* for paradise in the Qur'an are offered to jihadist martyrs (Qur'an 3:157, 4:74; Bukhari 4:53:352; Muslim 20:4645, 20:46). In essence, Muhammad dismissed Jesus's sacrifice as something weak and meaningless, and he replaced it with the greatest motivation to murder "infidels" (i.e., anyone who isn't a Muslim) in the name of spreading Islam.

Qur'an 3:157 (Shakir) [jihad = guaranteed forgiveness]
And if you are slain in the way of Allah or you die, certainly forgiveness from Allah and mercy is better than what they amass.

Qur'an 4:74 (Shakir) [jihad = vast reward]
Therefore let those fight in the way of Allah, who sell this world's life for the hereafter; and whoever fights in the way of Allah, then be he slain or be he victorious, we shall grant him a mighty reward.

Bukhari 4:53:352 [jihad = admission to paradise]
Allah's Apostle said, "Allah guarantees him who strives in His Cause and whose motivation for going out is nothing but Jihad in His Cause and belief in His Word, that He will admit him into Paradise (if martyred) or bring him back to his dwelling place, whence he has come out, with what he gains of reward and booty."

Muslim 20:4646 [jihad = guaranteed forgiveness]
"In case you are killed in the way of Allah and you always fought facing the enemy, never turning your back upon him your sins will be blotted out."

Muslim 20:4645 [jihad sacrifice = elevated position in paradise]
"Whoever cheerfully accepts Allah, Islam and Muhammad is entitled to enter Paradise. But there is another act which elevates the position of a man in Paradise to a grade one hundred times higher, jihad in the way of Allah! Jihad in the way of Allah!"

In stark contrast to Christianity, the Qur'an encourages Muslims to speak and/or do whatever it takes to get people to convert to Islam.

This includes using force, and when it comes to sacrifice, Muslims are encouraged to sacrifice their lives for the sake of jihad, which includes physical combat in many verses. Muslims who say jihad is a struggle devoid of violence are either ignorant of their Qur'anic scriptures or they are actively deceiving.

> The Qur'an contains at least 109 verses that call Muslims to war with nonbelievers for the sake of Islamic rule. Some are quite graphic, with commands to chop off heads and fingers and kill infidels wherever they may be hiding. Muslims who do not join the fight are called "hypocrites" (Qur'an 3:167), and warned that Allah will send them to hell if they do not join in the slaughter.[92]

The Qur'an contains many open-ended imperatives to commit violent acts against non-Muslims, in an attempt to force them to convert to Islam, until such time that Islam dominates the entire world (Qur'an 8:39). Since faithful Christians and Jews as a whole would object to forced conversion more than any other non-Muslim group, Islam is not just a theological declaration of war; it is also a military declaration of war against Christians and Jews in particular, which Islamic terrorists have been waging to this very day.

> **Qur'an 8:39 (Shakir)** [bold emphasis added]
> And **fight with them until** there is no more persecution and **religion should be only for Allah**; but if they desist, then surely Allah sees what they do.

In the future, the violence of the Antichrist will grow with each passing day of his reign of terror until it becomes so destructive, if God does not intervene, he will destroy the entire planet (Matthew 24:22, Mark 13). The Qur'an calls for this kind of violence, and with the advent of Iran and other Islamic nations obtaining nuclear power, this level of destruction is at hand.

6.3 What Do the Statistics Say?

As mentioned earlier, the peaceful portions of the Qur'an were actually inspired by Christian and Jewish writings, and drafted during Muhammad's early years in Mecca. Muslims who claim that Islam is a peaceful religion quote these portions of the Qur'an as proof. Most Muslims are *Mecca* Muslims, following the peaceful elements of their religious routines and disregarding the violent mandates.

The portions of the Qur'an Muhammad wrote later in his life, while he was in Medina, took a radically dark turn. In his later writings, Muhammad nullified his earlier peaceful teachings; this is known as *abrogation.* A search on the internet for "Muhammad" and "abrogation" will provide a wealth of information about this.

Abrogation also applies to the Bible. The Old Testament law, handed down from God through Moses, taught the Israelites right from wrong, but it also brought condemnation (Romans 8:3; 2 Corinthians 3:9). With that condemnation, harsh consequences were mandated. However, Jesus abrogated a great deal of Mosaic law on a number of occasions, both in His words (Matthew 5, the Sermon on the Mount, and many other scriptures) and in His actions. He saved an adulterous woman from stoning (John 8:7), offered salvation to another adulterous Samaritan woman (John 4), and called a tax collector, considered a thief, to be one of his apostles (Matthew 9:9–13). Jesus poured the Old Testament law through His filter of love and transformed it with a supernatural peace that transcends all understanding (Philippians 4:7).

So the Old Testament of the Bible started out harsh, but Jesus abrogated it to such an extent that the New Testament outlines a blueprint for the most peaceful religion in the world. As for Muhammad, he did exactly the opposite; he started out his Qur'an as a peaceful book and ended it as the most violent book in the world (Qur'an 8:39, etc.).

Islamic terrorists quote from the Medina portions of the Qur'an, and technically speaking (in a legalistic sense), their interpretation of the Qur'an is more accurate than the Mecca Muslims' interpretation because they are taking Muhammad's abrogation into account.

While most Muslims are Mecca Muslims, exactly how many are *Medina* Muslim*s*?

Alarmingly, there is a staggering estimated 750 million Medina Muslims (i.e., potential jihadists) in the world at this time, based on the voting records of Islamic-governed nations.[8] It turns out that psychopaths who spout off jihadist rhetoric in their political platform speeches are very popular these days; the Daniel Pipes website has much to say about this.[9] It's a sobering reality that this level of evil is brewing all over the planet.

Another website that has a compiled a list of Muslim opinion polls concerning terrorism is the Religion of Peace website.[10] Below is a sampling of some of its statistics:

> **ICM Poll:** Twenty percent of British Muslims sympathize with 7/7 bombers. http://www.telegraph.co.uk/news/uknews/1510866/Poll-reveals-40pc-of-Muslims-want-sharia-law-in-UK.html
>
> **NOP Research:** One in four British Muslims say 7/7 bombings were justified. http://www.cbsnews.com/stories/2006/08/14/opinion/main1893879.shtml&date=2011-04-06, http://www.webcitation.org/5xkMGAEvY
>
> **Channel Four (2006):** Thirty-one percent of younger British Muslims say 7/7 bombings were justified compared to 14 percent of those over forty-five.
>
> http://www.policyexchange.org.uk/images/publications/living%20apart%20together%20-%20jan%2007.pdf

People-Press: Thirty-one percent of Turks support suicide attacks against Westerners in Iraq.

http://people-press.org/report/206/a-year-after-iraq-war

YNet: One-third of Palestinians (32 percent) supported the slaughter of a Jewish family, including the children.

http://pajamasmedia.com/tatler/2011/04/06/32-of-palestinians-support-infanticide/, http://www.ynetnews.com/articles/0,7340,L-4053251,00.html

World Public Opinion: Sixty-one percent of Egyptians approve of attacks on Americans.

Thirty-two percent of Indonesians approve of attacks on Americans.

Forty-one percent of Pakistanis approve of attacks on Americans.

Thirty-eight percent of Moroccans approve of attacks on Americans.

Eighty-three percent of Palestinians approve of some or most groups that attack Americans (only 14 percent oppose).

Sixty-two percent of Jordanians approve of some or most groups that attack Americans (21 percent oppose).

Forty-two percent of Turks approve of some or most groups that attack Americans (45 percent oppose).

A minority of Muslims disagreed entirely with terror attacks on Americans (Egypt 34 percent, Indonesia 45 percent, and Pakistan 33 percent).

About half of those opposed to attacking Americans were sympathetic with al-Qaeda's attitude toward the United States.

http://www.worldpublicopinion.org/pipa/pdf/feb09/STARTII_Feb09_rpt.pdf

Pew Research (2010): Fifty-five percent of Jordanians have a positive view of Hezbollah.

Thirty percent of Egyptians have a positive view of Hezbollah.

Forty-five percent of Nigerian Muslims have a positive view of Hezbollah (26 percent negative).

Forty-five percent of Indonesians have a positive view of Hezbollah (30 percent negative).

http://pewglobal.org/2010/12/02/muslims-around-the-world-divided-on-hamas-and-hezbollah/

Pew Research (2010): Sixty percent of Jordanians have a positive view of Hamas (34 percent negative).

Forty-nine percent of Egyptians have a positive view of Hamas (48 percent negative).

Forty-nine percent of Nigerian Muslims have a positive view of Hamas (25 percent negative).

Thirty-nine percent of Indonesians have a positive view of Hamas (33 percent negative).

http://pewglobal.org/2010/12/02/muslims-around-the-world-divided-on-hamas-and-hezbollah/

Pew Research (2011): Twenty-one percent of Muslim Americans say there is a fair to great amount of support for Islamic extremism in their community.

http://www.people-press.org/2011/08/30/section-6-terrorism-concerns-about-extremism-foreign-policy/

ICM Poll: Eleven percent of British Muslims find violence for political ends acceptable.

http://www.danielpipes.org/blog/2005/07/more-survey-research-from-a-british-islamist

Pew Research (2010): Fifteen percent of Indonesians believe suicide bombings are often or sometimes justified.

Thirty-four percent of Nigerian Muslims believe suicide bombings are often or sometimes justified.

http://pewglobal.org/2010/12/02/muslims-around-the-world-divided-on-hamas-and-hezbollah/

Sixteen percent of young Muslims in Belgium say terrorism is "acceptable."

http://www.hln.be/hln/nl/1275/Islam/article/detail/1619036/2013/04/22/Zestien-procent-moslimjongens-vindt-terrorisme-aanvaardbaar.dhtml

Populus Poll (2006): Twelve percent of young Muslims in Britain believe that suicide attacks against civilians in Britain can be justified. One in four support suicide attacks against British troops.

http://www.danielpipes.org/blog/2005/07/more-survey-research-from-a-british-islamist

Pew Research (2007): Twenty-six percent of younger Muslims in America believe suicide bombings are justified.

Thirty-five percent of young Muslims in Britain believe suicide bombings are justified (24 percent overall).

Forty-two percent of young Muslims in France believe suicide bombings are justified (35 percent overall).

Twenty-two percent of young Muslims in Germany believe suicide bombings are justified (13 percent overall).

Twenty-nine percent of young Muslims in Spain believe suicide bombings are justified (25 percent overall).

http://pewresearch.org/assets/pdf/muslim-americans.pdf#page=60

Pew Research (2011): Eight percent of Muslims in America believe suicide bombings are often or sometimes justified (81 percent never).

Twenty-eight percent of Egyptian Muslims believe suicide bombings are often or sometimes justified (38 percent never).

http://www.people-press.org/2011/08/30/muslim-americans-no-signs-of-growth-in-alienation-or-support-for-extremism/

Pew Research (2007): Muslim-Americans who identify more strongly with their religion are three times more likely to feel that suicide bombings are justified.

http://pewresearch.org/assets/pdf/muslim-americans.pdf#page=60

ICM: Five percent of Muslims in Britain tell pollsters they would not report a planned Islamic terror attack to authorities.

Twenty-seven percent do not support the deportation of Islamic extremists preaching violence and hate.

http://www.danielpipes.org/blog/2005/07/more-survey-research-from-a-british-islamist.html

Federation of Student Islamic Societies: About one in five Muslim students in Britain (18 percent) would not report a fellow Muslim planning a terror attack.

http://www.danielpipes.org/blog/2005/07/more-survey-research-from-a-british-islamist

ICM Poll: Twenty-five percent of British Muslims disagree that a Muslim has an obligation to report terrorists to police.

http://www.danielpipes.org/blog/2005/07/more-survey-research-from-a-british-islamist

Populus Poll (2006): Sixteen percent of British Muslims believe suicide attacks against Israelis are justified.

Thirty-seven percent believe Jews in Britain are a "legitimate target."

http://www.danielpipes.org/blog/2005/07/more-survey-research-from-a-british-islamist

Pew Research (2013): At least one in four Muslims do not reject violence against civilians (study did not distinguish between those who believe it is partially justified and never justified).

http://www.pewforum.org/uploadedFiles/Topics/Religious_Affiliation/Muslim/worlds-muslims-religion-politics-society-full-report.pdf

Pew Research (2013): Fifteen percent of Muslims in Turkey support suicide bombings (also 11 percent in Kosovo, 26 percent in Malaysia, and 26 percent in Bangladesh).

http://www.pewforum.org/uploadedFiles/Topics/Religious_Affiliation/Muslim/worlds-muslims-religion-politics-society-full-report.pdf

PCPO (2014): Eighty-nine percent of Palestinians support Hamas and other terrorists firing rockets at Israeli civilians.

http://www.jihadwatch.org/2014/08/poll-89-of-palestinians-support-jihad-terror-attacks-on-israely

Pew Research (2013): Only 57 percent of Muslims worldwide disapprove of al-Qaeda. Only 51 percent disapprove of the Taliban. Thirteen percent support both groups, and one in four refuse to say.

http://www.pewglobal.org/2013/09/10/muslim-publics-share-concerns-about-extremist-groups/

BBC Radio (2015): Forty-five percent of British Muslims agree that clerics preaching violence against the West represent "mainstream Islam."

http://www.comres.co.uk/polls/bbc-radio-4-today-muslim-poll/

Palestinian Center for Political Research (2015): Seventy-four percent of Palestinians support Hamas terror attacks.

http://www.timesofisrael.com/support-for-hamas-skyrockets-following-war-poll-shows/

Pew Research (2014): Forty-seven percent of Bangladeshi Muslims says suicide bombings and violence are justified to "defend Islam." One in four believed the same in Tanzania and Egypt. One in five Muslims in the "moderate" countries of Turkey and Malaysia also believe the same.

http://www.pewglobal.org/2014/07/01/concerns-about-islamic-extremism-on-the-rise-in-middle-east/

The Polling Company CSP Poll (2015): Nineteen percent of Muslim-Americans say that violence is justified in order to make Sharia the law in the United States (66 percent disagree).

http://www.centerforsecuritypolicy.org/wp-content/uploads/2015/06/150612-CSP-Polling-Company-Nationwide-Online-Survey-of-Muslims-Topline-Poll-Data.pdf

The Polling Company CSP Poll (2015): Twenty-five percent of Muslim-Americans say that violence against Americans in the United States is justified as part of the "global Jihad" (64 percent disagree).

http://www.centerforsecuritypolicy.org/wp-content/uploads/2015/06/150612-CSP-Polling-Company-Nationwide-Online-Survey-of-Muslims-Topline-Poll-Data.pdf

The Sun (2015): Following the November 2015 attacks in Paris, one in four young Muslims in Britain (and one in five overall) said they sympathize with those who fight for ISIS.

http://www.thesun.co.uk/sol/homepage/news/politics/6758207/1-in-5-British-Muslims-have-sympathy-for-jihadis-in-poll.html

Pew Research (2007): Five percent of American Muslims have a favorable view of al-Qaeda (27 percent can't make up their minds). Only 58 percent reject al-Qaeda outright.

http://pewresearch.org/assets/pdf/muslim-americans.pdf#page=60

Pew Research (2011): Five percent of American Muslims have a favorable view of al-Qaeda (14 percent can't make up their minds).

http://www.people-press.org/2011/08/30/muslim-americans-no-signs-of-growth-in-alienation-or-support-for-extremism/

Pew Research (2011): One in ten native-born Muslim-Americans have a favorable view of al-Qaeda.

http://people-press.org/2011/08/30/muslim-americans-no-signs-of-growth-in-alienation-or-support-for-extremism/

al-Jazeera (2006): About half (49.9 percent) of Muslims polled supported Osama bin Laden.

http://www.partisanlines.com/threads/al-jazeera-arabic-poll-49-9-support-osama-bin-laden.712/

Pew Research: Fifty-nine percent of Indonesians supported Osama bin Laden in 2003.

Forty-one percent of Indonesians supported Osama bin Laden in 2007.

Fifty-six percent of Jordanians supported Osama bin Laden in 2003.

http://www.forbes.com/2010/02/15/iran-terrorism-al-qaida-islam-opinions-columnists-ilan-berman.html

Pew Global: Fifty-one percent of Palestinians supported Osama bin Laden.

Fifty-four percent of Muslim Nigerians supported Osama bin Laden.

http://pewglobal.org/files/pdf/268.pdf

MacDonald Laurier Institute: Thirty-five percent of Canadian Muslims would not repudiate al-Qaeda.

http://www.torontosun.com/2011/11/01/strong-support-for-shariah-in-canada

http://www.macdonaldlaurier.ca/much-good-news-and-some-worrying-results-in-new-study-of-muslim-public-opinion-in-canada/

World Public Opinion: Muslim majorities agree with the al-Qaeda goal of Islamic law.

Muslim majorities agree with the al-Qaeda goal of keeping Western values out of Islamic countries (Egypt 88 percent, Indonesia 76 percent, Pakistan 60 percent, and Morocco 64 percent).

http://www.worldpublicopinion.org/pipa/pdf/feb09/STARTII_Feb09_rpt.pdf

ICM Poll: Thirteen percent of Muslims in Britain support al-Qaeda attacks on America.

http://www.danielpipes.org/blog/2005/07/more-survey-research-from-a-british-islamist

World Public Opinion: Attitude toward Osama bin Laden:

Egypt: 44 percent positive, 17 percent negative, and 25 percent mixed feelings

Indonesia: 14 percent positive, 26 percent negative, and 21 percent mixed feelings (39 percent did not answer)

Pakistan: 25 percent positive, 15 percent negative, and 26 percent mixed feelings (34 percent did not answer).

Morocco: 27 percent positive, 21 percent negative, and 26 percent mixed feelings

Jordanians, Palestinians: Jordanians combined for 27 percent positive, 20 percent negative, and 27 percent mixed feelings. Palestinians were 56 percent positive, 20 percent negative, and 22 percent mixed feelings.

http://www.worldpublicopinion.org/pipa/pdf/feb09/STARTII_Feb09_rpt.pdf

Pew Research (2010): Forty-nine percent of Nigerian Muslims have favorable view of al-Qaeda (34 percent unfavorable).

Twenty-three percent of Indonesians have favorable view of al-Qaeda (56 percent unfavorable).

Thirty-four percent of Jordanians have favorable view of al-Qaeda.

Twenty-five percent of Indonesians have “confidence” in Osama bin Laden (59 percent had confidence in 2003).

One in five Egyptians have "confidence" in Osama bin Laden.

http://pewglobal.org/2010/12/02/muslims-around-the-world-divided-on-hamas-and-hezbollah/

Pew Research (2011): Twenty-two percent of Indonesians have a favorable view of al-Qaeda (21 percent unfavorable).

http://www.people-press.org/2011/08/30/muslim-americans-no-signs-of-growth-in-alienation-or-support-for-extremism/

Gallup: Fifty-one percent of Pakistanis grieved Osama bin Laden (only 11 percent were happy about his death).

Forty-four percent of Pakistanis viewed Osama bin Laden as a martyr (only 28 percent as an outlaw).

http://www.americanthinker.com/blog/2011/05/majority_of_our_pakistani_alli.html

Zogby International 2011: Majorities in all six countries said they viewed the United States less favorably following the killing of the Al-Qaeda head [Osama bin Laden] in Pakistan.

http://www.washingtonpost.com/blogs/checkpoint-washington/post/arab-worlds-views-of-us-president-obama-increasingly-negative-new-poll-finds/2011/07/12/gIQASzHVBI_blog.html

Populus Survey: Eighteen percent of British Muslims would be proud or indifferent if a family member joined al-Qaeda.

http://www.danielpipes.org/blog/2005/07/more-survey-research-from-a-british-islamist

Policy Exchange (2006): Seven percent of Muslims in Britain admire al-Qaeda and other terrorist groups.

http://www.danielpipes.org/blog/2005/07/more-survey-research-from-a-british-islamist

WordPress Survey (2014): Informal poll of Saudis in August 2014 showed 92 percent agreed that Islamic State (ISIS) "conforms to the values of Islam and Islamic law."

http://muslimstatistics.wordpress.com/2014/08/24/92-of-saudis-believes-that-isis-conforms-to-the-values-of-islam-and-islamic-law-survey/

Hurriyet Daily News/Metropoll (2015): Twenty percent of Turks support the slaughter of Charlie Hebdo staffers and cartoonists.

http://www.ibtimes.co.uk/metropoll-42-turkish-public-believe-muslims-are-real-victims-charlie-hebdo-attack-1486355

al-Jazeera Poll (2015): Eighty-one percent of respondents support the Islamic State (ISIS).

http://www.breitbart.com/national-security/2015/05/25/shock-poll-81-of-al-jazeera-arabic-poll-respondents-support-isis/

The Polling Company CSP Poll (2015): Thirty-three percent of Muslim-Americans say al-Qaeda beliefs are Islamic or correct (49 percent disagree).

http://www.centerforsecuritypolicy.org/wp-content/uploads/2015/06/150612-CSP-Polling-Company-Nationwide-Online-Survey-of-Muslims-Topline-Poll-Data.pdf

The Polling Company CSP Poll (2015): Thirty-eight percent of Muslim-Americans say Islamic State (ISIS) beliefs are Islamic or correct (43 percent disagree).

http://www.centerforsecuritypolicy.org/wp-content/uploads/2015/06/150612-CSP-Polling-Company-Nationwide-Online-Survey-of-Muslims-Topline-Poll-Data.pdf

ICM (Mirror) Poll 2015: One and a half million British Muslims, about half the total population, support the Islamic State.

http://www.mirror.co.uk/news/uk-news/muslim-leader-isis-supporting-brits-disenfranchised-6018357

Clarion Project Study (2015): About 11.5 percent of Arabs support ISIS, or about 42 million.

http://www.clarionproject.org/analysis/isis-has-least-42-million-supporters-arab-world

Palestinian Center for Policy and Survey Research (2015): Two-thirds of Palestinians support the stabbing of Israeli civilians.

http://www.france24.com/en/20151214-two-thirds-palestinians-support-knife-attacks-poll

Social Trends Survey (2016): Twenty-one percent of Turks says ISIS represents Islam; 10 percent would not categorize it as a terrorist organization.

http://www.trust.org/item/20160112154230-7c2sb/

Al-Arabiya: Thirty-six percent of Arabs polled said the 9/11 attacks were morally justified, 38 percent disagreed, and 26 percent were unsure.

http://www.alarabiya.net/articles/2011/09/10/166274.html

Gallup: Some 38.6 percent of Muslims believe the 9/11 attacks were justified (7 percent "fully," 6.5 percent "mostly," and 23.1 percent "partially").

http://elderofziyon.blogspot.com/2008/05/that-tiny-percentage-of-radical-muslims.html,

http://www.washingtoninstitute.org/templateC06.php?CID=1154

See also: http://wikiislam.net/wiki/Muslim_Statistics_(Terrorism) for further statistics on Islamic terror.

Germany Statistics Report: Migrants swell crime by 65 percent in Germany. https://muslimstatistics.wordpress.com/2015/10/13/germany-muslim-migrants-swell-crime-by-65/

> **Denmark Statistics Report:** Muslims are around 450 percent more criminal than non-Muslims https://muslimstatistics.wordpress.com/2014/09/10/denmark-muslims-are-around-450-more-criminal-than-non-muslims/
>
> **Norway Statistics Report:** Norway deports a record number of Muslims to reduce crime—31 percent improvement.

The above is just a sampling because these stats are like the Energizer bunny; they keep going and going. An even larger library of stats related to the religion of Islam is found on the Muslim Statistics website.[11]

Are these statistics not enough to show that the religion of Islam is not as *peaceful* as the mainstream media makes it out to be? In light of these numbers, the above 750 million potential jihadists estimate may not be that far off because that number correlates closely to the opinions of Muslims worldwide.

This is not to suggest that 750 million Muslims are willing to strap on a suicide vest and sprint for the nearest crowd with the intention of pulling the pin, but rather to point out that 750 million Muslims are more inclined to sympathize with a suicide bomber than with the innocent people who are killed in such attacks. It is these people, who have been indoctrinated to think of innocent civilians as infidels worthy of death, that terrorists target for radicalization.

Not too long ago, I stumbled upon a pro-Islamic website that spoke of Hitler in glowing terms. I was surprised to discover how easy it was to find this information. I simply did a Google search for "Hitler" and "Islam," and one of the first links that came up was this Islamic website with an article that referred to Hitler as a "great statesman."[12] The man burned men, women, and children alive. The Nazis penned up large flocks of geese near the infamous gas showers to try to drown out the noise of the screaming victims. How exactly is that a great statesman?[13]

Of course, there are a few articles out there that attempt to refute the mountain of evidence showing exactly how violent Islam really is. Huffington Post columnist Omar Alnatour, for example, published an article titled "Muslims Are Not Terrorists: An Actual Look at Terrorism and Islam."[14] This article is ridiculously inaccurate. There are hundreds, if not thousands, of surveys and government statistics collected worldwide that prove beyond a shadow of a doubt how inaccurate this article is.

For starters, the first so-called fact on the website, "Non-Muslims make up the majority of terrorism in the United States," singles out the United States for a beneficial statistic. Of course Islamic terrorism is lower in the United States than pretty much anywhere else in the world; it's not even worth comparing because the Muslim population is so low in the United States, for now. However, even singling out the United States for a favorable statistic reveals an intentional obscuring of the facts.

Digging into what the article identifies as "Christian terrorists" in the United States, overzealous abortion clinic protestors, who yell angry slogans, hit people with antiabortion signs, and sometimes try to block entrances to abortion clinics, are considered "terrorists" on par with ISIS psychopaths beheading children in front of their parents. What kind of comparison is that?

Referencing the sum total of the worst antiabortion "terrorism" on the ultraprogressive Think Progress website (one of the supporting links), singling out the United States, and dating all the way back to 1977 reveals a grand total of eight murders, seventeen attempted murders, forty-two bombings, 181 arsons, and thousands of incidences of other criminal activities.[15] All of these stats lumped together, without any details, greatly obscures the facts, but a rudimentary application of logic can see through it.

For example, out of the forty-two bombings and 181 arsons, how is it that only eight people were murdered? Obviously these bombings and arsons had to occur during nonwork hours when the buildings were empty (much unlike Islamic terrorists who seek populated locations for a higher death toll). Is that really the same kind of terrorism we see with Islamic extremists who seek more fatalities rather than less?

In short, these Christian terrorists in the United States, with its population exceeding three hundred million people, account for eight murders in thirty-nine years. Now pause for a moment and consider that about three thousand innocent people were murdered on a single day, September 11, 2001. This is not to downplay *any* murder, but obviously there is something profoundly skewed with Alnatour's so-called facts, even when singling out the United States in order to obtain a favorable statistic to downplay Islamic terrorism.

Another website article titled "Are All Terrorists Muslims? Not Even Close," written by Dean Obeidallah, is yet another deplorable example of misdirection and obscured facts. Once again the columnist focuses on areas with smaller Muslim populations, namely Europe and the United States, specifically avoiding Muslim nations. He also defines activities such as "price tag" wars, committed by Jews, as a form of terrorism.[16] What exactly are price tag wars? Vandalism. How can anyone think to compare vandalism with bombs, torture, and beheading?

Simply looking at the statistics found on countless opinion polls and government websites, such as the US Department of State's Bureau of Counterterrorism, will reveal just how far off the mark these Muslim apologists are with their attempts to downplay Islamic terrorism.[17] Out of 452 suicide attacks worldwide in 2015, all but two of them (with one of those in contention) were conducted by Muslims; that's 99.66 percent.[18] What's more, BBC News reported a 61 percent spike in global terrorism in 2013, and in 2014, 66 percent of terrorism worldwide was attributed to Muslims.[19]

When it comes to violence, Muslim apologists certainly have their work cut out for them. Violence stemming from Islamic ideology is off the charts, and that same violence is exactly what the Antichrist will use in his rise to power.

6.4 No Regard for the Desire of Women

This next character trait that identifies the Antichrist with the religion of Islam is a peculiar phrase mentioned in the book of Daniel.

> **Daniel 11:37 (ASV)** [bold emphasis and bracketed comments added]
> Neither shall he [the Antichrist] regard the God of his fathers, **nor the desire of women**, nor regard any god: for he shall magnify himself above all.

What does this scripture mean by the Antichrist having no regard for the desire of women?

Some have postulated that the Antichrist might be a homosexual. There is an argument for this, which I will address later. However, I think there is stronger evidence that suggests Daniel 11:37 is not referring to homosexuality. If the Antichrist were a homosexual, Daniel 11:37 would speak of a desire *for* women, not the desire *of* women. The desire *of* women more accurately refers to the Antichrist's opinion of what women desire. Taking this into account, what is the general consensus among Muslims when it comes to women's rights? Do women have a fair shake in Islamic countries? Are they treated equally?

Starting with the first Muslim, how did Muhammad treat women? Did he have any regard for their desires? Perhaps, if one considers a fifty-four-year-old man allowing his nine-year-old "wife" the luxury of playing with her dolls, so long as she provides him with enough sex whenever he wants it.

Muhammad married a six-year-old girl, Aisha, and he consummated that marriage when she turned nine years old. Aisha was still swinging on swings and playing with dolls.

> **Muslim 8:3310** [bold emphasis added]
> 'A'isha (Allah be pleased with her) reported: Allah's Apostle (may peace be upon him) married me when

> I was six years old, and I was admitted to his house when I was nine years old.
>
> **Bukhari 8:73:151** [bold emphasis added]
> **I used to play with the dolls in the presence of the Prophet**, and **my girlfriends also used to play with me**. When Allah's Apostle used to enter (my dwelling place) they used to hide themselves, but the Prophet would call them to join and play with me.
>
> Note: Playing with the dolls and similar images is forbidden for adult Muslim women, but it was allowed for Aisha at that time, as she was a little girl and had not yet reached the age of puberty.[20]

Those who debate the topic of child brides, will eventually discover that the age-of-sexual-consent laws are a relatively recent development in world history. The first age-of-consent laws appeared in England some eight hundred years ago, restricting the age of sexual consent to twelve years old.[21] The existence of these laws, however, does not necessarily mean that it was common for girls to get married at the age of twelve back then.

Even with these details, for a man in his fifties to marry a six-year-old and then have sex with her at nine years old is disturbing to say the least. Did Muhammad not have enough wives already? He actually set the limit at four wives with all of his followers (Qur'an 4:3), but then he made a special exception for himself (Qur'an 33:50).

> **Qur'an 4:3 (Shakir)** [bold emphasis added]
> And if you fear that you cannot act equitably towards orphans, then **marry such women as seem good to you, two and three and four**; but if you fear that you will not do justice (between them), then (marry) only one or what your right hands possess; this is

> more proper, that you may not deviate from the right course.
>
> **Qur'an 33:50 (Shakir)** [bold emphasis added]
> O Prophet! surely **We have made lawful to you your wives** whom you have given their dowries, **and those whom your right hand possesses out of those whom Allah has given to you as prisoners of war, and the daughters of your paternal uncles and the daughters of your paternal aunts, and the daughters of your maternal uncles and the daughters of your maternal aunts** who fled with you; **and a believing woman if she gave herself to the Prophet, if the Prophet desired to marry her—specially for you, not for the (rest of) believers**; We know what We have ordained for them concerning their wives and those whom their right hands possess in order that no blame may attach to you; and Allah is Forgiving, Merciful.

Even if an ardent defender of Muhammad's sex with a nine-year-old uses the historical "man of his times" argument and relies on the lack of sexual consent laws to justify Muhammad's actions, does that *really justify* a fifty-four-year-old man having sex with a nine-year-old girl who still plays with dolls?

I have read about this on a number of websites and in the Hadiths (there are many more than those I listed above). I can scarcely comprehend how so many Muslims defend this aspect of Islam, which is *still in practice today*, and refuse to call it pedophilia or child molestation. For an old man to have sex with a young girl in this day and age is unconscionable and has no viable defense. Yet this behavior is ardently defended, even by Christians in some cases, in the name of political correctness.

Jerry Vines spoke boldly at a Southern Baptist Convention, stating, "Islam was founded by Muhammad, a demon-possessed pedophile who had twelve wives, and his last one was a nine-year-old girl." Of course, Vines was wrong. Muhammad had fifteen to seventeen wives, not including his concubines; Mary, his Coptic slave; and the wives of the military commanders he killed or captured in battle.[22]

Yet C. Welton Gaddy, speaking on behalf of Southern Baptists, stated, "Historically, Baptists have been passionate supporters of religious liberty and its corollaries of church/state separation and have had an appreciation for pluralism."[23]

Naturally, CAIR (Council on American-Islamic Relations) felt compelled to chime in, with spokeswoman Hodan Hassan proclaiming, "This kind of hate-filled rhetoric is very shocking," and "It is especially surprising to see it coming from someone of that stature making such a statement concerning a religion that is practiced by one-fifth of the world's population."[24]

What is missing in these responses is that Muhammad was indeed having sex with a nine-year-old girl who still played with dolls. Pointing out this detail, I suppose, is "hate-filled rhetoric," which should simply be dismissed because so many people have such adoration for Muhammad.

Child brides are just the beginning. Women just can't win in Islam, even faithful Muslim women. Certainly there are many wonderful Muslim men who love their mothers, wives, and daughters, but culturally speaking, women in Islamic countries are far from being treated as equals. The best that women can hope for is the status of half a man because that is all they are allocated as far as legal testimony is concerned (Qur'an 2:282).

> **Qur'an 2:282 (Shakir)** [bold emphasis added]
> O you who believe! when you deal with each other in contracting a debt for a fixed time, then write it down; and let a scribe write it down between you with fairness; and the scribe should not refuse to write as Allah has taught him, so he should write; and let him who owes the debt dictate, and he should

> be careful of (his duty to) Allah, his Lord, and not diminish anything from it; but if he who owes the debt is unsound in understanding, or weak, or (if) he is not able to dictate himself, let his guardian dictate with fairness; **and call in to witness from among your men two witnesses; but if there are not two men, then one man and two women from among those whom you choose to be witnesses**, so that if one of the two errs, the second of the two may remind the other …

I have long wondered what the incentive is for a woman to remain a Muslim, other than to avoid family and community rejection, beatings, or getting killed by their families, husbands, or random strangers in the neighborhood looking for easy targets. The best Muslim women can hope for in Islamic heaven (a place not many women get to enjoy, according to Muslim 36:6597) is to share a man with seventy-one other women for all eternity, fulfilling his every whim. What kind of heaven is that? Where's the love? Where's the *regard for women*?

> **Muslim 36:6597** [bold emphasis added]
> Ibn Abbas reported that Allah's Messenger (may peace be upon him) said: I had a chance to look into the Paradise and I found that majority of the people was poor and **I looked into the Fire and there I found the majority constituted by women.**

Even Jannah (*Islamic heaven*), does not have any regard for women, and the profoundly oppressive treatment of women so pervasive in Islamic culture is fueled by the spirit of the Antichrist.

In contrast to Islamic heaven, Jesus taught that we will transcend sex when we get to heaven (Luke 20:36) and that men and women are equals (Galatians 3:27–29).

> **Galatians 3:27–29** [bold emphasis added]
> For as many of you as were baptized into Christ have put on Christ. There is neither Jew nor Greek, there is neither slave nor free, **there is neither male nor female, for you are all one in Christ Jesus**. And if you are Christ's, then you are Abraham's offspring, heirs according to promise.

Concerning the equality of men and women, compare and contrast the way the Qur'an deals with sex within the confines of marriage (Qur'an 2:223) with what the Bible says (1 Corinthians 7:3–5).

> **Qur'an (Shakir) 2:223** [bold emphasis added]
> **Your wives are a tilth for you, so go into your tilth when you like**, and do good beforehand for yourselves, and be careful (of your duty) to Allah, and know that you will meet Him, and give good news to the believers.

> **1 Corinthians 7:3–5** [bold emphasis added]
> The **husband should give to his wife her conjugal rights**, and likewise **the wife to her husband**. For the wife does not have authority over her own body, but the husband does. Likewise the husband does not have authority over his own body, but the wife does. **Do not deprive one another, except perhaps by agreement for a limited time**, that you may devote yourselves to prayer; but then come together again, so that Satan may not tempt you because of your lack of self-control.

Muhammad used the Bible for much of his inspiration, but he drastically deviated from it in countless ways, and sex within the confines of marriage is one of those deviations. The Bible treats men and women with equal care and consideration. When it comes to sex, the Bible makes an appeal out of love; spouses shouldn't "deprive" each other, and there is also a caveat in which they can have mutual agreements to not have sex for limited periods of time. The Qur'an, in contrast, simply declares that a man can go to his wife for sex whenever he wants, period.

Muhammad's treatment and overall opinion of women was beyond deplorable. To him, they were nothing more than sex objects, mostly destined for hell (Muslim 36:6597). This contrasts greatly with the teachings we find in the Bible.

The Bible describes in numerous scriptures how Jesus elevated the status of women. In an article titled "The Bible Is Crystal Clear on Male-Female Equality," author and apologist Anne Graham Lotz observed the following regarding God's elevation of the status of women through His Son Jesus:

- His mother Mary was declared a "favored one" by the angel Gabriel (Luke 1:28).
- His first miracle was performed in response to a plea from His mother (John 2:1–11).
- His first revelation of Himself as Messiah was to a woman (John 4:25–26).
- His greatest miracle was performed at the request of two women (John 11:1–44).
- His death was memorialized by a woman (John 12:1–8).
- Women were included in His expanded group of disciples (Mark 15:41).
- Women stayed with Him throughout His crucifixion, even after the men had left (Matthew 27:55–56).
- Women observed His burial (Matthew 27:61).
- Following His resurrection, He appeared first to a woman (John 20:1–16).
- He commissioned women as the first evangelists (Matthew 28:1–10, John 20:17).
- Women were included in the group of disciples who met daily for prayer after the ascension of Jesus (Acts 1:14).

- Ancient prophecy was fulfilled when the Spirit of God was given equally to men and women at Pentecost (Acts 2:17).
- Women were among the first believers, or Christians, who made up the early church (Acts 5:14, 8:12, 12, 17:4).
- The first church in Europe was begun with a group of women who met in the home of a woman (Acts 16:13–15).
- Many women staffed the early church (Romans 16:12, Philippians 4:3).
- A woman co-led at least one early church (1 Corinthians 16:19).[25]

Contrasting with this, in Islamic countries, the treatment of women as nothing more than sex objects and punching bags is rampant. The majority of these practices have been reinforced and woven into the fabric of Islamic culture throughout the centuries because of Muhammad's teachings. Perhaps the most prominent Islamic teachings that deal with the treatment of women and the expression of sexuality are the various descriptions of heaven provided by Muhammad and his later followers.

6.4.1 The Heaven of Islam

In the Bible, we are told that all the hardships and sacrifices endured in this life will be rewarded in heaven, which is defined as an "eternal and exceeding weight in glory" (2 Corinthians 4:17), because God the Father dwells there (2 Corinthians 5:8). God's presence is described as the fullness of joy (Psalm 16:11), which I can personally attest to. God's presence is pure love, and His love transcends any physical pleasure experienced in this world.

As for *Islam's* version of heaven, the reason for wanting to go there is not to be with Allah but rather to have thousands of servants, as well as eternal sex slaves known as *houri* (Qur'an 37:40–4, 44:51–55, 52:17–20, 55:54–59, 55:70–77, 56:37–40, 78:31–34, and Tirmidhi 4:21:2687).

> **Tirmidhi, 4:21:2687** [Islamic heaven = 72 wives] "The smallest reward for the people of Paradise is an abode where there are 80,000 servants and 72 wives, over which stands a dome decorated with pearls, aquamarine …"

Muhammad made his appeals to men, and sex sells; hence, many Qur'anic surahs speak of an endless supply of sex in heaven (Qur'an 37:41–48, 44:51–55, 52:17–20, 55:54–59, 55:70–77, 56:37–40, 78:31–34). As for the women, I can't wrap my mind around why any of them would want this version of heaven.

> **Qur'an 37:41–48 (Shakir)** [bold emphasis added] For them is a known sustenance, fruits, and they shall be highly honored, In gardens of pleasure, on thrones, facing each other. A bowl shall be made to go round them from water running out of springs, white, delicious to those who drink. There shall be no trouble in it, nor shall they be exhausted therewith. **And besides them will be chaste women, restraining their glances, with big eyes (of wonder and beauty)**.

> **Qur'an 44:51–55 (Shakir)** [bold emphasis added] Surely those who guard (against evil) are in a secure place, In gardens and springs; they shall wear of fine and thick silk, (sitting) face to face; thus (shall it be), and **we will wed them with Houris pure, beautiful ones**. They shall call therein for every fruit in security;

> **Qur'an 52:17–20 (Shakir)** [bold emphasis added] Surely those who guard (against evil) shall be in gardens and bliss rejoicing because of what their Lord gave them, and their Lord saved them from the punishment of the burning fire. Eat and drink pleasantly for what you did, **reclining on thrones**

set in lines, and we will unite them to large-eyed beautiful ones.

Qur'an 55:54–59 (Shakir) [bold emphasis and bracketed comment added]
Reclining on beds, the inner coverings of which are of silk brocade; and the fruits of the two gardens shall be within reach. Which then of the bounties of your Lord will you deny? **In them [the houris] shall be those who restrained their eyes; before them neither man nor jinni shall have touched them.** Which then of the bounties of your Lord will you deny? As though they were rubies and pearls. Which then of the bounties of your Lord will you deny?

Qur'an 55:70–77 (Shakir) [bold emphasis and bracketed comments added]
In them [fair wives] are goodly things, beautiful ones. Which then of the bounties of your Lord will you deny? **Pure ones [houris] confined to the pavilions**. Which then of the bounties of your Lord will you deny? **Man has not touched them before them nor jinni**. Which then of the bounties of your Lord will you deny? **Reclining on green cushions and beautiful carpets**. Which then of the bounties of your Lord will you deny?

Qur'an 56:37–40 (Shakir) [bold emphasis added]
Loving, equals in age, for the sake of the **companions** of the right, **a numerous company** from among the first, and **a numerous company** from among the last.

> **Qur'an 78:31–34 (Shakir)** [bold emphasis added]
> Surely for those who guard (against evil) is achievement, gardens and vineyards, and **voluptuous women of equal age**; and a pure cup.

As I read descriptions of heaven in various Qur'an surahs and Hadiths, I kept seeing the word *houris* over and over again. What exactly is a houri? For starters, the houris are female sex slaves with a fair complexion and wide eyes, who are given to Muslim men in addition to their wives. It doesn't end there, however. The more I researched, the more comical the houris became.

The houris are always Caucasian, not sure why. The houris also have contrasting attributes. For example, they are described as young and childlike—bashful, innocent, and chaste—yet they also have fully developed, high-pointed breasts for the enjoyment of their husband-masters. The houris are also perpetually young virgins, who never have been touched, yet through some form of pornographic osmosis, they are *sexperts* intent on pleasing their husband-masters for all eternity.

An article on www.FaithFreedom.org, titled "Houri, the Islamic Sex Slave in Paradise," details the following:

> The only hair on her body is on her head and eyebrows; the houri has a permanent Brazilian wax. A houri does not suffer any of the disabilities of ordinary women; they do not urinate, menstruate, or have any vaginal discharge … A houri will not become pregnant, therefore, there is no need to wear a condom in paradise. She will never look at any man other than her master-husband. She will never desire another man; Allah has formed her brain so that she does not have the ability to think of anyone or anything other than Allah or her master-husband … In an after-life Islamic [ethereal] brothel, women have no choice; they must have sex with any man that selects them …

> Yet much of the supporting evidence for the existence of [heavenly] Islamic booty-call robot girls comes directly from the Qur'an itself.[26]

Modern Islamic apologists try to downplay the materialism and sexual descriptions associated with Islam's version of heaven, but according to the *Encyclopedia of Islam*, even orthodox Muslim theologians, such as Al-Ghazali (who died in AD 1111) and Al-Ash'ari (who died in AD 935), have admitted sensual pleasures into paradise.

Qur'anic commentator Al-Suyuti (who died in AD 1505) believed that seventy-two virgins were just the starting point. Not only would there be seventy-two virgins, but they would also be *renewable*, and men would have *eternal* erections as well. Outside the context of sex, having an eternal erection would be a ridiculous embarrassment, not to mention a handicap! Al-Suyuti's version of heaven must therefore be an eternal orgy.

> Each time we sleep with a houri we find her a virgin. Besides, the penis of the Elected never softens. The erection is eternal; the sensation that you feel each time you make love is utterly delicious and out of this world and were you to experience it in this world you would faint. Each chosen one [i.e., Muslim] will marry seventy [sic] houris, besides the women he married on earth, and all will have appetizing vaginas.[27]

Islam is so fixated on sex that Muslims refuse to believe Jesus is the Son of God because Muhammad could not conceive of God having a Son through any other means than sex with Mary. Muhammad even wrote in the Qur'an that Jesus was born of a virgin by God's divine command (Qur'an 3:47), yet he simply thought of Jesus as a fatherless miracle. He could not accept the fact that Jesus is the literal Son of God (Qur'an 4:171) because that somehow had to involve sex with Mary.

Qur'an 3:47 (Shakir) [bold emphasis added]
She said: My Lord! When shall there be a son (born) to I me, and **man has not touched me**? He said: Even so, **Allah creates what He pleases**; when He has decreed a matter, **He only says to it, Be, and it is.**

Qur'an 4:171 (Shakir)
Allah is only one Allah; far be It from His glory that He should have a son!

Because of this misconception, Muhammad mistakenly believed that Christians elevated Mary to the status of God (Qur'an 5:17, 5:70–75, 5:116–117). This gave him a completely inaccurate definition of the Christian Trinity. Christians believe there is only one God, who manifests in three identities: the Father, Son, and Holy Ghost. They are all unique and yet one God at the same time. The Trinity is a God thing, somewhat beyond human comprehension, sort of how time exists as past, present, and future, or the third dimension is expressed as height, width, and depth; each element is unique, yet all work together as a unified whole. In any case, Mary is not part of the Trinity, but Muhammad thought Christians believed that she was.

Qur'an 5:17 (Shakir) [bold emphasis added]
Certainly they disbelieve who say: Surely, **Allah—He is the Messiah, son of Marium**. Say: **Who then could control anything as against Allah when He wished to destroy the Messiah son of Marium and his mother and all those on the earth?** And Allah's is the kingdom of the heavens and the earth and what is between them; He creates what He pleases; and Allah has power over all things.

Note: Why bother mentioning that Mary could be destroyed if not trying to refute the assumption that she is an immortal god that cannot be killed?

Qur'an 5:70–75 (Shakir) [bold emphasis added]
They are unbelievers who say, "**God is the Messiah, Mary's son.**" For the Messiah said, "Children of Israel, serve God, my Lord and your Lord. Verily whoso associates with God anything, God shall prohibit him entrance to Paradise, and his refuge shall be the Fire; and wrongdoers shall have no helpers." **They are unbelievers who say, "God is the Third of Three (thalithu thalathatin).**" No god is there but One God. If they refrain not from what they say, they shall afflict those of them that disbelieve a painful chastisement. Will they not turn to God and pray His forgiveness? God is All-forgiving, All-compassionate. The Messiah, son of Mary, was only a Messenger; Messengers before him passed away; **his mother was a just woman; they both ate food**. Behold, how We make clear the signs to them; then behold, how they perverted are!

Note: Why bother mentioning that Mary was just a woman who ate food if not trying to refute the assumption that she is an immortal god who does not need to eat?

Qur'an 5:116–117 (Shakir) [bold emphasis added]
And when Allah will say: O Isa son of Marium! did you say to men, **Take me and my mother for two gods besides Allah** he will say: Glory be to Thee, it did not befit me that I should say what I had no right to (say); if I had said it, Thou wouldst indeed have known it; Thou knowest what is in my mind, and I do not know what is in Thy mind, surely Thou art the great Knower of the unseen things. I did not say to them aught save what Thou didst enjoin me with: That serve Allah, my Lord and your Lord, and

> I was a witness of them so long as I was among them, but when Thou didst cause me to die, Thou wert the watcher over them, and Thou art witness of all things.
>
> Note: This is a clear indication that Muhammad believed Allah refuted the claim that Jesus and His mother were gods.

Reflecting on Muhammad's misconception of the Trinity, and his description of Jannah (Islamic heaven), it is evident that sex was a central theme of his theology.

Concerning sexuality in Islamic culture, Muhammad promoted an extreme double standard between his male and female followers. Today, Muslim women typically wear hijabs (veils), so no one can see what they look like. Great extremes are implemented when it comes to keeping women under wraps, literally. Female sexuality is treated as one of the greatest taboos in Islamic culture, and because of that, women are shut up, covered up, and locked up. As for the men, they can have multiple wives, prostitutes, concubines, sex slaves—pretty much anything goes. This all harkens back to these teachings on Islamic heaven.

In a way, it makes perfect sense that one of the side effects of Islamic culture, with normal contact between men and women so highly restricted, is the carnal desires of men that have leaked into the sexual fantasies of Islamic heaven. This likely stems from maintaining such an extreme degree of control over female sexuality.

6.4.2 The Child Brides of Islam

I already mentioned that when Muhammad was in his fifties, he married a six-year-old and had sex with her when she turned nine years old. By doing this, Muhammad established a precedent of "normalcy" in Islamic culture that stands to this day.

One would think that the trauma of a young preteen girl forced into a marriage with a man she may not even know would be bad enough, but that's actually just the beginning for many child brides.

Following is a narrative I have extrapolated and paraphrased from an article on the Answering Islam website, titled "What Is So Bad about Child Brides?"[28]

First is the radical departure of family and friends, and the introduction into a new home with a man who demands to have sex. These young girls—many of them eight, nine, and ten years old—have no idea what sex is; they're still playing with toys and coloring with crayons. They want to go to the park, not the bed! But their parents endorsed this madness, essentially selling them off to a child molester, following Muhammad's "perfect example."

So what happens next, when such young children who are not fully developed get pregnant? The nightmare that never ends, that's what. It's called a *fistula*.

Because these impregnated children are not fully developed, they can become pregnant but are not capable of having the baby. The baby ends up lodged in the birth canal, damaging the girl's bladder among other things. The girls can't get a cesarean; these are poor people. So on the first day of labor, the baby dies. Three days later, when the baby's decomposed corpse softens, it finally comes out. In the process, it rips up the poor child, and those wounds don't heal without surgery. Because these people are poor, surgery is out of the question. Most likely they don't even know that surgery can fix this problem, but even if they did know, they wouldn't be able to afford it.

So now the man who impregnated his child wife is upset, and he blames his child wife for this complete and utter failure to conceive a child for him. She is most likely sick with fever after such a horrendous ordeal and having a decomposing baby in her womb for three days. But of course that's all her fault; she must have done something to incur the wrath of Allah, and she brings shame on her husband and their family's honor.

As she slowly recovers, racked with physical pain and the emotional trauma of losing her baby, combined with the anger and rejection of her husband, she realizes within about twelve hours that she is constantly leaking urine and feces. This is a fistula; it is a result of the severe damage she incurred from the pregnancy she was not ready for.

Her husband does not want anything to do with her anymore, so he kicks her out. She has nowhere to go, so she hopes to return home. If she is fortunate, her parents might offer a shack far enough from the house to keep her stench away from them. In that place, she would be treated somewhat like a disgusting animal that no one wants to feed. However, many of these children are no longer welcome back with their parents because they failed their husband, which dishonors their family. Those girls end up homeless and permanently destitute, as bad if not worse than a leper.

This scenario is rampant in Nigeria, but it occurs all over the Muslim world. In Nigeria alone, vesicovaginal fistula (VVF) is affecting four hundred thousand to eight hundred thousand women, with twenty thousand new cases occurring annually and 90 percent of them going untreated.[29–30] Thanks to Muhammad's perfect example, between three and four million women in the Muslim world suffer from this fate that makes their lives a living hell.

In Iran, back in 2010, more than forty-three thousand marriages of girls younger than fifteen years of age were officially recorded. Many child-bride marriages end in divorce because more and more children cannot endure the trails that they face. In Western culture, divorce is painful, but the bulk of that pain is associated with the failure of the relationship. In Islamic culture, divorced women are viewed as a disgrace to their entire families, so on top of the pain of the failed relationship, there is an additional burden—a level of shame and rejection that far exceeds anything we have to deal with in Western society. Because of this shame and rejection, the girls sometimes leave their abusive husbands only to return to abusive parents, or they end up on the streets, forced into prostitution.[31]

6.4.3 The Practice of Female Genital Mutilation (FGM)

Another aspect of daily life for many Islamic women is the practice of female genital mutilation (FGM), a.k.a. female circumcision, mostly concentrated in twenty-seven African countries, Yemen, and Iraqi Kurdistan, and found elsewhere in Asia, the Middle East, and among diaspora communities around the world.[32]

Since the practice of FGM predates Islam, there are some outspoken Islamic critics of the practice who claim that FGM is a purely cultural phenomenon that has nothing to do with Islam. While it is true that FGM predates Islam, the Hadiths have made it *Fitra* (i.e., a preferred practice), commensurate with other hygienic activities, as taught by many Muslim clerics and widely practiced in many Muslim homes (Bukhari 7:72:777, 7:72:779, 8:74:312; Malik 49:3:3; Muslim 2:495–496; Dawud 41:5251).[33–34]

> **Bukhari 7:72:777** [bold emphasis added]
> Allah's Apostle said, "Five practices are characteristics of the Fitra: **circumcision**, shaving the pubic region, clipping the nails and cutting the moustaches short."

> **Bukhari 7:72:779** [bold emphasis added]
> I heard the Prophet saying. "Five practices are characteristics of the Fitra: **circumcision**, shaving the pubic hair, cutting the moustaches short, clipping the nails, and depilating the hair of the armpits."

> **Malik 49:3:3** [bold emphasis added]
> Yahya related to me from Malik from Said ibn Abi Said al-Maqburi from his father that Abu Hurayra said, "There are five things from the fitra: cutting the nails, trimming the moustache, removing the hair from the armpit, shaving the pubic region and **circumcision**."

> **Muslim 2:495–496** [bold emphasis added]
> Abu Huraira reported: Five are the acts quite akin to the Fitra, or five are the acts of Fitra: **circumcision**, shaving the pubes, cutting the nails, plucking the

> hair under the armpits and clipping the moustache. Abu Huraira reported: Five are the acts of fitra: **circumcision**, removing the pubes, clipping the moustache, cutting the nails, plucking the hair under the armpits.

Those who argue that there is nothing in Islam that mandates female circumcision neglect to mention all of these Hadiths, due to their unspoken assumption that these Hadiths only apply to men, but that is merely an interpretational license that some choose to believe. Because no gender is specified in these Hadiths, many Muslims do interpret them to mean that women must be circumcised as well.

Islamic culture in general makes a huge deal about ensuring that females are strictly regulated in countless variations of restrictions. Consider the following excerpt from the Ayatollah Khomeini's *Little Green Book*:

> A woman who has contracted a continuing marriage does not have the right to go out of the house without her husband's permission; she must remain at his disposal for the fulfillment of any one of his desires, and may not refuse herself to him except for a religiously valid reason. If she is totally submissive to him, the husband must provide her with her food, clothing, and lodging, whether or not he has the means to do so.[35]

In different Islamic countries, women often have no choice in who or when they will marry; women are often not allowed out of the house without a male escort; women cannot be alone in a house with a man who is not their husband, father, or brother; women are sometimes stoned to death if incapable of proving their innocence in an accusation of adultery; women are not allowed to drive; women are mandated to be covered from head to toe; and on and on it goes.

This desire for Muslim men to maintain such ultimate control over women has therefore become a sufficient justification for some of them to implement the most severe form of FGM, which involves a complete clitoridectomy (removal of the clitoris) and infibulation (excision of the genitalia and stitching/narrowing of the vaginal opening). Following this procedure, the female in question will no longer enjoy sex, which will reduce her desire to have premarital sex or commit adultery. For a control-freak Muslim man, that is a definite benefit.

This most severe form of FGM has sacred Islamic literature outside of the Hadiths to support it, and many Islamic theologians will argue in defense of it. The Answering Islam website describes a classic manual of Islamic sacred law *Umdat al-Salik*, which has been purposefully mistranslated into English by Ahmad ibn Naqib al-Misri and titled *Reliance of the Traveler*. According to a corrected translation, the Arabic law states the following:

> **Circumcision is obligatory (for every male and female)** by cutting off the piece of skin on the glans of the penis of the male, but **circumcision of the female is by cutting out the clitoris** (this is called HufaaD).[36]

This particular form of FGM is widely practiced in Egypt, where the Shafi'i school of Sunni law is practiced.

With modern science, we now know that FGM has nothing to offer women except barbaric, medieval torture, followed by a wide range of moderate to severe health risks and painful injuries, many of which can last a lifetime. According to an article by the human rights organization, European Network, titled *Effects of FGM*, the practice is an inhuman torture that can inflict hemorrhagic shock and neurogenic shock so severe the victim dies.[37]

To their credit, many Muslims have spoken out against the practice of FGM, but they repeatedly make the claim that it is only a cultural phenomenon, and it has nothing to do with the religion of Islam. To support this claim, they point to statistics from a few primarily Christian countries where FGM is practiced (Eritrea, and Ethiopia for example).[38] However, those who are practicing FGM in those Christian countries are often discovered to be Muslims. For example, one in every twenty Muslim women in the London borough of Southwark have been a victim of female genital mutilation.[39]

Despite various websites insisting that FGM has nothing to do with religion, seven out of the top eight countries where FGM is rampant are Muslim majority nations. FGM is forced on as many as six thousand girls every day, totaling about 130 million (with over two million annually). The vast majority of them are Muslims.[40–41]

6.4.4 The Issue of Rape and Sex Slaves

Another element of Islam that disregards the desire of women is the fact that Islam permits the rape of women who are considered to be "infidels," a.k.a. non-Muslims. Many Muslims will contest this notion vehemently, but consider what needs to be explained in order to defend all of the Qur'an surahs and Hadiths that speak of Muhammad and his men having sex with those referred to as slaves and "those whom your right hand possesses" and "those whom Allah has given to you as prisoners of war" (Qur'an 23:1–6, 33:50, 70:22–30, and many more). Does anyone honestly believe that any of this sex was consensual? What woman in her right mind would get turned on and want to have sex with a man who just murdered her mother, father, husband, children, and friends?

> **Qur'an 23:1–6 (Shakir)** [bold emphasis added]
> Successful indeed are the believers, Who are humble in their prayers, And who keep aloof from what is vain, And who are givers of poor-rate, '**Except before their mates or those whom their right hands possess**, for they surely are not blamable …

The "mates" in question are wives, and "those whom their right hands possess" are slaves.

> **Qur'an 33:50 (Shakir)** [bold emphasis added]
> O Prophet! surely **We have made lawful to you your wives** whom you have given their dowries, **and those whom your right hand possesses out of those whom Allah has given to you as prisoners of war**, and the daughters of your paternal uncles and the daughters of your paternal aunts, and the daughters of your maternal uncles and the daughters of your maternal aunts who fled with you; and a believing woman if she gave herself to the Prophet, if the Prophet desired to marry her—specially for you, not for the (rest of) believers; **We know what We have ordained for them concerning their wives and those whom their right hands possess** in order that no blame may attach to you; and Allah is Forgiving, Merciful.

"Lawful," in this case, means they are allowed to have sex with their wives and those whom they possess, a.k.a. slaves.

> **Qur'an 70:22–30 (Shakir)** [bold emphasis added]
> Except those who pray, those who are constant at their prayer And those in whose wealth there is a fixed portion. For him who begs and for him who is denied (good) And those who accept the truth of the judgment day And those who are fearful of the chastisement of their Lord—Surely the chastisement of their Lord is (a thing) not to be felt secure of—**And those who guard their private parts, except in the case of their wives or those whom their right hands possess**—for these surely are not to be blamed …

"Guarding their private parts" is a reference to abstaining from sex. Here, the Qur'an is basically saying that successful believers are those who indulge in sexual activities with their wives and their sex slaves. These activities happened in Muhammad's day, and they're still happening today by Muslims following Muhammad's example. Members of ISIS, for example, actually rape women and children as a form of worship to Allah.[42]

One article on the Answering Muslims website, which detailed this information about Muhammad's slave trade activities, had a list of comments following the article. Various Muslim apologists were arguing the point that all of the sex that Muhammad and his men had with their prisoners of war was consensual.[43] I cannot comprehend how anyone can be so diluted. The extent of their logic was the equivalent of a Monty Python skit. As the bickering went back and forth in various threads, one Muslim stated that no one can ever prove this sex was nonconsensual, to which one counter response was that Muslims are still doing this today, simply following Muhammad's example. Look at the actions of ISIS.

At the mention of ISIS, a stream of Muslim posters interjected into the feed the same preposterous Nazi garbage I listed earlier. They spouted off that ISIS is a Jewish Zionist organization, it's all lies, and on and on, sounding like Hitler, convulsing and screaming in a spittle-infused tirade of Jew-hating psycho-babble. If this had occurred in a debate forum, all anyone would have to do is back away from the podium and stare in awestruck silence.

Muhammad's men sometimes had questions about all of this sex they were having with their sex slaves. "Should we maybe try to avoid getting them pregnant?" they questioned.

Muhammad's response was (my paraphrase), "Does it matter? If they do, it's all good, it must be Allah's will" (Muslim 8:3371, 8:3384).

> **Muslim 8:3371** [bold emphasis added]
> Abu Sirma said to Abu Sa'id al Khadri (Allah he pleased with him): 0 Abu Sa'id, did you hear Allah's Messenger (may peace be upon him) mentioning al-'azl? He said: Yes, and added: **We went out with Allah's Messenger** (may peace be upon him) on the expedition to the Bi'l-Mustaliq **and took captive some excellent Arab women; and we desired them,**

> **for we were suffering from the absence of our wives**, (but at the same time) we also desired ransom for them. So **we decided to have sexual intercourse with them** but by observing ‘azl (Withdrawing the male sexual organ before emission of semen to avoid-conception). But we said: We are doing an act whereas Allah’s Messenger is amongst us; why not ask him? So we asked Allah’s Messenger (may peace be upon him), and he said: **It does not matter if you do not do it**, for every soul that is to be born up to the Day of Resurrection will be born.

> **Muslim 8:3384** [bold emphasis added]
> Jabir (Allah be pleased with him) reported that a man came to Allah’s Messenger (may peace be upon him) and said: **I have a slave-girl** who is our servant and she carries water for us and **I have intercourse with her, but I do not want her to conceive**. He said: Practice ‘azl, if you so like, but what is decreed for her will come to her. The person stayed back (for some time) and then came and said: **The girl has become pregnant**, whereupon he said: **I told you what was decreed for her would come to her**.

Muhammad’s men came to him with another sex-related question about their slaves: “What if our slave girls are pregnant? Can we still have sex?”(my paraphrase).

Muhammad’s response was (my paraphrase), “Allah says you should wait until she finishes having her period.”

> **Dawud 11:2153** [bold emphasis added]
> Should I tell you what I heard the Apostle of Allah (peace be upon him) say on the day of Hunayn: It is not lawful for a man who believes in Allah and the last day to water what another has sown with

> his water (meaning intercourse with women who are pregnant); **it is not lawful for a man who believes in Allah and the Last Day to have intercourse with a captive woman till she is free from a menstrual course**; and it is not lawful for a man who believes in Allah and the Last Day to sell spoil till it is divided.

And again Muhammad's men came to him with yet another question about their sex slaves. Some of the women were married, and their husbands were still alive. Up to this point, they were holding off because … well … their husbands were still alive. What to do about this conundrum? My paraphrase, "Muhammad, gee, this married slave of mine, she's married, but her husband is also my slave. Can I …?"

Muhammad's response was (my paraphrase), "Sure, you can have sex with your wives, and you can have sex with your slaves as well. Allah says it's cool because they're your property."

In the Qur'an, Muhammad tells his men that they are forbidden to have sex with all married women except "those whom your right hand possesses," i.e., slaves (Qur'an 4:24). When it comes to slaves, it is okay to have sex with them. This is a little vague by itself, but a corresponding Hadith sheds light on the backstory to this verse, making it crystal clear (Dawud 11:2150).[44–45]

> **Qur'an 4:24 (Shakir)** [bold emphasis added]
> And **all married women except those whom your right hands possess** (this is) Allah's ordinance to you, **and lawful for you are (all women) besides those**, provided that you seek (them) with your property, taking (them) in marriage not committing fornication. Then as to those whom you profit by, give them their dowries as appointed; and there is no blame on you about what you mutually agree after what is appointed; surely Allah is Knowing, Wise.

> **Dawud 11:2150** [bold emphasis added]
> Abu Said al-Khudri said: **"The apostle of Allah sent a military expedition to Awtas** on the occasion of the battle of Hunain. They met their enemy and fought with them. **They defeated them and took them captives. Some of the Companions of the apostle of Allah were reluctant to have intercourse with the female captives in the presence of their husbands** who were unbelievers. **So Allah, the Exalted, sent down the Quranic verse, 'And all married women (are forbidden) unto you save those (captives) whom your right hands possess.' That is to say, they are lawful for them when they complete their waiting period."**

The slave business was a big hit with Muhammad and his men. They had more sex than they knew what to do with, so the more slaves they had the merrier. To that end, Muhammad was given guidance from his graceful, ample-giving Allah on how to institute a breeding program with their slaves, singling out breeders who were in the best physical shape—that is, "those who are fit."[46]

> **Qur'an 24:32 (Shakir)** [bold emphasis added]
> And **marry those among you who are single and those who are fit among your male slaves and your female slaves**; if they are needy, Allah will make them free from want out of His grace; and Allah is Ample-giving, Knowing.

Leading by example, Muhammad established a cultural precedent of rape concerning non-Muslim women. Probably all of these women suffered from PTSD, and many were in a state of extreme shock. The closest thing to sexual consent with any of them would be if they were catatonic vegetables that had lost their will to fight back, or if they succumbed to the effects of the Stockholm syndrome.

In the Qur'an, the word *rape* will not be found because Muhammad did not even recognize its existence. In the Qur'an, the factors that determine whether or not sex is lawful have nothing to do with a woman's consent. As for the idea of marriage, Muhammad had a very different concept of a legal marriage. For example, Muhammad freed and married two of his slave girls, Safiyah and Juwairiyah, but these unions beg the question of what Islam constitutes as freedom or marriage.

In Safiyah's case, Muhammad attacked her village; murdered her husband, a Jewish rabbi named Kinana; and purportedly "manumitted" (freed) her but then immediately married her on the same day (Bukhari 1:8:367). I wonder exactly how free she was, and I certainly question the validity of her so-called marriage.[47] This is the pinnacle of legalism in Islam. Does anyone want to argue the point that Safiyah was in love with Muhammad?

As for Juwairiyah, she agreed to marry Muhammad as a means of rescuing her village from destruction shortly after it was attacked without warning (Dawud 29:3920, Bukhari 3:46:717). On this occasion, the Hadiths praise Muhammad for his overwhelming mercy.

The element of rape in Muhammad's conquests never officially ended. The Islamic terrorists who wage jihad today are fully aware of this fact. Slavery is still practiced in the Sudan, Niger, Mauritania, and a few other corners of the Muslim world.[48] As for the violence of rape, it is still frequently excused in cases where infidel women are concerned, and it is also widely disregarded *even with Muslim women*, in order to protect family honor.

Consider the case of Anni Cyrus, just one example of an Iranian girl who now lives in the United States. When she lived in Iran, she was raped, and shortly afterward she was threatened with ninety-five lashes if she told the government or police about the incident because it would bring shame on her family.

> "If this (a rape) were about to happen in the Islamic Republic of Iran, well, it couldn't happen," Cyrus

> said. "I'll tell you why: there's no such a word as rape. None. Because to their eyes," Cyrus continued, "if it happened between a wife and a husband, there's no such a thing as rape, because the wife is the man's property. She does not get to say no—or yes. Now, if it happens to just a girl or a woman by a stranger or someone who's not married to them—again, it cannot happen. Because it was her fault. She seduced him."[49]

In her interview with Glasnov Gang Productions, Anni gave a stern warning to Obama regarding his often-public declarations of warm acceptance of Islam in America.

> "What I am trying to tell you … watch Obama say, 'Let there be no doubt that Islam is part of America,'" Cyrus said. "Well, I want you to know—let there be no doubt (that) raping your mother, your sister, your wife, your daughter is part of Islam."[50]

Thanks to Western influence, rape is at least technically considered a crime now in *some* Islamic countries, but it is seldom reported because it is viewed as a stain on a family's honor, as it was in Anni's case. In some countries, such as Libya, it can even carry with it an honor killing death sentence.[51]

In many instances, rape automatically carries with it the connotation that the woman provoked it. Some Muslim clerics preach this message of blaming rape on women, making sure to instill fear in women so they will adhere to all the Islamic restrictions. Australian Sheik Feiz Muhammad, for example, said a rape victim "has no one to blame but herself. She displayed her beauty to the entire world … to tease men and appeal to their carnal nature."[52]

In a 1999 study in Turkey, it was discovered that 33 percent of police officers agreed with the assessment that "some women deserve rape," and 66 percent agreed that "the physical appearance and behaviors of women tempt men to rape."[53] In another study in

Saudi Arabia, 87 percent of men blamed women for sexual assault.[54] This prevailing attitude of blaming the victim has led many men to disregard the crime of rape as no big deal. One in three African men *openly admit to rape*,[55] and 87 percent of the female students at Imam Muhammad Bin Saud University were abused by faculty staff.[56] Examples of this nature are endless.

Those few brave women who step forward and blow the whistle are often tasked with an exceptionally heavy burden of proof because rape is nearly impossible to prove in many Islamic nations. According to the Qur'an, sexual relations can only be proven if witnessed by four males willing to testify of the event (Qur'an 24:4, 13). Muhammad established this precedent in order to protect his family's honor from the accusation of adultery made against his wife Aisha. While Aisha was actually suspected of committing adultery, Muhammad's ruling in this situation mutated over the years into a means of protecting rapists.

Married women struggle to avoid being accused of adultery when reporting rapes, and in instances where the woman is not married, the woman or girl can be prosecuted severely. If it is discovered that a girl who reports a rape was not a virgin, as in the case of a fifteen-year-old Maldives girl who was raped in 2013, the consequences are even more severe. The Maldives girl was sentenced to one hundred lashes and eight months of house arrest for having premarital sex. This was discovered while investigating her rape by her own stepfather, who also impregnated her and then killed their baby.[57]

It is this kind of behavior we can expect from the Antichrist, who will have no regard for the desire of women.

6.4.5 What Happens to Women Who Speak Out in Islam?

In the middle of the most hostile Islamic territory where women are severely oppressed, there are some extraordinarily brave souls who dare to speak out. A number of these women are listed on this website: www.IranHumanRights.org.[58] There are thousands of others who are locked up and being tortured, or they have already been raped and executed.

Not many of these women have the opportunity to tell their stories, but one of them, Ladan Pardeshenas, survived imprisonment. With the help of friends in the People's Mojahedin Organization, she managed to escape Iran during one of her trips to the hospital for brain surgery, which was the result of one of her tortures.

Ladan was first arrested in 1980 as a supporter of the People's Mojahedin Organization, a human rights organization most recognized for their warnings about religious fundamentalism being the primary obstacle to freedom, democracy, and equality. For speaking out in favor of these democratic ideals, Ladan was held in Evin Prison for four years, as well as six months in Gezel Hesar Prison.

In prison women were tied to a short bench, blindfolded, and flogged on their backs and the soles of their feet with a cable. They were threatened with rape on a regular basis. Then there was "the scale," where one arm was twisted up over their shoulder and the other arm from underneath, and then bound behind their backs. Then they were suspended from the ceiling and left like that for twelve hours.

Ladan still bears scars from this torture; she lost the hearing in her right ear and most of the sight in her left eye. She suffers constant pain in her arms and legs, and because of the constant head injuries, she now suffers long periods of headaches and dizziness. This is all a normal part of her life now.

Ladan was not alone in prison. Her younger sister, Nassrin Pardehshenas, who was only eighteen years old, was also with her. They eventually raped and executed her. The worst torture of all was psychological, being forced to watch the torture of other prisoners. Sometimes women who had children were tortured in front of their children. Ladan was forced to witness her sister's torture.[59]

In Elvin Prison, simply *torturing* the female prisoners wasn't enough for the Ayatollah Khomeini, so he institutionalized the practice of raping the prisoners prior to their execution. In 2009, the Iranian Political Prisoner's Action Committee published a list of 1,400 females who were raped by prison guards in so-called marriages, conducted specifically to prevent them from *going to heaven.* Many of these females were under the age of seventeen.[60–62]

In 1999, Ladan was living in Italy, still serving as a leading women's rights activist for Iranian women. After her escape, the Tehran regime stopped at nothing to terrorize her and members of her family, both in and out of Iran.

> During the Gulf War in 1991, Ladan sent her two sons, aged two and four, to Holland for safekeeping. One of the regime's agents kidnapped her eldest son while he was living in The Netherlands. A few days later, they threw her four-year-old son to his death from the fourth floor of a building.[63]

6.4.6 The Ayatollah Khomeini's Unique Contribution to Women

When it comes to the treatment of women and the overall aspect of human sexuality, the culture of Islam, along with its Islamic icons (such as the Ayatollah Khomeini), present a perfect picture of the heart of the Antichrist. God gave sex to humanity as the apex of intimacy and enjoyment between a husband and wife, so it stands to reason that Satan would attack this union so vehemently.

The perfect rendition of Satan's version of human sexuality would include a convoluted legal system that paints a pretty picture on the outside, but on the inside, it conceals an incomprehensibly twisted perversion that knows no bounds. This is exactly what Islam has morphed into, and a prime example of this satanic perversion comes from the late Ayatollah Khomeini.

The Shiite title *ayatollah* is defined as "a title in the religious hierarchy achieved by scholars who have demonstrated highly advanced knowledge of Islamic law and religion."[64] With this in mind, consider what the former Ayatollah Khomeini, a man enlightened by Islamic doctrine, published in his *Little Green Book* regarding religious regulations all Shiite Muslims should strive to adhere to:

- If a man who has married a girl who has not reached puberty possesses her sexually before her ninth birthday, inflicting traumatisms upon her, he has no right to repeat such an act with her.[65]
- If a man sodomizes the son, brother, or father of his wife after their marriage, the marriage remains valid.[66]
- A temporary marriage, even though only one of convenience, is nevertheless legal.[67]
- Temporary marriage: If the father or paternal grandfather of a boy has him marry a woman for a temporary marriage, he may prematurely cancel it in the boy's interest, even if the marriage was contracted before the boy reached the age of puberty. If, for example, a fourteen-year-old boy has been married off to a woman for a period of two years, they may return her freedom to the woman before this time has run its course, but a continuing marriage cannot be broken in this way.[68]

Anyone reading through the *Little Green Book* will become immediately aware of the degree of legalism at work. This book also reads like a Freudian fantasy; the detail that Khomeini went into concerning every possible aspect of sexual intercourse is ridiculous. Then there are the disturbing *fatwas* listed above.

The first fatwa I mentioned speaks of men having sex with girls who have not yet reached puberty. Legalistically speaking, this can even include *infants*, which many claim it does in a practice known as *thighing*, specifically addressed in other fatwas[69–70] and explicitly detailed in the *Tahrir al-Wasilah*, fourth volume, made available by the Institute for Compilation and Publication of Imam Khomeini's Works.[71]

A legalistic Muslim reading this fatwa about "inflicting traumatisms" upon his prepubescent or even infant wife can simply ask himself, "What is a traumatism? Is thighing an infant traumatism? The baby does not mind; the baby does not know what is happening to her. Thank you, *Little Green Book.*" The *Little Green Book* might as well be called the Big Green Light for child molesters.

Pedophiles frequently employ deceptive tactics in what they do, grooming their victims over time, training them, desensitizing them to a sexual reality that they should never be exposed to at such young ages. This fatwa is nothing short of a pedophile's legal permit, allowing them to do whatever their sick, twisted imaginations can contrive, as long as no one can determine from external appearances that no traumatisms have happened to the children in question.

The second fatwa on the list is another green light for a pedophile to rape his own son! In the very least, child molestation is downplayed in this fatwa as something having no significance on the validity of a man's marriage to his wife. I suspect this was drafted in response to Iranian women demanding a divorce from their sick husbands who were abusing their children. It could mean more than that, however; this fatwa speaks of sodomy incest with any male member of a family.

If Khomeini is going to address something as outlandishly twisted as a man sodomizing his son, brother, or father, why not go the extra mile and declare that men should not be sodomizing their male family members at all, under any circumstance, period? In my opinion, a man who does that deserves the Elvin Prison that Ladan endured, but no, Khomeini doesn't want to go there. He would rather talk about not eating animal excrement and the meat of sodomized animals, as in the fatwa below:

> It is forbidden to consume the excrement of animals or their nasal secretions. But if such are mixed in minute proportions into other foods their consumption is not forbidden. The meat of horses, mules, or donkeys is not recommended. It is strictly forbidden if the animal was sodomized while alive by a man. In that case, the animal must be taken outside the city and sold.[72]

Take special note of the wording: "if the animal was sodomized 'while alive'." What's that supposed to mean? Who is actually going to sodomize a dead donkey? This is absolutely ridiculous!

Who knows, maybe dead animals are all the rage in Iran; perhaps my multicultural grasp of the world I live in is not what it should be, but I digress. I will say, however, it's worth pointing out that while Khomeini took the time to write about these legal regulations regarding sodomy, he did not once say that sodomy with one's own children was forbidden.

He talks all about not eating the meat of sodomized animals and the fact that sex doesn't count if penetration doesn't go beyond the circumcision ring. Yes, all these details are explicit and extremely important in the *Little Green Book*, but when it comes to not committing sodomy with one's own children or whatever animals happen to be around, no hint of that is mentioned.

Finally, the last two fatwas listed discuss the topic of temporary marriage, of which the *Little Green Book* has much to say. I find it laughable that any Shiite would condescendingly speak of the "Western infidels" and their filthy, sinful lifestyles, as Khomeini did throughout his writings, when in fact there are many fatwas that provide a means of *institutionalized promiscuity* for men. In many cases, these temporary marriages morphed into forced prostitution, a.k.a. *slavery*. That's legalism at its finest.

So the Ayatollah Khomeini, the supreme religious authority over all Shiite Muslims not too long ago, wrote an insane *Little Green Book*, among many others, such as the *Tahrir al-Vasyleh*. These books are chock-full of the most intensely profane content imaginable, yet this man was highly revered all over Iran, with his picture emblazoned on every street corner.

As the supreme religious authority over all Shiite Muslims, Khomeini had the option to write some new fatwas, such as "Fathers, don't sodomize your children!" but instead he chose to write about other things because I don't think Khomeini was all that concerned about children. In fact, there is a well-documented story about

Khomeini raping a four-year-old girl. Apparently traumatizing the poor little girl wasn't an issue.

The story below is documented in the book *For Allah, Then for History,* by an author with the alias of Husayn al-Musawi.[73] A former companion of Khomeini, the author was present to testify about this event, when Khomeini was visiting a friend of his named Sayyid Sahib.

> Sayyid Sahib was joyous with our visit, and we arrived at his house around the time of Dhuhr. So, he prepared for us a lavish dinner, and called some of his relatives, who came to see us, and the house became crowded in celebration of our presence.
>
> Sayyid Sahib then requested that we spend that night at his home, to which the Imam agreed. When it was night time, we were given our supper, and the guests would take the Imam's hand and kiss it, and they would ask him questions, with him answering their questions.
>
> When it was time to sleep, the guests had all left, except for the inhabitants of the house. Al-Khomeini laid his eyes on a young girl who, despite being only four or five years of age, was very beautiful.
>
> So, the Imam requested from her father, Sayyid Sahib, that he spend the night with her in order to enjoy her. Her father happily agreed, and Imam al-Khomeini spent the night with the girl in his arms, and we could hear her crying and screaming [through the night].[74]

A number of YouTube videos have different Islamic scholars and imams rightfully ticked off about Khomeini; most of them are probably Sunni Muslims. Just because some Islamic literature places a stamp of approval on things like terrorism, and dismisses spousal abuse, rape, sodomy, child abuse, and so forth, does not mean that *all* Muslims buy into it.

As for the Muslims who *do* approve of these things, the Antichrist will be right at home among them.

6.4.7 Homosexuality, Chai Boys, and Bacha Bazi

The Ayatollah Khomeini's violent, perverse mind was inspired by the literature that preceded him. Even the act of sodomy with boys has its roots in the Qur'an, directly penned by the hand of Muhammad, long before Khomeini was born. Consider these surahs from the Qur'an, which speak of perpetual young boy-servants in heaven:

> **Qur'an 52:24**
> And there will go round boy-servants of theirs, to serve them as if they were preserved pearls.
>
> **Qur'an 56:17**
> They will be served by immortal boys.
>
> **Qur'an 76:19**
> And round about them will (serve) boys of everlasting youth. If you see them, you would think them scattered pearls.

Reading these surahs should beg the question for any inquisitive reader, what would be the purpose of beautiful immortal slave boys in heaven? Why don't they grow up? What did they do so wrong that they can never be men and enjoy heaven like other men? Why are they perpetual slaves, with no rights, for all eternity? What is their purpose? Do the aspects of their beauty, permanently stunted growth, and eternal destiny as slaves place them in the same somewhat nonhuman category as the houris?

As I previously stated, sex sells, and I suspect it was Muhammad's intention to recruit more men when he contrived the concept of the robot-like, sex-slave houris. These immortal boys are no exception; they're obviously the pedophilic homosexual version of the houris. Muhammad likely encountered a number of men in his travels who had acquired a pedophilic appetite for young boys as a product of their culture, which is still prevalent today.

Much of Middle Eastern society is nothing short of a prison when it comes to the availability of women for the average man, and what happens in prison? Men who are not normally homosexuals start acting out with homosexual behavior. With so many young, defenseless boys running around—and the majority of the women off limits because the wealthy men gobbled them all up with four wives each and unlimited slave girls, all hiding out in various homes, fearful and forbidden to step outside—it doesn't take a rocket scientist to see that this is a recipe for pedophilic disaster.

Around the time Muhammad passed away, it was common in Arabic poetry to glorify homosexual pedophilia. Most likely inspired by Muhammad's reference to the "immortal boys" and "scattered pearls" I mentioned above, the famous Arabic poet Abu Nuwas penned this poem, among others, about "smooth-faced boys":

O the joy of sodomy!
So now be sodomites, you Arabs.
Turn not away from it—
therein is wondrous pleasure.
Take some coy lad with kiss-curls
twisting on his temple
and ride as he stands like some gazelle
standing to her mate.
A lad whom all can see girt with sword
and belt not like your whore who has
to go veiled.
Make for smooth-faced boys and do your
very best to mount them, for women are
the mounts of the devils.[75]

I can hear the clamor of millions of Muslims right about now, quoting the Qur'an's account of the people of Lut, which is the Qur'an's version of the biblical story of Sodom and Gomorrah (Qur'an 7:81, 26:165–166, 27:55, 29:28–29). Complementing this clamor is the harsh penalties prescribed for homosexuals throughout the Muslim world. However, there is a convenient loophole Muhammad provided for those of the pedophilic persuasion. All of the Qur'an surahs that speak about the homosexual behavior of the people of Lut refer to *men* and *not children*.

For the sake of consistency, I have generally been quoting from the Shakir translation of the Qur'an, but in these particular surahs, there is a minor difference among the translations worth pointing out.

While the Shakir and Pickthall translations use the word *males* in some of these surahs, the Sahil International, Yusuf Ali, Muhamad Sarwar, Mohsin Khan, and Arberry translations all translate the word as *men*.

Qur'an 7:80–81 (Shakir) [bold emphasis and bracketed comment added]
And (We sent) Lut when he said to his people: What! Do you commit an indecency which anyone in the

world has not done before you? Most surely you come to **males [men]** in lust besides females; nay you are an extravagant people.

Qur'an 26:165–166 (Shakir) [bold emphasis and bracketed comment added]
What! Do you come to the **males [men]** from among the creatures And leave what your Lord has created for you of your wives? Nay, you are a people exceeding limits.

Qur'an 27:55 (Shakir) [bold emphasis added]
What! do you indeed approach **men** lustfully rather than women? Nay, you are a people who act ignorantly.

Qur'an 29:28–29 (Shakir) [bold emphasis and bracketed comment added]
And (We sent) Lut when he said to his people: Most surely you are guilty of an indecency which none of the nations has ever done before you; What! Do you come to the **males [men]** and commit robbery on the highway, and you commit evil deeds in your assemblies? But nothing was the answer of his people except that they said: Bring on us Allah's punishment, if you are one of the truthful.

Islam has given rise to a great deal of what most people in Western culture would define as pedophilia. I have already discussed the prevalence of pedophilia involving girls in the Islamic world. When Muhammad married six-year-old Aisha and had sex with her at nine years old, he set the example for others to follow. He also wrote in the Qur'an about the provisions for having sex with women, including in those provisions girls who had not yet had a period—that is, they were prepubescent (Qur'an 65:4).

> **Qur'an 65:4 (Shakir)** [bold emphasis and bracketed comment added]
> And (as for) those of your women who have despaired of menstruation, if you have a doubt, [about whether to have sex with them or not] their prescribed time shall be three months, **and of those too who have not had their courses**; and (as for) the pregnant women, their prescribed time is that they lay down their burden; and whoever is careful of (his duty to) Allah He will make easy for him his affair.

Concerning pedophilia with boys, Muhammad made sure to include slave boys in his version of heaven, and slaves have no rights; they are merely one's property. What's more, when he condemned the homosexual practices of the people of Lut, he specifically narrowed this activity as it relates to *men*, thereby leaving the door open when it comes to *homosexual pedophilia*. These aspects of the Qur'an, combined with the prisonlike culture of limited access to women, has created a homosexual pedophilic incubation chamber in many Muslim communities throughout the Islamic world.

It is this environment of generational sodomy committed against young boys that inspired the fatwas of the Shiites. It is also this environment that is spreading like wildfire with the recent migration of thousands of Muslims throughout the world. In 2015, in the United Kingdom, for example, Islamic child-sex grooming cases increased by 32 percent in a single year and have spread to every town and city in the United Kingdom. Gangs of sex offenders roam the streets searching for prey.[76]

What do homosexuality and pedophilia have to do with the Antichrist? First of all, as I already mentioned, scripture states that the Antichrist will have no regard for the desire of women (Daniel 11:37).

> **Daniel 11:37** [bold emphasis and bracketed comments added]
> Neither shall he [the Antichrist] regard the God of his fathers, **nor the desire of women**, nor regard any god: for he shall magnify himself above all.

While I believe this scripture refers to the desires that women have, which the Antichrist will care nothing about, it might also mean that the Antichrist will be attracted to males rather than females. Moreover, it could further mean that both assessments are true. The Antichrist might be a homosexual who also cares nothing for women. Either way, the religion of Islam fits the bill.

Concerning homosexuality in general, I speculate that it would not be unreasonable to consider that the Antichrist might be attracted to the homosexual lifestyle, precisely because it is defined in both the Old and New Testaments as an abomination against God (Leviticus 18:22, 20:13; 1 Corinthians 6:9–10; Romans 1:26–28, 32). As for homosexual pedophilia, this adds yet another level of depravity. Whether the Antichrist will be a homosexual pedophile or not, he would certainly appreciate the multicultural environments where homosexual pedophilia is practiced.

> **Leviticus 18:22** [bold emphasis added]
> **You shall not lie with a male as with a woman**; it is an abomination.

> **1 Corinthians 6:9–10**
> Do you not know that the unrighteous will not inherit the kingdom of God? Do not be deceived: neither the sexually immoral, nor idolaters, nor adulterers, nor men who practice homosexuality, nor thieves, nor the greedy, nor drunkards, nor revilers, nor swindlers will inherit the kingdom of God.

> **Romans 1:26–28, 32** [bold emphasis added]
> For this reason God gave them up to dishonorable passions. For their women exchanged natural relations for those that are contrary to nature; and the men likewise gave up natural relations with women and were consumed with passion for one another, men committing shameless acts with men and receiving in themselves the due penalty for their error. And since they did not see fit to acknowledge God, God gave them up to a debased mind to do what ought not to be done … Though they know God's decree that those who practice such things deserve to die, **they not only do them but give approval to those who practice them**.

In the West, homosexual activists don't just live a sinful lifestyle, they are proud of it, hence the term "gay pride." They furthermore condemn those who do not approve of it, which directly correlates with Romans 1:32: "they not only do them [sins], but give approval to those who practice them."

While homosexuality is a sin, just like any other sin, such as fornication (sex outside of marriage, which is unfortunately widely accepted as the norm in Western culture), what sets it apart is that homosexual activists are attempting to redefine it as no longer a sin but rather something to be proud of.

God shows compassion for people who recognize their sin, struggle with it, and humbly ask for mercy and forgiveness in their struggle (Luke 18:11). Jesus had more compassion for those struggling in sin who were willing to acknowledge their need for His mercy and grace, rather than those who were self-righteous and believed they were *better* than such sinners. Promoting a deception in which homosexuality is redefined as no longer being a sin places those who are deceived in a jeopardizing situation, where they are no longer willing to admit their sin and therefore *incapable of repenting*. That's a very bad situation to be in.

In essence, homosexual activists are at war with God when they actively promote the homosexual lifestyle in gay pride parades and during dedicated days like Harvey Milk Day, which is celebrated every May 22. Their main purpose of getting involved in politics is to reach the younger generation and indoctrinate children to reject the word of God.

This sort of defiance against God is exactly what the Antichrist loves. I do not say these things to demean homosexuals but rather just the opposite: to appeal to them to repent and turn from their sin. They should at least be willing to admit to the sin for what it is and struggle with the addiction. Trying to make excuses for it, by declaring they were born with a particular orientation, is worthless. Everyone on Earth was born with an *orientation to sin*, and Jesus declared as much (Mark 10:18), but that doesn't justify any sin. The Bible explains in no uncertain terms that the homosexual lifestyle is contrary to nature. The sooner homosexuals admit this, the better off they will be, even if it means … a struggle.

Combining the homosexual lifestyle with the practice of pedophilia is, as I previously stated, one step deeper into the quagmire of sin. Even most homosexuals, who have wholeheartedly accepted homosexuality as a perfectly acceptable alternative lifestyle, will commonly reject the practice of pedophilia, for now.

There are clear-cut verses in the Qur'an that denounce homosexuality, but views on it are changing in the Islamic world in spite of this. Over twenty Muslim majority nations have legalized same-sex marriages, at least in part (Albania, Azerbaijan, Bahrain, Bosnia, Herzegovina, Burkina Faso, Chad, Djibouti, Guinea-Bissau, Lebanon, Iraq, Jordan, Kazakhstan, Kosovo, Kyrgyzstan, Mali, Niger, Tajikistan, Turkey, the West Bank in Palestine, most of Indonesia, and Northern Cyprus).[77]

On this particular aspect of Islamic society, there is wide variation. On the one hand, these twenty-plus countries endorse homosexual marriage, while in other Muslim majority countries, homosexuals are given the death sentence. It all comes down to how they interpret the Qur'an.

As for homosexual pedophilia, it is widespread throughout the Islamic world. Many Muslims might do their best to excuse, minimize, or outright deny allegations of child abuse in Islamic countries, but ever since US troops have spent time in the Middle East, the secret is out. Many US soldiers have been shocked beyond belief by what they have witnessed in public, and they have returned home with disturbing memories.

In a report posted by Christopher Allard concerning the immigration of Syrian Muslim refugees, he provided details about his active-duty army experiences as a medic, spending three years overseas in Iraq and Afghanistan. According to his testimony, picking up the body parts of friends and working hard to save the lives of those who were trying to kill him and his men were just the beginning of the horrors he faced. In light of his experiences, he gives dire warnings about allowing the culture of Islam to spread into the United States.

> During my first deployment to Iraq, in 2006, my unit voluntarily ran a children's burn clinic outside of the Forward Operating Base (FOB). It was a constant target for attacks. You would think that people wouldn't shoot mortars or rockets at their own children, but you would be wrong. We saw hundreds of children, from infants to 18 year olds. The overwhelming majority of the kids we saw, 90% or more, were clear cases of abuse.
>
> These parents were literally dunking their kids in boiling water, or throwing hot chai at their kid's faces. Yes, we're talking about babies, toddlers, kids not even old enough to understand why their parents would do these things to them; hundreds of kids.
>
> We saw quite a few of these kids that were sexually abused, both girls and boys. Their parents acted as if

> nothing was wrong with this, even when confronted by our doctors. This is the mentality of their society, not the viewpoint of a few individuals. These beliefs have been accepted by the vast majority of these people. Many were educated, well-dressed, well-spoken men, and yet, they still raped their own children, and kept "chai boys."
>
> Fast forward a couple of years, and I find myself in Helmand Province, in Afghanistan. We had a group of Afghanis that were paid to help guard our little mud hut in the middle of an Afghan village. These guys also kept a "chai boy," about 11 years old, who was there to serve them sexually. We heard him being sexually assaulted many times, but there was nothing we could do about it. We asked the police, the Afghan Army, and we were told the same thing every time. It's their culture, accepted as the norm.[78]

Other soldiers have equally disturbing tales. In the documentary *This is What Winning Looks Like*, in December 2012, US Marine Major Bill Streuber heard that three chai boys had been shot dead while fleeing the Afghan police headquarters. A fourth was shot point blank in the knee as punishment for trying to escape. This was the police headquarters, where groups of young boys were routinely abducted, held captive, and abused as sex slaves by police officers in the police station. The police were among the worst offenders of this activity; those who tried to escape were severely wounded or murdered.[79]

In another documentary, *The Dancing Boys of Afghanistan* (2010), Afghan police officials put on a show about how they insist sex traffickers will be arrested, but later that very same day, two of the same officers were filmed at a *bacha bazi* party.

> "I have told them not to keep them," Khan insists to Major Steuber. Despite the fact that one of the boys tried to poison a police chief, he maintains that "these little boys stay willingly in the patrol bases and offer their asses in the night."[80]

Major Steuber proposed a joint raid the next morning to apprehend the child molesters, but the Afghan authorities canceled the operation at the last minute. According to the documentary, Khan has since quietly retired, and no one was ever charged or arrested for all of this flagrant child abuse.

And these people are our allies.

Major Streuber's tale is one among many concerning rampant child abuse in the Middle East.

> In 2010, the San Francisco Chronicle reported that for centuries Afghan men have taken boys, roughly 9 to 15 years old, as lovers. Some research suggests that half the Pashtun tribal members in Kandahar and other southern towns are bacha bazi, the term for an older man with a boy lover. Literally it means "boy player." The men like to boast about it.
>
> "Having a boy has become a custom for us," Enayatullah, a 42-year-old in Baghlan province, told a Reuters reporter. "Whoever wants to show off should have a boy." The authors of "Pashtun Sexuality" venture that the practice of bacha bazi is a function of a culture of extreme fear of female sexuality. The Chronicle article cites a 29-year-old who told a reporter, "How can you fall in love if you can't see her face? We can see the boys, so we can tell which are beautiful."

> The State Department has called bacha bazi a "widespread, culturally sanctioned form of male rape." For instance, one military intelligence reservist related a story about an Afghan colonel who stood before a judge after he hurt a chai boy by violently raping him: "His defense was, 'Honestly, who hasn't raped a chai boy? Ha ha.' The judge responded, 'You're right. Case dismissed.'"[81]

In another incident, Sergeant First Class Charles Martland, a Green Beret who earned the Bronze Star for valor, and his commanding officer, Captain Daniel Quinn, received word from a local interpreter that an Afghan Local Police (ALP) commander, Rahman, kidnapped a boy, chained him to a post in his house for two weeks, and raped him repeatedly. The boy's mother tried to ask for help but was beaten severely by the ALP commander's brother as a result.

Disgusted with what he heard, Captain Quinn verified the facts of this incident with other ALP commanders in neighboring villages, and then he and Martland confronted Rahman. The situation quickly escalated out of control.

The Pentagon categorically denied allegations that it had any official policy when it came to looking the other way concerning child abuse cases, but at the same time, they placed Martland under a gag order. It literally took an act of Congress, Rep. Duncan Hunter, R-California, to obtain Martland's statement.

> "After the child rapist laughed it off and referenced that it was only a boy, Captain Quinn picked him up and threw him," Martland wrote. Martland then proceeded to "body slam him multiple times," kick him in the rib cage, and put his foot on his neck.[82]

After Martland conducted a series of body slams, removing Rahman from the camp, Rahman returned a short while later and reported the incident to higher ranking army officials. Captain Quinn resigned as a result, and Martland was informed that he would be kicked out of the army.

While I do not claim that Western culture is morally superior, primarily because much of Western society has drifted so far away from the God of the Bible, I will make the claim that the Judeo-Christian heritage has inspired the idea that people are born with God-given inalienable rights. These rights form what we now know of as *basic human rights*, and they should apply to *everyone*, not just Americans. I already outlined how the Bible has elevated the status of women in the world, but the Bible doesn't stop there. The Bible also has a great deal to say about children.

While children are frequently overlooked and treated as an annoyance to usher out of the way, Jesus rebuked His disciples on one occasion for doing this. He then made a point to highlight children for special consideration (Matthew 19:13–15). Jesus also pointed out on another occasion that believers must have the faith of a child, and He further warned that anyone who deceives children into sinning will sorely regret it (Matthew 18:1–6).

> **Matthew 19:13–15** [bold emphasis added]
> Then children were brought to him that he might lay his hands on them and pray. The disciples rebuked the people, but Jesus said, **"Let the little children come to me and do not hinder them, for to such belongs the kingdom of heaven."** And he laid his hands on them and went away.
>
> **Matthew 18:1–6** [bold emphasis added]
> At that time the disciples came to Jesus, saying, "Who is the greatest in the kingdom of heaven?" And calling to him a child, he put him in the midst of them and said, **"Truly, I say to you, unless you turn and become like children, you will never enter the kingdom of heaven. Whoever humbles himself like this child is the greatest in the kingdom of heaven. Whoever**

> **receives one such child in my name receives me, but whoever causes one of these little ones who believe in me to sin, it would be better for him to have a great millstone fastened around his neck and to be drowned in the depth of the sea."**

Jesus spoke of children a number of times and *always* in a positive context for literal children. As for the Antichrist, he will do anything and everything to reap a harvest of destruction in as many ways as possible. This includes laying the groundwork for his arrival by establishing an environment that matches his characteristics—a place rich with the culture of killing innocents through terrorism and other means, and the destruction of the quality of life for women and children. To that end, the spirit of the Antichrist is spreading throughout the earth; his influence is affecting every sphere of human society.

6.5 The Exceeding Pride of the Antichrist

Another characteristic of the Antichrist is his pride. Consider these words about the Antichrist in scripture (Daniel 8:25, 11:12, 11:36; 2 Thessalonians 2:3–4; Revelation 13:5):

> **Daniel 8:25** [bold emphasis added]
> By his cunning he shall make deceit prosper under his hand, and **in his own mind he shall become great**. Without warning he shall destroy many. And he shall even rise up against the Prince of princes, and he shall be broken—but by no human hand.

> **Daniel 11:12** [bold emphasis added]
> And when the multitude is taken away, **his heart shall be exalted**, and he shall cast down tens of thousands, but he shall not prevail.

> **Daniel 11:36** [bold emphasis added]
> And the king shall do as he wills. **He shall exalt himself and magnify himself above every god, and shall speak astonishing things against the God of gods**. He shall prosper till the indignation is accomplished; for what is decreed shall be done.

> **2 Thessalonians 2:3–4** [bold emphasis added]
> Let no one deceive you in any way. For that day will not come, unless the rebellion comes first, and the man of lawlessness is revealed, the son of destruction, **who opposes and exalts himself against every so-called god or object of worship**, so that he takes his seat in the temple of God, **proclaiming himself to be God.**

> **Revelation 13:5** [bold emphasis added]
> And the beast was given **a mouth uttering haughty and blasphemous words**, and it was allowed to exercise authority for forty-two months.

One of the most telling characteristics of overweening pride is an extreme adverse reaction to criticism. Muhammad is a perfect example of this character trait.

Following a major defeat in the Battle of Uhud in AD 625,[83] Muhammad's followers were relatively weak. Muhammad therefore encouraged them to endure insults for a time (Qur'an 3:186). This had nothing to do with humility but rather served the purpose of building up strength, all the while *plotting revenge*.

> **Qur'an 3:186 (Shakir)** [bold emphasis added]
> You shall certainly be tried respecting your wealth and your souls, and **you shall certainly hear** from those who have been given the Book before you and from those who are polytheists **much annoying talk;**

and if you are patient and guard (against evil), surely this is one of the affairs (which should be) determined upon.

Just a few years later, after Muhammad and his men recovered, they murdered these same critics, members of the Jewish tribes of ad-Nadir and Qurayza, following the Battle of the Trench in AD 627.[84]

After that battle, Muhammad's power dramatically increased, and he spent this time in Medina, where the Qur'an shed the false humility of Qur'an 3:186 and adopted the violent posture of Qur'an 33. Muhammad and his men attacked the Jewish strongholds in Medina, captured them, and decapitated six hundred male Jews of the Qurayza tribe. They also enslaved all the women and children. This was when Muhammad married Safiyah, the beautiful Jewess whose husband he murdered.[85–86]

At this later time, the Qur'an shifted dramatically from prescribing patience to prescribing "slay without mercy." Qur'an 33:61 is particularly poignant.

Qur'an 33:26–27 (Shakir) [bold emphasis added]
And He **drove down those of the followers of the Book** who backed them from their fortresses and He cast awe into their hearts; **some you killed** and **you took captive** another part. And **He made you heirs to their land and their dwellings and their property**, and (to) a land which you have not yet trodden, and Allah has power over all things.

Qur'an 33:57 (Shakir) [bold emphasis added]
Surely (as for) those who speak evil things of Allah and **His Messenger**, Allah has **cursed them** in this world and the hereafter, and He has prepared for them a chastisement bringing disgrace.

> **Qur'an 33:61 (Shakir)** [bold emphasis added]
> They shall have a curse on them: whenever they are found, they shall be seized and slain (without mercy).

The Hadiths pick up where Muhammad left off, providing various examples of how Muhammad's followers butchered anyone who *said anything insulting to or about Muhammad.*

> **Bukhari 5:59:369** [bold emphasis and bracketed comment added]
> Allah's Apostle said, **"Who is willing to kill Ka'b bin Al-Ashraf who has hurt [insulted] Allah and His Apostle?"** Thereupon Muhammad Maslama got up saying, "O Allah's Apostle! **Would you like that I kill him?" The Prophet said, "Yes."** Muhammad bin Maslama said, "Then **allow me to say a (false) thing** (i.e. to deceive Ka'b)." **The Prophet said, "You may say it."** … "I have got the best Arab women who know how to use the high class of perfume." Muhammad bin Maslama requested Ka'b, "Will you allow me to smell your head?" Ka'b said, "Yes." Muhammad smelt it and made his companions smell it as well. Then he requested Ka'b again, "Will you let me (smell your head)?" Ka'b said, "Yes." **When Muhammad got a strong hold of him, he said (to his companions), "Get at him!" So they killed him and went to the Prophet and informed him. (Abu Rafi) was killed after Ka'b bin Al-Ashraf."**

> **Bukhari 3:106** [bold emphasis added]
> The Prophet said, "Do not tell a lie against me for **whoever tells a lie against me** (intentionally) then he **will surely enter the Hell-fire.**"

Dawud 38:4348 [bold emphasis and bracketed comment added]

A blind man had a slave-mother who used to abuse [insult] the Prophet (peace be upon him) and disparage him. He forbade her but she did not stop. He rebuked her but she did not give up her habit. **One night she began to slander the Prophet** (peace be upon him) and abuse him. **So he took a dagger, placed it on her belly, pressed it, and killed her.** A child who came between her legs was smeared with the blood that was there. When the morning came, the Prophet (peace be upon him) was informed about it. He assembled the people and said: I adjure by Allah the man who has done this action and I adjure him by my right to him that he should stand up. Jumping over the necks of the people and trembling the man stood up. He sat before the Prophet (peace be upon him) and said: Apostle of Allah! **I am her master; she used to abuse you and disparage you. I forbade her, but she did not stop, and I rebuked her, but she did not abandon her habit. I have two sons like pearls from her, and she was my companion. Last night she began to abuse and disparaged you. So I took a dagger, put it on her belly and pressed it till I killed her. Thereupon the Prophet** (peace be upon him) **said: Oh be witness, no retaliation is payable for her blood.**

Dawud 38:4349 [bold emphasis added]

A Jewess used to abuse the Prophet (peace be upon him) and disparage him. **A man strangled her till she died. The Apostle of Allah** (peace be upon him) **declared that no recompense was payable for her blood.**

The above Hadiths are just a small sampling of the story of Muhammad and his followers permanently silencing their critics.

One of the popular ways that people voiced their beliefs and concerns about society in Muhammad's day was through satirical poetry. Muhammad and his men made a hit list of all the poets who criticized them, and they executed them one by one. Their names are listed on a web page titled "Muhammad's Dead Poet Society."

Murdered poets who critiqued/criticized Muhammad:

- March 624: Al-Nadr bin al-Harith
- March 624: Uqba bin Abu Muayt
- March 624: Asma bint Marwan
- April 624: Abu Afak
- September 624: Kab bin al-Ashraf
- September 624: Ibn Sunayna
- July-August 625: A one-eyed Bedouin
- After January 630: Close call for Abdullah bin Sad
- After January 630: One of Abdullah bin Katal's two singing girls
- After February 630: Close call for Kab bin Zuhayr [87]

These examples of how to address anyone who speaks critical of Muhammad or his writings are still widely in effect all around the world. That is not to say that *all* Muslims consider Muhammad and the Qur'an beyond reproach, to the extent of recommending the death penalty to critics, but a great many Muslims certainly believe punishment is definitely in order for the critics of Islam. Consider these statistics:

> **NOP Research:** Seventy-eight percent of British Muslims support punishing the publishers of Muhammad cartoons. http://www.cbsnews.com/stories/2006/08/14/opinion/main1893879.shtml&date=2011-04-06

http://www.webcitation.org/5xkMGAEvY

British Survey: Sixty-two percent of British Muslims do not believe in the protection of free speech. Only 3 percent adopt a "consistently pro-freedom of speech line."

http://www.cbsnews.com/stories/2006/08/14/opinion/main1893879.shtml&date=2011-04-06 / http://www.webcitation.org/5xkMGAEvY

ICM Poll: Fifty-eight percent of British Muslims believe insulting Islam should result in criminal prosecution.

http://www.danielpipes.org/blog/2005/07/more-survey-research-from-a-british-islamist

Wenzel Strategies (2012): Fifty-eight percent of Muslim-Americans believe criticism of Islam or Muhammad is not protected free speech under the First Amendment.

Forty-five percent believe mockers of Islam should face criminal charges (38 percent said they should not).

Twelve percent of Muslim-Americans believe blaspheming Islam should be punishable by death.

Forty-three percent of Muslim-Americans believe people of other faiths have no right to evangelize Muslims.

Thirty-two percent of Muslims in America believe Sharia should be the supreme law of the land.

> http://www.andrewbostom.org/blog/2012/10/31/sixty-percent-of-us-muslims-reject-freedom-of-expression/ / http://www.answeringmuslims.com/2012/10/poll-nearly-half-of-us-muslims-believe.html.[88]

Modern-day examples of Muslims demanding that the critics of Islam be silenced are common in the news.

> When author Salman Rushdie published "The Satanic Verses," a 1988 novel deemed offensive to Muhammad, the Ayatollah Khomeini pronounced a death sentence in the form of a fatwa that was supported by a majority of Muslims.
>
> After a Danish newspaper published cartoons of Muhammad in 2006, an imam (who had been welcomed to Denmark as an immigrant), traveled back to the Middle East and whipped up hatred that resulted in deadly rioting on three continents. Demonstrators in London held signs reading "Massacre Those Who Insult Islam."
>
> In the years since, there have been many incidents in which Muslims have whipped themselves into a violent frenzy over perceived insults to Islam. At the same time, such outrage is notably lacking when innocent people, including other Muslims, are murdered in the name of this same religion.[89]

Another relatively recent example of Islamic outrage concerns a video titled *The Qur'an Challenge*, created by comedian Steven Crowder. In the video, Crowder gives a few examples of why he thinks the Qur'an is not "a peaceful book" as many Muslims claim. Ironically, for creating this video, he received countless death threats.

Crowder then produced a follow-up video, *Jesus vs. Muhammad*, which received even more Muslim backlash and was addressed with a fatwa prescribing the death penalty for Steven Crowder.[90]

The religion of Islam is *anything but tolerant* when it comes to criticism. Much unlike Muhammad, Jesus never killed anyone, nor did He damn anyone to hell for speaking against Him personally. The closest Jesus came to rebuking those who accused Him of lying or operating under satanic power was to warn them not to speak against the Holy Spirit. While Muhammad considered any criticism against him to be on par with any criticism against Allah (Qur'an 33:57), Jesus said He would forgive anyone who said anything against Him personally (Matthew 12:32).

> **Matthew 12:32** [bold emphasis added]
> And **whoever speaks a word against the Son of Man will be forgiven**, but whoever speaks against the Holy Spirit will not be forgiven, either in this age or in the age to come.

Jesus furthermore directed His disciples to forgive their critics of everything in countless scriptures, and in his letters to the churches, the apostle Paul continued to direct believers to do the same (Romans 12:14).

> **Romans 12:14**
> Bless those who persecute you; bless and do not curse them.

Jesus was known for His boundless humility, which He took with Him to the cross. Muhammad, however, rejected the sacrifice Jesus made on the cross because he just didn't get it. He was so far removed from that kind of humility that he directly opposed this fundamental tenet of Christianity. This is the sort of pride that will align directly with the character of the Antichrist, who will also reject Jesus's death on the cross because *that is what an "anti" Christ does.*

6.6 The Geographic Region of the Antichrist

A decade ago, using scripture, I predicted in *Aliens and the Antichrist* that the Antichrist will rise to power in the Middle East, either out of Lebanon or Syria.[91] Many who study prophecy seem to fixate only on Rome, or other oddities like national symbols or economic treaties. Because of this, they speculate that a pope or a US president will be the Antichrist. What these speculations dismiss, however, is that the regions within both the ancient Roman Empire and the ancient Grecian Empire actually intersect in the Middle East, with ancient Assyria right in the middle. Understanding these prophecies makes the most compelling case for the Antichrist rising to power in the Middle East.

Currently ISIS is operating in this exact region, and Iran is well on its way to obtaining nuclear power. This region is historically a hotbed of Antichrist activity. In mid-February 2014, twenty-one Coptic Christians were beheaded because of their faith, and their last words were "Lord, Jesus Christ."[92] More Christians are targeted and murdered because of their faith, more than ever before, by Islamic terrorists. Their preferred method of execution in these murders is beheading. This is prophecy, plain as day (Revelation 20:4).

> **Revelation 20:4** [bold emphasis added]
> And I saw the souls of those who had been **beheaded** because of their testimony about Jesus and because of the word of God.

If ISIS is not something the Antichrist will arise out of directly, it has to be a close predecessor because all the signs are lining up. We can't go on much longer until the return of Jesus. That cannibalistic, jihadist, psychopathic general in Syria may very well be the Antichrist, for all we know; it actually would not be that far-fetched.[93–94] Some reports say Osama Bin Laden was very popular in Pakistan while he was hiding there. Fierce, ruthless jihadist tyrants are exactly what Islamic extremists want.

Author Joel Richardson agrees with this assessment about where the Antichrist will rise to power, but interestingly enough, he derived his conclusions taking a completely different angle than the scriptures I presented in *Aliens and the Antichrist.* While I focused on prophecies that point to specific geographic regions, Richardson came to his conclusions through his focus on Islam and the Ottoman Empire.

CHAPTER 7

COMPARING CHRISTIAN AND ISLAMIC ESCHATOLOGY

I started this book by highlighting prophecies in the Bible that speak of an otherworldly connection with the strong delusion to come in the future. Because this strong delusion will be led by a figure known as the Antichrist, I shifted my focus to the Antichrist and explained specific character attributes that he will have, which perfectly align with the religion of Islam. I then pinpointed the geographic location where the Antichrist will rise to power, which happens to be an Islamic stronghold.

I will now address the topic of Islamic eschatology (End Times prophecy); the Qur'an and Hadiths convey a near-perfect mirror image of biblical eschatology. I say mirror image because they are nearly identical, and yet they are exact opposites.

It shouldn't be taken lightly that the faiths of over four billion people on this planet, Christians and Muslims, include two versions of prophetic visions that are nearly identical, yet they represent opposing viewpoints as to which side of a great future battle to be on. Those who proclaim jihad are right in one respect—a "holy war" is coming—but which side is holy is the big question.

To summarize a portion of *The Islamic Antichrist*, when the facts are analyzed, the following becomes glaringly obvious. The Bible and the Qur'an and Hadiths tell nearly the exact same story, but the identities of the protagonists and antagonists are swapped. In the table below, the first two characters are clear comparisons made by Joel Richardson, but I deviate from his analysis on the last character, known as the *Dajjal*.

Table 1: Mirror Image of Prophetic Characters

Bible		Qur'an/Hadiths
Antichrist	=	Mahdi (Muslim Messiah)
False Prophet	=	Muslim Jesus
Two witnesses/Jesus returned/ Antichrist	=	Dajjal(s)

This is an ugly conclusion with horrific ramifications. On the stage of world events, this is a global collision that we're all headed for, whether we like it or not. Almost everyone will be forced to accept Islam or fight a losing battle. This is the essential premise of the Qur'an and Hadiths, as well as the Bible, almost.

According to Qur'an and Hadith prophecies, after a global slaughter of all non-Muslims is complete, a natural world of Islamic supremacy will commence and continue throughout all generations. The Bible, on the other hand, also speaks of a near-global slaughter, but the conclusion of that battle is not an eternal Islamic caliphate.

7.1 Satan's Tactic of Reversing the Roles

Satan has been refuting God's word since he first opened his mouth to Adam and Eve. His favorite ploy is to swap the antagonists with the protagonists. For example, recall my earlier mention of the Tower of Babel (Genesis 11). While the Bible establishes that these people were sinful and met with God's judgment, *The Epic of Gilgamesh* describes Gilgamesh (whom the Hebrews referred to as Nimrod) as a hero who defied the "evil entity" that brought about the flood of Noah. Building a massive tower was Gilgamesh's way of defying that so-called evil entity to escape any future flood.[1–2] This was from the perspective of the ancient Sumerians who wrote *The Epic of Gilgamesh* from their satanically inspired perspective, rather than from the biblical perspective, which identifies Nimrod with the Hebrew word for "rebel."

Babylonian, Assyrian, Egyptian, Greek, Norse, Chinese, Hindu Vedas, and every other ancient mythology found throughout the world (over six hundred that we know of) state that the gods once mingled openly in the affairs of humanity.[3] These were beings of immense power; people worshipped them, and in some cases, they had intercourse and bore children with them. Their children became demigods. These demigods were also worshipped and were considered the heroes of old by pretty much everyone, *except for the authors of the Bible*.

Greek mythology, for example, still resonates today with identifiable names such as Hercules and Perseus, described as benevolent heroes from the Greek perspective. In contrast to this, the biblical narrative paints an entirely different picture.

> **Genesis 6:4–5** [bold emphasis added]
> There were giants in the earth in those days; and also after that, when the sons of God came in unto the daughters of men, and they bore children to them, the same became **mighty men** which were of old, **men of renown**. And God saw that the **wickedness** of man was great in the earth, and that **every imagination of the thoughts of his heart was only evil continually**.

According to the biblical narrative, these sons of God were in complete disobedience to the true Creator God. Greek mythology has Zeus, considered the benevolent father of the Greek gods, as the biggest philanderer of all time. As for the Bible, Zeus and the rest of his gang, who were having intercourse with humans, were fallen angels in utter contempt and rebellion against the one true God. Zeus may have even been Satan. When the apostle John encountered Jesus after He ascended (Revelation 2:12–13), Jesus made a connection with the Greek Zeus and Satan by stating that Satan's real, literal throne was the Pergamum. This was the location of Zeus's temple at that time.

> **Revelation 2:12–13** [bold emphasis added]
> "And to the angel of the church in Pergamum write: 'The words of him who has the sharp two-edged sword. "'**I know where you dwell, where Satan's throne is.** Yet you hold fast my name, and you did not deny my faith even in the days of Antipas my faithful witness, who was killed among you, where Satan dwells."

The same thing happened with Egypt's so-called gods. God placed them under His divine judgment, declaring that people should have nothing to do with them (Exodus 12:12, 23:32; 1 Corinthians 10:20).

In summation, both these examples concerning the actions of the fallen angels are ancient texts that depict satanic beings as heroes. Scripture, however, stands alone, revealing the true nature and intent of these beings. The Bible calls them out for what they really are. These ancient texts are "doctrines of devils" (1 Timothy 4:1) inspired by Satan, other fallen angels, and demons/devils.

To help people easily identify what constitutes *satanic doctrine* inspired by the spirit of the Antichrist, the Bible speaks of specific tests. I mentioned a few of these tests in *Aliens and the Antichrist*, and Joel Richardson points them out as well (1 John 2:22–23, 4:1–3; 2 John 1:7).

> **1 John 2:22–23** [bold emphasis added]
> **Who is the liar but he who denies that Jesus is the Christ? This is the antichrist**, he who denies the Father and the Son. **No one who denies the Son has the Father**. Whoever confesses the Son has the Father also.

> **1 John 4:1–3** [bold emphasis added]
> Beloved, do not believe every spirit, but test the spirits to see whether they are from God, for many false prophets have gone out into the world. **By this you know the Spirit of God: every spirit that confesses that Jesus Christ has come in the flesh is from God, and every spirit that does not confess Jesus is not from God. This is the spirit of the antichrist**, which you heard was coming and now is in the world already.

> **2 John 1:7** [bold emphasis added]
> For many **deceivers** have gone out into the world, **those who do not confess the coming of Jesus Christ in the flesh. Such a one is the deceiver and the antichrist**.

Elaborating on the above scriptures, Richardson describes how these tests are used to identify key truths in scripture that must never be refuted.[23]

1. **Jesus is the Christ—that is, Messiah/Savior**. The greatest evidence for Jesus's preeminence is His death on the cross, in which He sacrificed Himself to atone for the sins of the world. No one is perfect, and everyone has sinned and falls short of God's perfect standard, except for God Himself. He therefore endured the cross for the sake of perfect justice, to pay the price for sin. He was the only one who could pull this off. What's more, because He is God, the all-powerful essence of perfect love, He wielded power over death and rose from the dead. This is this same power He grants to those who accept Him as their Savior.
2. **Jesus Christ has come in the flesh**. Jesus took the form of a physical human being through the immaculate conception of Mary. This is God's level of intimacy. He is the righteous

judge because He was one of us and walked a lifetime in our shoes. The fact that Jesus is literally God's biological Son was first prophesied in Genesis 3:15, when God the Father said that the *seed of the woman* (Eve) would crush the *seed of the serpent* (Satan), putting an end to the disastrous results of Adam and Eve's sin.

3. **Jesus and His Father are as one**. This is the doctrine of the Trinity, which speaks of God as a unified Being, coexisting in three manifestations. When I first became a Christian, I didn't understand the Trinity until I read the New Testament. I knew Jesus was the Son of God, but the more I studied the things He said, the more I began to understand that He and His Father, as well as the Holy Spirit, are one Supreme Being. One scripture that explains how Jesus actually played a part in creation is Colossians 1:13–20. This scripture is about Jesus.

Colossians 1:13–20 [Bold emphasis added]
Who hath delivered us from the power of darkness, and hath translated us into the kingdom of his dear Son: In whom we have redemption through his blood, even the forgiveness of sins: **Who is the image of the invisible God**, the firstborn of every creature: **For by him were all things created, that are in heaven, and that are in earth, visible and invisible, whether they be thrones, or dominions, or principalities, or powers: all things were created by him, and for him: And he is before all things, and by him all things consist**. And he is the head of the body, the church: who is the beginning, the firstborn from the dead; that in all things he might have the preeminence. For it pleased the Father that **in him should all fullness dwell**; And, having made peace through the blood of his cross, by him to reconcile all

things unto himself; by him, I say, whether they be things in earth, or things in heaven.

In addition to these tests, I have two more to add. These are as follows:

4. **True prophets are accurate**. Those who give false prophecies that don't come to pass are false prophets (Deuteronomy 18:20–22). A common example of this are date setters, people who definitively declare that some huge event will occur on a specific date, but that date comes and goes and nothing happens. The only way I will ever make a declaration about something specific happening on a specific date is if an angel, or God Himself, informs me directly, and that hasn't happened yet. So far, all I have is a strong impression that we are on the edge of a precipice.
5. **Those who speak in the name of other gods are false prophets.** Even if someone declares prophecies that do come to pass, if that same person professes allegiance with other gods (other religious systems), that person is a false prophet.

Deuteronomy 18:20–22 [bold emphasis added]
"But the prophet who presumes to speak a word in my name that I have not commanded him to speak, or who speaks in the name of other gods, that same prophet shall die." And if you say in your heart, "How may we know the word that the LORD has not spoken?"—**when a prophet speaks in the name of the Lord, if the word does not come to pass or come true, that is a word that the Lord has not spoken**; the prophet has spoken it presumptuously. You need not be afraid of him.

Deuteronomy 13:1–4 [bold emphasis added]
If a prophet or a dreamer of dreams arises among you and gives you a sign or a wonder, and the sign

> **or wonder that he tells you comes to pass, and if he says, "Let us go after other gods," which you have not known, "and let us serve them," you shall not listen to the words of that prophet or that dreamer of dreams.** For the Lord your God is testing you, to know whether you **love** the Lord your God with all your heart and with all your soul. You shall walk after the Lord your God and fear him and keep his commandments and obey his voice, and you shall serve him and hold fast to him.

With these litmus tests spelled out, explaining in specific detail how to spot a deception that is fueled by the *spirit of the Antichrist*, guess where Islam falls within the spectrum? As it turns out, Islam not only fails all of these tests but also outright attacks them with utmost distain.

Islam denies that Jesus is the Son of God (Qur'an 5:17, 9:30, 10:68, 19:88–92), Islam denies the Trinity (Qur'an 5:73), and Islam blatantly rejects the notion that Jesus ever died on the cross (Qur'an 4:157–158).

> **Qur'an 4:157–158 (Shakir)** [bold emphasis added]
> And their saying: Surely we have killed the Messiah, Isa son of Marium, the messenger of Allah; and **they did not kill him nor did they crucify him**, but **it appeared to them so (like Isa)** and most surely those who differ therein are only in a doubt about it; **they have no knowledge respecting it, but only follow a conjecture**, and **they killed him not for sure. Nay! Allah took him up to Himself**; and Allah is Mighty, Wise.
>
> **Qur'an 5:73 (Shakir)**
> Certainly they disbelieve who say: Surely Allah is the third (person) of the three; and there is no god but the one Allah, and if they desist not from what they say,

> a painful chastisement shall befall those among them who disbelieve.

> **Qur'an 9:30 (Shakir)** [bold emphasis added]
> And the Jews say: Uzair is the son of Allah; **and the Christians say: The Messiah is the son of Allah**; these are the words of their mouths; they imitate the saying of those who disbelieved before; **may Allah destroy them**; how they are turned away!

> **Qur'an 10:68 (Shakir)** [bold emphasis added]
> They say: Allah has taken a son (to Himself)! Glory be to Him: He is the Self-sufficient: His is what is in the heavens and what is in the earth; **you have no authority for this; do you say against Allah what you do not know?**

> **Qur'an 19:88–92 (Shakir)**
> And they say: **The Beneficent Allah has taken (to Himself) a son. Certainly you have made an abominable assertion**. The heavens may almost be rent thereat, and the earth cleave asunder, and the mountains fall down in pieces, That they ascribe a son to the Beneficent Allah. And it is not worthy of the Beneficent Allah that He should take (to Himself) a son.

As for the other two tests, Islam *attempts* to pass them, first by borrowing prophecies from the Bible about End Times events, and secondly, through declaring that the word *Allah* is the same God as mentioned in the Bible. However, the Qur'an tweaks End Times prophecies into their mirror-image *opposite*, and the name Allah actually has pagan origins. Moreover, the Allah of Muhammad is nothing at all like the God of the Bible.

If anyone questions the above Qur'an references about the identity of Jesus, simply ask any Muslim. Even *moderate* Muslims will most likely agree on all three tests that have to do with Jesus. If they don't, I don't think they can justifiably call themselves Muslims because the Qur'an considers the identity of Jesus as God's literal biological Son a *blasphemous* doctrine.[24]

Keep in mind the prophecies regarding the Antichrist and his egomaniacal, loud-mouthed, brazen lies. Scripture says he will magnify himself and speak great things—blasphemies against God, the tabernacle, and God's people. So what sort of examples might these great things, these blasphemies be?

How about pronouncing a curse on those who believe that Jesus is God's Son? As I just pointed out, the Qur'an says this. Additionally, Muslims deny the Trinity, and some deny it with such venomous hatred that a newsletter titled *Invitation to Islam*, published by a Muslim group from Toronto, stated that …

> Murder, rape, child molesting, and genocide … are all some of the appalling crimes which occur in our world today … But there is something which outweighs all of these crimes put together: It is the crime of shirk."[25]

What is *shirk*? Shirk is the sin of idolatry and includes believing in the Trinity. So Christians who believe in the Trinity are worse than child molesters, rapists, and maniacal murderers of entire races of people. Really?

From the Islamic perspective, at worst, believing that Jesus has the authority to forgive sins is blasphemy, punishable by death. At best, Jesus giving His life on the cross for mankind makes no sense.

Author Joel Richardson referred to this sentiment when he recalled the following bumper sticker suggestion from a Muslim on an internet discussion group: "Why would God die to save His own creation?"[26] In response to this question, I have a question of my own. Which of the below two options makes the most sense?

Option 1: A God who endorses hate-filled suicide to kill unbelievers and use it as a fear tactic to emphasize the importance of rules and force others into submission (Qur'an 47:4).

Or …

Option 2: A God who endorses love-motivated self-sacrifice to try to save unbelievers and use it to demonstrate the value of human life and stop the cycle of violence (Luke 6:27–38).

The entire Muslim quandary over why God would sacrifice Himself to save His creation likens God the Creator to a manufacturer of merchandise. That's not God, and His creation is not *merchandise*. God is a Creator like a divine parent of infinite love who decided to have children, and I know there must be many Muslims who believe this. God's Creation is not a *thing*. People are created in the *image of God* (Genesis 1:26) and well worth the price of an incredible sacrifice. In fact, the price is so high that humanity does not have the ability to pay it. All our righteousness combined does not even come close (Isaiah 64:6, Psalm 14:3, Mark 10:18).

7.2 Who Is the Mahdi?

As previously stated, I credit author Joel Richardson for illuminating me on an entirely new perspective regarding the strong delusion. His work has forced me to readdress the strong delusion, now with a prophetic eye focused on the religion of Islam.

In addition to Richardson's research, I also stumbled across Lisa Haven's research,[4] as well as information on the Answering Islam website.[5] Haven is an internet blogger who references the works of Islamic eschatologist Dr. Muhammad Al-'Areefi.[6] The findings of all three of these sources are combined in the table below.[7]

Table 2: Antichrist = Mahdi (Twelve Similarities)

The Biblical Antichrist	The Muslim Mahdi (i.e., Muslim Messiah, the 12th Imam)
1. The Antichrist will be a leader who has the ability to speak boldly. **Daniel 7:8** "[a]nd a mouth speaking great things." **Revelation 13:5** "And he was given a mouth uttering haughty and blasphemous words …"	**1.** The Mahdi will be a leader who has the ability to speak boldly. **Bihar al-Anwar, vol. 52, p. 32; Al-Hurr al-Amili, Ithbat al-Hudat, vol. 6, p. 19** "He will be so powerful that if he … shouts among the mountains, hard rocks will turn into powder …"
2. The False Prophet will arrive to promote the Antichrist to the world and deceive people into worshipping him as their divine leader. **Revelation 19:20** "And the beast was captured, and with it the false prophet who in its presence had done the signs by which he deceived those who had received the mark of the beast and those who worshiped its image …"	**2.** A Muslim Jesus (not to be confused with the Christian Jesus) will return to promote the Mahdi to the world and convince people into accepting him as their divine leader. **Bukhari 3:43:656** "Allah's Apostle said, 'The Hour will not be established until the son of Mary (i.e., Jesus) descends amongst you as a just ruler, he will break the cross, kill the pigs, and abolish the Jizya tax. Money will be in abundance so that nobody will accept it (as charitable gifts).'"

3. The Antichrist will have a powerful army that will do damage to the earth, ultimately causing all to follow him under his military leadership. **Revelation 13:4–5, 7–8** "And they worshiped the dragon, for he had given his authority to the beast, and they worshiped the beast, saying, "Who is like the beast, and who can fight against it?" … Also it was allowed to make war on the saints and to conquer them. And authority was given it over every tribe and people and language and nation, and all who dwell on earth will worship it, everyone whose name has not been written before the foundation of the world in the book of life …"	**3.** The Mahdi will have a powerful army that will do damage on the earth, ultimately causing all to follow him under his military leadership. **Abdulrahman Kelani, *The Last Apocalypse, An Islamic Perspective* (Fustat 2003), p. 34–35** "Mahdi will receive a pledge of allegiance as a caliph for Muslims. He will lead Muslims in many battles of jihad." **Ibn Maja, *Kitab al-Fitan* #4084 as quoted by Kabbani, p. 231** "If you see him, go and give him your allegiance …" **Al-Sadr and Mutahhari, *The Awaited Savior*** "[the Mahdi will] fight against the forces of evil, lead a world revolution, and set up a new world order based on justice, righteousness, and virtue."[8]

4. The Antichrist will be a world leader and rule for seven years. **Daniel 9:27** "And he shall make a strong covenant with many for one week [seven years] ..." **Revelation 13:7** "[A]nd authority was given it over every tribe and people and language and nation ..."	**4.** The Mahdi will be a world leader and rule for seven years. **Dawud 36:4272** "the Mahdi will be of my stock, and will have a broad forehead a prominent nose. He will fill the earth will equity and justice as it was filled with oppression and tyranny, and he will rule for seven years."[9] **Ayatullah Baqir al-Sadr and Ayatullah Muratda Mutahhari, *The Awaited Savior* (Karachi, Islamic Seminary Publications), prologue, p. 4** "Fight against the forces of evil, lead a world revolution and set up a new world order ..." **Tabarani, quotes by Mufti A. H. Elias and Muhammad Ali ibn Zubair Ali** "The prophet said: There will be four peace agreements between you and the Romans. The fourth will be mediated through a person who will be from the progeny of Hadrat Aaron [Honorable Aaron-the brother of Moses] and will be upheld for seven years ..."[10]
5. The Antichrist will change times and laws. **Daniel 7:25** "He ... shall think to change the times and the law ..."	**5.** The Mahdi will more than likely adopt the Islamic calendar, thus changing the times. In addition he will promote Sharia law, thereby changing the laws. **Dawud 36:4273** "He ...will divide the property, and will govern the people by the Sunnah of their Prophet (peace be upon him) and establish Islam on Earth ..." **Dr. Waleed A. Muhanna, "A Brief Introduction to the Islamic (Hijri) Calendar"** "It is considered a divine command to use a [hijra] calendar with twelve [purely] lunar months without inter-calculation, as evident from ... the Holy Qur'an."[11]

6. The first of the four horsemen of the apocalypse rides a white horse; this is not Jesus but rather a violent conqueror. **Revelation 6:2** "And I looked, and behold, a white horse! And its rider had a bow, and a crown was given to him, and he came out conquering and to conquer." Note: This imposter is not to be confused with Jesus, who is also on a white horse, distinguished by the titles King of Kings and Lord of Lords (Revelation 19:11).	**6.** The Mahdi comes riding on a white horse. Ironically, Muslims who believe this quote (with Revelation 6:2 as their source) view the white horse rider in that passage as their Mahdi, when in fact the Bible does not present this character as a good guy. **Izzat and 'Arif, *Al Mahdi and the End Times*** "It is clear that this man is the Mahdi who will ride the white horse and judge by the Qur'an (with justice) and with whom will be men with marks of prostration (zabiba) on their foreheads."[12]
7. The Antichrist and False Prophet will promote a one-world religion. **Revelation 13:15** "[t]he image of the beast … might cause those who would not worship the image of the beast to be slain."	**7.** The Mahdi will make Islam the only acceptable religion. **Dawud 36:4273** "He … will govern the people by the Sunnah of their prophet and establish Islam on the earth."[13]
8. The Antichrist will execute infidels through beheading. **Revelation 20:4** "[I] saw the souls of those who had been beheaded for the testimony of Jesus and for the word of God, and those who had not worshiped the beast or its image and had not received its mark on their foreheads or their hands …"	**8.** The Mahdi will execute infidels (anyone who does not believe in Islam) through beheading. **Qur'an 8:12 (Shakir)** "I will cast terror into the hearts of those who disbelieve. Therefore strike off their heads and strike off every fingertip of them." **Qur'an 47:4 (Shakir)** "So when you meet in battle those who disbelieve, then smite the necks …"[14]

9. The Antichrist will kill anyone who opposes him, with a special emphasis on killing Jews and Christians. **Revelation 13:7** "Also it was allowed to make war on the saints and to conquer them …" **Revelation 12:4** "[A]nd the dragon [Antichrist] stood before the woman [Israel] who was about to give birth, so that when she bore her child he might devour it."	**9.** The Mahdi will kill anyone who opposes Islam, with a special emphasis on killing Jews and Christians.[15] **Qur'an 5:51 (Shakir)** "do not take the Jews and the Christians for friends; they are friends of each other; and whoever amongst you takes them for a friend, then surely he is one of them; surely Allah does not guide the unjust people." **Qur'an 9:5 (Shakir)** "slay the idolaters wherever you find them, and take them captives and besiege them and lie in wait for them in every ambush …"
10. The Antichrist will attack and conquer Jerusalem. **Zachariah 14:2** "For I will gather all the nations against Jerusalem to battle, and the city shall be taken …"	**10.** The Mahdi will conquer Jerusalem.[16] **Muslim 41:6985** "Jerusalem will be the location of the rightly guided caliphate and the center of Islamic rule, which will be headed by Imam al-Mahdi."
11. The Antichrist performs many signs, wonders, and miracles. **2 Thessalonians 2:9** "The coming of the lawless one is by the activity of Satan with all power and false signs and wonders," **Revelation 12:13–14** "It performs great signs, even making fire come down from heaven to earth in front of people, and by the signs that it is allowed to work in the presence of the beast it deceives those who dwell on earth …"	**11.** The Mahdi performs many signs, wonders, and miracles. **Hakim Mustadrak, related by Abu Sa'id al-Khudri (4:557 and 558), as quoted by Kabbani, 233** "In the last days of my Ummah [universal Islamic community], the Mahdi will appear. Allah will give him power over the wind and the rain and the earth will bring forth its foliage. He will give away wealth profusely, flocks will be in abundance, and the Ummah will be large and honored …"[17]

12. The Antichrist will make people receive a mark on the hand or forehead to pledge allegiance to him. **Revelation 13:16–17** "Also it causes all, both small and great, both rich and poor, both free and slave, to be marked on the right hand or the forehead, so that no one can buy or sell unless he has the mark, that is, the name of the beast or the number of its name."	**12.** Followers of the Mahdi usually mark themselves with headbands on the foreheads. Muslims receive *bismillah* (in the name of Allah), unbelievers receive *bismilkafir* (in the name of unbelievers)

While Haven's list is quite expansive, she missed two items linking the Antichrist to the Mahdi, both of which Richardson spotted. The first of these is significant because it will unmistakably identify the Antichrist when it happens. The second item is something I have speculated in the past, concerning the Ark of the Covenant.

Table 3: Antichrist = Mahdi (Three More Similarities)

The Biblical Antichrist	The Muslim Mahdi (i.e., Muslim Messiah, the 12th Imam)
1. The Antichrist will rule from the temple in Jerusalem, sitting on a throne in God's temple. **2 Thessalonians 2:4** "[Antichrist] who opposes and exalts himself above every so-called god or object of worship, so that he **takes his seat in the temple of God**, proclaiming himself to be God." See also **Zechariah 14:2**, **Ezekiel 38:9–12**, and **Daniel 9:27**.	**1.** The Mahdi will rule from the Dome of the Rock (temple) in Jerusalem. **Tirmidhi as quoted in Zubair, *Signs of Qiyamah*, 42, and Abdullah, Islam, Jesus, Mehdi, Qadiyanis, and Doomsday, 54** "[Armies carrying] black flags will come from Khurasan [Iran]. No power will be able to stop them and they will finally reach Eela [the Dome of the Rock in Jerusalem] where they will erect their flags …"[18] **Izzat and 'Arif, *Al Mahdi and the End Times*** "Jerusalem will be the location of the rightly guided caliphate and the center of Islamic rule, which will be headed by Iam al-Mahdi."[19]
2. The Antichrist will bring forth the Ark of the Covenant, in order to sit on it in God's temple. **2 Thessalonians 2:4** "[Antichrist] who opposes and exalts himself above every so-called god or object of worship, so that he **takes his seat in the temple of God**, proclaiming himself to be God." Note: If this deception is to be most effective, God's throne might be the mercy seat on top of the Ark of the Covenant. The whereabouts of the Ark of the Covenant is currently unknown. However, this scripture indicates it might be found in the future.	**2.** The Mahdi will bring forth the Ark of the Covenant. **Izzat and 'Arif, *Al Mahdi and the End Times*** "As-Suyuti mentioned in al-Hawi that 'at the hands of the Mahdi the Ark of the Covenant will be brought forth from the Lake of Tiberias and taken and placed in Jerusalem.'"[20]

This is quite a bit of evidence that links the Antichrist with the Mahdi, and Joel Richardson has even more to add than this, but I believe what I have listed here is enough to get the point across.

In the future, the people of the world will have to choose which version of the End Times prophecy to believe, Islam or Christianity. Concerning this choice, consider the words of the prophet Daniel, who spoke of the "god of fortresses" to which the Antichrist will give honor.

> **Daniel 11:37–39** [bold emphasis and bracketed comments added]
> He [Antichrist] shall pay no attention to the gods of his fathers, or to the one beloved by women. **He shall not pay attention to any other god**, for he shall magnify himself above all. **He shall honor the god of fortresses** instead of these. A god whom his fathers did not know he shall honor with gold and silver, with precious stones and costly gifts. **He shall deal with the strongest fortresses with the help of a foreign god.** Those who acknowledge him he shall load with honor. He shall make them rulers over many and shall divide the land for a price.

The interpretation of the word *fortresses* relates to war and the use of force. Strong's Enhanced Lexicon states the following:

> **H4581**
> מעז מעז מעוז מעוז
> mâʿôz mâʿûz mâʿôz mâʿûz
> *maw-oze', maw-ooz', maw-oze', maw-ooz'*
> From H5810; a fortified place; figuratively a defense: force, fort (-ress), rock, strength
> (-en), (X most) strong (hold).

From the context of Daniel's prophecy, the Antichrist does not regard any god insomuch as he uses the religion of a particular warlike god in order to serve his purposes. The name Allah actually has pagan origins that refer to an ancient warlike moon god of "violence and revolution."[21] As for the word *Islam*, it means "to submit." Clearly both of these words refer to the warlike nature of Islam.

Moderate Muslims claim that Islam calls for a *peaceful submission*, but Islamic texts, history, and Islamic leaders today openly declare and actively demonstrate exactly the opposite. The black flags of Islam are a declaration of war against all unbelievers. Consider the words of none other than Sheik Omar Bakri Muhammad, a Sharia law court judge in Great Britain. He is also the secretary general of the Islamic World League and spokesman for the International Islamic Front.

> The punishment of those who wage war against Allah and His apostle and strive to make mischief in the land is only this, that they should be murdered or crucified or their hands and their feed should be cut off on opposite sides or they should be imprisoned; this shall be as a disgrace for them in this world, and in the hereafter they shall have a grievous chastisement.[22]

Those at war against Allah, for those who need clarification, are non-Muslims. They include innocent, defenseless people who simply refuse to convert to Islam. Islam's version of submission is to *force* the entire world to *submit* to the will of Allah, or *die*. Using force is the central theme of Islamic eschatology. These are not my words; these words come directly from the Qur'an (47:4).

> **Qur'an 47:4 (Shakir)**
> So when you meet in battle those who disbelieve, then smite the necks until when you have overcome them, then make (them) prisoners …

There are volumes upon volumes of historical records that document the mindless, rampant bloodshed of Islam because of these words.

In America, Muslims are free to wear their turbans, promote the Qur'an, and worship the Allah of Muhammad all they want. This is because America is founded on a constitution inspired by a Judeo-Christian heritage, which advocates freedom. If an American wants to have a Nazi swastika tattooed on his forehead like Charles Manson, he or she is free to do it … but good luck on the job interview!

Islam, on the other hand, has no respect for religious freedom. Islam promotes a "god of force" and serves as the perfect vehicle the Antichrist will use to achieve his goal of world domination.

But do not be dismayed; Jesus knew this day would come.

> **John 16:1–4** [bold emphasis added]
> "I have said all these things to you to keep you from falling away. They will put you out of the synagogues. Indeed, **the hour is coming when whoever kills you will think he is offering service to God**. And they will do these things because they have not known the Father, nor me. But I have said these things to you, that when their hour comes you may remember that I told them to you."

7.3 Who Is the False Prophet?

As Joel Richardson put it, "Jews are waiting for the Messiah, Christians are waiting for Jesus, and Muslims are waiting for both the Mahdi (Muslim Messiah) *and* Jesus. All religions describe them as men coming to save the world."[27]

When I first read this in Richardson's book, it threw me for a loop. The Qur'an says that Jesus is coming back to the earth in the future? How can Muslims not believe that Jesus rose from the dead, yet at the same time believe He is still alive and will return to the earth in the future? If He is still alive, doesn't that mean He has conquered death at least in another way?

I've already mentioned that Muslims believe Jesus avoided the cross (Qur'an 4:157–158) and ascended into heaven to be with Allah, similar to Enoch or Elijah's ascensions. That is where He has been all this time, with God. Therefore, the Bible and the Qur'an describe Jesus as having the unique role of an individual who has physically ascended into heaven and will return to earth in the future.

Before I read Richardson's book, I always thought the Antichrist would claim to be Jesus. I was surprised to be enlightened by something I had never considered. What if the *False Prophet* is the one who will claim to be Jesus? Would that not give the False Prophet a certain degree of clout, especially if the things he said fell in line with so many New Age beliefs circulated today? If the False Prophet is the one who claims to be Jesus, his role is already established in Islam; he will definitely be able to appeal to Christians on the fence, and New Agers will eat up every word he says.

As it is, New Agers tweak the words of Jesus when He spoke of His Father as being God (Luke 2:49) and when He spoke of being one with His Father (John 8:48–59, 10:30). After all, they say, *are not we all the children of God?* Are not we all one with God, those who embrace the light within us?

Of course Jesus meant specifically what He said; He is *literally* God's biological Son. The archangel Gabriel declared this to Mary (Luke 1:31, Matthew 1:23), and the Father personally declared this to His Son Jesus when the Holy Spirit descended upon Him during His baptism (Matthew 3:17, Mark 1:11) and also at the Mount of Transfiguration (Matthew 17:5, 2 Peter 1:17).

Muslims deny these claims, and New Agers tweak them or, worse yet, elevate themselves to the status of Jesus. Therefore a False Prophet Muslim Jesus, who gives credence to a new flavor of Islam with its charismatic star-child guru in chief, will be a perfect deceiver for these two groups of people. Only faithful Christians and Jews will refuse to convert and will not be taken in.

As for nominal Christians and Jews, the fact that the *real* Jesus is the Head of the Christian church and also a Jew will place the False Prophet Muslim Jesus in a unique position to unify these two groups under an Islamic banner. So in the future, if someone shows up in a grand display claiming to be Jesus, but he refutes the identify of God's only begotten Son as Christians have always believed him to be, this will be the pinnacle of deception. The False Prophet, in fact, may very well be even *more deceptive* than the Antichrist.

While Lisa Haven focused on the parallels between the Antichrist and the Mahdi, Joel Richardson went further in his analysis and cross-referenced other characters of equal if not even greater relevance to the strong delusion. While the Antichrist seems to carry the grandmaster title of evil, it is the False Prophet who may be the most deceptive. Without him, many people will never believe in or accept the Antichrist. Otherwise, the False Prophet would not be necessary.

So what is it about the False Prophet that will make him so convincing?

Below is a summary of Richardson's parallels between the Bible's False Prophet and Islam's Muslim Jesus:

Table 4: False Prophet = Muslim Jesus (Five Similarities)

The False Prophet	The Muslim Jesus
1. Supporting/subordinate role of the Antichrist. **Revelation 13:11–14** "Then I saw another beast … It had two horns like a lamb and it spoke like a dragon. It exercises all the authority of the first beast in its presence, and makes the earth and its inhabitants worship the first beast, whose mortal wound was healed. It performs great signs, even making fire come down from heaven to earth in front of people, and by the signs that it is allowed to work in the presence of the beast it deceives those who dwell on earth …"	**1.** Supporting/subordinate role of the Mahdi. **Muslim 1:0293** "The Messenger of Allah said: A section of my people will not cease fighting for the truth and will prevail until the Day of Resurrection. He said: Jesus son of Mary would then descend and their [Muslims'] commander [the Mahdi] would invite him to come and lead them in prayer, but he would say: No, some amongst you are commanders over some."[28] **Veliankode, *Doomsday Portents and Prophecies,* 350** "Jesus Christ will decline the offer and invitation of Imam Mahdi to come and lead the Muslims in prayer, and say his prayers behind the Mahdi."[29] **Sais I-Nursi, "The Fifth Day," 493** "Jesus (peace be upon him) will come and will perform the obligatory prayers behind the Mahdi and follow him."[30] **Al-Sadr and Mutahhari, *The Awaited Savior*, prologue, 3** "[Jesus] will be following the Mahdi, the master of the time, and that is why he will be offering his prayers behind him."[31]

2. The False Prophet will enforce the rule of the Antichrist. **2 Thessalonians 2:9–12** "The coming of the lawless one is by the activity of Satan with all power and false signs and wonders, and with all wicked deception for those who are perishing, because they refused to love the truth and so be saved. Therefore God sends them a strong delusion, so that they may believe what is false, in order that all may be condemned who did not believe the truth but had pleasure in unrighteousness." **Revelation 13:11–13** "Then I saw another beast [The False Prophet] … It exercises all the authority of the first beast in its presence, and makes the earth and its inhabitants worship the first beast …" **Revelation 13:15** "And it [The False Prophet] was allowed to give breath to the image of the beast, so that the image of the beast might even speak and might cause those who would not worship the image of the beast to be slain."	**2.** The Muslim Jesus will enforce the rule of the Mahdi. **Kabbani, *Approach of Armageddon?* 237** "When Jesus returns he will personally correct the misrepresentations and misinterpretations about himself. He will affirm the true message that he brought in his time as a prophet, and that he never claimed to be the son of God. Furthermore, he will reaffirm in his second coming what he prophesied in his first coming bearing witness to the seal of the Messenger, Prophet Muhammad. In his second coming many non-Muslims will accept Jesus as a servant of Allah Almighty, as a Muslim and a member of the community of Muhammad."[32] **Hakim Mustadrak (2:651) #4162, related by Harayra, quotes in Kabbani, *Approach of Armageddon?* 237** "The Prophet said: verily Isa ibn Maryam shall descend as an equitable judge and fair ruler …"[33] **Veliankode, *Doomsday Portents and Prophecies*, 351** "Jesus, the son of Mary will descend and will lead them judging amongst them according to the holy Qur'an and the Sunnah of the Prophet Muhammad."[34]

3. False Prophet is an executioner using beheading as his modus operandi. **Revelation 13:14–15** "and by the signs that it is allowed to work in the presence of the beast it deceives those who dwell on earth, telling them to make an image for the beast that was wounded by the sword and yet lived. And it was allowed to give breath to the image of the beast, so that the image of the beast might even speak and might cause those who would not worship the image of the beast to be slain." **Revelation 20:4** "... I saw the souls of those who had been beheaded for the testimony of Jesus and for the word of God, and those who had not worshiped the beast or its image and had not received its mark on their foreheads or their hands ..."	**3.** The Muslim Jesus is an executioner. **Veliankode, *Doomsday Portents and Prophecies*, 358** "Jesus, the son of Mary will soon descend among the Muslims as a just judge ... Jesus will, therefore, judge according to the law of Islam ... all people will be required to embrace Islam and there will be no other alternative."[35] **Al-Misri, *Reliance of the Traveler*, 603** "The time and the place for [the pole tax] is before the final descent of Jesus. After his final coming, nothing but Islam will be accepted from them, for taking the poll tax is only effective until Jesus's descent."[36] **Zubair, *Signs of Qiyama*** "Isa [Jesus] kills the Dajjal at the Gate of Hudd, near an Israeli airport, in the valley of 'Ifiq.' The final war between the Yahudis will ensue, and the Muslims will be victorious."[37] **Veliankode, *Doomsday Portents and Prophecies*, 218** "In the Last Hour Muslims will fight with Jews. Since the Jews are an integral part of the army of the Dajjal, and Muslims are the soldiers of the Prophet Jesus, they will fight each other and the Muslims will become triumphant until even a stone or a tree would say: Come here, Muslim, there is a Jew hiding behind me; kill him."[38]

4. The False Prophet will be empowered by a strong delusion that will cause people to believe him. **2 Thessalonians 2:11–12** "… Therefore God sends them a strong delusion, so that they may believe what is false, in order that all may be condemned who did not believe the truth but had pleasure in unrighteousness."	**4.** The Muslim Jesus will be empowered by a strong delusion that will cause people to believe him. **Qur'an 4:159** [bracketed comment added] "And there is not one of the followers of the Book [Christians and Jews] but most certainly believes in this before his death, and on the day of resurrection he (Isa) shall be a witness against them."[39] **Shafi and Usmani, *Signs of the Qiyama and the Arrival of the Maseeh*, 60** "confirm that he is alive and has not died and he is not God or the Son of God but merely His [Allah's] slave and Messenger, and Isa [Jesus] will testify against those who had called him son of God, the Christians, and those who had belied him, the Jews."[40] **Al-sadr and Mutahhari, *The Awaited Savior*, prologue, 3** "Jesus will descend from heaven and espouse the cause of the Mahdi. The Christians and the Jews will see him and recognize his true status. The Christians will abandon their faith in his godhead [sic]."[41]

In reviewing Richardson's list of parallels, I noticed the Mahdi will also abolish the *jizya* tax. Richardson didn't point this parallel out that I noticed, but having control over taxation is controlling the economy, and the Bible states that the False Prophet will exercise this authority.

Table 5: False Prophet = Muslim Jesus (One More Similarity)

False Prophet	Muslim Jesus
The False Prophet will control the economy [buying and selling] in the Antichrist kingdom. This will be a means that he will use to force people to accept the Antichrist. **Revelation 13:11; 16–17** [bracketed comment and bold face added] "Then I saw another beast rising out of the earth. **It had two horns like a lamb and it spoke like a dragon.** ... Also **it causes all**, both small and great, both rich and poor, both free and slave, **to be marked on the right hand or the forehead, so that no one can buy or sell unless he has the mark, that is, the name of the beast or the number of its name.**"	The Muslim Jesus will control the economy in the form of tax regulations in the Mahdi kingdom. This will be a means that he will use to force people to accept Islam. **Dawud 37:4310** [bold emphasis added] "The Prophet said: there is no prophet between me and him, that is, Jesus. He will descent [sic] [to the Earth] ... He will break the cross, kill swine, and **abolish jizyah** [penalty tax for non-Muslims]. Allah will perish all religions except Islam."[42]

Notice in Revelation 13:15–18 that the apostle John refers to the False Prophet as a beast who is "like a lamb" yet speaks "like a dragon." As Richardson points out, this is one of the most telling signs that the False Prophet will claim to be Jesus because Jesus is directly symbolized as a lamb earlier in the book of Revelation (5:6). This lamb who speaks like a dragon, however, is a *false* lamb; he is a dragon in disguise.

7.4 Who Is the Dajjal?

While Islamic eschatology presents a mirror-image opposite of biblical eschatology, with clear cross-references of the Antichrist to the Mahdi, and the False Prophet to the return of a Muslim Jesus, pinning down the identity of the Dajjal, which is the Hadith's version of the End Times' Antichrist, is not as clear cut.

Joel Richardson espouses the theory that the basic pattern of swapping the protagonists with the antagonists simply continues with the Dajjal. Since the Hadiths all identify the Dajjal as the Antichrist, the Dajjal will claim to be Jesus the Messiah because he *really will be* Jesus the Messiah.

According to the Hadiths, however, the Dajjal is not a perfect match for the real Jesus for a number of reasons.

For starters, Islamic prophecies are flawed; the earth will not end up an Islamic caliphate of men with harems of robot sex slaves and eternal erections. When the *real* Jesus returns, He will be with the saints of heaven, and it's game over. The tyranny of the Antichrist and the False Prophet will be done, end of story.

> **Revelation 19:11–21** [bold emphasis added]
> Then I saw heaven opened, and behold, a white horse! The one sitting on it is called Faithful and True, and in righteousness he judges and makes war. **His eyes are like a flame of fire**, and on his head are many diadems, and he has a name written that no one knows but himself. He is clothed in a robe dipped in blood, and the name by which he is called is The word of God. **And the armies of heaven, arrayed in fine linen, white and pure, were following him on white horses. From his mouth comes a sharp sword with which to strike down the nations, and he will rule them with a rod of iron**. He will tread the winepress of the fury of the wrath of God the Almighty. On his robe and on his thigh he has a name written, King of kings and Lord of lords. Then I saw an angel standing in the sun, and with a loud voice he called to all the birds that fly directly overhead, **"Come, gather for the great supper of God, to eat the flesh of kings, the flesh of captains, the flesh of mighty men, the flesh of horses and their riders, and the flesh of all men, both free and slave, both small and great." And I saw the beast and the kings of the earth with their armies gathered to make war against him who was sitting on the horse and against his**

> **army. And the beast was captured, and with it the false prophet who in its presence had done the signs by which he deceived those who had received the mark of the beast and those who worshiped its image. These two were thrown alive into the lake of fire that burns with sulfur. And the rest were slain by the sword that came from the mouth of him who was sitting on the horse**, and all the birds were gorged with their flesh.

Contrasting with this scripture, the Hadiths describe a Muslim Jesus descending to the earth between the wings of two angels (Muslim 41:7015), not on a white horse followed by the saints of heaven. Now, if the Bible included a description of the arrival of the False Prophet, I have a hunch it would be exactly like this Muslim Jesus. As for the Dajjal, the Hadiths talk about him quite a bit, but only some of the Hadiths sound like they could pertain to the real Jesus, and they are not within the context of eschatology. The primary reason for this is simple: The Dajjal, as the *real* Jesus, cannot just show up and instantly wipe out all opposition as the *real* Jesus will do when He returns. The Dajjal's character, therefore, actually matches some of the Bible's descriptions of the Antichrist. This, of course, tweaks the premise of the mirror-image eschatology that Joel Richardson has brought to light, but not entirely.

The Dajjal is particularly prominent in the Hadiths. Since he poses the greatest discrepancy to Richardson's thesis about Islamic eschatology being a mirror image of the Bible's eschatology, I saw something in his character that had a unique prophetic significance. I believe that by finding out more about how the Dajjal can fit in biblical prophecy, I might be able to extract from the enemy's game plan (the Hadiths) more information that will help me understand biblical prophecy more fully. Richardson started this process, showing how the Antichrist will most likely be the Mahdi, and how a Muslim Jesus will most likely be the False Prophet. I simply wish to continue this process and make it more complete concerning the Dajjal.

So who is the Dajjal, really? Is he the *real* Jesus? What if he's someone else? Does the Bible provide any clues?

Starting with the Qur'an Explorer website,[43] which contains eighteen thousand Hadiths translated into English, I extracted 134 Hadiths about the Dajjal. I imported them into a custom-built database where I cataloged them for analysis. As I studied them, I found thirty-four recurring themes. In addition to analyzing the Hadiths, I also conducted research on Islamic prophecy websites to see what Muslim scholars say about the Dajjal.

Along with these Islamic sources, for everything new I learned, I queried the Bible for an interpretation. It took me quite a while, but I eventually found enough information about the Dajjal to formulate a theory about his *true identity*.

To begin with, there is not just one Dajjal but thirty of them (Bukhari 9:88:237; Dawud 37:4319, 37:4320). This is not too surprising because the Bible states in several places that there is more than one Antichrist (Matthew 24:24; Mark 13:22; 1 John 2:18, 2:22, 4:3; 2 John 1:7), and the Hadiths are copying the Bible for much of their inspiration.

Just as the Bible speaks of *many* Antichrists, yet highlights one (or two) in particular that will crown them all, the Hadiths do the same with their Dajjals, though they are much less consistent than the Bible. For example, only one in my sample of 134 Hadiths states directly that the Dajjal will be a Jew (Muslim 41:6995). There are also two other Hadiths that give this strong indication because he has seventy thousand Jewish followers (Muslim 41:6979, 41:7034).

Strangely, however, there are thirteen Hadiths in my sampling that describe the Dajjal in the presence of the Muslim Jesus, while he is in the middle of the "tawaf around Kaaba" (Bukhari 4:55:649, 4:55:650, 7:72:789, 9:87:128, 9:88:237, 9:88:242; Dawud 35:4230; Malik 49:49.2.2; Muslim 1:323, 1:324, 1:327, 41:7023, 41:7024).

The Kaaba, also referred to as the Kaaba Muazzama, is a building at the center of Islam's most sacred mosque, Al-Masjid al-Haram, in Mecca, al-Hejaz, Saudi Arabia. It is the most sacred Muslim site in the world. I might be wrong, but I don't think non-Muslims are allowed anywhere near it.

What's more, the Hadiths above describe the Dajjal conducting the tawaf around Kaaba. This is part of the Muslim pilgrimage known as the *Hajj* and *Umrah*, which all faithful Muslims must attempt to do at least once in their lifetime. This prayer is the pinnacle of Islamic religious activity; there is no way anyone would be doing it if he or she were not a Muslim.

So right away, within the Hadiths, the Dajjal has a massive whopper of a discrepancy with his identity, without trying to find out who he is in the Bible. We can't even tell if he's a Jew or a Muslim. Now almost any Muslim will agree that the Dajjal will be a Zionist Jew, yet no Jew is allowed anywhere near the Kaaba, much less making the Muslim pilgrimage. So what's up with that?

After my investigation into this mysterious Dajjal character, I have come to the conclusion that he may be a representation of four different people: Jesus, the two witnesses of the book of Revelation, and the Antichrist (or, more accurately, one of them because there might be two). I will now elaborate on each of these possibilities.

7.4.1 The Dajjal as the Real Jesus

Many Hadiths about the Dajjal list him as someone associated with hell and/or the grave, almost as if to warn Muslims about him if they are near death's door or in a personal spiritual battle against him. These are generally the vaguest references about him, and I have placed these Hadiths under the category of Punisher or Afflicter. In my sample, a total of thirty-five Hadiths fall into this category: Bukhari 1:3:86, 1:4:184, 1:12:795, 2:18:162, 2:23:459, 3:46:719, 5:59:652, 6:60:230, 8:75:376, 8:75:379, 8:75:386, 8:75:387, 8:75:388, 9:88:240, 9:88:243, 9:92:390; Dawud 14:2526; Malik 12:12.2.4, 15:15.8.3; Muslim 4:1216, 4:1218, 4:1219, 4:1220, 4:1221, 4:1224, 4:1225, 4:1773, 4:1977, 31:6133, 35:6534, 40:6859, 41:7003, 41:7015, 41:7035, and 41:7037.

For the sake of brevity, below is only one of these Hadiths.

> **Bukhari 2:23:459** [bold emphasis added]
> Allah's Apostle used to invoke (Allah): "Allahumma ini a'udhu bika min 'adhabi-l-Qabr, wa min 'adhabi-nnar, wa min fitnati-l-mahya wa-lmamat, wa min fitnati-l-masih ad-dajjal. (O Allah! I seek **refuge with you from the punishment in the grave** and from the **punishment in the Hell fire** and from the afflictions of life and death, and **the afflictions of Al-Masih Ad-Dajjal**."

Another category of Hadiths shows the Dajjal exercising one of his most convincing powers of deception. In his presence is something that looks like heaven, paradise, a garden, or refreshing water, and also in his presence is something that looks like hell or fire. Muslims are instructed to not believe the Dajjal under any circumstances. When he shows them heaven, it's actually hell, and when he shows them hell, it's actually heaven (Bukhari 4:55:554, 4:56:659, 9:88:244; Dawud 35:4232; Muslim 41:7011, 41:7012, 41:7013, 41:7010, 41:7014, 41:7019).

Again, for the sake of brevity, three of these Hadiths follow.

> **Bukhari 4:55:554** [bold emphasis added]
> Allah's Apostle said, "Shall I not tell you about the Dajjal a story of which no prophet told his nation? **The Dajjal** is one-eyed and **will bring with him what will resemble Hell and Paradise, and what he will call Paradise will be actually Hell**; so I warn you (against him) as Noah warned his nation against him."

> **Muslim 41:7014** [bold emphasis added]
> Abu Huraira reported Allah's Messenger (may peace be upon him) as saying: May I not inform you about the Dajjal what no Apostle of Allah narrated to his people? He would be blind and **he would bring along with him an Image of Paradise and Hell-Fire and**

what he would call as Paradise that would be Hell-Fire and I warn you as Noah warned his people.

Dawud 35:4232 [bold emphasis added]
Then the Antichrist (Dajjal) will come forth **accompanied by a river and fire**. He who **falls into his fire will certainly receive his reward**, and have his load taken off him, **but he who falls into his river will have his load retained and his reward taken off him**.

The nebulous wording of many of these Hadiths indicates to me that they are designed to lead Muslims astray at a very critical moment, perhaps at a time when they are at death's door, or if they already have passed beyond death's door, or if they ever receive a visitation from Jesus in person. These Hadiths are Satan's preemptive strike of deception, his best attempt at keeping Muslims deceived even when they are seeing the real Jesus standing right in front of them.

Consider the possibility of a Muslim who has died, and his or her spirit sees a spark of light in the midst of the deepest void. At the end of that tunnel of light, the lost Muslim soul encounters Jesus, who is the Way, the Truth, and the Life (John 6:14); He is also the *door* (John 10:7–9).

John 10:7–9 [bold emphasis added]
So Jesus again said to them, "Truly, truly, I say to you, **I am the door** of the sheep. All who came before me are thieves and robbers, but the sheep did not listen to them. **I am the door**. If anyone enters by me, he will be saved and will go in and out and find pasture."

So there Jesus stands as the literal door to heaven, and a conversation ensues. The Muslim asks, "Who are you?" Or perhaps there is a universal recognition of who Jesus is, at least in appearance. Either way, the answer that Jesus gives is not what the Muslim expects.

"I am Jesus. I'm here to let you know that heaven is right behind me, and …"

"Wait … wait a second here, what's going on around here? Why am I seeing Jesus, son of Mary?"

"Yea, she was my mom," Jesus replies, "and my Dad, well, they're both behind me …"

To this, the Muslim's defenses immediately set off a red flag, Dajjal alert! Beep! Beep! Beep! With every ounce of will, the Muslim tries desperately to recall a Hadith of protection against someone he perceives as a blasphemer standing before him. In spite of this, Jesus emits unconditional love and continues with His dialogue.

"Hey, buddy, I don't have one eye; I have both of my eyes. Obviously something is wrong with your Hadiths, no? Yes, I am Jewish, but …"

"This can't be right!" the Muslim protests.

"Look, I'm not lying to you. Even your own book says I was born of a virgin; how do you suppose that happened?"

Finally, the Muslim remembers one of those Hadiths of protection for times like this (Muslim 4:1225, 4:1766), and he starts madly chanting, "and I seek refuge with Thee from the trial of Masih al-Dajjal," to which Jesus twiddles his thumbs and waits.

> **Muslim 4:1225** [bold emphasis added]
> Ibn 'Abbas reported that the Messenger of Allah (may peace he upon him) used to teach them this supplication (in the same spirit) with which he used to teach them a Surah of the Qur'an. He would thus instruct us: "Say, O Allah I we seek refuge with Thee from the torment of Hell, and I seek refuge with Thee from the torment of the grave, **and I seek refuge with Thee from the trial of Masih al-Dajjal**, and I seek refuge with Thee from the trial of life and death."
> Muslim b. Hajjaj said: It has reached me that Tawus

> said to his son: Did you make this supplication in prayer? He said: No. (Upon this) he (Tawus) said: Repeat the prayer. Tawus has narrated this hadith through three or four (transmitters) with words to the same effect.

"Just let me know when you're through," Jesus replies. After a while, the frustrated Muslim soul eventually comes to the conclusion that Jesus isn't going anywhere and that Hadith doesn't appear to be doing anything … *or is it?* He's not in hell yet, but then again, the darkness behind him doesn't look so pleasant. But wait, Jesus said that beautiful, exceptionally compelling light behind Him is *heaven.* Remember what those Hadiths warned? That might actually be hell!

What happens next is up to God, and it all depends on what is in the Muslim's heart. Ultimately, those who have true love in their hearts should know the truth when they hear it because the sheep know the voice of their shepherd (John 10:16). I suspect that Jesus's voice, which is the voice of love, is capable of transcending any religious indoctrination, but sadly, many will reject His voice of unconditional love. Many do not understand it, nor will they ever; in fact, they detest it because that voice convicts them of all the sin in their hearts that they refuse to acknowledge.

Now I personally believe that there may be a window of opportunity for accepting Jesus after passing from this life, just like in the illustration I provided above. This window of opportunity could possibly last up until Judgment Day. If this is the case, I think that Satan, being aware of that window of opportunity, inspired these Hadiths to address it.

I can now hear Christians rattling off Hebrews 9:27, which states that judgment comes after death, but it doesn't say that judgment comes *immediately* after death. Also, if Hebrews 9:27 is to be taken as a hard inflexible "rule" of the afterlife, how does it reconcile with all the people in the Bible who were resurrected from the dead, yet later in life they *died a second time*? Lazarus falls into this category, among several others. This scripture, therefore, has at least one obvious exception.

> **Hebrews 9:27**
> And just as it is appointed for man to die once, and after that comes judgment…

Setting aside the idea of an extended window of opportunity to repent and accept Jesus, there will eventually come a time when any opportunity for salvation will be lost forever (Matthew 7:21–23, 25:12; Luke 13:27).

> **Matthew 7:21**
> "Not everyone who says to me, 'Lord, Lord,' will enter the kingdom of heaven, but the one who does the will of my Father who is in heaven."

So these Hadiths that speak of encountering someone who looks like Jesus, sounds like Jesus, says He's Jesus, and even has what appears to be a vision of heaven and hell with Him … well, *I think He's Jesus*. However, not all of these Hadiths are so clear cut.

While some Hadiths speak of the Dajjal's heaven-and-hell deception, which could be the power Jesus holds as the *door to heaven*, some of these same Hadiths also speak of other Dajjal attributes that are most likely *not* referring to Jesus. For example, Jesus doesn't have one eye, yet there are several Hadiths that speak of a one-eyed character who wields a power to deceive with heaven and hell.

I think the reason these Hadiths are jumbled about the Dajjal is because there is more than one main Dajjal, but from Satan's point of view, it doesn't matter. Why would it? If a Muslim were to encounter the *real* Jesus, and that Muslim was stubbornly insistent on adhering to Islamic doctrine, he or she would most likely conclude that the real Jesus was the Dajjal, even if He has both of His eyes.

I think the same goes for the two witnesses in the book of Revelation. In the future, when these two Jewish guys start preaching the Gospel and garner thousands of Jewish followers, whether they have one eye or not, I think most Muslims will consider them to be Dajjals. Because of this, Satan will have achieved his goal of deception, even though his prophecies are not entirely accurate.

7.4.2 The Dajjal as the Two Witnesses

The Bible states that in the End Times, there will be two men who will wield supernatural power to preach the Gospel wherever they go, and nobody will be able to stop them.

> **Revelation 11:1–14** [bold emphasis added]
> Then I was **given a measuring rod** like a staff, and I was told, **"Rise and measure the temple of God and the altar** and those who worship there, **but do not measure the court outside the temple;** leave that out, for it is given over to the nations, and **they will trample the holy city for forty-two months**. And **I will grant authority to my two witnesses**, and they will **prophesy for 1,260 days,** clothed in sackcloth." These are **the two olive trees** and **the two lampstands that stand before the Lord of the earth**. And **if anyone would harm them, fire pours from their mouth and consumes their foes. If anyone would harm them, this is how he is doomed to be killed. They have the power to shut the sky, that no rain may fall during the days of their prophesying, and they have power over the waters to turn them into blood and to strike the earth with every kind of plague,** as often as they desire. And when they have finished their testimony, **the beast** that rises from the bottomless pit **will make war on them and conquer them and kill them**, and **their dead**

> **bodies will lie in the street of the great city that symbolically is called Sodom and Egypt, where their Lord was crucified.** For three and a half days some from the peoples and tribes and languages and nations will gaze at their dead bodies and refuse to let them be placed in a tomb, and **those who dwell on the earth will rejoice over them and make merry and exchange presents, because these two prophets had been a torment to those who dwell on the earth.** But after the three and a half days a breath of life from God entered them, and they stood up on their feet, and great fear fell on those who saw them. Then they heard a loud voice from heaven saying to them, "Come up here!" **And they went up to heaven in a cloud**, and their enemies watched them. And at that hour there was a great earthquake, and a tenth of the city fell. Seven thousand people were killed in the earthquake, and the rest were terrified and gave glory to the God of heaven. The second woe has passed; behold, the third woe is soon to come.

Since the olive tree has been a long-standing symbol for Israel, the general consensus about these two witnesses is that they are Jewish. Because they are described as standing before the Lord, yet they end up on Earth preaching the Gospel for forty-two months, and they are supernaturally empowered, most theologians also believe they will come from heaven. These two people are most widely speculated to be Enoch and Elijah (the two men who ascended to heaven without physically dying) or Moses and Elijah (the two men who met with Jesus on the Mount of Transfiguration) (Matthew 17:3).[44]

These men will definitely be considered Dajjals to Muslims for at least eight reasons I have enumerated below, though there are probably more correlations than this:

1. **The two witnesses will most likely be Jewish**, and at least one Hadith states this verbatim about the Dajjal (Muslim 41:6995). The two witnesses will most likely have many Jewish followers, especially if they come at a time when the Jews are on the run during the reign of the Antichrist (Isaiah 16:1–5, Ezekiel 20:33–35, Matthew 24:15–21, Revelation 12:5–17). It makes sense that the two witnesses will appear at that time when Israel needs them the most for protection from the Antichrist. Corresponding with this, the Hadiths state that the Dajjal (at least *one* of them) will have seventy thousand Jewish followers, which again identifies him as most likely being Jewish (Muslim 41:7034, 41:6979).

   Muslim 41:6995 [bold emphasis added]
   Abu Sa'id Khudri reported: Ibn Sa'id said to me something for which I felt ashamed. He said: I can excuse others; but what has gone wrong with you, O Companions of Muhammad, that you take me as Dajjal? **Has Allah's Apostle** (may peace be upon him) **not said that he would be a Jew** whereas I am a Muslim …

2. **The two witnesses will be supernaturally empowered to tell the truth**, to publically proclaim the Gospel to the whole world, including Muslim nations, where they will also most likely be helping the Jews escape the Antichrist. Muslims will definitely see their preaching as a massive deception, and their supernatural signs and wonders (causing plagues, turning water into blood, etc.) will automatically identify them to Muslims as deceiving Dajjals (Dawud 37:4305, 37:4320; Muslim 31:6134, 4:1219, 4:1220, 41:7015).

   Dawud 37:4305 [bold emphasis added]
   The Prophet (peace be upon him) said: **Let him who hears of the Dajjal (Antichrist) go far from him**

for I swear by Allah that **a man will come to him thinking he is a believer and follow him because of confused ideas roused in him by him.**

3. **The two witnesses will most likely accept new believers into their fold to protect them, along with the Jews** (Revelation 12:6, 12:13–16). I draw this conclusion from the fact that the two witnesses will most likely be helping the Jews in the wilderness to fend off the Antichrist's attacks. Simultaneously, they will also preach the Gospel to Muslims, and any Muslims who accept their testimony will have a better chance of survival if they join the Jews and the two witnesses. This is what the Hadiths prophesy about the actions of the Dajjal. The Hadiths state that there will be a time when Muslims will gather in two cities, Mecca and Medina, and the Dajjal will not enter those cities (Bukhari 3:30:103, 3:30:104, 3:30:105, 3:30:106, 7:71:627, 9:88:239, 9:88:240, 9:88:246, 9:88:247, 9:88:248, 9:93:565; Malik 45:45:4.16; Muslim 41:6994, 41:6995, 41:6996, 41:7015, 41:7028, 41:7030, 41:7032, 41:7033, 41:7034, 7:3186, 7:3187). Rather than invading these cities, he (or they) will respectfully land in the barren flat plains outside Medina, and all Muslims who no longer want to be Muslims will rush out of the city to join him (or them) and a large group of Jews.

   Muslim 41:7015 [bold emphasis added]
   He would come to the people and invite them (to a wrong religion) and **they would affirm their faith in him and respond to him**.

   Bukhari 3:30:105 [bold emphasis added]
   The Prophet said, "**There will be no town which Ad-Dajjal will not enter** except Mecca and Medina, and there will be no entrance (road) (of both Mecca and Medina) but the angels will be standing in rows

> guarding it against him, and then **Medina will shake with its inhabitants thrice** (i.e., three earthquakes will take place) and **Allah will expel all the nonbelievers and the hypocrites from it**."
>
> **Muslim 41:7034** [bold emphasis added]
> Anas b. Malik reported that Allah's Messenger (may peace be upon him) said: **The Dajjal would be followed by seventy thousand Jews** of Isfahan wearing Persian shawls.

Note that these Hadiths are mostly in the context of End Times prophecy and not personal encounters, or have anything to do with near-death experiences. That being said, I don't see the events immediately following Jesus's return involving a prolonged period of Jesus running around and preaching the Gospel. That's the job of the two witnesses and the believers on the earth, *prior* to the return of Jesus. As I said above, when Jesus returns it's game over, and the majority of the people left on the earth at that time will fully align with either the Antichrist or the Jews. The job of separating the wheat from the tares will be complete (Matthew 13:30), and the two witnesses will play a pivotal part of that process.

The *real* Jesus will then effortlessly wipe out all opposition when He arrives in what is described as an anticlimactic battle. No ups and downs, no win-some-lose-some business. Revelation 19:20–21 describes the final battle when Jesus returns in two sentences: "These two [the Antichrist and False Prophet] were thrown alive into the lake of fire that burns with sulfur. And the rest were slain by the sword that came from the mouth of him who was sitting on the horse." There you go, done. There's nothing in there about running around and having personal confrontations, side-show parlor trick miracles of killing people just to resurrect them (as the Hadiths contend), or any prolonged battles with anyone. Therefore, these Hadiths that refer to the Dajjal with Jewish followers are almost certainly a reference to the two witnesses.

The only prophetic Bible scriptures about the future that refer to the *real* Jesus possibly witnessing to masses of people are the scriptures that speak of the survivors of the Great Tribulation. This only happens *after* Jesus wipes out the Antichrist, the False Prophet, and all their minions because these scriptures are in the context of the aftermath of battle (Zechariah 12:10; Zechariah 14; Romans 11:26; Revelation 7:3–4; 14:1, 14:3).

4. **The two witnesses may have a divine connection for obtaining supernatural provision** (Revelation 12:6). This is the time when the Jews are on the run from the Antichrist, and they seek refuge in the abandoned city of Petra (Isaiah 16:1–5, 26:20–21, 63:108), which is out in the middle of the desert (déjà vu for Israel). In this barren place, the Jews will receive *nourishment* for 1,260 days. This time frame happens to be the exact same amount of time allocated to the two witnesses. Concerning the Hadiths, they describe the Dajjal's miraculous ability to obtain an abundance of food and water (Bukhari 9:88:238; Muslim 25:5352, 41:7015, 41:7021, 41:7004). The city of Petra, in particular, has an incredibly complex system of ancient plumbing; all it needs is water to come back to life.[45]

Revelation 12:6 [bold emphasis and bracketed comments added]
And **the woman [Israel/the Jews] fled into the wilderness**, where she has a place [possibly Petra] prepared by God, in which **she is to be nourished for 1,260 days**.

Muslim 41:7015 [bold emphasis and bracketed comment added]
He [the Dajjal] would then **give command to the sky and there would be rainfall upon the earth and it would grow crops**. Then in the evening,

their **pasturing animals would come to them with their humps very high and their udders full of milk and their flanks stretched. He would then come to another people and invite them**. But **they would reject him and he would go away from them and there would be drought for them** and nothing would be left with them in the form of wealth ... **He would then walk through the wasteland and say** to it: **Bring forth your treasures, and the treasures would come out and collect (themselves) before him** like the swarm of bees.

Muslim 41:7021 [bold emphasis added]
Mughira b. Shu'ba reported that none asked Allah's Apostle (may peace be upon him) about Dajjal more than I asked him. I (one of the narrators other than Mughlra b. Shu'ba) said: What did you ask? Mughira replied: **I said that the people alleged that he would have a mountain load of bread and mutton and rivers of water**. Thereupon he said: He would be more insignificant in the eye of Allah compared with all this.

5. **The two witnesses will defend themselves, and maybe others with them, using supernatural fire** (Revelation 11:5). The Dajjal, likewise, will use supernatural fire, which Muslims are trained via the Hadiths to ignore and mindlessly charge into. This will be to their detriment (Bukhari 9:88:244; Dawud 35:4232; Muslim 41:7011, 41:7012, 41:7013).

Revelation 11:5 [bold emphasis and bracketed comments added]
And if anyone would harm them [the two witnesses], **fire pours from their mouth and consumes their**

foes. If anyone would harm them, this is how he is doomed to be killed.

Dawud 35:4232 [bold emphasis added]
Then the **Antichrist (Dajjal) will come forth accompanied by a river and fire. He who falls into his fire will certainly receive his reward, and have his load taken off him**, but he who falls into his river will have his load retained and his reward taken off him. I then asked: What will come next? He said: **The Last Hour will come**.

The above Hadith is one that can refer to Jesus or the two witnesses, though I think it more aptly applies to the two witnesses because it is connected with the Last Hour. As for the fire in question, it seems to be used as a destructive weapon rather than a vision of the fires of hell.

6. **The two witnesses will have the ability to control the weather and cause it to stop raining** (Revelation 11:6), which is a direct correlation with one of the Dajjal's listed powers (Muslim 41:7115).

Revelation 11:6 [bold emphasis added]
They have the power to shut the sky, that no rain may fall during the days of their prophesying, and they have power over the waters to turn them into blood and to strike the earth with every kind of plague, as often as they desire.

Muslim 41:7115 [bold emphasis added]
He would come to the people and invite them (to a wrong religion) and they would affirm their faith in him and respond to him. **He would then give command to the sky and there would be rainfall**

upon the earth and it would grow crops. Then in the evening, their posturing animals would come to them with their humps very high and their udders full of milk and their flanks stretched. **He would then come to another people and invite them. But they would reject him and he would go away from them and there would be drought for them and nothing would be left with them in the form of wealth.**

7. **The two witnesses will prophesy for 1,260 days, a.k.a. forty-two months**, which is close to at least one Hadith that estimates the duration of the Dajjal's reign of terror as possibly forty months (Muslim 41:7023).

   Revelation 11:3 [bold emphasis added]
   I will **grant authority to my two witnesses**, and **they will prophesy for 1,260 days**.

   Muslim 41:7023 [bold emphasis added]
   The **Dajjal would appear in my Ummah and he would stay (in the world)** for forty—I cannot say whether he meant forty days, **forty months** or forty years …

8. **The two witnesses will most likely have a supernatural transportation ability.** Concerning Elijah, the most consistent speculation for one of the identities of the two witnesses, remember how he left the earth in that nifty flying chariot of Israel (2 Kings 2:12)? A similar chariot was most likely witnessed by Ezekiel (Ezekiel 1, 10) and perhaps further used to transport the apostle Philip much later (Acts 8:39). With this in mind, take note of the interesting description in the book of Revelation as to how the Jews will escape from the Antichrist. If the two witnesses play a part in this escape, it seems likely to me that they may assist Israel with their mode

of transportation. The Hadiths also tend to support this idea because the Dajjal has a supernatural transportation ability to visit every town on Earth during his short allotment of time (Muslim 41:6996, Bukhari 3:30:105). His mode of travel is described in some sources as a magic mule that travels at impossible speeds, and in other sources, it is "a cloud driven by the wind" (Muslim 41:7115).

Revelation 12:14 [bold emphasis and bracketed comments added]
But **the woman [Israel/the Jews] was given the two wings of the great eagle so that she might fly from the serpent into the wilderness**, to the place where she is to be nourished for a time, and times, and half a time, [aka forty-two months, or 1,260 days].

Muslim 41:6996 [bold emphasis and bracketed comments added]
I am Dajjal and would be soon permitted to get out and so **I shall get out and travel in the land, and will not spare any town where I would not stay for forty nights** [months] except Mecca and Medina as these two (places) are prohibited (areas) for me and I would not make an attempt to enter any one of these two.

Bukhari 3:30:105 [bold emphasis added]
The Prophet said, **"There will be no town which Ad-Dajjal will not enter** …"

Muslim 41:7115 [bold emphasis added]
We said: Allah's Messenger, **how quickly would he walk upon the earth?** Thereupon he said: **Like cloud driven by the wind.**

7.4.3 The Dajjal as the Antichrist

Last but not least, I believe the Dajjal may also represent the Antichrist, or at least *one of them* because I have come to the conclusion that there will most likely be two main Antichrists in the End Times. The role of the first is a lesser role, functioning to build up and catapult the fame of his successor, the Mahdi. They are related to each other as part of the same beast, in the sense that they are both devout Muslims. This provides the automatic assumption that they will deny the divinity of Jesus, which by definition is blasphemy.

My working theory about these men is that they come from rival Muslim nations; one will be Sunni, and the other will be Shiite. The Dajjal, who will be the first and lesser Antichrist, will lead the Islamic nation in the south. The Mahdi, the greater Antichrist, will lead the nation in the north.

The first clue that led me to this theory is the most distinguishing characteristic about the Dajjal, which is listed in a total of twenty-eight Hadiths out of my sample of 134. These Hadiths reveal the Dajjal as having one eye (Bukhari 4:52:290, 4:54:562, 4:55:553, 4:55:554, 4:55:649, 4:55:650, 5:59:685, 7:72:789, 8:73:194, 9:87:128, 9:87:153, 9:88:241, 9:88:242, 9:88:245, 9:93:504, 9:93:505; Dawud 37:4306; Muslim 1:323, 1:324, 1:325, 1:327, 41:7000, 41:7005, 41:7009, 41:7014, 41:7015, 41:7010; Malik 49:49.2.2).

Many other Hadiths describe other physical attributes about the Dajjal, such as his reddish complexion; his stout, or obese, build (Bukhari 4:55:650, 9:87:153, 9:88:242; Muslim 1:323, 1:325, 1:327); and his curly hair (Bukhari 4:55:649, 7:72:789, 9:87:128, 9:87:153, 9:88:242; Muslim 1:323, 1:324, 1:325, 1:327, 41:7010, 41:7015).

These details highlight the fact that this Dajjal character is definitely a person and not a symbol as many Muslims hypothesize, concerning the one eye of Horus (an Egyptian god with one eye).

7.4.4 The One-Eyed Dajjal False Flag Theory

I believe at least one source Muhammad's followers may have used that inspired the Dajjal is found in the Bible, in the book of Zachariah. Consider the following passage:

> **Zechariah 11:16–17** [bold emphasis added]
> For behold, I am raising up in the land **a shepherd who does not care for those being destroyed**, or **seek the young or heal the maimed or nourish the healthy**, but devours the flesh of the fat ones, tearing off even their hoofs. **"Woe to my worthless shepherd, who deserts the flock! May the sword strike his arm and his right eye!** Let his arm be wholly withered, **his right eye utterly blinded!"**

The dead giveaway that the Hadiths drew on this scripture is the specific reference to a right eye, which a number of Hadiths make sure to mention (Bukhari 9:87:128, 4:55:649, 5:59:685, 7:72:789, 9:87:153, 9:93:504; Malik 49:49.2.2; Muslim 1:323, 1:324, 1:325, 41:7005).

> **Bukhari 9:87:128** [bold emphasis and bracketed comments added]
> Allah's Apostle said, **"I saw myself (in a dream) near the Ka'ba last night, and I saw a man [the Muslim Jesus / a.k.a. False Prophet]** with whitish red complexion, the best you may see amongst men of that complexion having long hair reaching his earlobes which was the best hair of its sort, and he had combed his hair and water was dropping from it, and **he was performing the Tawaf around the Ka'ba** while he was leaning on two men or on the shoulders of two men. I asked, 'Who is this man?' Somebody replied, **'(He is) Messiah, son of Mary' [aka the Muslim Jesus/False Prophet]. Then I saw another man with very curly hair, blind in the right eye**

> **which looked like a protruding out grape.** I asked, **'Who is this?'** Somebody replied, **'(He is) Messiah, Ad-Dajjal.'"**

Bible commentaries, such as Matthew Henry's,[46] John Gill's,[47] and the *Bible Reader's Companion*,[48] believe Zechariah's prophecy refers to the spiritual blindness of Israel's leadership, which was prevalent in Jesus's day and alluded to in the New Testament (Matthew 23:16, 23:19, 24:5; John 9:39). My New International Version (NIV) commentary also points to the Old Testament (Jeremiah 23:5), which mentions one of the pharaohs of Egypt whose arm was wounded as a judgment from God.[49]

> **Matthew 23:16** [bold emphasis added]
> "Woe to you, **blind guides**, who say, 'If anyone swears by the temple, it is nothing, but if anyone swears by the gold of the temple, he is bound by his oath.'

An interesting aspect about the passage in Zachariah is that it hints at the possibility of a Jewish Antichrist because of the symbol of the shepherd and his flock, which is indicative of someone with authority over Israel. I still think the Dajjal Antichrist is Muslim, but he may have Jewish ancestry, which would make him a better fit with many Hadiths. Mixed ancestry is common in Israel. For example, in the crime-infested city of Lod, Israel, where at least one Hadith says the Dajjal will be killed by the Muslim Jesus (Muslim 41:7015), the demographic is quite diverse.

> The district is around 70% Arab, 20% Ethiopian and 10% elderly veteran Israelis. In addition to racial tension between the Arabs and the Ethiopians, there are schisms within the Arab community among the Bedouin, Israeli Arabs from the Lod area, and **"mixed" families of Arabs from Israel married to Palestinians from the West Bank.**[50]

Dropping back to a much earlier time, when the man Israel (aka Jacob) was still alive, yet on his deathbed, he gave prophecies for each of his sons. Reuben was stoked; Jacob said Reuben was "his firstborn, his might" (Genesis 49:3). The other brothers received their prophecies as well. Judah was very pleased; he would be like a lion cub. Wow, how totally cool is that? Then it came Dan's turn.

> **Genesis 49:17**
> **Dan shall be a serpent in the way, a viper by the path** that bites the horse's heels so that his rider falls backward. I wait for your salvation, O Lord.

Ouch. Dan's expression was probably something like "Yo, Dad, what's up with that? That's harsh! Seriously, nothing good? A snake, that's all you got?" Poor Dan.

Thus, Jacob immediately follows Dan's prophecy with my paraphrase, "Be patient, salvation will come." Actually Jacob was blind at that time, so he couldn't see Dan's face, but maybe he sensed it.

Anyway, it could be that Judas Iscariot was from the tribe of Dan, as some speculate,[51] but Jacob's prophecy could also link to more than one person as many prophecies do.

So the scriptures give some evidence that the Antichrist may have a Jewish lineage, but numerous Hadiths indicate that the one-eyed Dajjal is a Muslim because he is either in the presence of the Kaaba or conducting the tawaf around the Ka'ba. Moreover, other Hadiths state that the Dajjal will arise from Muhammad's *house*, or his *community* (Dawud 35:4230; Muslim 41:7023; 41:7024). That must mean he is a Muslim or that he starts out as one, but it doesn't rule out some Jewish ancestry.

> **Dawud 35:4230** [bold emphasis added]
> Then will come a test which is pleasant. Its murkiness is due to the fact that **it is produced by a man from the people of my house [a Muslim]**, who will assert that he belongs to me, whereas he does not, for my

friends are only the God-fearing. Then the people will unite under a man who will be like a hip-bone on a rib. Then there will be the little black trial which **will leave none of this community without giving him a slap [possibly excommunicated from his community]**, and when people say that it is finished, it will be extended. During it a man will be a believer in the morning and an infidel in the evening, so that **the people will be in two camps: the camp of faith which will contain no hypocrisy, and the camp of hypocrisy which will contain no faith [possibly Sunni vs. Shiite]. When that happens, expect the Antichrist (Dajjal)** that day or the next.

Muslim 41:7023 [bold emphasis and bracketed comment added]
He then reported that Allah's Messenger (may peace be upon him) said: **The Dajjal would appear in my Ummah** [translated as "community"] and he would stay (in the world) for forty—I cannot say whether he meant forty days, forty months or forty years …

Muslim 41:7024 [bold emphasis and bracketed comment added]
Shu'ba said like this and 'Abdullah b Amr reported Allah's Messenger (may peace be upon him) having said: **The Dajjal would appear in my Ummah [community]** …

Returning to Zechariah 11:16–17, note that Revelation 13:3 says the beast (a symbol representing both the Antichrist, and his kingdom), will receive a fatal wound to his head. Having one eye definitely falls into the category of a severe head injury. In the case of the Dajjal, his eye injury is described as bulging out like a grape (Bukhari 4:55:649,

4:55:650, 5:59:685, 7:72:789, 9:87:128, 9:87:153, 9:88:242, 9:93:504; Malik 49:49.2.2; Muslim 1:323, 1:324, 1:327, 41:7005).

> **Bukhari 4:55:649** [bold emphasis added]
> The Prophet mentioned the Messiah Ad-Dajjal in front of the people saying, Allah is not one eyed while Messiah, **Ad-Dajjal is blind in the right eye and his eye looks like a bulging out grape** …

John's revelation states that the wound of the Antichrist ties directly to a miracle. As I read over Revelation 13, a theory about this multiheaded beast began to take shape. First the beast has seven heads with ten crowns, which is a reference to ten kings, and then one of these heads is wounded. Shortly after that, it is miraculously healed. What could this mean?

The Hadiths say that the Muslim Jesus will kill the one-eyed Dajjal (Muslim 41:6924, 41:7015, 41:7023), but Revelation states that the Antichrist's fatal wound will be healed. Could it be that the beast in this scripture refers to two individuals, as well as the two heads of Islam, the Sunni and the Shiites? Perhaps the leader of a northern nation will ally himself with an otherworldly power (the False Prophet), defeat the southern nation, and be hailed as a hero. He will then become so universally popular among *all* Muslims that he will unite the Shiites and Sunni (which would take a miracle to do), bringing back the caliphate of their glory days. In this manner, his wound will be miraculously healed.

Perhaps a Sunni leader down south in Egypt, reviled even by many Muslims, will be killed by a Shiite leader from Syria. Their dispute will probably include a covenant that the Syrian leader might have with Israel, among other things. With this possibility in mind, consider this extended narration of Revelation 13, with my speculations in bracketed comments.

Revelation 13:1–14 [bold emphasis and bracketed comments added]

And I saw a **beast [the Antichrist kingdom taking shape] rising out of the sea, with ten horns and seven heads [seven heads refer to the seven world empires; Egypt, Assyria, Babylon, Medo-Persian, Greek, Rome, and the last Antichrist kingdom; ten kings are part of Antichrist kingdom; all are eventually consumed by the Antichrist]**, with ten diadems **[ten kings]** on its horns and blasphemous names on its heads, **[as they will all receive when accepting the Islamic faith]**. And the beast that I saw was like a leopard; its feet were like a bear's, and its mouth was like a lion's mouth. And to it the dragon gave his power and his throne and great authority. **One of its heads [one of the ten kings] seemed to have a mortal wound [a literal and most likely fatal wound] but its mortal wound was healed [perhaps a reference to a return to the Caliphate, led by the arrival of the Mahdi, who unites the two Muslim factions of Sunni and Shiites]**, and the whole earth marveled as they followed the **beast [now symbolized as the Mahdi in charge of the new Caliphate]**. And they worshiped the dragon, for he had given his authority to the beast, and they worshiped the beast, saying, **"Who is like the beast, [the Mahdi, with his otherworldly alliance(s)] and who can fight against it?"** And the beast was given a mouth uttering haughty and blasphemous words, and **it was allowed to exercise authority for forty-two months, [aka 1,260 days, or three and a half years]. It opened its mouth to utter blasphemies against God, blaspheming his name and his dwelling, that is, those who dwell in heaven.** Also **it was allowed to make war on the saints and to conquer them**. And

> authority was given it over every tribe and people and language and nation, and all who dwell on earth will worship it, everyone whose name has not been written before the foundation of the world in the book of life of the Lamb that was slain. If anyone has an ear, let him hear: If anyone is to be taken captive, to captivity he goes; if anyone is to be slain with the sword, with the sword must he be slain. Here is a call for the endurance and faith of the saints. **Then I saw another beast [the False Prophet, a.k.a. Muslim Jesus] rising out of the earth. It had two horns like a lamb [appearance of Jesus] and it spoke like a dragon [words of Satan].** It exercises all the authority of the first beast in its presence, and **makes the earth and its inhabitants worship the first beast, [the False Prophet Muslim Jesus gives his authority to the Mahdi] whose mortal wound was healed [by his defeating the Dajjal, and uniting Sunni and Shiite Muslims]. It performs great signs, even making fire come down from heaven to earth in front of people**, and by the signs that it is allowed to work in the presence of the beast [the Mahdi] it deceives those who dwell on earth, telling them to make an image for the beast that was wounded by the sword and yet lived.

For Islam to be the primary vehicle that Satan will use to achieve his goals, which it is specifically tailored to do, Satan needs it to be as prophetically close to the word of God as he can get it, in order to fool as many Christians as possible. However, with the roles of protagonists and antagonists reversed, the main bad guy can't be the *real* Jesus because the real Jesus will be the one to put an end to all End Times conflict when He arrives.

I don't think Satan has enough confidence (or self-deception) to know for sure that he will win this match, but he still wants to deceive as many souls as possible, win or lose. Therefore, in order for Satan to guarantee the most successful deception, he needs his own bad guy to play the part of the Dajjal Antichrist, and this false flag bad guy must be convincing enough to even convince Christians that he *is* the Antichrist in the Bible. In some respects, he *might actually be* the Antichrist in the Bible, as I have shown above.

At the same time, if anyone is to consider the Mahdi a good guy, he has to be the one to defeat this Antichrist character and save the world. He can't do this with the real Jesus, but he can certainly do it if he installs a fake Antichrist of his own. This isn't a problem for Satan because he has had plenty of practice establishing Antichrists throughout the millennia.

Concerning this entire false flag scenario, I believe scripture alludes to it in Revelation (12:4) and in the book of Daniel (8:10–12). This main battle between a northern and southern kingdom, which appears to involve otherworldly participants (the host and stars) will catapult the Antichrist (Mahdi) to global fame.

> **Daniel 8:10–12** [Bold emphasis added]
> It grew great, even to the **host of heaven**. And **some of the host** and **some of the stars** it **threw down to the ground and trampled on them**. It became great, even as great as the Prince of the host. And the regular burnt offering was taken away from him, and the place of his sanctuary was overthrown. And a host will be given over to it together with the regular burnt offering because of transgression, and it will throw truth to the ground, and it will act and prosper.

> **Revelation 12:4** [bold emphasis and bracketed comments added]
> **His [the devil's] tail swept down a third of the stars of heaven** and cast them to the earth. And **the dragon [the devil]** stood before the woman who was about to

> give birth, so that when she bore her child he might devour it.

Interestingly, at least one Hadith lays out this false flag scenario exactly as I have theorized; it is one of the main signs of the End Times, a.k.a. the Last Hour, according to the Hadiths (Bukhari 9:88:237).

> **Bukhari 9:88:237** [bold emphasis added]
> Allah's Apostle said, **"The Hour will not be established (1) till two big groups fight each other whereupon there will be a great number of casualties on both sides and they will be following one and the same religious doctrine**, (2) till about thirty Dajjals (liars) appear, and each one of them will claim that he is Allah's Apostle, (3) till the religious knowledge is taken away (by the death of Religious scholars) …

This false flag war is also succinctly spoken of in Daniel 11:5–34, which documents the centuries of conflict among Muslim rivalries, concerning a king of the north and a king of the south. As for Israel, the "glorious land" (Daniel 11:16, 11:41), it is unfortunately stuck in the middle of this conflict.

Near the end of Daniel 11, the final confrontation describes the Mahdi Antichrist king of the north invading the south. This is the lengthiest Bible excerpt in this book, but I feel it is worth including this entire passage, along with my bracketed comments, because it makes the entire false flag scenario very clear, showing how the Dajjal Antichrist fits into the picture with the Mahdi Antichrist.

> **Daniel 11:27–45** [bold emphasis and bracketed comments added]
> **And as for the two kings, their hearts shall be bent on doing evil [they are both Antichrists].** They

shall **speak lies at the same table [treaties, etc., routinely broken, which is common among Islamic nations]**, but to no avail, for the end is yet to be at the time appointed. And he shall return to his land with great wealth, but **his heart shall be set against the holy covenant [the king of the north will have an agreement with Israel, which he plans to violate]**. And he shall work his will and return to his own land. "**At the time appointed [the End Times] he [the Mahdi, king of the north]** shall return and come into the south, but it shall not be this time as it was before. For ships of Kittim shall come against him, and **he shall be afraid and withdraw, and shall turn back and be enraged and take action against the holy covenant [he will violate his agreement with Israel]**. He shall turn back and pay attention to those who forsake the holy covenant. **Forces from him [the Mahdi Antichrist] shall appear and profane the temple and fortress, and shall take away the regular burnt offering. And they shall set up the abomination that makes desolate**. He shall seduce with flattery those who violate the covenant **[the Mahdi will be very convincing and not even need war to win over some nations]**, but the people who know their God shall stand firm and take action. And the wise among the people shall make many understand, though for some days they shall stumble by sword and flame, by captivity and plunder **[this is a time for great persecution against Christians and Jews]**. When they stumble, **they shall receive a little help, [perhaps the two witnesses here, as well as angels]**. And many shall join themselves to them with flattery **[those who are not serious about their faith will cave in to the Mahdi's deception]**, and some of the wise shall stumble, so that they may be refined, purified, and made white **[perhaps some people initially cave in to the Mahdi's threats/deceptions, but then they come to their senses, such as the Muslims who flee Mecca and Medina]** until the time of the end, for it still awaits the appointed time.

"And the king **[Mahdi]** shall do as he wills. **He [the Mahdi] shall exalt himself and magnify himself above every god, and shall speak astonishing things against the God of gods [at this point, the Mahdi is making adjustments to Islam to accommodate his claims. The False Prophet will assist in this process. A Shiite Mahdi will have a greater advantage at doing this because he places greater emphasis on prophets following Muhammad. Islamic eschatology (End Times prophecy) is standard doctrine for Shiites, but not for Sunni]**. He shall prosper till the indignation is accomplished; for what is decreed shall be done. **He shall pay no attention to the gods of his fathers [again diverting from traditional Islam], or to the one beloved by women [he could care less about women]**. He shall not pay attention to any other god, for he shall magnify himself above all. He shall honor the god of fortresses **[this is probably related to his source of power, which I think will be a New Age flavor of Islam with otherworldly allies, including the False Prophet]**, instead of these. A god whom his fathers did not know he shall honor with gold and silver, with precious stones and costly gifts. **He shall deal with the strongest fortresses with the help of a foreign god [his otherworldly allies, with highly advanced *supernatural* technology]**. Those who acknowledge him he shall load with honor. He shall make them rulers over many and shall divide the land for a price.

> **"At the time of the end, the king of the south [the Dajjal Antichrist] shall attack him, but the king of the north shall rush upon him like a whirlwind [probably like the whirlwind that swept Elijah into a sky chariot], with chariots and horsemen [again, these are probably not normal chariots; who fights with chariots these days?], and with many ships, [possibly intergalactic/inter-dimensional ships included here]**. And he shall come into countries and shall overflow and pass through. **He shall come into the glorious land [Israel]**. And **tens of thousands shall fall [the Hadiths speak of the Dajjal involved in war (Dawud 37:4281, 37:4282, 37:4283; Muslim 41:6924, 41:6930, 41:6979)]**, but **these shall be delivered out of his hand: Edom and Moab and the main part of the Ammonites [this is when the Jews in Israel escape the Antichrist, perhaps assisted by the two witnesses]**. He shall stretch out his hand against the countries, and **the land of Egypt [the Dajjal Antichrist, king of the south]** shall not escape. He shall become ruler of the treasures of gold and of silver, and all the precious things of Egypt, and the Libyans and the Cushites shall follow in his train. But news from the east and the north shall alarm him, and he shall go out with great fury to destroy and devote many to destruction. And he shall pitch his palatial tents between the sea and the glorious holy mountain. **Yet he shall come to his end, with none to help him [when Jesus arrives with the saints of heaven and puts a stop to the Great Tribulation]**.

The Mahdi Antichrist who is the king of the north will be from ancient Assyria, which is mainly modern Syria, but it could also be Lebanon. As for the lesser Dajjal Antichrist king of the south, he will come from Egypt (Daniel 11:42–43). In summation, the Mahdi

Antichrist king of the north will come from Syria, and with the help of the False Prophet, he will kill the Dajjal Antichrist king of the south in Egypt. This victory will be hailed throughout the world.

Elements of this same epic, false flag battle are also alluded to in the book of Ezekiel, with Gog, the chief prince of Meshech and Tubal, eventually invading Israel after conquering many other nations (Ezekiel 38–39).

Many Hadiths that speak of the Dajjal refer to Old Testament scriptures when they state that Noah and the prophets gave ample warnings about the Antichrist (Bukhari 4:52:290, 4:54:562, 4:55:553, 5:59:685, 8:73:194, 9:88:241, 9:93:505; Dawud 40:4738; Muslim 41:7000, 41:7014). This is true; some of those prophecies are shown above. Drawing inspiration directly from the Bible makes some Hadiths much closer to the truth than they normally would be; thus, the deception promoted in the Hadiths is even more powerful as a result.

> **Bukhari 4:52:290** [bold emphasis added]
> "I **warn you about him (i.e., Ad-Dajjal)** and there is no prophet who did not warn his nation about him, and **Noah warned his nation about him**, but I tell you a statement which no prophet informed his nation of. **You should understand that he is a one-eyed man** and Allah is not one-eyed."

It is interesting that Noah, in particular, is singled out in the Hadiths in reference to the Dajjal Antichrist and the End Times. Jesus singled out the days of Noah as well, when He said the world would return to the days of Noah in the End Times (Matthew 24:37, Luke 17:26).

Concerning the Dajjal, some of his powers and actions can fit with Jesus, as I have already explained, but others most certainly do not. For example, while Jesus has the ability to resurrect people from the dead, he would not hack a person to bits with a sword and then immediately resurrect him like some kind of street magician.

Jesus did many amazing miracles, but He never outright murdered people just to prove He could resurrect them, as the Hadiths state the Dajjal will do (Bukhari 3:30:106, 9:88:246; Muslim 41:7015, 41:7017, 41:7019). If there is any merit to these Hadiths about a resurrecting murderer, they must be speaking about the Dajjal Antichrist.

CHAPTER 8

OTHERWORLDLY INFLUENCES THROUGH THE AGES

I started this book about the coming strong delusion with a discussion about extraterrestrial life, and then I shifted my focus to the religion of Islam, which shares multiple characteristics with the Antichrist and also contains a mirror image of End Times prophecy that aligns with the Bible.

Now I will come full circle and reveal exactly how the Bible, as well as the Qur'an and Hadiths, has documented an extensive interaction of otherworldly beings in the affairs of human society since the dawn of time. That otherworldly interaction will soon come to the forefront and play a prominent role in the days to come.

8.1. The Days of Noah

Scripture has been telling us all along that we are not alone in the universe. It starts as early as Genesis chapter 1 with the definition of heaven, or more accurately, *the heavens*, because *shamayim* in Hebrew is a plural word referring to the abode of the sun, moon, and stars (Genesis 1:14–18).

> **Genesis 1:14–18** [bold emphasis and bracketed comment added]
> And God said, **"Let there be lights in the expanse of the heavens [see Strong's Enhanced Lexicon for**

shamayim] to separate the day from the night. And let them be for signs and for seasons, and for days and years, and **let them be lights in the expanse of the heavens** to give light upon the earth." And it was so. And God made the **two great lights—the greater light to rule the day and the lesser light to rule the night—and the stars**. And **God set them in the expanse of the heavens** to give light on the earth, to rule over the day and over the night, and to separate the light from the darkness. And God saw that it was good.

H8064
שׁמה שׁמים
shâmayim shâmeh
shaw-mah'-yim, shaw-meh'
The second form being dual of an unused singular; from an unused root meaning to be lofty; the sky (as aloft; the dual perhaps alluding to the visible arch in which the clouds move, as well as to the higher ether where the celestial bodies revolve): air, X astrologer, heaven (-s).

The Hebrews of ancient times understood that the heavens, or outer space, is where angels dwelled, both faithful and fallen. It is for this reason that the prophets warned the Israelites not to worship the host of heaven, and throughout scripture, the heavens are linked with angelic beings and false gods in myriad ways (Genesis 6:2–4; Job 1, 2, 38; Deuteronomy 4:19, 17:3; 2 Kings 17:16, 21:3–5; 2 Chronicles 33:3–5; Nehemiah 9:6; Jeremiah 8:2; Daniel 8:10; Acts 7:42).

The Bible consistently reiterates the same message of otherworldly beings from the cosmos involved in the affairs of humanity. At almost every pivotal junction in the affairs of humanity, there is evidence of otherworldly intervention from both fallen and faithful angels.

2 Kings 17:16 [bold emphasis and bracketed comment added]
And they abandoned all the commandments of the Lord their God, and made for themselves metal images of two calves; and they made an Asherah and **worshiped all the host of heaven and served Baal [notice the worship of the host of heaven is linked to serving Baal, a demonic entity]**.

Nehemiah 9:6 [bold emphasis and bracketed comments added]
"You are the Lord, you alone. **You have made heaven [shamayim or outer space]** the **heaven of heavens [the third heaven, probably a glorified planet]**, with **all their host [life forms]**, **the earth** and **all that is on it**, **the seas** and **all that is in them**; and you preserve all of them; and **the host of heaven [angelic beings among the stars, and possibly other lower life forms] worships you**."

As Nehemiah 9:6 states so succinctly, the heavens are populated with life. I believe the "host of heaven" refers to angels, as well as other life forms that might not be angels, but they have to be intelligent, sentient beings in order to *worship* God. I am a Christian, and I believe in the existence of extraterrestrial life, not just because of the stories I heard or even what I have seen with my own eyes, but mostly because of what I read in the Bible.

On the very first day I started reading the Bible after I became a born again Christian, I immediately pictured the days of Noah as an incredible sci-fi/fantasy film. That Russell Crowe movie about Noah (2014) was based on the Kabballah. Too bad. I think if they had used the Bible, it could've been a lot like one of those planets in *Star Wars* and actually be highly accurate. There were all sorts of freaky hybrids running around back then (all flesh was corrupted, Genesis 6:12), and some probably had supernatural power just as the ancient texts indicate. The book of Enoch, chapter 7, should have been the source for that movie, not the Kabbalah.

Enoch dates to Genesis chapters 5 and 6, describing the days of Noah. The otherworldly Watchers descended from the heavens and interacted with humanity, exactly like an episode of *Star Trek* in which they blew off the prime directive. It's the same thing, with only one key difference. In *Star Trek*, it's all about science and evolution, and God is a question mark. In reality, however, God's throne is on a glorified planet; all the angels know exactly where it is, and they make a point to travel there and worship Him in person on a regular basis.

There is no greater pleasure, no greater joy, than being in the direct manifest presence of God, the Creator of the universe. No one can ever fully explain Him. He is still very much a mystery to the angels of heaven, but at the same time, they *know* Him. He is very personal and loving without bounds.

Concerning Enoch, exactly what happened to him? One minute, he's hanging out with the Watchers, and the next minute …

> **Genesis 5:20–53**
> Enoch walked with God, and he was not, for God took him.

God physically snatched Enoch off the earth and took him to heaven. Some speculate that he could have vanished, but why would that be the case when the prophet Elijah was taken to heaven in a flying angelic chariot later on (2 Kings 2:12), and even Jesus floated into the sky and disappeared into a cloud (Acts 1:9–11)? In the future, the two witnesses will also float up into the sky and disappear into a cloud (Revelation 11:12).

Enoch was most likely taken to heaven in an intergalactic, interdimensional spacecraft, just like them. He never physically died, and this is yet another clue about the nature of heaven. It is a real, *physical* place, integrated into the multidimensional structure of the universe. If this were not the case, physical people would not be able to go there, and there would be no point in bringing the heavenly city of New Jerusalem, with all of its angelic inhabitants and people, to the Earth in the future (Revelation 21:2). There would be no further point in a physical resurrection of the dead (1 Corinthians 15:50–53).

Some might argue that this same scripture states that flesh and blood cannot inherit the kingdom of God, but this must be a reference to *mortal* flesh and blood because there is definitely a resurrection from the dead. Our flesh will be changed, *translated* into a new, immortal nature. It should be understood, therefore, that this new nature consists of a type of atomic structure, otherwise God would not bother to resurrect our dead bodies.

> **1 Corinthians 15:50–53** [bold emphasis and bracketed comments added]
> I tell you this, brothers: **flesh and blood cannot inherit the kingdom of God**, nor does the perishable inherit the imperishable. Behold! I tell you a mystery. We shall not all sleep, but **we shall all be changed, in a moment, in the twinkling of an eye**, at the last trumpet. For the trumpet will sound, and **the dead will be raised imperishable, and we shall be changed**. For this perishable body must put on the imperishable, and **this mortal body must put on immortality**.

Until the saints are physically resurrected, they reside in heaven as disincarnate spirits, and this is probably the main reason why so many people think of heaven as a nonphysical reality. I'm fairly certain, however, that the deceased saints are looking forward to the resurrection of their physical bodies, or there would be no point in this future event.

So the days of Noah, as described in Genesis 6 and especially in the book of Enoch, are mostly about otherworldly beings interacting with humanity. The majority of these beings were evil, and they almost wiped out the entire planet. Their influence in human society was so profound as they manipulated, exploited, and perverted humanity for their own selfish pursuits, God had to start all over again.

Following the flood of Noah, where is the next pit stop that otherworldly intervention into the affairs of humanity becomes evident?

8.2. The Tower of Babel

As I have already touched on, the ancient *Epic of Gilgamesh* discloses details about what appears to be the Tower of Babel, and Gilgamesh was most likely the biblical King Nimrod in Genesis 11. Based on the epic, Gilgamesh was a Nephilim, and his purpose for building the Tower of Babel was directly related to his defiance against God.

The Epic of Gilgamesh is a downloadable PDF available at several locations on the internet, and there is also an interesting website that extracts some of the details regarding his otherworldly encounters/visions, though I certainly don't agree with Sitchin's grand conclusions.[1]

I find the clearest and most noteworthy portion of *The Epic of Gilgamesh*, on tablet 1, which states the following:

> Two thirds of him is god, one third of him is human.
> The Great Goddess [Aruru] designed (?) the model
> for his body, she prepared his form ...[2]

As the Bible indicates, the activities associated with the Tower of Babel were sinful and associated with pride. While the Bible is not specific about those details, *The Epic of Gilgamesh* fills in the gaps and gives an indication that Nephilim activity was in play in that region. The above reference even seems to indicate that Gilgamesh may have been a product of genetic engineering.

When it comes to God intervening in the affairs of humanity, He has the power to do this simply by willing things to be the way He chooses. This is how most people view *all* of the miraculous things associated with God. However, scripture gives many examples where God delegates various tasks to His angels, and in these cases, I don't rule out the use of angelic technology as a means of accomplishing various miracles.

In the case of the Tower of Babel, the scrambling of the people's language could have been accomplished by God simply willing it to happen, but it also could've been God's angels using some sort of mental manipulation technology of a devastating sort.

Trashing someone's language is a pretty trippy thing to do; so much ties into language. Culture and a fundamental way of thinking go along with the words, syntax, and linguistic variations of language. To simply zap thousands of people and alter their languages so they divide into smaller groups is quite an amazing feat.

> **Genesis 11:5–9** [bold emphasis and bracketed comments added]
>
> And the Lord came down to see the city and the tower, which the children of man had built. And the Lord said, "Behold, they are one people, and they have all one language, and **this [building a tower in defiance of God] is only the beginning of what they will do**. And nothing that they propose to do will now be impossible for them. Come, **let us [either God with some angels or the Trinity] go down and there confuse their language**, so that they may not understand one another's speech." So **the Lord dispersed them from there over the face of all the earth**, and they left off building the city. Therefore its name was called Babel because there the LORD confused the language of all the earth. And from there the Lord dispersed them over the face of all the earth.

8.3. Sodom and Gomorrah

Another pivotal point in human history was the time of the great patriarch Abraham when God established his covenant with him. God guided Abraham to the land of Canaan, where it just so happened to be that Nephilim activity was at an all-time high. I don't think this was a coincidence. The corruption in the area was so extreme that God destroyed a total of four cities on the southern side of the Dead Sea (which might not have been the Dead Sea at that time but rather a freshwater oasis before this event).

God knew the Nephilim would continue to infest that area, so He had Abraham establish a stronghold there to keep otherworldly forces at bay.

The cities of Sodom, Gomorrah, Admah, and Zeboiim were wiped off the face of the earth (Genesis 14:2). The nearby city of Bela (Zoar) was spared because it was not as corrupt as the others (Genesis 15:16).[3]

Back in 2005, archaeologist Steve Collins found these cities.[4] Even today, the area is so packed with sulfur that the rocks are flammable at the light of a match.[5]

8.4. Jacob's Ladder

Not long after the destruction of Sodom and Gomorrah, Abraham's son Isaac insisted that his son Jacob not choose a wife from the daughters of Canaan (Genesis 28:1). I don't think this was racism; I think there was more to it. Many of those daughters of Canaan *weren't entirely human.*

Later on, Jacob, Abraham's grandson, received a vision from God. While I know dreams are symbolic in nature, and Jacob may very well have seen what appears to be a normal ladder, could it be that Jacob's ladder actually resembled an intergalactic spaceport? The fact that he called that place "the gate of heaven" stands out to me.

Along with this vision, he received a message from God concerning his destiny. Basically put, his descendants would spread all over the face of the earth from this place, and through them, Jesus would eventually be born and save the world. Concerning his mandate to maintain a presence in this specific geographic region, God declared that He would bring Jacob back to that area, and He would not leave him until this was accomplished. This was a prophetic promise that God gave to Jacob, regarding the angelic help the Israelites would receive in the future in order to wipe out the remaining Nephilim in the land of Canaan.

> **Genesis 28:11–17** [bold emphasis and bracketed comments added]
>
> And he [Jacob/Israel] came to a certain place and stayed there that night, because the sun had set. Taking one of the stones of the place, he put it under his head and lay down in that place to sleep. **And he dreamed, and behold, there was a ladder set up on the earth, and the top of it reached to heaven. And behold, the angels of God were ascending and descending on it!** And behold, **the Lord stood above it and said,** "I am the Lord, the God of Abraham your father and the God of Isaac. **The land on which you lie I will give to you and to your offspring.** Your offspring shall be like the dust of the earth, and you shall spread abroad to the west and to the east and to the north and to the south, and **in you and your offspring shall all the families of the earth be blessed. Behold, I am with you and will keep you wherever you go, and will bring you back to this land. For I will not leave you until I have done what I have promised you."** Then Jacob awoke from his sleep and said, "Surely the Lord is in this place, and I did not know it." And he was afraid and said, "How awesome is this place! This is none other than the house of God, and **this is the gate of heaven.**"

Every time I read this passage, I'm reminded just how hard core Jacob was; he would've been right at home in the infantry, using *a rock* for his pillow.

8.5. Moses, Egypt, and the Exodus

Just as God hinted to Jacob, the Israelites were detoured from their residency in the promised land of Canaan. A famine struck the land, which sent the Israelites off on a wild tangent into the land of Egypt for the next four hundred years. This wasn't an accident. Egypt was yet another hotbed of Nephilim activity. Just look at its advanced knowledge and technology still evident today, four thousand years later. Look at its hieroglyphs, packed with stories about the gods. I wouldn't be surprised if many of the hieroglyphics of half-humanoid, half-animal hybrids were real creatures that lived in that area. The book of Enoch indicates as much.

Egyptian mythos fits the typical pattern of Watcher/Nephilim activity. The confrontation between God and satanic forces, waged through Moses and Pharaoh, is yet another indication that a great deal of otherworldly activity was going on in that region. God inflicted ten plagues on Egypt to which the sorcerers of Egypt were able to replicate, at least on a smaller level, up to the fourth plague. Egyptian sorcerers were in touch with demonic powers operating in that area.

What did God do in Egypt? He set the record straight. He wasn't pleased with the Egyptians worshipping imposters and enslaving His people; it was wretched and going nowhere fast. Egypt reached the height of its civilization, and at the same time, it was an immoral cesspool, and God used the Israelites to put an end to it.

While the Israelites escaped Egypt, a pillar of cloud at day and a pillar of fire at night kept the Egyptian forces at bay and split the Red Sea in half. This was not a natural phenomenon as some have suggested, regarding the possibility of a fierce wind that could blow the water in one direction. Scripture states that the Israelites crossed on dry ground with a *wall of water on each side* of them. What's more, this wind was clearly not affecting the Israelites because a wind that is powerful enough to split the Red Sea in half would also be strong enough to swipe everything else out of the way, including people. That isn't what happened; therefore, the wind in question was more like a force field projected specifically against the water, and avoiding the people.

> **Exodus 13:21**
> And the Lord went before them **by day in a pillar of cloud** to lead them along the way, and **by night in a pillar of fire to give them light, that they might travel by day and by night**.
>
> **Exodus 14:19–22** [bold emphasis added]
> Then the **angel of God who was going before the host of Israel** moved and went behind them, and **the pillar of cloud** moved from before them and stood behind them, **coming between the host of Egypt and the host of Israel**. And **there was the cloud and the darkness. And it lit up the night without one coming near the other all night**. Then Moses stretched out his hand over the sea, and **the Lord drove the sea back by a strong east wind all night and made the sea dry land, and the waters were divided**. And the people of Israel went into the midst of the sea on **dry ground**, the waters being **a wall to them on their right hand and on their left**.

Again I emphasize that while scripture attributes this miracle to God, the presence of the strangely shaped cloud at day, which also emanated light (fire) at night, says to me that God sent His angels to take care of this task. God was most likely with them, and Exodus 14:19 even states that the angel of God moved and the pillar of cloud moved, indicating that the two were independent of one another.

Perhaps God sometimes entered that pillar spacecraft to join His angels, and other times He was outside of it. Either way, the pillar was obviously technology, amazing technology that we can't match to this day. At the same time, this is God in these scriptures, the real God who created the universe. He doesn't need technology, but His angels do because they appear to be using it in these passages of scripture.

8.6. Israel in the Desert

While in the desert, Moses climbed the Mountain of God, and received the Ten Commandments from God. What did this look like?

> **Exodus 24:9–18**
> Then Moses and Aaron, Nadab, and Abihu, and seventy of the elders of Israel went up, and **they saw the God of Israel. There was under his feet as it were a pavement of sapphire stone, like the very heaven for clearness. And he did not lay his hand on the chief men of the people of Israel; they beheld God, and ate and drank** [wow, dinner with God, how cool is that?]. **The Lord said to Moses, "Come up to me on the mountain and wait there, that I may give you the tablets of stone, with the law and the commandment, which I have written for their instruction."** So Moses rose with his assistant Joshua and Moses went up into the mountain of God. And he said to the elders, "Wait here for us until we return to you. And behold, Aaron and Hur are with you. Whoever has a dispute, let him go to them." Then Moses went up on the mountain, and the cloud covered the mountain. **The glory of the Lord dwelt on Mount Sinai**, and the **cloud covered it six days.** And on the seventh day he called to Moses out of the midst of the cloud. **Now the appearance of the glory of the Lord was like a devouring fire on the top of the mountain** in the sight of the people of Israel. **Moses entered the cloud** and went up on the

> mountain. **And Moses was on the mountain forty days and forty nights.**

The preincarnate Jesus is an enigmatic being, full of wonder and mystery. Jesus stated that no one has seen the face of God (John 6:46), and He was referring to His Father. The apostle John reiterated this to emphasize the point (John 1:18, 1 John 4:12). God the Father is *invisible*, but the Son is the Father's manifestation in visible form in this world because Jesus is "the image of the invisible God, the firstborn of all creation" (Colossians 1:15). This fact reconciles these scriptures about no one ever seeing God with other scriptures where people obviously did see God; He was simply the preincarnate Jesus.

> **Colossians 1:15**
> He is the image of the invisible God, the firstborn of all creation.

> **1 John 4:12** [bold emphasis and bracketed comments added]
> No one has ever seen God [the Father]; if we love one another, God abides in us and his love is perfected in us.

> **John 1:18** [bold emphasis and bracketed comments added]
> No one has ever seen God [the Father]; the only God [Jesus], who is at the Father's side, he has made him known.

> **John 6:46**
> It is written in the Prophets, "And they will all be taught by God." Everyone who has heard and learned from the Father comes to me—not that anyone has seen the Father except he who is from God; he has seen the Father.

On top of Mount Sinai, Moses spent some quality time with God (the preincarnate Jesus), and probably a group of His faithful angels as well. I'm pretty sure Moses entered a powerful, intergalactic, interdimensional spacecraft and enjoyed his stay there, utterly fascinated by everything he saw and experienced.

Moses was given all sorts of instructions about how the Israelites should treat each other ethically. God established His laws with Moses, and the Mosaic Law was unlike anything the world had ever known. It was far different from the many pagan mythologies that spanned the globe, some even mandating the sacrifice of their children and institutionalized prostitution.

Moses was also told how to construct the Ark of the Covenant, among other things (Exodus 25). The ark served as a conduit for God's power, by which God communicated with Moses (Exodus 25:22). The Israelites carried it with them wherever they went, roughly a half mile ahead of the group (Joshua 3:4). It was used to part the Jordan River (Joshua 3:15–16, 4:7–18) and was nothing short of a weapon of mass destruction when the Philistines once captured it in battle (1 Samuel 5).

Shortly after all this amazing stuff with God at the mountain, God told Moses to send out a recon team to the land of Canaan (Numbers 13). What they discovered blew them away. While they were off on a four-hundred-year detour in Egypt, their home was invaded by the Nephilim. These beings were like cockroaches; wiping them out in the flood of Noah slowed them down a bit, but they returned with a vengeance. These Nephilim giants were so formidable that the Israelites were terrified to enter their Promised Land, even in spite of eating dinner with God and witnessing the massive glowing column in the sky every single day!

As a result of their lack of faith (or *trust* in this case because they even *saw* God; they *knew* He existed), God would not allow that generation to enter the Promised Land. For forty years, the Israelites wandered the desert with that mysterious column floating in the sky above them, tending to their needs and providing them with food and water.

Even the food that God provided, *manna*, was a highly advanced technology. There was always the right amount, and it had only enough preservatives in it to last one day—unless it was the day before the Sabbath, in which case it lasted through the Sabbath (Exodus 16:16–35). If we had a sample of the manna today, I suspect we would discover it had the perfect amount of nutrients with all the essential fats, proteins, carbs, calories, vitamins, minerals, and things we don't even know exist yet, all of which would constitute a perfect diet.

8.7. Entering the Promised Land

Upon entering the Promised Land, the Israelites were instructed to drive out the Canaanites. Canaan had been festering with Nephilim for forty years, so by the time the Israelites finally crossed the Jordan River, those Nephilim were everywhere.

Now, when the Israelites left Egypt forty years prior, it must have created quite a stir in the surrounding nations. Moses, an obscure desert nomad, wandered out of the barren wasteland and confronted Pharaoh, the most powerful king in his day. "Let my people go," he declared to the king's face.

"Who sent you?" queried Pharaoh, probably thinking this desert vagrant baked his brains out in the sun.

"I AM sent me. I know, trippy name, huh? But you better listen, or things are going to go south really quick."

And thus the ten plagues of Egypt commenced, providing a spectacle to the world. They ended with Egypt releasing its entire slave labor force, but then waffling after that decision was made and tearing off after them with an army of chariots. Then the most amazing thing happened: the Red Sea split in half, and the Israelites crossed on dry ground. When Pharaoh's army had the tenacity to pursue them, wham! In one fatal swoop, they were completely decimated.

After this outlandish demonstration of power, otherworldly miracles surrounded the Israelites for forty years in the desert, with a column of fire hovering above them in the night sky. Then, just in case anyone forgot about the Red Sea incident, God decided a little reminder was in order. When the Israelites entered the Promised Land, God split the Jordan River so the Israelites could cross on dry ground.

This miracle was an act of mercy aimed at the Canaanites; God was reminding them what they were up against. In military terms, this is called a *show of force*, and it serves the explicit purpose of minimizing casualties. In this case, however, I think it served the purpose of dividing the wheat from the tares. What do I mean by this?

One would think that the inhabitants of Jericho would have hightailed it out of there after seeing all these ridiculous displays of power, but no, they held fast, defiant in the face of all those miracles coming their way. Why is that?

Could it be that some among them were powerful Nephilim imbued with supernatural power and worshipped as gods, or maybe they even had otherworldly allies they thought might bail them out? Obviously they had to have a lot of faith in *something* to think they could defy a group of people who crossed the Jordan River on dry ground. How else does one explain their complacent attitude with the audacious miracles surrounding the Israelites?

Jericho, the formidable walled city fortress of Canaan, was the first city the Israelites attacked, and it was leveled to the ground with the mere blowing of trumpets. This was the most astounding defeat of a city anyone had ever seen. It's no mistake that this powerful stronghold was the first place the Israelites attacked; doing this was another show of force, but those Canaanites remained entrenched in the land of Canaan, refusing to budge. For many years after this, the Israelites battled the Canaanites, and in many of those battles, they fought the Nephilim.

8.8. The Prophets of Old

The Nephilim were problematic for the Israelites throughout the time of the judges and also after Israel made the transition from judges to kings. During this time, God continued to send His prophets through the ages to guide mankind. These prophets served as intermediaries between humanity and God, who often worked through His angels.

8.8.1 Nephilim Confrontations

Who hasn't heard of King David's battle against Goliath, the nine-and-a-half-foot-tall freak with six fingers on each hand and six toes on each foot (1 Samuel 17:4–7)? Goliath wasn't the only one who fit this description. Someone named Elhanan also killed a giant with six fingers on each hand and six toes on each foot (2 Samuel 21:20, 1 Chronicles 20:5–6).

I have found that when it comes to Goliath's height, there is considerable debate among scholars concerning variations in ancient manuscripts. Most scholars believe that Goliath was six and a half feet tall rather than nine and a half. I personally think the nine-and-a-half-foot-tall manuscript is the accurate one. King Og's bed was about thirteen feet long (Deuteronomy 3:11), yet all the websites I found with scholars downplaying Goliath's height leave out this reference to King Og.[6–7]

Something that also is commonly overlooked in these debates is that Goliath had six fingers on each hand and six toes on each foot, and Goliath wasn't the only giant with this characteristic. With the two instances of this I quoted above, scripture indicates this may have been a normal characteristic for the Nephilim.

While polydactylism (extra digits) is not that uncommon, mostly due to inbreeding,[8] I think it's noteworthy to see two examples of it with a perfect distribution of digits (six fingers on each hand and six toes on each foot, as opposed to just one hand, one foot, only hands, or only feet).

Interestingly, the famous alien autopsy video associated with Area 51 features an alien with six fingers on each hand, and devices in the alien spacecraft associated with the autopsy show handprint mold mechanisms with six fingers, indicating this is a normal characteristic for at least one species of gray aliens. The Mona Lisa moon-base extraterrestrial also had six fingers.[9]

Whether Goliath was a real giant or not, a great many theologians blatantly excuse the fact that scripture clearly says the Nephilim were sired from angelic beings crossing with humans, and countless other details surround them that give clear evidence of their otherworldly origins.

To these squabbles over Goliath's height, I say these theologians don't know the half of it. If they could just catch a glimpse of what was really going on back in ancient times, their jaws would drop to such an extent that it would take a surgeon to reattach them. If they were there to dine with God, if they saw the column in the sky above Israel and crossed the Red Sea with the Israelites, or if they joined Enoch in one of his many visitations with the Watchers, they would no doubt stop debating about how tall Goliath was.

The ancient world was very different from today in many ways. From the astronomical ages of antediluvian people (the people of Noah's day lived to be several hundred years old on average) to otherworldly visitors, miracles and the practice of magic, and the wide variety of Nephilim present on the earth, the ancient world resembled J. R. R. Tolkien's *Lord of the Rings* more than any would ever expect.

I believe there really were giants, just as the Bible says, and no, they were not six-and-a-half-foot giants. The Nephilim were *giants*, no kidding.

Pretty much every time I search the internet for any new findings on Nephilim, I see more discoveries that have been made and new websites, such as www.6000Years.org.[10] It's true that there are numerous hoaxes, most of which are easily debunked photos, but some are not so easily dismissed, even by experts. Some are also definitely real, such as the twenty-inch skull found in Peru.[11]

What does our trustworthy friend Snopes.com have to say about these things? Snopes simply declares that they are *all fake*, period. For proof, it cites a biologist's argument about the so-called square-cube law.

> In any case, we don't need to know the specific origins of these photos to definitively determine that they're fakes. The square-cube law makes it a physical impossibility that humanoids of the size represented by these bones could ever have existed.[12]

I don't claim to be an expert in biology, but I do know there is an extinct species of gorilla, Gigantopithecus, that stood up to ten feet tall, and this species coexisted with humans at one point.[13] How is it a biological impossibility for people to reach this stature when we have the fossils of gorillas that have? Exactly why does the square-cube law apply only to humans and not gorillas?

I realize there are a lot of hoaxes out there, and Snopes points out several photos that have been exposed as hoaxes, but to simply declare that *every single* picture and reported discovery of giant humans is false, based on a biological "rule" that is not applied logically or consistently, is arrogant and preposterous.

8.8.2 Chariots of Fire

Giants are not the only otherworldly aspect of ancient times that carried over into the age of the kings of Israel and Judah in the Old Testament. Scripture gives many other examples of otherworldly interactions between heavenly beings and people.

Elisha, the prophet of God, along with his servant, saw an entire armada of sky chariots on one occasion; they were apparently cloaked from normal eyesight (2 Kings 6:14–22). This is a fascinating story because these sky chariots did not use any kind of conventional warfare that we can imagine. These sky chariots somehow altered the consciousness of an entire army, with a much smaller version of the mental tweaking that occurred at the Tower of Babel.

Here, the angels made an entire army susceptible to the power of suggestion to such an extent that Elisha led them directly into enemy territory, where they were forced to surrender without a single casualty. This narrative may very well be the source that inspired

George Lucas's idea for the "Jedi mind trick" because that is exactly what happened.

> **2 Kings 6:14–22** [bold emphasis and bracketed comments added]
> So he sent their horses and chariots and a great army, and they came by night and surrounded the city. **When the servant of the man of God [Elisha] rose early in the morning** and went out, behold, **an army with horses and chariots was all around the city**. And the servant said, "Alas, my master! What shall we do?" He said, "**Do not be afraid, for those who are with us are more than those who are with them.**" Then Elisha prayed and said, "O Lord, please **open his eyes that he may see [the sky chariots were cloaked from normal vision]**." So the Lord opened the eyes of the young man, and he saw, and behold, **the mountain was full of horses and chariots of fire all around Elisha**. And when the Syrians came down against him, Elisha prayed to the Lord and said, "**Please strike this people with blindness**." So **he struck them with blindness** in accordance with the prayer of Elisha. **And Elisha said to them, "This is not the way, and this is not the city [in other words, these are not the droids you are looking for]. Follow me, and I will bring you to the man whom you seek."** And he led them to Samaria. As soon as they entered Samaria, Elisha said, "O Lord, open the eyes of these men [so] that they may see." So **the Lord opened their eyes and they saw, and behold, they were in the midst of Samaria**. As soon as the king of Israel saw them, he said to Elisha, "My father, shall I strike them down? **Shall I strike them down?**" He answered, "**You shall not strike them down. Would you strike down those whom you**

> **have taken captive with your sword and with your bow? Set bread and water before them [so] that they may eat and drink and go to their master."**

As I said before, the first time I read the Bible it was like reading the *Lord of the Rings* and *Star Wars*, all rolled up in one. Elisha was a Jedi knight!

This wasn't the first time Elisha was in the company of sky chariots. Earlier, he watched as Elijah was beamed up in a "whirlwind" into a flying chariot of fire, with horses of fire (2 Kings 2:11). This most likely also happened with Enoch earlier on (Hebrews 11:5). The same thing could have happened with Moses as well, both on the Mountain of God and after he died.

Scripture states that God buried Moses (Deuteronomy 34:6), yet Moses was with Elijah when he met with Jesus on the Mount of Transfiguration (Matthew 17:3). Why would Elijah be a physical person and Moses a ghost? Some consider the possibility that God sent the archangel Michael to return for Moses, resurrect him, and bring him to heaven later on. Why else would Satan enter a heated argument with Michael about the body of Moses (Jude 1:9)?

> **Jude 1:9** [bold emphasis added]
> But when **the archangel Michael, contending with the devil, was disputing about the body of Moses,** he did not presume to pronounce a blasphemous judgment, but said, "The Lord rebuke you."

Angelic armies with their "chariots of God" were further reported by the prophet King David, as well as the prophet Isaiah. I think Isaiah saw something in the End Times in his visions.

> **Psalm 68:17**
> The chariots of God are twice ten thousand, thousands upon thousands; the Lord is among them; Sinai is now in the sanctuary.

> **Isaiah 66:15**
> "For behold, the Lord will come in fire, and his chariots like the whirlwind, to render his anger in fury, and his rebuke with flames of fire."

A flying chariot might have parked outside when the archangel Gabriel arrived to give his prophecies to Daniel (Daniel 9:21, 10:13). Since these sky chariots have advanced cloaking, pretty much any instance of angelic visitation can include them, though that may not always be the case. Gabriel is a pretty powerful dude; he might be like the Q in *Star Trek* and not need a sky chariot.

The prophet Zechariah also saw strange things, such as a flying scroll (Zechariah 5:2) and flying chariots with colored horses (Zechariah 6), but his visions tend to read more like dreams than actual encounters with physical manifestations of angels. I find this to be one of the difficulties that comes with interpreting scripture.

When it comes to dreams, images may be strange and clearly symbolic, such as the various beasts mentioned in the books of Daniel and Revelation. They do translate to literal meanings, but the images themselves are dreamlike. However, in most passages that refer to sky chariots, as well as interactions with angels and God, those are usually not dreams. A dream *did not* take Elijah to heaven. On most occasions, the Old Testament prophets actually saw and spoke with literal angels standing right in front of them, as if they were *real physical people*. These were physical manifestations while they were fully awake and going about their business during any given day or night.

Zechariah's visions do not fall into this category of physical manifestations; however, I don't rule him out. He definitely saw the future, and I wouldn't be surprised if he interacted with angels and saw elements of their technology as well.

8.8.3 King Solomon's Jinns

As I studied the Qur'an and Hadiths regarding End Times prophecy, a number of passages in the Qur'an and Hadiths that refer to otherworldly beings interacting with humanity did not escape my attention. Among them are some unusual details about King Solomon.

Scripture states that King Solomon was the wisest king who ever lived (1 Kings 4:29–34). Unfortunately, much of his wisdom had to do with ruling as a king, and it was linked more to his intelligence than to his love for God because scripture states that his heart turned away from God.

> **1 Kings 11:1–11** [bold emphasis added]
> Now King Solomon loved many foreign women, along with the daughter of Pharaoh: Moabite, Ammonite, Edomite, Sidonian, and Hittite women, from the nations concerning which the Lord had said to the people of Israel, "You shall not enter into marriage with them, neither shall they with you, for surely they will turn away your heart after their gods." Solomon clung to these in love. He had 700 wives, princesses, and 300 concubines. And **his wives turned away his heart**. For **when Solomon was old his wives turned away his heart after other gods**, and his heart was not wholly true to the Lord his God, as was the heart of David his father. For **Solomon went after Ashtoreth the goddess of the Sidonians, and after Milcom the abomination of the Ammonites**. So Solomon did what was evil in the sight of the Lord and did not wholly follow the Lord, as David his father had done. Then **Solomon built a high place for Chemosh the abomination of Moab**, and **for Moloch the abomination of the Ammonites**, on the mountain east of Jerusalem. **And so he did for all his**

> **foreign wives, who made offerings and sacrificed to their gods**. And **the Lord was angry with Solomon, because his heart had turned away from the Lord, the God of Israel, who had appeared to him twice and had commanded him concerning this thing, that he should not go after other gods**. But he did not keep what the Lord commanded. Therefore the Lord said to Solomon, "Since this has been your practice and you have not kept my covenant and my statutes that I have commanded you, I will surely tear the kingdom from you and will give it to your servant."

God appeared to King Solomon twice. Later, when Solomon completed the building of the Tabernacle of God, he sacrificed to the Lord, and fire came down from heaven and burned the sacrifice in front of all the people of Israel. God's glory then filled the tabernacle with such force that the priests could not enter it. King Solomon witnessed all of this.

> **2 Chronicles 7:1–4** [bold emphasis added]
> As soon as Solomon finished his prayer, **fire came down from heaven and consumed the burnt offering and the sacrifices**, and **the glory of the Lord filled the temple. And the priests could not enter the house of the Lord, because the glory of the Lord filled the Lord's house**. When **all the people of Israel saw the fire come down and the glory of the Lord on the temple**, they bowed down with their faces to the ground on the pavement and worshiped and gave thanks to the Lord, saying, "For he is good, for his steadfast love endures forever." Then the king and all the people offered sacrifice before the Lord.

In light of all of this revelation, how is it that King Solomon turned away from God?

I suspect that pride was the primary culprit. Something similar happened to many other rulers of the past, all of which followed the template established by Satan/Lucifer. Satan/Lucifer was a king at one time, an angelic king over an angelic kingdom in an earlier version of the Garden of Eden that existed before Adam and Eve were created (Ezekiel 28, Isaiah 14). Satan was involved in trade, he became rich and powerful, and he was exceptionally intelligent and probably talented in almost every way. All of this led to his exceeding pride, and in that pride he rebelled against God.

King Solomon followed the same pattern.

Solomon was also involved in trade (1 Kings 10:22), and he became exceedingly rich, powerful, and wise. God gave specific instructions to the Israelites not to multiply wives to themselves (Deuteronomy 17:17), but Solomon thought he knew better. Later on, a combination of his wives' beliefs, his curiosity, and his prideful overconfidence led him down the slippery slope of pagan practices until he was deeply involved in the worship of false gods.

What exactly does the Qur'an say about King Solomon, especially with respect to worshipping false gods?

For starters, the Qur'an does not say anything *negative* about King Solomon whatsoever, especially with respect to false gods or apostasy. The Qur'an only praises Solomon for his wisdom and accomplishments (Qur'an 27:15), and it states that he went to heaven when he died (Qur'an 38:39–40).

The Bible also says good things about Solomon but exposes his fatal flaws, which led to his apostasy. The Bible reveals these flaws about King Solomon in 1 Kings, but at the same time, the Bible also includes entire books written by King Solomon, the Songs of Solomon, and Ecclesiastes. These books, therefore, were written either before Solomon fell into sin or afterward if in fact he later repented before death, which no one really knows.

Qur'an 27:15 (Shakir)

And certainly we gave knowledge to Dawud and Sulaiman [Solomon], and they both said: Praise be to Allah, Who has made us to excel many of His believing servants.

Qur'an 38:39–40 (Mohsin Khan) [bold emphasis added]
[Saying of Allah to Sulaiman (Solomon)]: "This is our gift, so spend you or withhold, no account will be asked." And verily, **he enjoyed a near access to us, and a good final return (Paradise)**.

Concerning Solomon's wisdom and knowledge, while the Bible states that Solomon spoke *about* trees, beasts, birds, reptiles, and fish (1 Kings 4:33–34), the Qur'an states that Solomon spoke *with* birds (Qur'an 27:16), and he understood the speech of ants (Qur'an 27:18–19). He also had supernatural beings, known as *jinns*, serve him as soldiers (Qur'an 27:16). Some suggest that Muhammad was inspired by the Talmud regarding these stories.[14]

1 Kings 4:33–34
He spoke of trees, from the cedar that is in Lebanon to the hyssop that grows out of the wall. He spoke also of beasts, and of birds, and of reptiles, and of fish. And people of all nations came to hear the Wisdom of Solomon, and from all the kings of the earth, who had heard of his wisdom.

Qur'an 27:16 (Shakier) [bold emphasis added]
And Sulaiman was Dawud's heir, and he said: O men! **We have been taught the language of birds**, and we have been given all things; most surely this is manifest grace. And **gathered for Solomon were his soldiers of the jinn and men and birds**, and **they were [marching] in rows**. And **his hosts of the jinn and the men and the birds were gathered to him, and they were formed into groups**.

> **Qur'an 27:18–19 (Mohsin Khan)** [bold emphasis added]
> Till, when **they came to the valley of the ants, one of the ants said: "O ants! Enter your dwellings, lest Sulaiman (Solomon) and his hosts crush you**, while they perceive not." So he [Sulaiman **(Solomon)**] **smiled, amused at her speech and said: "My Lord! Inspire and bestow upon me the power and ability that I may be grateful for Your Favors** which You have bestowed on me and on my parents, and that I may do righteous good deeds that will please You, and admit me by Your Mercy among Your righteous slaves."

These are some bizarre stories, and paramount among them is Solomon commanding jinn soldiers.

There's more than meets the eye about these jinns. The Qur'an gives a peculiar statement about Solomon controlling the wind in such a way that he was able to make a two-months' journey in a single day and night (Qur'an 34:12–13). This ability is stated in the context of Solomon's affiliation with the mysterious jinns. These beings also created a "fountain of molten copper," whatever that is. The fact that this fountain is mentioned directly after Solomon's ability to travel through the wind at amazing speeds leads me to believe it is most likely the Arabic equivalent of a chariot of fire that flies through the sky.

> **Qur'an 34:12–13 (Shakir)** [bold emphasis and bracketed comments added]
> And **(We made) the wind (subservient) to Sulaiman [Solomon], which made a month's journey in the morning and a month's journey in the evening**, and **We made a fountain of molten copper to flow out for him**, and **of the jinn there were those who worked before him by the command of his Lord**;

> and **whoever turned aside from Our command from among them, We made him taste of the punishment of burning. They made for him what he pleased of fortresses and images, and bowls (large) as watering-troughs and cooking-pots that will not move from their place**; give thanks, O family of Dawud! And very few of My servants are grateful.

The Muslim tradition about Solomon's mode of travel harkens to the legend of the flying carpet, despite the fact that no carpet is mentioned in the Qur'an.[15] A long time ago, some prominent Muslim probably figured there had to be *something* that the wind was carrying that Solomon could ride on (or in), so the idea of the carpet was conceived, but the Qur'an actually speaks of a fountain. A fountain, incidentally, is usually round, and the fountain in this Qur'an surah has the appearance of molten copper. Does this not sound similar to Ezekiel's "flying wheel within a wheel, engulfed in flames" (Ezekiel 1:13–16)?

> **Ezekiel 1:13–16** [bold emphasis added]
> As for the likeness of the living creatures, **their appearance was like burning coals of fire**, like **the appearance of torches moving to and fro** among the living creatures. And **the fire was bright**, and **out of the fire went forth lightning**. And the living creatures darted to and fro, like the appearance of a **flash of lightning**. Now as I looked at the living creatures, I **saw a wheel on the earth** beside the living creatures, one for each of the four of them. As for the appearance of the **wheels** and their construction: their appearance was like the gleaming of beryl. And the four had the same likeness, their appearance and construction being as it were **a wheel within a wheel**.

Unraveling Qur'an 34:12 requires a more thorough understanding of what the jinns really are. In light of their technology, which includes flying chariots in my opinion, my guess is that these beings were either the Watchers (angels) or their Nephilim progeny, or both.

According to one Islamic website, the jinns are described like this [with bold emphasis added]:

> Islamic belief **divides sentient beings into three categories**. In order of creation, they are: **the angels** (malayka), **the hidden ones** (jinn), **and humankind** (nas or banu adam). **Angels are made out of light, jinn out of fire, men out of earth** (sometimes translated as mud or clay). **Angels are considered neither male nor female** and **have no free will. Jinn, like humans, are gendered, and have free will.** (This is why, **in Islamic thought, Satan is a jinn, not an angel**; it would be impossible for an angel to disobey the will of God.) **Jinn may be benevolent, evil, or neutral, but are generally regarded as less trustworthy and more prone to trickery than people, even if they are benign.**[16]

I don't agree with these definitions, which were most likely derived from early Gnosticism, teachings that promoted the idea that all matter is inherently evil (hence, angels *were* made of light). The Gnostics also believed a lot of other things that are not biblical.

During the days of the early Christian church, Gnostic teachings diverged from orthodox Christianity to such an extent that some theologians argue the apostle John wrote the book of 1 John to specifically address these heresies.[17] John insisted that Jesus came in the *flesh*, and anyone who taught otherwise, as the Gnostics did, was inspired by the spirit of the Antichrist (1 John 4:2–3). John's statement that this "spirit of the Antichrist" was already in the world in his day was his acknowledgement of the deception the Gnostics promoted.

> **1 John 4:2–3** [bold emphasis added]
> By this you know the Spirit of God: **every spirit that confesses that Jesus Christ has come in the flesh is from God, and every spirit that does not confess Jesus is not from God. This is the spirit of the antichrist**, which you heard was coming and now **is in the world already**.

It's ironic that Muhammad chose to import some Gnostic teachings into the Qur'an because Islam's version of heaven includes many descriptions of material wealth, a multitude of servants, and of course, an eternal orgy for all Muslim men. These all constitute a material universe and an extremely carnal one at that, which is the antithesis of Gnosticism.

Interestingly, Muhammad borrowed just enough Gnosticism to demote Jesus from the status of God and to redefine the abhorrently evil Nephilim (if the jinns are Nephilim) as neutral (rather than pure evil as the Bible states). He then abandoned Gnosticism altogether when it came to his carnal version of heaven.

Concerning the angels, I don't think they are made out of light (i.e., pure photonic energy). The Bible makes no direct statement to this effect. Describing a being as an angel of light does not necessarily mean it is *made* of light. Angels might very well *emit* light, similar to the way Moses's and perhaps Stephan's faces glowed when they were in the presence of God (Exodus 34:35, Acts 6:15), but as for their atomic structure, I think the angels were *made* just like us and were later translated into their higher angelic forms.

I also don't buy the idea that all angels are male; the Bible doesn't say this anywhere, and I think it is merely the product of a male-centric culture that the assumption is made. In the future, all females who are *saved* will be translated to be like the angels who are in heaven (Luke 20:35–36). How can they be like the angels in heaven if there are *no female angels?*

Lastly, knowing a little about AI (artificial intelligence), the greatest determining factor of true sentience is free will. Without free will, angels would be nothing more than simplistic robots, which would make them lesser than humans, not greater, as the Bible says they are (Psalm 8:5, Hebrews 2:7). To that end, all truly sentient beings have free will, including angels and jinns. What's more, the Bible gives every indication that Satan was an angel, and an extremely powerful and influential angel at that (Job 1, 2; Ezekiel 28; Isaiah 14; Revelation 12:7–9). In summation, angels most certainly have free will. There would be no such thing as a fallen angel if they didn't.

While I disagree with the above characteristics of the three categories of sentient beings outlined in the Qur'an, I do agree with some elements of these categories.

First, there are angels and there are humans, and they are intrinsically different from one another; the Bible makes this abundantly clear. Their biggest difference is angels are immortal and imbued with supernatural power, whereas humans are mortal and lacking in the supernatural department.

Secondly, there are also beings that are not as high in power, glory, or abilities as angels, yet they are highly intelligent, they are not human (at least entirely), and at least some of them exercise supernatural power. The Nephilim fit all of these characteristics. They are part angel, part human, and possibly also part angel, part animal. The jinns, therefore, can directly cross-reference to the Nephilim. They might also be defined as other forms of life that God created, which have not yet been officially identified by science. Such forms of life that are higher than humans but lower than angels could include certain extraterrestrials, or they might even be terrestrial and transdimensional for all we know. The point is the range between humans and angels is vast; the possibilities are endless.

In King Solomon's case, I believe the jinns associated with him were most likely Nephilim because scripture states that Solomon worshipped the false gods of Ashtoreth, Milcom, Chemosh, and Moloch. This fact alone establishes Solomon's possible connection with either the Watchers of Enoch, a.k.a. the sons of God of Genesis 6, or their Nephilim progeny. Since we know the Nephilim were on the earth in open contact with people back in Solomon's day, this connection is even easier to establish.

Is it such a great leap to conjecture that Solomon, one of the wisest men who ever lived, may have figured out a way to take advantage of the Nephilim, or strike an agreement with them or the Watchers?

What if Solomon learned sorcery and harnessed demonic power through sorcery? One scripture that might give a clue about this is the fact that Solomon spoke of a "silver cord" that is snapped in the context of dying (Ecclesiastes 12:1, 6–7). Astral projectors have long reported seeing a silver cord that connects their spirit bodies to their physical bodies while they are separated from them. How did Solomon know about this silver cord?

> **Ecclesiastes 12:1, 6–7** [bold emphasis added]
> **Remember also your Creator in the days of your youth**, before the evil days come and the years draw near of which you will say, "I have no pleasure in them" … **before the silver cord is snapped**, or the golden bowl is broken, or the pitcher is shattered at the fountain, or the wheel broken at the cistern, and the dust returns to the earth as it was, and the spirit returns to God who gave it.

The ability to astral project is a skill that leads to many other psychic abilities. People who learn and develop various psychic abilities eventually get to a point where they are capable of harnessing a great deal *more* power when they enter the realm of sorcery, and they learn how to overcome demonic entities and force them into servitude. This processes is documented extensively in the works of Carlos Castaneda, an anthropologist who claimed to be an apprentice of an Iroquois sorcerer back in the 1960s.[18]

Back in the day, I read a half dozen of Castaneda's books, which describe many details about the spiritual realms and sorcery, including Castaneda's battles with demons. I recall one of the conundrums that all sorcerers faced was keeping demonic powers at bay. They didn't call all of these beings demons, but their descriptions certainly aligned with demonic entities. The main way they kept their demon servants at bay was usually to pit them against each other, but sorcerers who eventually accumulated too many demons had the tendency to go insane. Suffice it to say, the life of a sorcerer was beyond chaotic.

Anyway, it seems to fit with King Solomon that he might have used the same logic of disobeying God regarding women and applied it to practicing sorcery as well. He accumulated vast knowledge, and it could be that some of that knowledge was *forbidden*. If he was a sorcerer, it's likely he was the most powerful sorcerer who ever lived because he would have been perverting God's gift of supernatural wisdom to do it. This is indeed the case if what the Qur'an says of Solomon has any merit: that he had an army of jinns under his command and used them and their technology for various means (i.e., construction projects, travel to distant lands, or even star-gazing, etc.).

I tend to believe the Qur'an's account of King Solomon on these details because it fits with the Qur'an's consistent contradiction of the Bible. For example, the Bible says that King Solomon fell into terrible sin, whereas the Qur'an counters that he did not. The Qur'an goes further to state that King Solomon had an army of jinns under his control, given to him *by the command of the Lord*. What's more, the jinns who refused to obey Solomon were burned (Qur'an 34:12–13). This sounds exactly like demonic underlings under the forced servitude of Satan, directly linked with sorcery.

This part about God giving a man control over an army of jinns (Nephilim)—powerful, supernaturally imbued, and utterly wicked beings—to use as his personal servants is something that exposes the origin of Islamic doctrine. It is actually the false gods to whom Solomon sacrificed, who would have granted him Nephilim servants, and not the God of Abraham, Isaac, and Jacob. Therefore, if Muhammad was inspired to write the Qur'an by a demonic entity, this information about King Solomon is exactly what one would expect.

Qur'an 34:12–13 (Shakir) [bold emphasis and bracketed comments added]
[O]f the jinn there were those who worked before him by the command of his Lord; and **whoever turned aside from Our command from among them, We made him taste of the punishment of burning. They made for him what he pleased of fortresses and images, and bowls (large) as watering-troughs and cooking-pots that will not move from their place**; give thanks, O family of Dawud! And very few of My servants are grateful.

8.9 Jesus's Day

When Jesus was born, the earth was once again filled with otherworldly signs and wonders. First we have the roving Star of Bethlehem, which came to rest over Jesus's house (Matthew 2:2, 2:9). This might have been an angelic flying chariot.

After this, the archangel Gabriel visited the temple of High Priest Zechariah and declared that his barren wife Elizabeth, an elderly woman at that time, would have the ability to conceive a child. When Zechariah expressed his doubts to Gabriel, Gabriel made him temporarily mute for his lack of faith (Luke 1:11–22).

When it comes to these miracles and many others in the Bible, I don't have any problem considering the possibility that God's angels used technology to make them happen. In my mind, that doesn't make them any less miraculous. The only point of miracles was to get people to believe in Jesus because He is the Son of God, the Creator of the Universe (Colossians 1:16). With that in mind, so what if angels altered the weather when Jesus rebuked the storm (Luke 8:24, Mark 4:39), and so what if angels zapped Jesus on the Sea of Galilee so He could walk on water (Matthew 14:22–33). That doesn't mean Jesus can't walk on water now that He's glorified because He can do anything now. However, when Jesus was alive before His crucifixion, He was bound by all the limitations of being human. He relied on His

Father, the Holy Spirit, and angels assigned to Him to accomplish the miracles He did (Philippians 2:5–8).

> **Philippians 2:5–8** [bold emphasis added]
> Have this mind among yourselves, which is yours in Christ Jesus, who, **though he was in the form of God, did not count equality with God a thing to be grasped, but made himself nothing, taking the form of a servant, being born in the likeness of men**. And being found in human form, **he humbled himself by becoming obedient to the point of death, even death on a cross.**

The fact that Jesus emptied Himself of His personal divine power, which is a theological concept known as *kenosis*, only makes sense. Jesus would not have truly experienced what it means to be human if He didn't do this. Jesus got hungry and tired; He experienced flatulence and defecation just like anyone else, and the list goes on. Some folks think my talking about Jesus in this manner is disrespectful, but I adamantly disagree. I think it is so far beyond awesome that God did these things that I don't even know where to start! Jesus is human in every way, though now He's glorified, and that's different from what He used to be. That being said, I reiterate the fact that He exercised His faith and relied entirely on His external connections with His Father, the Holy Spirit, and the angels to do the miracles He did during his life on Earth.

Jesus's miracles, therefore, could have been accomplished through a wide variation of means, and that might explain why sometimes He performed the same miracle in different ways, such as curing blindness. To one man, He mixed His spit with dirt (John 9:6–7); to another man, He spit in his eyes (Mark 8:22–25); and to yet a third, He simply declared, "Recover your sight!" (Luke 18:42).

For all we know, angels used technology to alter Jesus's saliva with a healing substance for the first two miracles, and the Holy Spirit performed the last miracle. I'm certain God had specific reasons for each of these variations, reasons that probably serve some symbolic, prophetic significance, but for the relevance I am establishing here, I am only pointing out one reason. I don't consider it a nonmiracle if angels used technology to assist Jesus in accomplishing some of His miracles.

Continuing on, shortly after the angel Gabriel visited Zechariah, he also visited Joseph, Jesus's stepfather, to warn him about King Herod's plans to murder all the firstborn male children in the region (Luke 1:11, 26–38; Matthew 1:20). This ended up saving Jesus's life.

Around this same time, a large group of angels appeared and announced the birth of Jesus to a group of shepherds in a field (Luke 2:8–15). I love this about God; He picks a group of obscure shepherds in the countryside to announce the singular most important event in the history of the world.

Human reasoning would have these angels appearing to the most powerful rulers on the planet, or sending them to a vastly populated city, to make a grand display of their announcement there. Today we have huge events with endless pomp and ceremony to make announcements, such as who will be the next president or who will win the Oscars. God, however, makes His announcements to the nobodies of society, a few guys out in a field watching some sheep. These were the garbage collectors, the gardeners, the janitors, the taxi drivers—the dime-a-dozen, nameless, faceless members of society in their day. This is God's way of saying that nobody is nameless or faceless to Him.

These angels that appeared to the shepherds could have simply been floating in the air as they are usually depicted, or the first angel that appeared opened a dimensional portal to the third heaven where the other angels were, or angelic flying chariots could have been visible as well. It could also be that angelic flying chariots opened a portal to the third heaven because any interdimensional, intergalactic vehicle would have to have the ability to generate a quantum singularity (a wormhole in space-time) in order to travel faster than light to get here. In any case, otherworldly beings were present on this momentous occasion.

Luke 2:7–15 [bold emphasis added]

And she gave birth to her firstborn son and wrapped him in swaddling clothes and laid him in a manger, because there was no place for them in the inn. And in the same region there were shepherds out in the field, keeping watch over their flock by night. And **an angel of the Lord appeared to them, and the glory of the Lord shone around them, and they were filled with fear**. And the angel said to them, "Fear not, for behold, I bring you good news of a great joy that will be for all the people. For unto you is born this day in the city of David a Savior, who is Christ the Lord. And this will be a sign for you: you will find a baby wrapped in swaddling clothes and lying in a manger." And **suddenly there was with the angel a multitude of the heavenly host praising God and saying, "Glory to God in the highest, and on earth peace among those with whom he is pleased!"** When the angels went away from them into heaven, the shepherds said to one another, "Let us go over to Bethlehem and see this thing that has happened, which the Lord has made known to us."

Angels probably have the ability to fly, but I doubt it's because of some dorky-looking bird wings they have on their backs, as countless artistic images render them. If they can levitate or fly, it is due to their supernatural power, not birds' wings. If they actually flew like birds, flapping wings on their backs, it would look ridiculous and anything but graceful. Simply look at the way birds fly and analyze the shapes of their bodies; birds are aerodynamically designed for flight, and humanoids are not.

Beyond this, every description of biblical encounters in which the prophets were actually speaking with angels face-to-face describe the angels as looking like men, and there are no wings on their bodies. When it comes to angels associated with wings, every Bible passage that describes them seems far more like technology than angels with wings. Take this and add the fact that angels use flying chariots, and the conclusion should be fairly evident that angels don't have literal wings.

The only caveat I might add to this tidbit about angels with wings is that visions (which might be out of body) can be highly subjective and/or symbolic. I touched upon this earlier when speaking about the visions of the Old Testament prophet Zechariah.

For example, frequently people who astral project (out of body) report that they see many bizarre things, such as a mixture of dreamlike images, symbols, or nonhuman entities. I personally know one such astral projector, Davey, a Christian who claims to astral project from time to time; it is something that simply started happening to him at a young age. He has encountered many different types of angels (as well as demons, unfortunately).

Davey informed me that some angels have wings and others do not, but it is his opinion that much of what he sees may be the product of his own expectations projected into the reality he is immersed in.

In the material universe, reality is concrete and it takes quite a bit to manipulate atomic structure. You generally can't change something just by looking at it. In nonphysical realities (or perhaps lesser-physical realities composed of finer particles than atoms), however, reality is subject to change using thoughts alone.

Whether angels have literal wings or not, many will hotly debate, but I would seek to eject myself from such debates even though I have my opinions, which I have just divulged. I don't think it is very important what angels look like. What *is* important is that we need to be able to look past our expectations and set aside anything nonessential when it comes to honing our discernment in the days ahead.

Angels, both faithful and fallen, as well as other members of the host of heaven who are not angels, will most likely be in *open contact* with humanity in the future. With respect to physical appearances, the good guys and bad guys might have no discernible differences between them. Our discernment of them should therefore not be based on whether or not they use technology, or if they have wings or not, but rather the content of their messages.

In the End Times, scripture states that an angel will be preaching the Gospel (Revelation 14:6). We should be able to trust the Gospel, no matter what the angels look like. We should likewise be able to identify deceivers, no matter what they look like. Discernment should always be based on the *fruit of one's actions* and the *content of one's words*, not on tangents like wings or the use of flying chariots, which I am almost certain do not look anything like the chariots we typically think of today.

> **Revelation 14:6** [bold emphasis added]
> Then **I saw another angel flying directly overhead**, with **an eternal gospel to proclaim to those who dwell on earth**, to **every nation** and **tribe** and **language** and **people**.

So angels announced the birth of Jesus, and they showed up again to minister to Jesus following His temptation with Satan (Matthew 4:11). I don't doubt that a flying chariot was present when Jesus was baptized (Matthew 3:16–17, Mark 1:11) or when Moses and Elijah met Jesus on the Mount of Transfiguration, along with a mysterious cloud that overshadowed them (Matthew 17:2–6, Mark 9:2–13, Luke 9:28–36).

Moses and Elijah dropped in to give Jesus His pep talk about going to the cross (Luke 9:31). That had to be a tough deal. Imagine being the one who had to talk with Jesus just before the cross. What did they say to Him?

Elijah: "Dude."

Moses: "Way."

Jesus, "I AM the Way."

> **Matthew 17:2–6** [bold emphasis added]
> And **he was transfigured before them**, and **his face shone like the sun, and his clothes became white as**

> **light**. And behold, **there appeared to them Moses and Elijah, talking with him**. And Peter said to Jesus, "Lord, it is good that we are here. If you wish, I will make three tents here, one for you and one for Moses and one for Elijah." He was still speaking when, **behold, a bright cloud overshadowed them, and a voice from the cloud said, "This is my beloved Son, with whom I am well pleased; listen to him."** When the disciples heard this, they fell on their faces and were terrified.

And finally, as I mentioned earlier in this book, when Jesus left this earth, he floated up into the sky and disappeared into a cloud, which was most likely a flying chariot (Acts 1:9).

8.10 The Early Church

After Jesus left the earth, the early church experienced many miraculous signs and wonders, many of which directly involved angels.

Angels broke the apostles out of jail (Acts 5:19, Acts 12:7–11), and when Jesus appeared to the apostle Paul on the road to Damascus (when Paul was still known as Saul and persecuted believers at that time), Jesus blasted him with a beam of light that no one else with Saul could see. Scientifically speaking, that might have been a type of laser. Jesus also cloaked Himself from everyone but Paul, but interestingly, He allowed them to hear His voice (Acts 9:1–19).

This is Jesus and He can do anything, so there is no need for technology; however, I find it interesting that Paul's blindness, which Jesus inflicted on him, was removed when something with the appearance of scales fell off his eyes (Acts 9:18). It could be that angels used some amazing technology to instantly place some blinding contacts (scales) on Paul's eyes in order to blind him; thus, curing him simply involved removing the blinders.

I see Jesus possibly involving angels in many of these miraculous details because God loves to delegate and get everyone involved. If all He wanted to do was get the job done Himself, what would be the point of creating everything in the first place? He didn't *need* creation; He *wanted* it. Rather than doing everything Himself, He generally assigns tasks, giving angels and people the *honor* of doing things for Him. That's His way, always has been.

I think when God is personally present, it's always for the personal touch—the relationship aspect, rather than the necessity of His power, which He can either delegate to angels or accomplish from afar if He wills it. Think about it; if God didn't bother to fight Satan personally when he rebelled, but instead sent Michael and some other angels to take care of it for Him (Revelation 12:7–12), why would He do any lesser task unless it was for personal, intimate reasons?

While I'm sure God's faithful angels were quite busy in the days of the early church, accompanying the apostles and possibly empowering many of their miracles, the enemy was madly at work as well. This is evident in the many demonic exorcisms that Jesus and the apostles conducted, casting out demons left and right.

I think exorcisms frequently involve angels showing up and adjusting their "frequencies" to the dimensions of these devils/demons, and literally evicting them in what Christians call spiritual warfare. This is literal warfare; these beings duke it out, and even the good angels can take a beating sometimes, but they have an infinite supply of backup. God's angels cannot be altogether stopped when God mandates something to happen, but they can be delayed as the archangel Gabriel was on one occasion, when delivering a message to the Old Testament prophet Daniel (Daniel 10:13).

While demons (the ghosts of the Nephilim) were losing a tremendous amount of territory, getting cast out of their victims in the days of the early church, people who operated in agreement with demonic entities were also losing ground. A man known as Simon the Sorcerer, for example, was losing influence among the people of his area when the apostles showed up, and the apostles put him in his place (Acts 9:3–8). The apostle Paul also put another sorcerer in his place, by giving him a taste of his own past experience when he cursed him with blindness (Acts 13:6–7). Perhaps another application of those blinder contacts was prescribed.

While the early church days do not give many examples of sky chariots, they were most likely present and cloaked when angels were in the area. One was also probably used to instantly transport the apostle Philip to a distant location (Acts 8:26–40). What's more, while the heavenly visions of Paul and John could have been dreams—or even out-of-body excursions of an astral nature since Paul honestly couldn't even tell if he was in his body or not—these trips may have also involved angelic sky chariots (2 Corinthians 12:1–7, Revelation 4:1).

8.11 Constantine the Great

The days of the early Christian church were riddled with horrific persecution, and in the midst of it all, the miracles continued. Some of these, which involved otherworldly powers intervening in the affairs of humanity, are documented in *Foxe's Book of Martyrs.*[19]

Much of the persecution toward the early Christian church was instigated by Rome, but on one momentous day, October 27, in AD 312, a man known as Constantine the Great saw something that caused him to conduct a complete 180-degree shift for the direction of his entire empire. The Christian History Institute website sums up Constantine's dramatic turnaround as follows:

> Throughout its first three centuries, the church went through unimaginable persecution from the Roman Empire, though all the time growing and spreading. So imagine what an extraordinary turn of events it was when the Roman Emperor himself became a Christian. Within one person's lifetime, the Empire went from the most savage of its severe persecutions of Christians to embracing Christianity.

> This text [website] tells the story of Emperor Constantine's conversion, and a little of how his new faith was reflected in his imperial policy. In addition to what you'll read below, he outlawed infanticide, the abuse of slaves and peasants, and crucifixion, and he made Sunday a day of rest.[20]

What on earth did Constantine see and/or experience that made him go from persecuting Christians to becoming one, somewhat like that dramatic turnaround of Saul of Tarsus to the apostle Paul?

> [A]bout noon, when the day was already beginning to decline, he saw with his own eyes the sign of a cross of light in the heavens, above the sun, and bearing the inscription, "By this symbol you will conquer." He was struck with amazement by the sight, and his whole army witnessed the miracle.[21]

What Constantine saw in the sky was most likely a physical manifestation because his entire army saw it. I suspect angels used some form of advanced technology to make this miracle happen.

Shortly after this experience, Constantine prayed to this unfamiliar God He believed sent him a sign, and this happened:

> In his sleep, the Christ of God appeared to him with the same sign which he had seen in the heavens, and commanded him to make a likeness of that sign which he had seen in the heavens, and to use it as a safeguard in all engagements with his enemies.[22]

I will not make the declaration that everything following this event was peaches and cream, far to the contrary. Initially the treatment of Christians was greatly improved (of course, it couldn't get any worse); however, the Roman Catholic Church was later infiltrated by satanic forces and used to perpetrate a continuation of the persecution of Christians, among others. Satan simply shifted gears, put on his institutionalized religion hat prepackaged with its own bag of tricks, and off he went.

8.10 Muhammad's Day

To counter the corruption within the Roman Catholic Church, some Christian prophecy researchers conjecture that God allowed the rise of Islam as a judgment against apostate Christians and Jews. The Roman Catholic Church, for example, martyred many devout Christians in its early history; some of these are documented in *Foxe's Book of Martyrs. Jesus Freaks* by dc Talk[23] and other books, such as *Martyrs and Miracles: The Inspiring Lives of Saints and Martyrs,*[24] also include many of these testimonies.

One element of early Islam these scholars highlight to support this theory is that Muhammad started out targeting Jewish and Christian apostates, but he allowed those who were faithful to their respective religions, which he called a "people of the book," to avoid slaughter by paying a jizya tax.

Some prophecy researchers also point to the fifth trumpet in the book of Revelation, which they propose is a reference to the rise of Islam aimed at stopping Roman Catholics from persecuting Protestant Christians (Revelation 9:1–12).[25–27] Some of these theories sort of fit, but Muhammad and his followers veered dramatically away from targeting only apostate Christians and Jews once they migrated to Medina, so the duration and extent of the spread of Islam does not match the biblical narrative. Revelation 9:5 specifically states that the "scorpions" were not allowed to kill anyone, but that was definitely not the case with Muhammad and his followers.

Concerning Muhammad's rise to power, there is widespread agreement among Christians, as well as Muslims, that this was directly attributed to Muhammad's direct contact with otherworldly entities. It is the alignment of these entities where Christians and Muslims disagree.

Muhammad claimed to have encountered both the jinns and the angels. (Many Christians would probably add a prefix to the angels in question).

About the jinns, Muhammad's descriptions of these beings as slaves of Solomon's army make them sound like another species of humanoid, physical people who one might interact with in a normal, matter-of-fact way as a part of daily life, yet the jinns had supernatural power and/or connections. This almost gives them a direct link to the Nephilim.

A number of Qur'an surahs and Hadiths can easily translate the jinns to the Nephilim. However, other elements of the Qur'an and Hadiths that speak of jinns add details about them that point to nonphysical beings. It is almost as if Muhammad and his men made little to no distinction between beings that are physical and those that are nonphysical. The Bible makes clear distinctions in this regard, whereas the Qur'an and Hadiths do not.

Concerning the biblical concept of angels, they are almost always described as physical beings. They eat, drink, have conversations, and grab/touch people (Genesis 19:1–22; Daniel 9, 10; and many others), destroy cities (Genesis 19:24–25), and fight in battles (2 Kings 19:35 and many others). Fallen angels even had sex with humans and sired hybrid offspring with them (Genesis 6, Jude 1:6, 2 Peter 2:4). It takes physical DNA to do that.

Angels are definitely physical beings; however, they also have the ability to enter dreams, and to *alter* their frequency and pop in and out of this dimension. They do this because of their supernatural power. Most people use the terminology that angels "assume a physical form," which is sort of true, but it isn't entirely accurate the way I understand it. Angels are what they are; they simply make an internal adjustment to their bodies and enter this dimension, much like a person can hold his or her breath and swim underwater. They aren't *creating* new bodies; they're simply *adjusting* their bodies.

What throws people off about angels is their supernatural abilities; they adjust their frequencies and walk through walls, teleport, manipulate the mind, inflict blindness, fly, visit people's dreams, appear and disappear, and so forth. Because of this, they are generally confused as being nonphysical. This is why the term *spiritual* has nonphysical connotations. Angels, however, are very physical, and this applies to both faithful and fallen angels.

Demons, on the other hand, are another matter; they are strictly nonphysical entities. They do not have the ability to assume physical form because they are physically dead. As I said earlier, the Hebrew word *rapha* is translated as "giants," as well as "ghosts." Demons are *the ghosts* of the Nephilim; they are composed of a much finer matter, affiliated with being nonphysical.

If disincarnate entities are very powerful, they might be able to muster up enough energy to generate some poltergeist activity, but for the most part, if they want to interact in this world, they search for viable hosts to feed off of. That is why scripture gives so many examples of people possessed by demons/devils.

One would think that people living in sin are the biggest targets for possession, and they probably are, but that is not always the case because the Bible has examples of possessed children. It could be that some people are natural conduits; this is most likely a spiritual gifting that some people have, and demons search for it. That doesn't seem fair, but keep in mind that if these same people dedicate their lives to Christ, their ability to channel the power of the Holy Spirit is most likely magnified.

In any case, demons possess people because they do not have bodies of their own. If they did, they wouldn't go through all the trouble to find hosts, possess them, and then risk an exorcism, after which one or more faithful angels might apprehend them and force them into hell. In order to avoid exorcisms, a general tactic for demons is to find natural conduits who are also living in sin because these people would normally avoid church and any faithful believers who might discern the situation and cast them out. Therefore, people who are natural conduits are most likely just fine if they live clean lives, especially if they are connected to the church and other believers.

There is only one exception to this general rule that I know of: fallen angels do not possess people or animals because they have bodies of their own. Satan is the exception; he has possessed a serpent in the past (Genesis 3), and he will most definitely possess a man in the future (the Antichrist).

As an immortal angel that cannot die (Luke 20:36), Satan has his own body. He might even end up being the literal father of the Antichrist in the future. If the *seed of the woman* was a literal seed (Jesus), why wouldn't the *seed of the serpent* be a literal seed as well (Genesis 3:15)? Regardless of these details, Satan has his own immortal body, but he has possessed a serpent in the past and will possess a man in the future. However, these actions are not committed out of necessity due to his lack of having a body. These possessions probably have to do with Satan's tactics more than anything else.

Aside from these two examples (the Antichrist and the serpent in the Garden of Eden), I know of no other instance in the Bible where a fallen angel has possessed someone or something. All other possessions in scripture are attributed to demons/devils.

In summation, I find the Bible is quite clear about the distinction between angels, physical beings with supernatural power that allows them to transcend the physical realm, and demons, nonphysical beings associated with possession. I discuss these distinctions in much more detail in *Aliens and the Antichrist*. As for the Nephilim, they were definitely physical beings.

The Qur'an and Hadiths, however, bounce all around this issue and mix up the two. One minute the jinns seem physical, and the next, they're flittering shadows and hidden observers. There may be a number of reasons why this occurs.

Muhammad and his followers were most likely encountering living Nephilim, as well as deceased Nephilim, and they simply grouped them all together under the label of jinn. Several factors contributed to this, some of which might make one's head swim to contemplate because the variations are endless.

I have derived a few speculations based on my own knowledge of the Bible and the paranormal, but in no way do I make any dogmatic claim of authority with these speculations; these are just "what if" scenarios.

Demons might exhibit physical attributes:

- Demons can be particularly powerful, probably more powerful than human ghosts because they are half angel. Because of this, they might have enough energy in their disincarnate bodies to emit or reflect light and give the appearance of being physical. They still don't have physical bodies as we understand what *physical* means—hence, they still want to possess people—but they might be able to give a pretty good illusion of being physical. They might further be able to move objects.
- If demons have enough power to make themselves visible to people, they might also be able to present themselves in any way they want, such as animals or people. This gives the illusion of shape-shifting. I have read that people who astral project can achieve this feat, so demons can probably do it as well.
- We know from scripture that demons possess people, and they can possess animals as well. People and animals possessed by powerful demons might exhibit some extraordinary supernatural abilities; teleportation might be one example. If possessed people or animals can perform these supernatural feats, it blurs the distinction of their physicality.

Nephilim might exhibit nonphysical attributes:

- Nephilim who were physically alive were very powerful, the stuff of legends. Most, perhaps even all, had supernatural power, and they most likely were not all giants. Many legends about them are of superheroes who were not giants. It could be that they were able to perform near-angelic feats, adjust their frequencies, and do things that seem to be nonphysical. For example, they might be able to make themselves invisible, fly, shape-shift, astral project, mentally manipulate or possess people or animals, and so forth. The previously mentioned sorcerer, Carlos Castaneda, claimed to be able to fly and shape-shift. If people can do these things (provided Castaneda's tales had any truth to them), then Nephilim could most likely do them as well.

- Some Nephilim may have had access to otherworldly technology obtained from their angelic parents. Who knows what sort of crazy things they were capable of, using angelic technology.

I started out this discussion of the physical and nonphysical attributes of jinns to fully disclose what they are from a biblical perspective. I think they were, and maybe still are, Nephilim, both alive and deceased. However, this definition only applies to *real* jinns.

Probably the most common references to the jinns in the Qur'an and Hadiths stem from superstitions. The jinns were pretty much blamed for anything that went wrong. If someone lost or misplaced something valuable, jinns stole it (Bukhari 4:54:533); if someone had evil thoughts pop into his or her head, they came from jinns (Qur'an 15:18; Muslim 26:5535, 26:5538, 26:5536); if kids went out at night and never returned, the jinns got them (Bukhari 4:54:533); and if someone saw a snake or a scorpion in his or her tent and yelled at it to get lost for three days, but it didn't listen, it was probably a jinni (Malik 54:54.12.33; Dawud 41:5231, 41:5236; Muslim 26:5557, 26:5559).

The Qur'an surahs and Hadiths have many references to jinns, and a lot of them amount to nothing more than superstitions. However, quite a few speak about the jinns as if they were a neighboring tribe—people Muhammad and his followers spoke with, traveled with, and knew intimate details about.

Calling a rustling noise in the bushes a jinni is one thing, but Muhammad and some of his followers claimed to have conversations with these beings (Bukhari 5:58:200, 5:58:206). They discussed what they ate (Bukhari 5:58:200; Dawud 1:39; Muslim 4:904, 4:903), big events that occurred in their lives (Bukhari 5:58:206, 6:60:443), and details about what they believed. These go way beyond simple superstitions.

The particulars about the jinns are fairly elaborate. Jinns listened to readings of the Qur'an (Qur'an 46:29, 72:1; Bukhari 5:58:199, 6:60:443; Muslim 4:902). Many of them claimed to have been *worshipped as gods*, as the Nephilim were; hence their direct link to the Nephilim (Qur'an 34:41, Bukhari 6:60:238–239, Muslim 43:7182–7184). Many jinns also became Muslims (Qur'an 46:29, 72:1; Bukhari 6:60:238–239, 6:60:443; Malik 54:54.12.33; Muslim 4:902, 26:5557, 26:5559, 43:7182–7184).

Superstitions don't convert to a particular religion.

Most superstitions link unrelated phenomenon with silly cause-and-effect scenarios. Breaking a mirror, walking under a ladder, or seeing a black cat crossing one's path are said to bring bad luck. Finding four-leaf clovers, carrying lucky charms as many baseball players do, or having a pretty lady kiss the dice to *charm* a gambling spree are said to bring good luck.

None of these superstitions involve intricate details like the jinns.

Legends and superstitions that have the most elaborate elements are often rooted in some form of truth. The Bible tells us exactly what we need to know about the Nephilim; the jinns are simply a diluted rendition of the Nephilim.

The Qur'an surahs and Hadiths that lean toward the superstitious elements of the jinns describe the jinns as hiding all around us (Bukhari 5:58:206; Muslim 4:902, 26:5535), and they are generally responsible for all kinds of mischief. I don't doubt this; whispering lies is something demons do, according to the Bible (1 Kings 22:19–23, 2 Chronicles 18:18–22, Revelation 16:13). These lies will have no effect on us if we simply hold to the truth.

What's more, just because demons flit about trying to cause problems doesn't mean they're responsible for *everything* that doesn't go our way. They further shouldn't be used as scapegoats to avoid accountability. The devil can't *make* people do anything; he and his minions simply present lies and temptations as best they can, and we choose to remain faithful or to believe the lies and sin. So whether or not demons are swimming around is almost irrelevant; they're primary power is limited by our free will, and we always have the divine authority in the name of Jesus to render them completely powerless.

Muhammad said all people have jinns assigned to them, and they are generally described as deceptive in nature (Qur'an 15:18; Muslim 26:5535–26:5536, 26:5538), except Muhammad's jinni was good, naturally (Muslim 39:6757).

I doubt each person has "assigned" jinns. There's too much division in the enemy's camp to follow orders to that extent. This is not to say that Satan does not have a hierarchy and a well-organized plan because he most certainly does. However, much of Satan's plan is coordinated chaos, with demons functioning more like street gangs run amok. Letting these evil beings go wherever they want and do the sort of things that they find fun is part of Satan's plan.

Satan and demons probably target specific people when they start causing problems with Satan's plans. For example, if a believer starts hanging around drug addicts and winning souls over to Christ, that's fewer drug addicts to leach energy off of. That's a problem. If believers of a specific church start making real progress in turning neighborhoods around, they're creating problems for Satan and his minions. In a situation like that, a more powerful demon might investigate the members of that church and search for weaknesses.

Maybe the pastor has a secret porn addiction, perhaps someone is committing adultery, or maybe the pastor's kids are doing drugs. Whatever the hidden sins are, demons will attempt to wreak as much havoc as possible, using those sins to take people out, and ultimately destroy the church. This is probably Satan's most common strategy, rather than specifically assigning his minions to *everyone*.

8.10.1 Muhammad's Battle with a Jinni

While many Qur'an surahs and Hadiths speak of the jinns as primarily invisible—their common reference among the three categories of beings is the "hidden ones"—they certainly aren't hidden all the time. Muhammad claimed to battle one of these creatures, and when he overcame it, he was tempted to chain it up in the mosque so everyone in his village could see it for themselves (Bukhari 1:8:450, 4:55:634, 6:60:332; Muslim 4:1104).

For this to truly happen, if it did, this jinni had to be a real, physical entity.

> **Bukhari 6:60:332** [bold emphasis added]
> The Prophet said, "**Last night a demon from the Jinns came to me** (or the Prophet said, a similar sentence) **to disturb my prayer, but Allah gave me the power to overcome him. I intended to tie him to one of the pillars of the mosque till the morning so that all of you could see him**, but then I remembered the Statement of my brother Solomon: 'My Lord! Forgive me and bestow on me a kingdom such as shall not belong to any other after me,' (38.35). The narrator then added: Then he (the Prophet) dismissed him, rejected. 'Nor am I one of the pretenders (a person who pretends things which do not exist),' (38.86).

What was this all about, some otherworldly creature attacking Muhammad for no apparent reason? One speculation is Muhammad might have been trying to copy Jesus's temptation in the wilderness, but that doesn't seem likely in this passage because it bears no resemblance to Jesus's temptations. This encounter has no temptation or dialogue at all; the creature simply attacked him. Jesus was never *physically attacked* by a demon. Instead, much the opposite occurred; Jesus directly confronted demons on many occasions. In at least one incident, He cast out a legion [over one thousand] of them (Mark 5:9, Luke 8:30). Note: In Jesus's day, a Roman legion represented just over one thousand troops.

This story of Muhammad's could possibly relate to another Hadith, in which Muhammad instructed his followers to fight anyone who passed in front of them while they were praying (Bukhari 4:54:495).

It is almost as if Muhammad lay awake at night thinking up things to get angry about. In this Hadith, Muhammad claims that anyone who walks in front of a Muslim while he is praying is a Satan.

> **Bukhari 4:54:495** [bold emphasis added]
> The Prophet said, **"If while you are praying, somebody intends to pass in front of you,** prevent him; and should he insist, prevent him again; and if he insists again, **fight with him (i.e., prevent him violently,** e.g., pushing him violently), because **such a person is (like) a devil."**
>
> Narrated Muhammad bin Sirin: Abu Huraira said, "Allah's Apostle put me in charge of the Zakat of Ramadan (i.e., Zakat-ul-Fitr). Someone came to me and started scooping some of the foodstuff of (Zakat) with both hands. I caught him and told him that I would take him to Allah's Apostle." Then Abu Huraira told the whole narration and added "He (i.e., the thief) said, 'Whenever you go to your bed, recite the Verse of "Al-Kursi" (2.255) for then a guardian from Allah will be guarding you, and Satan will not approach you till dawn.'" On that the Prophet said, **"He told you the truth, though he is a liar, and he (the thief) himself was the Satan."**

A simple word search for *Satan* in the Hadiths will reveal many instances where Muhammad and his followers called people a Satan or the Satan. This might be a kind of slang for someone who is being disrespectful.

Whether talking about jerks or jinns, the Hadith in which Muhammad wrestles a jinni is clearly distinguished in context from the general uses of the term *Satan* because Muhammad specifically wanted to chain it up so other people could *see it* in order to *believe it*. This highlights the believability factor. No one would care about seeing the village asshole chained up in the mosque, but to see a real supernatural being chained up would be quite another matter.

Muhammad made a big deal about this encounter, as if to boast that "Allah gave him power to overcome him." Then he used the excuse that only King Solomon had permission from Allah to command the jinns, so he decided to let it go, which I find highly inconsistent.

Why would King Solomon have greater power and authority than Muhammad if in fact Muhammad was the "greatest of all the prophets" as the Qur'an declares? For being the greatest of all prophets, Muhammad appears to fall short of King Solomon, even by his own admission. Moreover, I find it interesting that, out of all the prophets in the Bible Muhammad chose to respect as having greater authority than him, he chose a prophet who ended up falling into sin and turning away from God.

Regarding Muhammad's wrestling match with the jinni, it could be that Muhammad simply attacked someone in his village who walked in front of him while he was praying, and that event inspired him to concoct this wild tale. Seeing the reality of the demonic realm in Islamic terrorism today, however, I have little doubt that Muhammad and his followers were plagued with real demons. Another possibility is Muhammad could have been attacked by a human-sized Nephilim who was still alive.

8.10.2 The Night of the Jinns

Muhammad's encounters with the otherworldly jinns did not cease with the mindless attack mentioned above. On another night, he met a more civil jinni who escorted him on a journey known as "the night of the jinns." He was then introduced to a bunch of jinns as if they were a neighboring tribe (Muslim 4:903).

> **Muslim 4:903** [bold emphasis added]
> Dawud reported from 'Amir who said: I asked 'Alqama if Ibn Mas'ud was present with the Messenger of Allah

> (may peace be upon him) on **the night of the Jinn (the night when the Holy Prophet met them)**. He (Ibn Mas'uad) said: No, but **we were in the company of the Messenger of Allah** (may peace be upon him) **one night and we missed him. We searched for him in the valleys and the hills and said he has either been taken away (by jinn) or has been secretly killed**. He (the narrator) said, we spent the worst night which people could ever spend. **When it was dawn we saw him coming from the side of Hiri'**. He (the narrator) reported. We said: Messenger of Allah, we missed you and searched for you, but we could not find you and we spent the worst night which people could ever spend. He (the Holy Prophet) said: **There came to me an inviter on behalf of the Jinn and I went along with him and recited to them the Qur'an**. He (the narrator) said: **He then went along with us and showed us their traces and traces of their embers. They (the Jinn) asked him** (the Holy Prophet) **about their provision and he said: Every bone on which the name of Allah is recited is your provision. The time it will fall in your hand it would be covered with flesh, and the dung of (the camels) is fodder for your animals**. The Messenger of Allah (may peace be upon him) said: Don't perform istinja with these (things) for these are the food of your brothers (Jinn).

This Hadith clearly reveals that Muhammad was physically absent from his village, and everyone was looking for him all night long until he showed up the next morning. The story he relayed was that he struck an agreement with these beings to leave food for them. Their primary staple was bones (Bukhari 5:58:200, Dawud 1:39, Muslim 4:903–4:904), but jinns also have "animals" that eat camel dung. Exactly what is an animal that belongs to a jinni?

Just as I researched the Dajjal, I also researched the jinns, adding an additional forty-three Qur'an surahs and Hadiths to my Dajjal database, which is now a Dajjal-Jinn database. I find these tales about the jinns interesting because they might cover a wide range of entities, though I believe their primary definition resides with the Nephilim.

From these Hadiths about Muhammad's night of the jinns, I can't tell whether these jinns are physical or not. Muhammad sees them and converses with them as if they are normal people. However, their specific request of him is an indication that they might be disincarnate and simply making themselves visible. Either that or these neighboring-tribe jinns are physical Nephilim, making requests on behalf of their deceased relatives.

For starters, these jinns eat bones. Recalling my earlier discussion about bones, I have long considered the possibility that bones may contain some *residual spiritual energy* of the living, hence the association of hauntings with graveyards and the recently deceased. I also base part of this theory on an incident in the Bible, when Elisha's bones resurrected a man from the dead (2 Kings 13:21). Now I read in the Hadiths about these jinns who eat bones. Could it be that bones contain residual spiritual energy that demons can consume?

Concerning the dung to feed the jinns' animals, what sorts of animals might the jinns have? If the jinns in this Hadith are *living* Nephilim, their animals could simply be normal animals. However, animals don't eat dung.

Strike that, I've seen dogs … never mind.

Let's just say animals don't *live* on dung if any are disgusting enough to actually eat it, and most aren't. These animals of the jinns, therefore, don't represent normal animals. This is yet another indication that the jinns in this Hadith are nonphysical entities; they are most likely deceased Nephilim, a.k.a. demons. As for their unusual nonphysical animals, they could be unnatural mixed hybrids (Nephilim experiments), or perhaps transdimensional species originally created by God that we know nothing about (officially anyway).

If the jinns are highly intelligent, as well as powerful, there is no reason to suggest that they have not figured out how to capture and domesticate less intelligent creatures in their realm, whatever exotic species those creatures may be.

Then there's the possibility that the animals of the jinns are simply lower-ranking demons. Either way, they're subservient to the jinns, and strangely enough, they eat camel dung.

I have no way of knowing for sure if the below connection of *demons* to *dung* holds any merit, but the name Beelzebub, referenced in 2 Kings 1:2–3 and other places in the Bible, might owe its origins to these animals of the jinns.

Beelzebub is usually translated to mean "lord of the flies." The first part of this name comes from Baal; it derives from a Hebrew word for "lord," but it also refers to an ancient Canaanite god. As for the second part of this name, it might derive from a slurred pronunciation of *zebel*, a word used to mean "dung" in the Targum (the Aramaic translation of the Bible).[28] Therefore, the name Beelzebub may directly associate demons with dung, and maybe the reason why is that is what some types of demons actually eat.

I can just see a few demons sitting around the dinner table munching away, and one pipes up, "Wow, this tastes like crap."

"I know, delicious, huh?"

But on a serious note, since demons are noncorporeal entities, I suspect they don't necessarily munch on physical crap but rather consume a kind of residual life force it retains, similar to the residual life force in bones. Think about what all living creatures eat: things that were once alive. Demons might replenish their energy in a similar manner.

The only reason I mention this strange tangent is because the Hadiths make a point to talk about it in detail, and it provides yet a further clue as to the origin of the otherworldly jinns, and their animals in this case, which is downright odd. Without a doubt, I'm certain that the unseen realities surrounding us would boggle our minds if we could perceive them.

8.10.3 Other Jinn Details

The two primary Islamic sources I have researched about the jinns, in addition to the Qur'an and Hadiths, are the www.MissionIslam.com and www.Answering-Islam.org websites.[29–30] As I have said before, I don't consider my speculations as authoritative, but rather a simple comparative analysis of possibilities I see in the Bible and Islamic literature, and what I know about paranormal phenomenon. My general purpose in this analysis is to use the Bible and see what truth I can extract out of the Qur'an and Hadiths, if any.

The lore of the jinns is quite expansive. A simple word search in the Qur'an on the Qur'an Arabic Corpus website identifies thirty-two instances of the word *jinn*,[31] and the same search in the Hadiths listed on the Qur'an Explorer website will reveal fifty-three instances.[32] A related word, *shaytan*, and its plural equivalent, *shaytana*, are found more than eighty times in the Qur'an.[33]

I've discussed some of the oddities of the jinns, such as the difficulty in determining whether they are physical beings or not, and the fact that they are most likely Nephilim, both living and deceased. Muhammad's placement of the jinns as *higher* than humans, but *lower* than angels, correlates directly with the Nephilim.

However, there are a number of jinn attributes that do not correlate with the Nephilim, and this is due to two possibilities: Muhammad and the Hadith authors were wrong in some of their assumptions about the jinns, or they applied the label of jinn to a broad category of life forms and phenomena, including species that are Nephilim and those that are not Nephilim.

While I tend to believe that the references to jinns refer to the Nephilim, I don't rule out the possibility that God has created what we might define as *transdimensional* species on Earth as part of God's natural order of creation. Even so, I would still not classify them as *higher* than humans, as the jinns are classified, because God gave Adam and Eve dominion over the earth (Genesis 1:26).

Being less than human leaves plenty of room for many possibilities. Dolphins and whales, for example, are exceptionally intelligent, perhaps far more than we realize. Moreover, they might even have supernatural abilities we are not aware of. For all we know, dolphins are able to astral project and could be the source of a great deal of poltergeist activity. Wouldn't that be a trip?

What's more, there could also be transdimensional species that are not native to this dimension, but they have the ability to *adjust* their frequencies and pop in and out as they please, just like the angels do. Either way, whether native to this dimension or not, *all* of the dimensions of this multidimensional planet we call Earth were originally placed under the dominion of humans. Therefore, if a species were part of God's natural order of creation, it would most likely have *less* glory than humans (hence less intelligence and power) because humans have dominion over the earth.

That *was* the case until fallen angels sired the Nephilim, which fall outside of God's natural order of creation. Ever since this happened, it gave rise to angelic hybrids that defy the natural order.

Consider the possibility of a creature that is 80 percent angel and 20 percent animal. Depending on the animal, it might not be as intelligent as a human, but it could potentially wield a great deal of supernatural power and live a very long time. Some entities might have so much power (i.e., angelic glory) that they might not even exist in this dimension in their natural state—that is, frequency.

I theorize that the many variations of the Bigfoot species might actually be primate-angel Nephilim, with so much supernatural power that they can pop in and out of this dimension at will. I'm not the first to contrive this idea of a transdimensional Bigfoot species. Paranormal investigator Jon-Erik Beckjord espouses the idea as well. On the website Before It's News, a contributor known as Barlow states, "Many Bigfoot advocates distance themselves from the paranormal position and regard it as an embarrassment."[34]

How is it that an avid Bigfoot hunter can regard anyone's theory about Bigfoot an embarrassment? That's almost as bad as two Trekkies at a Star Trek convention, who speak fluent Klingon, arguing about the battleship specifications of a Klingon bird of prey.

Adding fuel to the Bigfoot debate is a five-year DNA study known as the Ketchum Bigfoot Study. National Geographic quotes this study and states that the findings reveal all the hair and dung samples are of natural species.[35] Numerous other researchers also quote this same study and declare that some of the findings point to an undiscovered species of primate.[36–38] I think what's happening is when the findings do not conclude a known species, scientists set it aside for further analysis. Those who are Bigfoot enthusiasts focus on those findings, some of which indicate an unknown species of primate. Those who are not Bigfoot enthusiasts consider these further-analysis findings to be inconclusive and are suspicious of human DNA contamination during the testing process.

Because these tests have to do with a search for humanlike DNA to begin with, there should be more scrutiny before dismissing the samples as having human DNA contamination, but I think what's happening here is scientists are using Occam's razor to dismiss things they have biased opinions about.

In any case, we *do* have many Bigfoot DNA samples, some of which indicate an unknown species of primate, but as far as catching one of these creatures, it's pretty much impossible. I therefore believe the transdimensional theory should not be so readily dismissed. And concerning the idea of a transdimensional species in general, I believe the definition of jinns as the hidden ones perfectly aligns with this concept.

So what else do the Qur'an and Hadiths say about the jinns? Following is a list of attributes that relate to them, along with a possible biblical explanation regarding the accuracy of said attributes:

8.10.3.1 Jinns Once Ruled the Earth

A number of Islamic sources report an extensive backstory to the Qur'an surah below:

> **Qur'an 2:30 (Shakir)** [bold emphasis and bracketed comments added]
> And when your **Lord said to the angels, I am going to place in the earth a khalif [humanity]**, they said: **What! wilt Thou place in it such as shall make mischief in it and shed blood**, and we celebrate Thy praise and extol Thy holiness? He said: Surely I know what you do not know.

This surah states that the angels were upset about God creating humanity, and the obscure reference to bloodshed leaves only a vague impression that angels were certain that humans were destined for corruption. This is most likely related to the Islamic teaching that angels have no free will, but humans and jinns do, which I think is entirely inaccurate.

Commentaries on this surah have more to add. According to the Mission Islam website, and paraphrased on the Questions on Islam website, this surah refers to a time when jinns once ruled the earth prior to Adam and Eve. Apparently these jinns of ancient times were horribly violent.

> "Two thousand years before (mankind) was created, there were Jinn on (the Earth), and they caused corruption on it and shed blood. Then Allah sent against them a troop of Angels who beat them and cast them away to islands in the seas. So, when Allah said: 'I am placing (mankind) generations after generations on Earth,' They (the Angels) said, 'Will You place therein one who will cause corruption and shed blood' (Al Baqarah, 2:30), That is: Just as those Jinn did? Then Allah said: 'I know that which you do not know.'"[39–40]

The commentary on the Questions on Islam website further states that Allah sent a being named Iblis (Islam's version of Satan, who is a type of jinn), along with some other angels, and they destroyed this civilization, scattering the surviving jinns to remote islands. God then created humans to rule the earth, and this is when the angels became upset with God's decision. This doesn't make much sense. How can a being lacking free will be upset? Anyway, this is also when Satan/Iblis allowed his success in destroying these jinns to go to his head, and he initiated his rebellion against God.

Obviously there are some major differences between Islam and the Bible. The aspect of free will, along with the origin of evil, are among the most fundamental of those differences. According to the Bible, *any act of evil* against another sentient being *is an act of rebellion against God.* Scripture is replete with examples of various sins ultimately pointing back to violations against God (Genesis 39:9, Exodus 10:16, Joshua 7:20, Judges 10:10, 2 Samuel 12:13, Psalm 51:4, etc.).

The Bible points to Satan as the first angel to conceive of evil and rebel against God (Isaiah 14, Ezekiel 28). The Bible also reiterates many times that all evil is a sin against God, but Islam is distinctly different by suggesting that evil existed as part of God's original creation, even before Satan/Iblis rebelled against God.

Setting aside the element of angels not having free will, and the origin of evil between Islam and the Bible, this Islamic commentary makes some sense from a biblical perspective if these jinns are the same entities as Nephilim. Why do I say this?

The Bible speaks about the pre-Adamite civilization indirectly when it refers to Lucifer's kingdom on Earth in the Garden of Eden, which had to be prior to the creation of Adam and Eve (Isaiah 14, Ezekiel 28). This kingdom was destroyed when Lucifer led a rebellion against God. I discuss this pre-Adamite period much more extensively in *Aliens and the Antichrist*, so for those who are interested in knowing more about those details, simply obtain a copy of that book.

Without getting too much into the weeds about the pre-Adamites, I will simply state that the horrific violence inflicted through the Nephilim in Noah's day may have occurred on the earth prior to Adam and Eve's creation as well because the pre-Adamites were a race of both mortal and immortal humanoids. (I say this because many of them were killed in the flood of Lucifer, so some of them had to be mortals.) If the immortals crossed with the mortals back then, that may have produced an earlier version of the Nephilim.

While many of Islam's details about this pre-Adamite period are highly inaccurate, the theme of evil jinns driven mad with violence and corrupting the entire earth remains consistent with the Nephilim narrative, both in the days of Noah and perhaps even prior to the creation of Adam and Eve.

8.10.3.2 Jinns Were Worshipped

The Qur'an states that the jinns were once worshipped (Qur'an 34:41, Muslim 43:7182–7184, Bukhari 6:60:238–239), which again is a direct reference to the Nephilim. These jinns most likely refer to those that populated the earth in Noah's day because I don't see Satan sharing his glory with them when he ruled his earthly kingdom predating Adam and Eve.

8.10.3.3 Jinns Have Differing Religion Beliefs

Some jinns became Muslims (Qur'an 46:29, 72:1; Bukhari 6:60:238, 6:60:443; Malik 54:54.12.33; Muslim 4:902, 26:5557, 26:5559, 43:7182–7184), and this makes sense for a hybrid species that has consistently rebelled against God since the dawn of time. According to some Hadiths, some jinns wholeheartedly embraced Islam, even to the point of using their supernatural power of shape-shifting to assume the form of a wolf and evangelize on behalf of Muhammad (Bukhari 3:39:517, 4:56:667, 5:57:15, 5:57:39).

> **Bukhari 3:39:517** [bold emphasis added]
> Narrated Unais bin 'Amr: Ahban bin Aus said, "I was amongst my sheep. Suddenly a wolf caught a sheep and I shouted at it. **The wolf sat on its tail and addressed me, saying, 'Who will look after it (i.e., the sheep) when you will be busy and not able to**

> **look after it? Do you forbid me the provision which Allah has provided me?'"** Ahban added, "I clapped my hands and said, 'By Allah, I have never seen anything more curious and wonderful than this!' On that the wolf said, "There is something (more curious) and wonderful than this; that is, Allah's Apostle in those palm trees, inviting people to Allah (i.e., Islam).' Unais bin 'Amr further said, "Then Ahban went to Allah's Apostle and informed him what happened and embraced Islam.)"

Concerning the topic of salvation for Nephilim/jinns, I am a firm believer in free will. Some teach that the Nephilim have no salvation, based on an obscure reference in Isaiah (Isaiah 26:14) and on God's judgments against the Nephilim in times past. These judgments, however, were made due to the extreme violence and sin initiated by the Nephilim, and not simply because they existed.

> **Isaiah 26:14** [bracketed comment and bold emphasis added]
> They are dead, they will not live; **they are shades [rapha]**, they will not arise; to that end you have visited them with destruction and wiped out all remembrance of them.

What this passage in Isaiah refers to are demons, specifically singled out with the Hebrew word *rapha.* In this context, it is true that *these* Nephilim, which are now deceased, have no salvation because they rejected God all the way to their graves. The book of Enoch also makes this assertion. As for any Nephilim that are alive in this day and age, there is no telling what percentage of angelic DNA they still have in their blood. Regardless of this, free will has always been the ultimate grounds on which salvation is based, and not DNA (Galatians 3:26–29).

> **Galatians 3:26–29** [bold emphasis added]
> [I]**n Christ Jesus you are all sons of God, through faith**. For as many of you as were baptized into Christ have put on Christ. There is **neither Jew nor Greek**, there is neither **slave nor free**, there is neither **male nor female**, for **you are all [all, as in anyone with freewill who accepts Christ]** one in Christ Jesus. And if you are Christ's, then you are Abraham's offspring, heirs according to promise.

There are reportedly people in the world today who are fully convinced that they are modern-day Nephilim. They believe this because of a history of alien abduction activity that has plagued their families for generations. Sadly, some of these people are even convinced that they have no salvation.

To counter this misconception, the general tactic taken by some theologians, such as Pastor Chris Ward, is to argue the point that there is no such thing as angelic hybrids.[41] While I do not agree with the premise that Nephilim are not angelic hybrids, I do agree that salvation applies to any intelligent life with free will. Again, salvation is not based on DNA but rather free will. Scripture reiterates this in myriad ways, such as the scripture above, and also in the Gospels (Matthew 28:19, Mark 16:15–16, Luke 9:2, John 3:16).

> **Mark 16:15–16** [bold emphasis added]
> And he said to them, "Go into all the world and **proclaim the gospel to the whole creation. Whoever believes and is baptized will be saved, but whoever does not believe will be condemned**."

God judged the Nephilim as he judges all life; He judge's humans by His same righteous standard when they act in rebellion against Him. God is therefore not at war with *genetics* but rather with entities that rebel against the nature of love (i.e., sin).

Now one could speculate that there might be something inherently problematic about crossing angels with other species. Something about this activity could create a genetic profile that is more prone to violence, but I am still compelled to emphasize that as long as an entity has free will that entity has a choice to do good. Jesus came to call the *sinners*, not the *righteous* (Matthew 9:13, Mark 2:17, Luke 5:32), and *all* have fallen short of the glory of God, which I believe applies to Nephilim and humans alike (Romans 3:23). Jesus grants the power to overcome sin, no matter how depraved; all it takes is faith. Therefore, there is hope for salvation for anyone alive who thinks he or she may be a modern-day Nephilim.

Moreover, anyone who is convinced that he or she is a Nephilim is probably ruling out a myriad of other possibilities. For example, even if someone has a lifetime of alien abductions or is part of a family of generational abductions, it doesn't guarantee that alien DNA was inserted into one's genetic profile. The exact details of genetic tinkering, if any, for any given alien abductee, are completely unknown (at least publicly).

As for someone having psychological issues stemming from the idea that he or she might not be saved, I consider that to be strong evidence that the person *is* saved. Why? Because those who are truly lost usually don't care about salvation, or repentance, or God; they prefer the darkness and don't want anything to do with the light. They generally label the idea of salvation, hinging on repentance and dependence on God's love, as weak, repulsive, and/or foolishness.

Concerning God's judgment, which applies to all whether they believe or not, the Qur'an and Hadiths contend that the jinns will be judged by God/Allah, right along with humans (Qur'an 37:158, 15:18; Bukhari 6:60:443). Of course, Muslims obviously believe that one must be a Muslim in order to be saved, whereas the Bible declares the words of Jesus as the path to salvation (John 3:16).

8.10.3.4 Jinns Were Created by Allah

The Qur'an states that Allah created the jinns (Qur'an 6:100, 51:56, 55:15, 15:27) in order to serve Allah (Qur'an 51:56), but if the jinns are Nephilim, they were not created by God but rather came about as a byproduct of fallen angels mating with humans (Genesis 6; Enoch 7).

The Qur'an and Hadiths also state that the jinns were created from fire (Qur'an 15:26–27, 55:15). This could have been inspired by an obscure verse in the book of Hebrews (Hebrews 1:7), but it was more likely extracted from Gnostic teachings.

> **Hebrews 1:7**
> Of the angels, he says, "He makes his angels winds,
> and his ministers a flame of fire."

I've read a number of commentaries on this passage, and none of them conclude that ministers are composed of *fire*. The context of this scripture begins with the preceding verse, which refers to the preeminence of Jesus. As for the association of wind and fire with angels, this may refer to angelic chariots, which are always accompanied by wind and fire.

8.10.3.5 Jinns Can Assume Physical Form

The Qur'an and Hadiths teach that jinns can assume the physical form of wolves (mentioned earlier), but mostly snakes (Dawud 41:5231, 41:5236; Malik 54:54.12.33; Muslim 26:5557). While there are many ancient legends about various gods with shape-shifting abilities, the Bible does not specify any Nephilim as having this supernatural power. However, the Bible does refer to the many legends about the Nephilim and declares that they were "men of renown" (Genesis 6:4).

The book of Enoch also states that among the teachings of the Watchers was magic/sorcery. The Bible speaks plainly about those who practiced the sin of sorcery and that people should repent of it (Acts 17:11). Therefore, there are enough clues in the Bible to indicate that the Nephilim may have had shape-shifting abilities they harnessed either with their innate supernatural abilities or through practicing sorcery.

The Bible further states that Satan, a fallen angel, operated through a snake in the Garden of Eden (Genesis 3), and an angel enabled a donkey to speak (Numbers 22:21–38). Moreover, the Bible narrates stories of demons possessing people (Matthew 17:14–23; Mark 5:1–20, 9:14–29; Luke 9:38–43) and animals (Matthew 8:31, Mark 5:12, Luke 8:26–37). Muhammad drew on all these scriptures to develop his teachings about the jinns.

8.10.3.6 Jinns Were Mortal

The Hadiths state that the jinns were mortal creatures, just like people (Qur'an 7:38, Muslim 35:6561).

> **Qur'an 7:38 (Shakir)** [bold emphasis added]
> He will say: **Enter into fire among the nations that have passed away before you from among jinn and men**; whenever a nation shall enter, it shall curse its sister, until when they have all come up with one another into it; the last of them shall say with regard to the foremost of them: Our Lord! These led us astray therefore give them a double chastisement of the fire. He will say: Every one shall have double but you do not know.

> **Muslim 35:6561** [bold emphasis added]
> Ibn 'Abbas reported that Allah's Messenger (may peace be upon him) used to say:" O Allah, it is unto Thee that I surrender myself. I affirm my faith in Thee and repose my trust in Thee and turn to Thee in repentance and with Thy help fought my adversaries. O Allah, I seek refuge in Thee with Thine Power; there is no god but Thou, lest Thou leadest me astray.

> Thou art ever-living that dieth not, **while the Jinn and mankind die.**"

This actually creates an inconsistency with Muhammad's teaching that Satan was a jinni, not an immortal fallen angel, because Satan has been around for so long. Islamic scholars therefore quote Qur'an 38:81–83 to suggest that Muhammad made a special exception for Satan's extensive lifespan.

> **Qur'an 38:81–83 (Shakir)**
> Ali: "Till the Day of the Time Appointed." He said: "Then by Thy Might I will surely make them live an evil life, all, except Thy servants from among them, the purified ones."

The Bible teaches that the Nephilim were mortals just like humans, and like humans, they have spirits that continue to exist after physical death. It can also be assumed that unrepentant Nephilim spirits became demons. It may therefore be for this very reason that there is confusion concerning the physicality of the jinns within the Qur'an and Hadiths. Some of these beings were probably living Nephilim, and others were deceased, yet the degree of supernatural power they wielded blurred the distinction of their physicality.

8.10.3.7 Jinns Can Have Children

The Qur'an makes an indirect reference to jinns having sex (Qur'an 55:56) and also having children in a passage that directly references Iblis/Satan (Qur'an 18:50).

> **Qur'an 18:50 (Shakir)**
> And when We said to the angels: Make obeisance to Adam; they made obeisance but **Iblis (did it not). He was of the jinn, so he transgressed the commandment of his Lord. What! Would you then take him and his offspring** for friends rather than

> Me, and they are your enemies? Evil is (this) change
> for the unjust.

Because the Nephilim were the product of reproduction, they were most likely able to reproduce as well. The earlier reference to Nimrod/Gilgamesh being two-thirds god is a direct reference to this. If the account of Gilgamesh is accurate, one of Gilgamesh's parents was a first generation Nephilim, and the other parent was a fallen angel.

8.10.3.8 Conclusion of the Jinns

Scripture tells us that the Nephilim were on the earth at an early time, and there is no scripture that declares them to be extinct. In light of this, it very well could be that some of Muhammad's encounters with jinns were actually Nephilim and/or their demon counterparts (ghosts of Nephilim). I say this because of the obvious satanic influences in Islamic doctrine that directly oppose the basic tenets of Christianity, and have also justified the extreme violence of raping, pillaging, murder, rampant abuse of women and children, pedophilia, racism, and slavery, among other things.

While many of these above attributes can be identified in many non-Muslim countries around the world, there is a clear concentration of basic human rights violations within Islamic nations. It is also evident that Islam specifically targets Christianity as its primary enemy; it's no mistake that the Dajjal will claim to be Jesus and not Moses, Buddha, the Dalai Lama, Confucius, or any gods from any other religion in the world.

Muhammad also picked out Jesus to return in the future, *and no one else*, yet his version of Jesus will be a *Muslim* who is *not* the Son of God. This is, by definition, a doctrine of the Antichrist. I believe the only explanation for this is satanic influence, so the conclusion that jinns were primarily Nephilim and/or demons intermingling with Muhammad and his early followers is consistent with the teachings of Islam.

8.10.4 Night Journey with Angel Gabriel

While Muhammad's associations with the jinns sound sensational, they actually pale in comparison to his trip from Mecca to "the furthest mosque" (Jerusalem), roughly 750 miles away as the crow flies. This was directly followed by his ascension to what he called the *seventh heaven*. Following are the details of Muhammad's night journey with Gabriel, most of which I obtained from two Islamic websites.[42–43]

Muhammad's night journey with Gabriel could very well be Muhammad's greatest fabrication, but there are interesting elements about this event that have a ring of truth, if taking Muhammad's interpretation out of the equation.

This Hadith is rather lengthy, so I trimmed it slightly with ellipses (…) and added bold emphasis and comments to the portions that have the most relevance for this analysis.

> **Bukhari 4:54:429** [bold emphasis and bracketed comments added]
>
> The Prophet said, "**While I was at the House in a state midway between sleep and wakefulness [possibly an altered state]**, (an angel recognized me) as **the man lying between two men**. **A golden tray full of [possibly surgical instruments]** wisdom and belief was brought to me and **my body was cut open from the throat to the lower part of the abdomen [a massive incision]** and then my abdomen was washed with Zam-zam water and (my heart was) filled with wisdom and belief. **Al-Buraq, a white animal, smaller than a mule and bigger than a donkey [was it really an animal that flies over 150 miles per hour and travels to other dimensions, or was it some sort of technology?] was brought to me and I set out with Gabriel. [At this point, the Qur'an and other Hadiths say Muhammad made**

a pit stop in Jerusalem 750 miles away (Qur'an 17:1, Muslim 1:309).] When I reached **the nearest heaven** Gabriel said to the heaven gate-keeper, 'Open the gate. ... **Then I met Adam** and greeted him and he said, 'You are welcomed O son and a Prophet.' Then we ascended to **the second heaven** ... Then **I met Jesus and Yahya (John)** who said, 'You are welcomed, O brother and a Prophet.' Then we ascended to **the third heaven** ... There **I met Joseph** and greeted him, and he replied, 'You are welcomed, O brother and a Prophet!' Then we ascended to **the 4th heaven** and There **I met Idris [most Muslims say this is Enoch, but Enoch does not translate to Idris]** and greeted him. He said, 'You are welcomed O brother and Prophet.' Then we ascended to **the 5th heaven** ... There **I met and greeted Aaron** who said, 'You are welcomed O brother and a Prophet." Then we ascended to **the 6th heaven** ... There **I met and greeted Moses** who said, 'You are welcomed O brother and a Prophet.' **When I proceeded on, he started weeping and on being asked why he was weeping, he said, 'O Lord! Followers of this youth who was sent after me will enter Paradise in greater number than my followers.' [Moses was not a prideful man like this]** Then we ascended to **the seventh heaven** ... There **I met and greeted Abraham** who said, 'You are welcomed o son and a Prophet.' Then I was shown Al-Bait-al-Ma'mur (i.e., Allah's House). I asked Gabriel about it and he said, This is Al Bait-ul-Ma'mur where 70,000 angels perform prayers daily and when they leave they never return to it (but always a fresh batch comes into it daily).' Then I was shown Sidrat-ul-Muntaha (i.e., a tree in the seventh heaven) and I saw its Nabk fruits which resembled the clay jugs of Hajr (i.e., a town in

> Arabia), and its leaves were like the ears of elephants, and four rivers originated at its root, two of them were apparent and two were hidden. I asked Gabriel about those rivers and he said, 'The two hidden rivers are in Paradise, and the apparent ones are the Nile and the Euphrates.' Then fifty prayers were enjoined on me. **I descended till I met Moses who asked me, 'What have you done?' I said, 'Fifty prayers have been enjoined on me.' He said, 'I know the people better than you, because I had the hardest experience to bring Bani Israel to obedience. Your followers cannot put up with such obligation. So, return to your Lord and request Him to reduce the number of prayers.'** I returned and requested Allah (for reduction) and He made it forty. I returned and (met Moses) and had a similar discussion, and then returned again to Allah for reduction and He made it thirty, then twenty, then ten, and then I came to Moses who repeated the same advice. **Ultimately Allah reduced it to five. When I came to Moses again, he said, 'What have you done?' I said, 'Allah has made it five only.' He repeated the same advice but I said that I surrendered (to Allah's Final Order)'" [Here Muhammad is declaring that he knows better than Moses]** Allah's Apostle was addressed by Allah, "I have decreed My Obligation and have reduced the burden on My slaves, and I shall reward a single good deed as if it were ten good deeds."

The main elements I will highlight about Muhammad's night journey with the angel Gabriel include his mode of transportation, an event that resembles heart surgery, and Muhammad's trip through various levels of heaven.

8.10.3.1 Was the Al-Buraq a Creature or Technology?

Muhammad's night journey initiated with the angel Gabriel (so the angel claimed) arriving with a creature known as an *al-buraq* (Bukhari 4:54:429, 5:58:227; Muslim 1:309, 1:314). They flew to Jerusalem for prayer (Qur'an 17:1, Muslim 1:309) and then ascended into the heavenly realms.

> **Qur'an 17:1 (Shakir)** [bold emphasis and bracketed comment added]
> Glory be to Him Who **made His servant to go on a night from the Sacred Mosque to the remote mosque [Jerusalem]** of which We have blessed the precincts, so that We may show to him some of Our signs; surely He is the Hearing, the Seeing.

The mosque in Jerusalem is a real physical place, which Muhammad described accurately to people in Mecca.[44] Muhammad also spoke of tethering his otherworldly steed and conducting prayer in the Jerusalem mosque, which are normal activities one might conduct while in a fully conscious state.

I think it is quite possible that an angel visited Muhammad, though I doubt it was Gabriel. It might also be possible that Muhammad rode on the back of a transdimensional creature, the al-buraq, but I think this al-buraq is more likely technology. Whatever it was, it flew over fifteen hundred miles round trip in a single night. Muhammad also spent time in prayer in Jerusalem, and he further left this dimension on an extended journey through the "seven levels" of heaven and then returned to his home, all in that same night.

A liberal estimate for Muhammad's time away from home is ten hours. If all Muhammad did was fly fifteen hundred miles in ten hours, he would have been flying at 150 miles per hour for ten hours straight. We know he had to fly faster than this to account for the other elements of his journey. Therefore, if this was simply Muhammad riding on the back of a creature as some movies depict for heroes riding dragons or winged horses, Muhammad would have been deaf from severe ear damage and blind. Why do I say this? I ride a motorcycle, and the wind starts damaging my ears at about forty miles per hour, and my eyes dry up as well. Without eye and ear protection, just five minutes at over 150 miles per hour would cause serious damage.

I can only think of a few possibilities to account for this discrepancy.

1. **Magic:** The creature was magical and therefore protected Muhammad from harm. This would probably be the typical Muslim response; magic/supernatural power explains all things and often requires no logic or consistency. However, even if a magic or a transdimensional creature of flight were used, why does the narrative provide a description of natural flight? I will speak more about this in a moment.
2. **A lie:** Muhammad had never traveled this fast before, so he did not realize that he had to include information in his *fabricated* tale about his need for ear and eye protection. If these details were included, this event would have an exceptional scientific accuracy in describing high-velocity flight on a flying beast, but these details are absent.
3. **Advanced technology:** This wasn't an actual creature but rather some form of technology like a *Star Wars* speeder bike with shielding or a transparent enclosure of some sort. I believe this is the most likely explanation. Near East and Persian art depict the al-buraq with a human face, which further supports the idea of technology associated with humanoid occupants (i.e., the angel), similar to biblical encounters associating angels with wheels within wheels and flying chariots of fire.[45]

Returning to the idea of a transdimensional creature, Muhammad specifically described details that preclude teleportation because the creature zipped across the sky rather than simply appearing in Jerusalem: "The animal's step (was so wide that it) reached the farthest point within the reach of the animal's sight." One would think that a transdimensional creature, with supernatural shielding to protect the person on its back, would simply use that same power to teleport, rather than fly like a bird. It is still possible this could be a creature with supernatural power; I just consider it unlikely.

According to *The Biography of Prophet Muhammad* by ibn Hisham,[46] Muhammad spotted a caravan below him while flying back home, and he spoke with them about their camel that had run away. He also made a second pit stop with another caravan and drank some of their water. An article titled "Muhammad: Aspects of His Biography," published at http://www.iman.co.nz/ by the Islamic Foundation of the United Kingdom, describes the narrative as follows:

> "In the valleys of Makkah," replied the Prophet, "I met a caravan, one whose camel had taken fright and run away. I warned them of this. Then I saw another caravan that had encamped for the night. Outside the principal tent stood a jar of water with a cover on it. I drank water from the jar and replaced the cover as it was before. This same caravan is now approaching Bayda and will shortly enter Makkah. It is led by a dark grey camel, carrying a double load, one half black and the other of various colors."[47]

Again I have to return to the concept of eye and ear protection; Muhammad would have never seen these caravans if he was flying over 150 miles per hour without eye protection. Either he was supernaturally protected from these effects or he was riding in or on something with shielding.

This particular follow-up of the story, if it is true, adds the most credibility to Muhammad's tale (that this event occurred, but not necessarily all the details) because it gives corroborating evidence that Muhammad knew about and accurately described two caravans out in the desert.

Another interesting story about things flying in the sky in Muhammad's time comes from another Hadith about lights in the night sky.

> **Bukhari 1:8:454** [bold emphasis added]
> **Once, on a dark night**, two of the companions of the Prophet departed (after a meeting with the prophet) **and were led by two lights like lamps (from the sky) lighting the road in front of them**. And, **when they parted (from each other), each of them was accompanied by one of these lights** till he reached his house.

Perhaps these lights were al-buraqs? Perhaps the al-buraqs were also fountains of molten copper or flying chariots of fire?

8.10.3.2 Did Aliens Perform Heart Surgery on Muhammad?

As soon as Muhammad encountered the angel claiming to be Gabriel, Gabriel did something very strange that is highly reminiscent of the alien abduction phenomenon. He conducted a surgical operation, making a massive incision from Muhammad's throat all the way to his lower abdomen. Gabriel then yanked out Muhammad's heart and did something to fix it, which Muhammad associated with wisdom and faith. He then washed his heart, reinserted it, and sutured him back up (Bukhari 4:54:429, 5:58:227; Muslim 1:309, 1:314).

This is outlandish. While the Bible speaks extensively of the heart, nowhere does it include a story about angels cutting people open, operating on their organs, and reinserting them.

Interestingly, this is not the first time the angel Gabriel (doubtful it was him) operated on Muhammad's heart. Gabriel conducted either the same or a similar operation on Muhammad when was a boy, long before the night journey (Muslim 1:311). According to the first event, it most likely occurred during broad daylight because there were a number of terrified boys who witnessed it; they thought Muhammad was being murdered! What's more, when Gabriel completed this operation, he left needle marks on Muhammad's chest.

> **Muslim 1:311** [bold emphasis added]
> Anas b. Malik reported that **Gabriel came to the Messenger of Allah** (may peace be upon him) **while he was playing with his playmates. He took hold of him and lay him prostrate on the ground and tore open his breast and took out the heart from it and then extracted a blood-clot out of it and said: That was the part of Satan in thee**. And then **he washed it with the water** of Zamzam in a **golden basin and then it was joined together and restored it to its place**. The **boys came running to his mother, i.e., his nurse, and said: Verily Muhammad has been murdered**. They **all rushed toward him** (and found him all right) **His color was changed**, Anas said. **I myself saw the marks of needle on his breast**.

The alien abduction phenomenon often involves people who are known as *contactees.* Most contactees have early memories of childhood abductions, and these abductions continue throughout their lives. Contactees can also belong to a family of contactees, with this same phenomenon spanning back for centuries in the same families. The prevalent theory is that the aliens are conducting genetic experimentation; hence, they focus on specific families for generations.

Contactees sometimes give accounts of horrific surgical procedures. In this particular Hadith, these other witnesses, coupled with a physical scar (or needle marks), are very telling of an actual alien abduction. According to this Hadith, as well as those who speak of Muhammad's night vision with heart surgery, Muhammad was probably a contactee, and some of his experiences relate to his abductions.

It could very well be that Muhammad's early childhood abductions created a high level of spiritual awareness in Muhammad at a young age. He knew there was much more to this reality than meets the eye. To make sense out of what he experienced, he immersed himself in any spiritual literature he could get his hands on. Over time, as he started to place labels on some of these things like the jinns, his entire theology of Islam began to take shape. Much comes from the Bible, some from the Talmud and other Gnostic sources, some from the Far East, and some probably even from Egyptian mythology or other sources (which I will mention in a moment). This Gabriel character, whoever he was, was also manipulating Muhammad and directing him down the spiritual path of Islam that he created.

Concerning Muhammad's journey through the seven heavens, this may be a mixture of fabrication and a coping mechanism whereby Muhammad was simply building an alternate reality in his own mind to make sense out of what happened to him.

A key difference between Muhammad and the biblical prophets is that Muhammad's abductors were not the good guys. Where Muhammad lived, the people were mostly apostates, and Muhammad's family clearly didn't accept the God of Abraham, Isaac, and Jacob as the Jews presented Him. There were probably other dark spiritual strongholds in that area as well, in order for this to happen to Muhammad. It is situations like this, where groups of people live far outside the will of God, that Satan establishes strongholds.

One of the most disturbing aspects of the alien abduction phenomenon is that aliens will sometimes target children. Those reading this might wonder why God would allow such a thing. I wonder this myself, and I'm pretty sure the answer has something to do with love and free will, but finding the exact words to articulate all the complex intricacies that lead to a child abduction takes a book of its own and spans far beyond my assessment here. Suffice it to say, there are many alien abduction cases that involve children, just as there are many children who are the victims of senseless crimes. The Bible also documents children who were possessed by demons, but no explanation is given as to how this came about.

The bottom line is we live in a sinful, cursed world, which Adam and Eve unleashed on us, and sometimes it appears as though Satan has the upper hand. Readers should take heart, however, that calling on the name of Jesus can cast demons out, and the name of Jesus will also stop an alien abduction in progress. I have personally corresponded with people who reported this to me from personal experience. They simply rebuke the aliens in the name of Jesus, as though they were rebuking demons, and the aliens leave hastily. Needless to say, those that bug out at the name of Jesus are the bad guys. It is therefore imperative that parents teach their children about Jesus early on so they will benefit from a relationship with Him, which reaps countless benefits in unfathomable ways.

8.10.3.3 Muhammad's Trip to the Seventh Heaven

So the angel Gabriel performed heart surgery on Muhammad, then he set him up with an al-buraq, and they flew to Jerusalem. Why did the angel go to Jerusalem of all places, the single most religiously charged location on the planet, even in Muhammad's day? By doing this, the angel with Muhammad made the Dome of the Rock a primary target for Islamic aggression for centuries to come. Too bad he didn't pick another spot!

After Muhammad spent time in prayer, he went to the seven heavens, as Muhammad referred to them (Qur'an 17:1; Bukhari 4:54:429, 5:58:227; Muslim 1:309; Malik 51:51.4.10; etc.). Concerning Muhammad's experiences in these realms, only a few basic details are mentioned:

1. Muhammad experienced his version of temptation when the angel Gabriel offered him wine or milk. Muhammad chose the milk, thereby equating wine with evil. What stands out about this temptation to me is the angel who Muhammad claimed was Gabriel was actually playing Satan's role as the tempter. That makes me wonder if he was actually Satan,

rather than Gabriel. Everything he did fits Satan's description much more than Gabriel's.

2. Muhammad met different people in the different levels of heaven; they are as follows:
   a. **First heaven:** Muhammad met Adam (and yet, no Eve).
   b. **Second heaven:** Muhammad met Jesus and John the Baptist (yup, Jesus is the lowest of the prophets in Muhammad's opinion, despite that even according to the Qur'an, He was born of a virgin, spoke as a baby, could create life and raise the dead, and is the only prophet who will return in the future to defeat the Dajjal Antichrist, all of which no prophet comes close to.)
   c. **Third heaven:** Muhammad met Idris, but who is Idris? (Muslims usually claim he was Enoch, despite the fact that the translation of the name Enoch is not Idris; hence, the name is left as Idris in English translations. What's more, absolutely nowhere in the Qur'an, or any Hadiths, is there any mention of Idris that associates him with Enoch (Qur'an 19:56, 21:85; Muslim 1:227, 1:309, 1:313, 1:314, 4:1916, 16:4139, 21:4749, 30:5779, 31:6051, 32:6246; Dawud 12:2207; Malik 2:2.1.3, 25:25.4.13, 51:51.5.15; Bukhari 6:60:480; etc.). Enoch wrote the book of Enoch, he was frequently visited by angels, and he never died. That's sort of a big deal, right? Might these tidbits be worth mentioning about Idris if he's really Enoch? Researching this mysterious character, I learned that Idris is most likely Osiris, taken directly from Egyptian mythology. Osiris translates to Idreesa in Aramaic. I've also read that Idris is not the only character listed in the Qur'an who is drawn from the mythologies of other religions.[48]
   d. **Fourth heaven:** Muhammad met Joseph, one of the twelve sons of Jacob.
   e. **Fifth heaven:** Muhammad met Aaron, Moses's brother, the first Levite chief priest of Israel.

f. **Sixth heaven:** Muhammad met Moses, and Moses cried because Muhammad had more followers than he did (Bukhari 4:54:429, 5:58:227; Muslim 1:314). Moses was not a proud man. Even when God first appointed him, he tried to avoid the job four times (Exodus 3:11, 4:1, 4:10, 4:13). He was a humble man and didn't want to be in the spotlight. The only reason his brother Aaron was brought into the picture is because Moses practically begged God to choose someone else (Exodus 4:13). Moses would never have cried if someone else brought more people to salvation than he did. He would have rejoiced! At one point, God was so angry with Israel, he was going to wipe it out and start over again with Moses's family (Deuteronomy 9:13–14, Exodus 32:12–14). If Moses was a proud man, he would have liked this idea, but the truth is he chose to risk taking on the wrath of God by interceding for Israel, rather than to accept that offer.

g. **Seventh heaven:** Muhammad met Abraham, who was in the highest heaven. It's interesting that Muhammad didn't meet King Solomon in one of these heavens. Solomon, according to Muhammad's own admission, had a level of authority that exceeded his own when it came to the jinns.

3. Muhammad made a point to outclass Moses on two counts. First, by having Moses cry for not amassing as many followers, Muhammad established bragging rights because he had a greater following. Secondly, Muhammad went back and forth between Allah and Moses regarding the number of times he and his followers should pray on a daily basis. The number starts with fifty, but Moses stopped Muhammad and advised him to return to Allah and bargain that number down because there was no way his followers would have been able to meet such a demand. Muhammad bounced back and forth between Allah and Moses until this number was reduced to five times, but Moses still advised Muhammad to drop that number even more. At this point, Muhammad put his foot

> down and said that five was good enough, and he would not return to Allah again. By doing this, he essentially overruled Moses because he demanded higher standards of piety than Moses did.

And such is the tale of Muhammad's night journey with Gabriel. To this day, Muslims sometimes debate where Muhammad tethered his al-buraq at the temple, and they frequently feud with Jews over pretty much everything at, in, near, or around that temple. The Dome of the Rock, a.k.a. Temple Mount, is considered the third holiest place for Muslims, and it's all because of Muhammad's claim that he ascended to the heavens from that very spot.

8.11 The Rise of World Civilizations

As the sands of time have trickled down through the centuries since the days of Muhammad, the *visible* signs of otherworldly interaction in this world have greatly diminished, but they're still around.

Otherworldly influences have gone underground, perhaps literally. They probably have underground bases, or bases at the bottom of the deepest oceans, but I think it would be rare if any of these secret bases integrate into human society as some claim. Most likely whatever interaction *they* have with us, it is strictly on *their* terms.

I don't doubt that the NSA (National Security Agency, aka No Such Agency) and other agencies with classified acronyms that no one knows about are concealing information about an extraterrestrial presence in, on, and around the earth. They know the truth about the famous Roswell incident, and they used Project Bluebook to cover their tracks for a while, but now their tactics have shifted to silence. We see UFOs roaming our skies all the time; that's always been the case, but now there are so many hoaxes that the real UFOs can come and go with impunity, and no one will ever know what's real and what's not. These days it's pretty much impossible to tell the *fake* videos and pictures from the *genuine articles*. These rampant hoaxes, therefore, have done more to cover up the extraterrestrial reality than any government ever did.

But they exist, and I say this based not on the "evidence" covered in countless UFO, extraterrestrial, and paranormal-type shows and books, or even my great-grandmother's testimony or my own personal encounter, but rather on what I know of scripture. They're real, and they read our mail (figuratively and probably literally). They're monitoring us and waiting for the right time, just as the Bible declares.

CHAPTER 9

The Grand Conclusion

All of the otherworldly details of this book, referenced in ancient manuscripts, are foreign to most people these days. They are abstract concepts, dismissed by most as ancient symbolism, poetry, figurative speech, and so on. Such things could not possibly be true.

Transdimensional angelic beings and their fantastical flying chariots of fire, roving stars, columns of fire, glorious clouds, and flying wheels within wheels; shape-shifting jinns and their fountains of molten copper, flying lamps and al-buraqs; bizarre angelic surgical operations, talking animals, and sorcery; six-fingered, six-toed giants; mutant hybrids with supernatural power; and people resurrected from the dead—this is all fairy tale stuff. It has to be, right? Who would ever believe these things?

And yet, we now have baboons with pigs' hearts[1] and mice with human rectums.[2] How weird is that? I suspect the reality of today would be every bit as strange to a person of ancient times as the ancient world would be for a person from this modern age. Consider how a person from Old Testament times would describe a fighter jet, nuclear power, laser holograms, brain mapping, artificial intelligence, or genetic engineering? Even these technologies are old school; now we're realistically looking at nanobots, intergalactic travel, planetary terraforming, invisibility shields, and much more. Our mathematics applied to quantum physics can see beyond this dimension to ten dimensions or more.[3] String theory, M theory, and others even more bizarre continue to diverge further from what we know of as reality, and yet so many still relegate the words of antiquity as mythological babble. Why is that?

The seers of today peer into the ancient past through the lens of ancient manuscripts, and they marvel and accept the truth of what they see. That is what I have attempted to do here. As for the prophets of old, they saw glimpses of our time, and they wrote about them in their time. We need to wake up, clarify our vision, and prepare ourselves for the days ahead. New discoveries of giants are reported all around the world, and yet they skirt the mainstream media, and websites like Snopes blast them all as fakes. Many are indeed fakes, but some of them *are probably real.* We need to start accepting new possibilities and stop automatically assuming certain things cannot be real.

It is no coincidence that the comic-book heroes we see so often in the movies today are becoming increasingly realistic. The same goes for sci-fi and fantasy films in general. These ideas are separate from reality, but at the same time, the pendulum has reached its mark; the clock has ticked, and now it swings the other way. More movies depict the multidimensional structure of the universe with ever-increasing clarity, and in countless ways, they remind us that the supernatural beings that were once openly among us are *returning.*

The Bible declares a time is coming when the saints of God will be "taken up" (1 Thessalonians 4:13–17, 1 Corinthians 15:51–58, Philemon 3:20–21).

What will that look like?

The prophets of old have spoken of a day that is coming when the two witnesses will appear to the people of the earth. These men will travel the globe, and their mode of transportation might very well be an angelic chariot of fire, or as Islamic literature suggests, a magic mule.

What will that look like?

When the two witnesses (Dajjals) travel to Medina, they will avoid two angels who will be guarding that area (Bukhari 3:30:103–106, 7:71:627, 9:88:246–248, 9:88:239–240, 9:93:565; Malik 45:45:4.16;

Muslim 7:3186–3187, 41:6994–6996, 41:7028, 41:7030, 41:7032–7033) and land on a flat barren plain outside of Medina. Then they will call everyone from the city to come join them (Bukhari 3:30:106, Muslim 41:7032).

What will that look like?

> **Bukhari 3:30:106** [bold emphasis added]
> "Ad-Dajjal will come and it will be forbidden for him to pass through the entrances of Medina. **He will land in some of the salty barren areas (outside) Medina ...**"
>
> **Muslim 41:7032** [bold emphasis added]
> Anas b. Malik reported that Allah's Messenger (may peace be upon him) said: There will be no land which would not be covered by the Dajjal but Mecca and Medina, and there would no passage out of the passages leading to them which would not be guarded by angels arranged in rows. **Then he (the Dajjal) would appear in a barren place adjacent to Medina and it would rock three times that every unbeliever and hypocrite would get out of it towards him**.

The veil is thin, and it grows thinner each day. Through all the years of my research, I believe I have been directed to a single event that will overshadow this world in the days ahead and usher in the strong delusion. A recurring vision I have had in my mind is of a savior-like man, illuminated in ethereal light, descending to Earth in a public spectacle for all to see. He will descend from an otherworldly, interdimensional, intergalactic spacecraft of unfathomable power, a technological wonder to behold.

The entire world will witness this event, and it will occur in a very public place. This man will look exactly like what we think Jesus looks like. This event may also be the initiation of *open contact*, in which *public disclosure* will no longer be an option.

For many years, I believed this man was going to be the Antichrist. Then I read Joel Richardson's book *The Islamic Antichrist*, which directed me to Islam's Muslim Jesus, a.k.a. the False Prophet. When I read the description of how this Muslim Jesus will descend to Earth between two angels, my jaw hit the floor. *This was my vision*; this was the primary source of the strong delusion unfolding before me, word for word, in the Hadiths and the Qur'an (Muslim 41:7015, 41:7023, 41:6924; Qur'an 43:63).

> **Qur'an 43:63 (Shakir)** [bold emphasis and bracketed comments added]
> And when Isa **[the False Prophet]** came with clear arguments he said: I have come to you indeed with wisdom, and that I may make clear to you part of what you differ in; so be careful of (your duty to) Allah and obey me:
>
> **Muslim 41:7015** [bold emphasis and bracketed comments added]
> [I]t would at this very time that Allah would send Christ, **[the False Prophet]** son of Mary, and **he will descend at the white minaret in the eastern side of Damascus wearing two garments lightly dyed with saffron and placing his hands on the wings of two Angels** …

The Bible does not tell us precisely where or how the False Prophet will arrive, but this Hadith does. He will descend to Earth between the wings of two angels.

What will this look like?

As I said before, I don't think angels have wings. They have been traditionally depicted with them in art because they are associated with the heavens, and they might have the ability to fly, but I *seriously doubt* that they fly like birds. When the real Jesus left this earth, He didn't sprout wings; He floated up into the sky and disappeared into a cloud (Luke 24:50–53, Acts 1:9). This event with the False Prophet will most likely be the reverse of the real Jesus's departure, with one exception. That cloud will not be described as a *cloud* by the people of today. In today's terminology, it will be a UFO.

> **Acts 1:9**
> And when he had said these things, as they were looking on, he was lifted up, and a cloud took him out of their sight.

Above is what I call **Arrival Scenario #1**, which aligns with the picture I have always had in my mind. This image is much clearer now. Rather than just seeing this image, I now hear the words of what this man will say. If Arrival Scenario #1 is on target, this charismatic angelic being from another world may very well repeat the words of Jesus, stating that *his kingdom is not of this world* (John 18:36), and he will be able to prove it by taking ambassadors from this world to another planet with an advanced civilization. This might even be the same place the angel who claimed to be Gabriel took Muhammad.

According to the Hadiths, seventy thousand angels journey to God's throne every day, and there probably is a real version of that angelic pilgrimage out in the cosmos, though I doubt they are limited to going only one time (Muslim 1:309).

In essence, **the False Prophet will be using the truth to tell a lie**. I'm convinced that the *real* Jesus does have a powerful, highly advanced kingdom that spans beyond this world, but it is not nearly as limited in scope as what the False Prophet will claim and/or reveal to be his kingdom.

Regarding this futuristic otherworldly kingdom of the False Prophet (if this will be his claim), I envision widespread media coverage, in which otherworldly dignitaries will meet and introduce the people of Earth to something we have sensed for a long time: we are not alone in the universe. There really is a *federation of planets* or a *new republic* ruled by a mysterious supreme being/Allah.

The False Prophet/Muslim Jesus will present a counterfeit; the entity he will identify as Allah, the cosmic ruler of the universe, will actually be Satan. Satan might even be his literal biological father (Genesis 3:15). The False Prophet might also have some story about being a genetic experiment for the benefit of mankind. Whatever he says, it will provide a scientific reason to answer the question about his amazing longevity, especially to Muslims, who believe he is mortal and will eventually die.

What's more, knowing how much Satan likes to counterfeit God, the False Prophet might be related to the Mahdi/Antichrist as well, since Jesus and John the Baptist were cousins. Why not? There are strong indications that both the False Prophet and the Mahdi/Antichrist will be Nephilim; such an otherworldly heritage will be yet another feather in the Mahdi's cap to claiming the status of a god. Moreover, this will not be anything new. The deception that is coming is simply a remake of the deceptions of old—new technology, better special effects, but the same old lie.

In reality, the real God of the universe, Yahweh, Elohim, Jehovah, and so forth, is in charge, but many of the *elements* of the False Prophet's deception will actually be *true*, which will make this deception even more cunning. The heavens are indeed populated with life, but God the Creator rules over all of them from a glorified planet in a higher dimension, where His throne resides (more info on this is found in *Aliens and the Antichrist*).[4] Satan will simply copycat this reality and establish another throne for his False Prophet on some other distant planet.

As soon as the False Prophet arrives, the world will be prepared for his arrival, and his words will flow as smoothly as a Shakespearian poet.

> Greetings people of Earth, you have been patiently awaiting for my return, and now that day has come. It is now time for me to reveal to you who I really am. While it is true that my kingdom is not of this world, I am no more a Son of God than any of you. I am

> unique in a certain way, but two thousand years ago, you did not understand. Now that you have evolved, you should be able to understand this truth.
>
> We have been watching over you since the beginning. My father came from an advanced race of enlightened beings in the Pleiades constellation. He is the source of my power and the light of my path. I am also not alone; there is another among you, who is also from my people, and it is to this man [the Mahdi] that you must owe your allegiance …

And so it will be that this *fake* Jesus, who will claim to set the record straight on his *true*, otherworldly identity, will explain his incredible longevity to both Muslims and Christians alike, and then he will confront the Dajjal/Antichrist, who might also have otherworldly allies. The False Prophet will overcome him, and the world will rejoice with great relief that this terror, this monstrosity of a man will finally be dealt with once and for all. This, however, will only be the beginning. Following this event, he will insist that the world accept the Mahdi as the rightful ruler of the world.

Another possibility has occurred to me, regarding the arrival of the False Prophet, which I find interesting. This is what I call **Arrival Scenario #2**.

Satan might have some grand scheme to have two beings that look exactly like what people might expect angels to look like: glowing humanoids with birds' wings, gently floating down to the earth with Jesus. Angels can pull this illusion off, no problem, so let's say Satan's fallen angels do this; they don a costume of angels' wings and cloak their ships. Now contrast this with God's faithful angels preaching the Gospel (Revelation 14:6), using their real angelic aerial vehicles and not bothering with the goofy bird-wing illusions.

> **Revelation 14:6** [bold emphasis added]
> Then **I saw another angel flying** directly overhead, **with an eternal gospel to proclaim to those who dwell on earth**, to every nation and tribe and language and people.

The two witnesses, likewise, will not bother with illusions. No matter how they arrive or what they do, that will be the real deal. Whatever that magic mule is, it'll be pretty awesome. For this reason, I see them most likely in the company of God's faithful angels (without wings), zipping about in otherworldly aerial vehicles.

The people of Earth will then be faced with a dilemma—an array of clashing paradigms, enough to boggle the mind—and put a lot of people in a state of catatonic shock. What to make of all this? Jesus said this would happen; people will be seriously freaked out!

> **Luke 21:25–26** [bold emphasis added]
> "**And there will be signs in sun and moon and stars**, and **on the earth distress of nations in perplexity** because of the roaring of the sea and the waves, **people fainting with fear and with foreboding of what is coming on the world**. For the powers of the heavens will be shaken."

Arrival Scenario #2 is an interesting take because it would pit the traditional ideas people have about angels and the heavens against the words and actions of the deceivers and those who are telling the truth.

The Antichrist/Mahdi and False Prophet might fit the bill perfectly, as far as meeting almost every expectation of what people *traditionally* think about angels, the nature of heaven, and the like. Contrasting with this will be the two witnesses and *real* angels, using otherworldly technology and basically flipping people out, because their revelation of the heavens as I have been describing in this book will seem all New Age and weird. It just won't seem right to them.

The two witnesses will also be able to call down fire from the sky, alter the weather, inflict plagues, and turn water into blood. The Antichrist/Mahdi and False Prophet likewise will be able to call down fire from the heavens and perform many signs and wonders.

However this all unfolds, be it Arrival Scenario #1, #2, or something else, physical appearances and traditional expectations will be such a distraction that only genuine believers of Christ, who *know* the voice and character of Jesus, will be able to hear the words of truth at that time (John 10:14, 10:27–28). Physical senses will be deceptive, and true believers will be *forced* to see with the eyes of their hearts (Ephesians 1:18) and judge what they see by its fruit (Matthew 7:16, Luke 6:44).

Continuing with my vision of Arrival Scenario #1 (the more likely of the two in my opinion), the False Prophet will specialize in deceiving Christians and other religions as a multifaceted religious guru with connections to all people. He will claim to be Jesus, appealing to Christians; he will claim to be a Muslim, appealing to Muslims; he will claim Jewish ancestry, appealing to Jews; he will have otherworldly origins, appealing to New Agers and other faiths. He will be the ultimate False Prophet.

As for the Antichrist/Mahdi, he will tap into this same deception, but his primary focus will be the role of a valiant Muslim warrior, catering to Muslim expectations. He will ride on a white horse (Revelation 6:2), and he will urge all Muslims to unite and break down the barriers between the Shiites and Sunnis.

> **Revelation 6:2**
> And I looked, and behold, a white horse! And its rider had a bow, and a crown was given to him, and he came out conquering, and to conquer.

Even now, Turkey's prime minister, Recep Tayyip Erdogan, is checking some of the blocks for the role of the Mahdi.[5] I don't think he will be the twelfth imam, though he is trying to unite Shiites and Sunnis, and on one occasion, he even tried to ride a horse. (That was a complete fiasco; there is a humiliating video circulating that is less than glamorous.[6] The skittish horse he picked was ready for the rodeo.)

The Antichrist/Mahdi will probably be able to tame a rodeo horse, and he will also be a commanding presence in his rise to power, advocating a return to the caliph. While he rises to power, a ruler from a country south of him—a man of extreme violence and perhaps imbued with supernatural power—will be taking the world by storm. I see this mysterious man of violence, whom I referred to earlier as the Dajjal/Antichrist (with the theory that there will be two Antichrists), closely associated with a terrorist group like the Muslim Brotherhood or ISIS. Most people will view him and his followers as universally evil, but many Muslims will align with him, just as many are aligned with ISIS, and many more will be sympathetic toward his cause.

This first and lesser Antichrist will have only one eye, fitting succinctly with many Islamic prophecies (Bukhari 9:87:128, 4:55:649, 5:59:685, 7:72:789, 9:87:153, 9:93:504; Malik 49:49.2.2; Muslim 1:323, 1:324, 1:325, 41:7005), as well as a few Bible scriptures (Zechariah 11:16–17, Revelation 13, Genesis 49:17). He might also have Jewish ancestry, though I think that connection more aptly applies to the two witnesses, who will be helping thousands of Jews most likely sheltered in the ancient city of Petra.

Tensions will escalate with this Dajjal/Antichrist figure, but then the key moment of the strong delusion, the arrival of the False Prophet, will take place and astonish the world. When this happens, the Antichrist/Mahdi (who probably won't be declared the Mahdi yet) will immediately seek out this otherworldly entity and align with him. The False Prophet will then endorse this Muslim leader as the true Mahdi, the twelfth imam, and signs and wonders will follow.

The False Prophet, seeking to fulfill his role in Islamic eschatology, will hunt down the first Dajjal/Antichrist and take him out. By this time, the world will be seeing many signs of otherworldly visitors as the words of Jesus come to pass. The days of Noah will be upon us, days when otherworldly beings interact with humanity in open contact (Matthew 24:37–42, Luke 17:26–37), days with otherworldly battles (Daniel 8:10; Revelation 12:4) when "the heavens will be shaken" (Matthew 24:29, Luke 21:26). The False Prophet will destroy this first Dajjal/Antichrist, and his alliance with the Antichrist/Mahdi will catapult the Mahdi to global fame.

In *Aliens and the Antichrist*, I hinted at the possibility of this false flag scenario when discussing the otherworldly battle narrated by the prophet Daniel.[7] Now that I have researched the Qur'an and Hadiths, I have become even more convinced that these battles are between warring factions within the enemy's camp because the enemy's game plan (i.e., Satan's prophetic strategy outlined in Islamic writings) also describes this exact scenario.

The arrival of the False Prophet is a diverging point for Islam, for when the Antichrist/Mahdi assumes complete control, he will establish a peace covenant with Israel and bring peace and prosperity to the world, *at least in the beginning*, for about three and a half years (Daniel 9:27). The rhetoric of the Mahdi/Antichrist will increase during this time until he eventually diverges from traditional Islam by claiming the status of a god. This will violate the portions of the Qur'an and Hadiths that insist upon monotheism, but by the time the Mahdi/Antichrist makes this transition, Muslims will be ready for it. Just as the False Prophet will creatively reinterpret Bible scriptures to remove his status as the only begotten Son of God, the Mahdi/Antichrist will also reinterpret the Qur'an and Hadiths to promote himself as a god.

The Mahdi/Antichrist's alliance with the False Prophet will greatly facilitate this transition; the mere presence of the False Prophet, with his divine otherworldly origins and his direct connections to different religions, will cause many people to abandon all they previously knew and accept this *new age of Islam* unfolding before them.

This is what I believe Daniel was referring to when he stated that the Antichrist will magnify himself and no longer pay attention to the gods of his fathers, but instead honor the "god of fortresses." The False Prophet, and/or his otherworldly father (who might literally, biologically be Satan) is the god of fortresses. Most of Islam will remain intact because it is a religion that will suit the Mahdi/Antichrist's ambitions for world domination; he will simply change those elements that impede his declaration of being a god.

> **Daniel 11:36–39** [bold emphasis and bracketed comments added]
> "And the king shall do as he wills. **He shall exalt himself and magnify himself above every god**, and shall **speak astonishing things against the God of gods**. He shall prosper till the indignation is accomplished; for what is decreed shall be done. **He shall pay no attention to the gods of his fathers, [he will abandon traditional Islam] or to the one beloved by women.** He shall not pay attention to any other god, for **he shall magnify himself above all. He shall honor the god of fortresses [the otherworldly False Prophet and/or his father, Satan] instead of these. A god whom his fathers did not know he shall honor with gold and silver, with precious stones and costly gifts [this may be a reference to a vast interstellar trade agreement, similar to what Satan had before]. He shall deal with the strongest fortresses with the help of a foreign god [as the Qur'an and Haditһs state, the Muslim Jesus/False Prophet will destroy the Dajjal/Antichrist].** Those who acknowledge him he shall load with honor. He shall make them rulers over many and shall divide the land for a price …"

As part of the tactics the Mahdi/Antichrist will use to convince the world he is their savior (in addition to working with the False Prophet to defeat the Dajjal/Antichrist in an otherworldly confrontation, as well as miraculous demonstrations of supernatural power) he will resolve a number of mysteries that have puzzled archaeologists for years. Right now, there are a few religious artifacts, such as the Ark of the Covenant and the black stone in the corner of the Kaaba, that evade discovery or scientific analysis. The Mahdi/Antichrist will have *no respect* for any religion whatsoever. Therefore, when he gains territory under his command, he will put an end to all speculations concerning any religious artifacts he finds.

He will probably find the Ark of the Covenant, return it to Jerusalem, and maybe even sit on the mercy seat (2 Thessalonians 2:4) when he claims to be a god. I speculated this tidbit in *Aliens and the Antichrist*,[8] and now Joel Richardson's *The Islamic Antichrist* states that Islamic scholars have been predicting the same event.[8]

When that ark is found, what will people think when its contents (the manna and pieces of the stone tablets with the Ten Commandments) are scientifically analyzed, and the evidence links them to highly advanced technology? Moreover, what if more ancient scrolls are found, as Islamic scholars also predict, that support the narrative of the Mahdi/Antichrist?[10] Even looking at the scriptures we have now, such as the book of Enoch, there is already a mountain of evidence supporting the ancient-astronaut narrative.

What more will be found?

As for the black stone embedded in the corner of the Kaaba, most people, even Muslims, think it is a meteorite, but why do Muslims treat it as such a holy object? What is so special about a meteorite, unless, of course, there's something more to it? What if it has some sort of technology imbedded inside of it just waiting to be revealed? Would that not be an eye-opener?

Along with my vision of a luminescent savior figure, descending from the sky beneath a UFO, I have always had a feeling that this earth we live on has countless secrets buried inside it—ancient yet highly advanced technology or evidence of species that would boggle the mind (such as the Nephilim, including their freakish animal-hybrid counterparts), all just waiting to be found. The Mahdi/Antichrist will find some of these relics, and his interpretation of these findings will support his claims of being a god worthy of worship, worthy of absolute obedience and submission to his rule, however violent it may be.

The Mahdi/Antichrist will also lead the world to end the suppression of highly advanced technology that has been occurring for a very long time. If there is a solution for free energy, he will use it. If we already have mastered antigravity but the military industrial complex has suppressed it, he will exploit it.

The exotic technology that the False Prophet will bring to this world will be far beyond anything we have. Interestingly, as I pointed out in *Aliens and the Antichrist*, the Bible even indicates that the False Prophet will give a mandate for the creation of true *artificial intelligence* (Revelation 13:11–18).[11]

> **Revelation 13:11–18** [bold emphasis added]
> Then I saw another beast rising out of the earth. **It had two horns like a lamb [a lamb like Jesus]** and **it spoke like a dragon [aligned with the Mahdi/Antichrist]**. It exercises all the authority of the first beast in its presence, and **makes the earth and its inhabitants worship the first beast**, whose **mortal wound was healed [unification of all Muslims]**. It performs great signs, even **making fire come down from heaven to earth** in front of people, and by the signs that it is allowed to work in the presence of the beast **it deceives those who dwell on earth, telling them to make an image for the beast** that was wounded by the sword and yet lived. **And it was allowed to give breath to the image of the beast, so that the image of the beast might even speak and might cause those who would not worship the image of the beast to be slain [the image of the beast is manmade, yet it has sentience]**. Also **it causes all**, both small and great, both rich and poor, both free and slave, **to be marked on the right hand or the forehead, so that no one can buy or sell unless he has the mark**, that is, the name of the beast or the number of its name. This calls for wisdom: let

> the one who has understanding calculate the number of the beast, for it is the number of a man, and his number is 666.

This passage of scripture states that this thing called the "image of the beast" will be a man-made entity. It will have a semblance of life (i.e., the False Prophet gives breath to the image). This image of the beast will be able to speak, and it will demand obedience. It will be integrated with a tracking system for all the people of the Antichrist kingdom (with the mark of the beast), and it will also tie into the economy of the beast kingdom. This is a blatantly obvious description of artificial intelligence, and it makes perfect sense that an otherworldly entity from a highly advanced civilization would introduce such technology to this world.

Another indication that the image of the beast will not be truly alive is that there is no mention of it when the False Prophet and the Antichrist are thrown into the lake of fire (Revelation 19:20). It is as if this thing, whatever it is, will simply be shut down, end of story.

As all the pieces fit together for the strong delusion, everything will appear to be going according to the plans of the Mahdi/Antichrist, though not everyone will accept him. Some will be suspicious, especially Jews in Israel, as well as many Christians. Whether there is a rapture of the church or not, the genuine Christians who are here at that time will not accept the Antichrist. These holdouts, refusing the mark of the beast, will exasperate the Mahdi/Antichrist and his minions to no end.

In the middle of the Mahdi/Antichrist's seven-year peace agreement with Israel, he will violate that agreement and initiate his violent campaign against the Jews, but then he will immediately be interrupted. Wars will tear him away, and around that same time, the two witnesses will show up to help the Jews. From the moment of their arrival, they will be a disrupting force in the plans of the Mahdi/Antichrist, but there won't be much he will be able to do about them. Their message, signs, and wonders will be a sight to behold.

The Mahdi/Antichrist and the False Prophet working together will not be able to stop the two witnesses for three and a half years, no matter how hard they try. At the end of those three and a half years, they will finally defeat them. However, three and a half days after that defeat, the two witnesses will rise from the dead, ascend to the sky, and enter a cloud. At this, the entire world will be utterly shocked (Revelation 11:11–12).

> **Revelation 11:11–12** [bold emphasis added]
> But after the three and a half days a breath of life from God entered them, and they stood up on their feet, and great fear fell on those who saw them. Then they heard a loud voice from heaven saying to them, "Come up here!" **And they went up to heaven in a cloud**, and their enemies watched them.

For the last three and a half years of the reign of the Mahdi/Antichrist, he will become so cruel and violent that he will resemble the Dajjal/Antichrist, whom the False Prophet defeated when he first arrived. In essence, the two Antichrists (Dajjal/Antichrist and Mahdi/Antichrist) will be like the same man—two heads of the same beast (Revelation 13:3)—but the Mahdi/Antichrist will be more powerful than his predecessor. By the end of his reign of terror, most of the people on Earth will be united under his command.

This now concludes my assessment of the strong delusion, concerning an otherworldly Islam about to break into this world in full force. It is my genuine hope and prayer that all of the people who read this, regardless of religion or background, will consider these words as *possible interpretations of scripture* regarding the End Times.

As events unfold on the world stage, if either arrival scenario I have presented in this book comes to pass, I am certain that anyone who has read this book will be much more prepared to accept these otherworldly encounters about to come their way and boldly trek into that uncertain future with assurance that the God of all creation has their back.

No matter what comes our way, whether there is a rapture or not, we should all strive to have hearts of faith found in Hebrews 11, hope found in Hebrews 6:19–20, love found in 1 Corinthians 16:14, and a boldness that transcends all fear (2 Timothy 1:7, 1 John 4:18).

> **Hebrews 6:19–20**
> We have this as a sure and steadfast anchor of the soul, a hope that enters into the inner place behind the curtain, where Jesus has gone as a forerunner on our behalf, having become a high priest forever after the order of Melchizedek
>
> **1 Corinthians 16:13**
> Let all that you do, be done in love.
>
> **2 Timothy 1:7**
> For God gave us a spirit not of fear but of power and love and self-control.
>
> **1 John 4:18**
> There is no fear in love, but perfect love casts out fear. For fear has to do with punishment, and whoever fears has not been perfected in love.

APPENDIX

The Gospel

John 3:16
God so loved the world that He gave His
Only begotten
Son, that whosoever believes in Him shall not
Perish, but have
Everlasting
Life

Following is my best attempt at explaining the Gospel.

Why God creates

The heart of the Creator of all things is love (1 John 4:16). Because God is love, He decided to create a beautiful universe and fill it with life. Why? So He can be with and love His children (1 Corinthians 2:9; Ephesians 1:4–5; John 1:1–2, 14). Love grows, and love enjoys loving relationships. God didn't want this relationship to disappear someday, either. He wants to spend eternity with His loving children, so He created His children as eternal beings (Acts 24:15, Daniel 12:2, Genesis 1:26–27).

> **1 John 4:16**
> So we have come to know and to believe the love that God has for us. God is love, and whoever abides in love abides in God, and God abides in him.

1 Corinthians 2:9
But, as it is written, "What no eye has seen, nor ear heard, nor the heart of man imagined, what God has prepared for those who love him"—

Ephesians 1:4–5
[E]ven as he chose us in him before the foundation of the world, that we should be holy and blameless before him. In love he predestined us for adoption through Jesus Christ, according to the purpose of his will …

John 1:1–2, 14
In the beginning was the Word, and the Word was with God, and the Word was God. He was in the beginning with God … And the Word became flesh and dwelt among us, and we have seen his glory, glory as of the only Son from the Father, full of grace and truth.
Note: God became flesh to be intimately linked to us, and to save us.

Acts 24:15
[H]aving a hope in God, which these men themselves accept, that there will be a resurrection of both the just and the unjust.

Note: All spirits are eternal, whether they are obedient and faithful to God or not. Everlasting damnation isn't God's desire, for He is not willing that any should perish, but it exists because it is a byproduct of free will. The fact that all spirits are eternal, however, is evident in that they exist for eternity, whether they are saved with God or eternally separated from God.

Daniel 12:2
And many of those who sleep in the dust of the earth shall awake, some to everlasting life, and some to shame and everlasting contempt.

Genesis 1:26–27
Then God said, "Let us make man in our image, after our likeness. And let them have dominion over the fish of the sea and over the birds of the heavens and over the livestock and over all the earth and over every creeping thing that creeps on the earth." So God created man in his own image, in the image of God he created him; male and female he created them.

Why evil exists

Of course, in order for God's children to truly love Him, they must freely choose to love Him. Therefore God decided to create life with free will (Genesis 2:16–17, Deuteronomy 30:19–20, Joshua 24:15).

Genesis 2:16–17
And the Lord God commanded the man, saying, "You may surely eat of every tree of the garden, but of the tree of the knowledge of good and evil you shall not eat, for in the day that you eat of it you shall surely die."

Note: While it isn't explicitly stated that humans have free will, it is implied by the fact that God created the tree of knowledge of good and evil, and gave Adam and Eve the choice of whether to obey Him and not eat it, or to disobey Him and eat it.

Deuteronomy 30:19–20

"I call heaven and earth to witness against you today, that I have set before you life and death, blessing and curse. Therefore choose life, that you and your offspring may live, loving the Lord your God, obeying his voice and holding fast to him, for he is your life and length of days, that you may dwell in the land that the Lord swore to your fathers, to Abraham, to Isaac, and to Jacob, to give them."

Note: Again, free will is implied by the fact that people obviously have the ability to choose life, and to love and obey God, as mentioned in this passage of scripture.

Joshua 24:15

"And if it is evil in your eyes to serve the Lord, choose this day whom you will serve, whether the gods your fathers served in the region beyond the River, or the gods of the Amorites in whose land you dwell. But as for me and my house, we will serve the Lord."

Because of the existence of free will, the opportunity to not choose to love and obey God exists. This can be a sad fact because many will choose not to love and obey God, but it must be so in order for love to bear true meaning. This is why evil exists. God allows evil to exist for a short season (on the scale of eternity), in order for all to choose Him with their own free will. Once this choice has been made throughout all creation, evil will pass away (Revelation 20:14–15).

Revelation 20:14–15

Then Death and Hades were thrown into the lake of fire. This is the second death, the lake of fire. And if anyone's name was not found written in the book of life, he was thrown into the lake of fire.

The meaning of life

The meaning of life is to choose to love and obey God, and have an eternal loving relationship with Him. Once this choice is made, the meaning of life grows to incorporate revealing this truth to others, so they may also choose to love and obey God, and have an eternal loving relationship with Him (1 Corinthians 2:9; Ephesians 1:4–6; John 1:1–2, 14).

> **1 Corinthians 2:9**
> But, as it is written, "What no eye has seen, nor ear heard, nor the heart of man imagined, what God has prepared for those who love him"—
>
> **Ephesians 1:4–6**
> [E]ven as he chose us in him before the foundation of the world, that we should be holy and blameless before him. In love he predestined us for adoption through Jesus Christ, according to the purpose of his will, to the praise of his glorious grace, with which he has blessed us in the Beloved.
>
> **John 1:1–2, 14**
> In the beginning was the Word, and the Word was with God, and the Word was God. He was in the beginning with God …And the Word became flesh and dwelt among us, and we have seen his glory, glory as of the only Son from the Father, full of grace and truth.

When free will is used for evil

Unfortunately, because of the existence of free will, sin came to pass, beginning in Genesis 3:6. What's worse, sin has a spreading effect once it is turned loose. There is no human means to stop its corruption. Sin was turned loose on the earth with the very first man and woman (Adam and Eve) and has spread throughout the entire earth since that time (Romans 3:23, 5:12–15).

> **Genesis 3:6**
> So when the woman saw that the tree was good for food, and that it was a delight to the eyes, and that the tree was to be desired to make one wise, she took of its fruit and ate, and she also gave some to her husband who was with her, and he ate.

> **Romans 3:23**
> [F]or all have sinned and fall short of the glory of God

> **Romans 5:12–15**
> Therefore, just as sin came into the world through one man, and death through sin, and so death spread to all men because all sinned—for sin indeed was in the world before the law was given, but sin is not counted where there is no law. Yet death reigned from Adam to Moses, even over those whose sinning was not like the transgression of Adam, who was a type of the one who was to come. But the free gift is not like the trespass. For if many died through one man's trespass, much more have the grace of God and the free gift by the grace of that one man Jesus Christ abounded for many.

Because God is perfect (Psalm 18:30), and there is no tolerance for sin, the penalty of sin is death (Genesis 2:17, Romans 5:12). God defines death as returning to the dust of the earth (Genesis 3:19) and calls it a curse, known as "the last enemy" (1 Corinthians 15:26). In essence, any rejection of God's rule is sin. It began with Adam and has since been endorsed by all humanity (Romans 5:12). So it appears there is a great dilemma because after sin was introduced into the world, all have been born into sin, living in bodies of flesh with a sinful nature. All are penalized with death even from birth.

> **Psalm 18:30**
> This God—his way is perfect; the word of the Lord proves true; he is a shield for all those who take refuge in him.
>
> **Genesis 2:17**
> "[B]ut of the tree of the knowledge of good and evil you shall not eat, for in the day that you eat of it you shall surely die."
>
> **Romans 5:12**
> Therefore, just as sin came into the world through one man, and death through sin, and so death spread to all men because all sinned—
>
> **Genesis 3:19**
> "By the sweat of your face you shall eat bread, till you return to the ground, for out of it you were taken; for you are dust, and to dust you shall return."
>
> **1 Corinthians 15:26**
> The last enemy to be destroyed is death.

God's method of dealing with sin

God knew that humanity needed a means of escaping sin. That's why the first thing He said about sin concerned His means of correcting it (Genesis 3:14–15). His Son, Jesus, first mentioned as the seed of the woman, was the answer. God knew that humanity would never have the ability to overcome sin and death (never did and never will, despite all the religions and doctrines in the world that claim otherwise). He therefore had to take care of this problem Himself.

Genesis 3:14–15
The Lord God said to the serpent, "Because you have done this, cursed are you above all livestock and above all beasts of the field; on your belly you shall go, and dust you shall eat all the days of your life. I will put enmity between you and the woman, and between your offspring and her offspring; he shall bruise your head, and you shall bruise his heel."

Jesus then embedded Himself inside the womb of a human female by the name of Mary and became a human being. The Creator of all things became human (John 1:1–2, 14; Colossians 2:9–10). Is this not amazing? His name was Jesus and still is because He is still alive. He lived a life of purity and obedience to God—a life of love, healing, and forgiveness. Because of His will power, He was able to live perfectly without sin (Hebrews 4:15). He then ended His life on Earth by sacrificing Himself for all (Romans 5:8–10, 1 Peter 3:18). Then by His power, He defeated death by rising from the dead (John 10:17–18, Romans 8:10–11).

John 1:1–2, 14
In the beginning was the Word, and the Word was with God, and the Word was God. He was in the beginning with God … And the Word became flesh and dwelt among us, and we have seen his glory, glory as of the only Son from the Father, full of grace and truth.

Colossians 2:9–10
For in him the whole fullness of deity dwells bodily, and you have been filled in him, who is the head of all rule and authority.

Hebrews 4:15

For we do not have a high priest who is unable to sympathize with our weaknesses, but one who in every respect has been tempted as we are, yet without sin.

Romans 5:8–10

[B]ut God shows his love for us in that while we were still sinners, Christ died for us. Since, therefore, we have now been justified by his blood, much more shall we be saved by him from the wrath of God. For if while we were enemies we were reconciled to God by the death of his Son, much more, now that we are reconciled, shall we be saved by his life.

1 Peter 3:18

For Christ also suffered once for sins, the righteous for the unrighteous, that he might bring us to God, being put to death in the flesh but made alive in the spirit …

John 10:17–18

"For this reason the Father loves me, because I lay down my life that I may take it up again. No one takes it from me, but I lay it down of my own accord. I have authority to lay it down, and I have authority to take it up again. This charge I have received from my Father."

Romans 8:10–11

But if Christ is in you, although the body is dead because of sin, the Spirit is life because of righteousness. If the Spirit of him who raised Jesus from the dead dwells in you, he who raised Christ Jesus from the dead will also give life to your mortal bodies through his Spirit who dwells in you.

God's calling

God offers the free gift of salvation to all who will ask and believe. He calls upon all of us to turn from our sinful ways and trust in what Jesus Christ has done for us. There is nothing we can do to remove our guilt before God. Doing good things doesn't remove our sin, and since all are sinners, nothing we can do can undo that; it's only by the mercy of God that we can be saved through what He has done (Ephesians 2:8–10). The gift of salvation is eternally rewarded, but those who refuse to repent and turn to God will have no place in His kingdom. Therefore, whoever rejects God's offer will suffer His wrath in the judgment to come, which the Bible clearly warns of. This terrifying prospect (2 Thessalonians 1:7–10) is a reality that Jesus spoke much of, warning people of their fate.

Ephesians 2:8–10

For by grace you have been saved through faith. And this is not your own doing; it is the gift of God, not a result of works, so that no one may boast. For we are his workmanship, created in Christ Jesus for good works, which God prepared beforehand, that we should walk in them.

2 Thessalonians 1:7–10

[A]nd to grant relief to you who are afflicted as well as to us, when the Lord Jesus is revealed from heaven with his mighty angels in flaming fire, inflicting vengeance on those who do not know God and on those who do not obey the gospel of our Lord Jesus. They will suffer the punishment of eternal destruction, away from the presence of the Lord and from the glory of his might, when he comes on that day to be glorified in his saints, and to be marveled at among all who have believed, because our testimony to you was believed.

God's justice

God is perfect justice (Psalm 19:7), perfect mercy (2 Corinthians 1:3–5), and all powerful (Romans 1:19–20). Jesus's sacrifice is the best example of all of these attributes. The fact that He died and paid the penalty of sin is justice. God accepts sacrifice and allowed His Son, Jesus Christ, to be sacrificed to atone for all of the sin in the world. The price had to be paid, but He picked up the tab! Whatever sins anyone has ever committed, past, present, or future, have all been atoned for. All people have to do is ask and believe.

> **Psalm 19:7** [bold emphasis added]
> The **law of the Lord is perfect**, reviving the soul; the testimony of the Lord is sure, making wise the simple …
>
> **2 Corinthians 1:3–5** [bold emphasis added]
> Blessed be the God and Father of our Lord Jesus Christ, **the Father of mercies and God of all comfort**, who comforts us in all our affliction, so that we may be able to comfort those who are in any affliction, with the comfort with which we ourselves are comforted by God. For **as we share abundantly in Christ's sufferings, so through Christ we share abundantly in comfort too.**
>
> **Romans 1:19–20** [bold emphasis added]
> For what can be known about God is plain to them, because God has shown it to them. For his invisible attributes, namely, **his eternal power and divine nature**, have been clearly perceived, ever since the creation of the world, in the things that have been made. So they are without excuse.

God's mercy

Jesus died, yet He is without sin; this is mercy. He didn't have to die. He is blameless, yet He died for all who would ask for Him to take their place (Romans 5:8, 1 Peter 3:18). This was the requirement in order for His sacrifice to truly atone for the sin of the world. If He were a sinner Himself, He'd only be getting the punishment He deserved. But because He is perfect, His crucifixion allowed Him to be made worthy to forgive all that would come to Him and ask His forgiveness.

> **Romans 5:8** [bold emphasis added]
> [B]ut God shows his love for us in that while we were still sinners, **Christ died for us**.

> **1 Peter 3:18**
> For Christ also suffered once for sins, the righteous for the unrighteous, that he might bring us to God, being put to death in the flesh but made alive in the spirit …

God's power

Being all powerful is displayed in Jesus's perfect life (the will power to live perfectly, Hebrews 4:15), in His miracles worked through faith in His Father's provision, and especially in His resurrection. He died to atone for sin, and He arose from the dead to prove that the atonement was not without meaning. He has power over death and will give that power to all who ask Him for forgiveness of sins, and salvation.

> **Hebrews 4:15**
> For we do not have a high priest who is unable to sympathize with our weaknesses, but one **who in every respect has been tempted as we are, yet without sin**.

Why Jesus is the only way to eternal life

Now when God allowed His Son to go to the cross, it wasn't easy. Would it be easy for any parent to allow his or her child to be murdered? He doesn't take His Son's death lightly, despite the fact that Jesus was resurrected. God stands outside of time and space, and He can see His son's death as if it were present for eternity. As humans, we have a minor experience of this in our memories, but God has perfect memory and visual clarity over all time-space. He can hear the cries of His Son, "Father, why have you forsaken me?" (Matthew 27:46, Mark 15:34) for all eternity.

> **Matthew 27:46**
> And about the ninth hour Jesus cried out with a loud voice, saying, "Eli, Eli, lema sabachthani?" that is, "My God, my God, why have you forsaken me?"

> **Mark 15:34**
> And at the ninth hour Jesus cried with a loud voice, "Eloi, Eloi, lema sabachthani?" which means, "My God, my God, why have you forsaken me?"

This is His means of saving humanity, and there is no other way. If there were, He would've taken it; neither He nor His Son desired the brutal murder of the cross. This is serious business, and it's why God allows for no other means of salvation. But, hey, I'm glad there is no other way because His way is the easiest, and the best, though it is sad that Jesus had to be crucified in order to make it happen. Nobody has to go through any rituals or punishments. All people have to do is lay aside their pride and stop trying to reach God by their own strength. All they have to do is look to Jesus because He is the Way, the Truth, and the Life; there is no way to the Father, except by Him (John 14:6).

> **John 14:6**
> Jesus said to him, "I am the way, and the truth, and the life. No one comes to the Father except through me.

How one might have eternal life

Salvation is a free gift. There's only one thing that people have to do to receive it. Ask Jesus for forgiveness of their sins and believe, as scripture states (John 3:16). He forgives all! No sin is unforgivable. Of course, one must have enough faith to ask such a question. This is a problem for many because they simply don't perceive what faith actually is. Let me make this even easier. Simply ask Jesus to forgive you of your sins and save you, and *hope* He's real. I assure you, in His infinite mercy, you will be saved if you do this. Put your hope in Him, and He and I promise you, you will not be let down. You don't even have to change your life *before* you come to Him. He'll take care of those details if your request is genuine. Just stop right now and send up a prayer to Him.

> **John 3:16**
> "For God so loved the world, that he gave his only Son, that whoever believes in him should not perish but have eternal life …"

There are other ways of rewording the act of asking God for salvation. For example, Acts 20:20–21 states that you must have "repentance toward God" and "faith in our Lord Jesus Christ." Repentance means a complete change of heart and mind regarding sin; you agree with God about your sin and want to live a life pleasing to Him. Faith in Jesus Christ entails accepting that He is the Son of the living God, that "Christ died for the ungodly," and that He conquered death through His resurrection (1 Corinthians 15:1–4, 15:21–22). But all of these Christian phrases simply boil down to believing in God enough to ask for forgiveness of sins from His Son, Jesus Christ, and allowing Him to work in our lives to transform us into better people. He carries the brunt of the workload, mainly because people are so spiritually puny.

> **Acts 20:20–21**
> [H]ow I did not shrink from declaring to you anything that was profitable, and teaching you in public and from house to house, testifying both to Jews and to Greeks of repentance toward God and of faith in our Lord Jesus Christ.

> **1 Corinthians 15:1–4**
> Now I would remind you, brothers, of the gospel I preached to you, which you received, in which you stand, and by which you are being saved, if you hold fast to the word I preached to you—unless you believed in vain. For I delivered to you as of first importance what I also received: that Christ died for our sins in accordance with the Scriptures, that he was buried, that he was raised on the third day in accordance with the Scriptures …

> **1 Corinthians 15:21–22**
> For as by a man came death, by a man has come also the resurrection of the dead. For as in Adam all die, so also in Christ shall all be made alive.

It's all that easy.

God bless you!

PS—Please let me know at jmilor@yahoo.com if you've read this and have asked Jesus to forgive you of your sins and save your soul. I would like to take the time to answer any of the questions you may have about being a new believer in Jesus Christ. God bless you again, and praise the Lord you're saved!

[illegible] into [illegible] come. He [illegible] the home of the workload [illegible] the people [illegible] any.

Acts 20:20–21

[illegible] and not [illegible] from [illegible] to [illegible] what was profitable [illegible] and [illegible] from house to house, testifying both [illegible] Christ.

1 Corinthians 15:1–4

[illegible] word [illegible] of the gospel [illegible] which [illegible] and [illegible] being saved [illegible] to you [illegible] what I also received [illegible] Christ died [illegible] according to the Scriptures, that [illegible] and that He was raised on the third day in accordance with the Scriptures.

1 Corinthians 15:21–22

[illegible] man came death, by man has come also the resurrection of the dead. For as in Adam all die, [illegible] also in Christ shall all be made alive.

[illegible]

Conclusion

[illegible] that you [illegible] and [illegible] your soul [illegible] would like to [illegible] is your [illegible] Christ [illegible] against [illegible]

NOTES

Chapter 1: My Great-Grandmother's Encounters

1. Rick Meyers, Equipping Ministries Foundation, e-Sword Bible software. http://www.e-sword.net/downloads.html (downloaded April 7, 2000). This free software contains multiple versions of the Bible, in addition to Strong's Enhanced Lexicon. I used this software for all of the Bible quotations in this article. Unless explicitly stated otherwise, I quote from the English Standard Version (ESV) for my Bible quotes.

Chapter 2: Christian Ufology

1. Finis Dake, *God's Plan for Man* (Lawrenceville, GA: Dake Publishing Inc., 1977). This book was first published in 1949.
2. Chuck Missler, *Return of the Nephilim—On Tape with Notes* (Coeur d' Alene, ID: Koinonia House Inc., 1997).
3. Tariq Malik, "Most Americans Believe Alien Life is Possible, Study Shows," Space.com, http://www.space.com/news/050531_alienlife_survey.html (last accessed April 11, 2016).
4. Wikipedia Encyclopedia Online, s.v. "Religion in the United States," http://en.wikipedia.org/wiki/Religion_in_the_United_States#cite_note-ARISKEY-4 (last accessed April 11, 2016).
5. Hugh Ross, Kenneth Samples, and Mark Clark, *Lights in the Sky & Little Green Men* (Colorado Springs, CO: NavPress Publications, 2002).
6. Kenneth R. Samples, "UFO Interview with Biola Magazine," *RTB30*, June 28, 2011, http://www.reasons.org/blogs/reflections/ufo-interview-with-biola-magazine (last accessed April 10, 2016).
7. Ibid.
8. Dr. Stephen Yulish, "Aliens Abductions Stopped by the Name of Jesus Christ," UFO Digest, http://www.ufodigest.com/news/0109/abductions-stopped.html (last accessed April 11, 2016).
9. Erick von Däniken, *Chariots of the Gods* (New York: Berkley Publishing Group, 1969).

10. Zecharia Sitchin, *The Twelfth Planet* (New York: HarperCollins, 1976). Throughout this book and others by this author, he promotes the idea that humanity is a genetically engineered species planted on Earth long ago.
11. Dr. Michael S. Heiser, *The Façade* (Bellingham, WA: Kirkdale Press, 2014). I had the honor of corresponding with Heiser and reviewing *The Façade* prior to its publication.
12. Dr. Barry Downing, *The Bible and Flying Saucers* (New York: Perseus Books Group, 1997). I was able to download a PDF of this book, with a reprint date of 1977, and an original copyright date of 1973.
13. Dr. Barry Downing, "The UFO Revelation," The Strong Delusion website, http://www.thestrongdelusion.com/images/stories/UFO%20Revelation.pdf (last accessed March 15, 2016).
14. Dr. Barry Downing, "Hermeneutical Rape," The Strong Delusion website, http://thestrongdelusion.com/index.php?option=com_content&task=view&id=1132&Itemid=9 (last accessed March 14, 2016).
15. Donald P. Coverdell, ThD, *The Mystery Clouds* (Orlando, FL: The Children's Bread Corp., 1986).
16. John W. Milor, *Aliens and the Antichrist* (Lincoln, NE: iUniverse, 2006); *Aliens in the Bible: A Biblical Perspective of Supernatural Entities, Realms of Existence, and Phenomenon* (Philadelphia, PA: Xlibris Corp., 1999).
17. John W. Milor, *Aliens and the Antichrist: Unveiling the End Times Deception* (Lincoln, NE: iUniverse, 2006).
18. Finis Dake, *God's Plan for Man* (Lawrenceville, GA: Dake Publishing Inc., 1977). This is an incredible book, containing thirty years of research, and an excellent reference for any Bible student.
19. Jim Cunningham, "UFOs: A Biblical Explanation," The Strong Delusion website http://thestrongdelusion.com/index.php?option=com_content&task=view&id=2445&Itemid=9 (last accessed March 16, 2016).
20. John W. Milor, *Aliens and the Antichrist* (Lincoln, NE: iUniverse, 2006), 19.
21. Ibid, 23.
22. Noah Shachtman, "Real-Life Hyperspace Drive," Military.com, http://www.defensetech.org/2006/01/05/real-life-hyperspace-drive/ (last accessed March 16, 2016). Few posters commenting on this article believe this is a real NASA project; however, I contend that projects like this are generally not released to the public until years after they've been developed. ETs use this technology, and we've been working on reverse engineering it since the 1940s. We probably figured it out a while back, and the only purpose of the article is to see what people think.
23. Finis Dake, *God's Plan for Man* (Lawrenceville, GA: Dake Publishing Inc., 1977), 112, 128, 947. Information about the flood of Lucifer.
24. John W. Milor, *Aliens and the Antichrist* (Lincoln, NE: iUniverse, 2006), 75.

Chapter 3: The Bible I Thought I Knew

1. John W. Milor, *The Eaglestar Prophecy* (Lincoln, NE: iUniverse Inc., 2003), 27.
2. Thomas R. Horn, "Britain Legalizes Nephilim Resurrection Plan," http://associate.com/groups/revfilesnews/0:1378read.html (last accessed March 7, 2016). If this link goes bad, simply search for Thomas Horn and the title of the article; there are several versions of it scattered across the internet.
3. "Tallest Man Living," Guinness World Records website, http://www.guinnessworldrecords.com/world-records/tallest-man-living (last accessed March 7, 2016).
4. David Hatcher Childress, "Archaeological Cover-Ups?" http://www.bibliotecapleyades.net/ciencia/supressed_inventions/suppressed_inventions19.htm (last accessed June 13, 2016). Elements of this research are also found in other places on the internet, such as the website Giants, http://www.genesis6giants.com/index.php?s=389 (last accessed March 7, 2016).
5. Scott Alan Roberts, *The Rise and Fall of the Nephilim* (Pompton Plains, NJ: New Page Books, 2012), 76.
6. Simcha Jacobovici, et al., "The Giants of Genesis," *The Naked Archaeologist*, 2:10, June 2008, 20.
7. Joe Taylor, "Giant Leg Bone," Genesis 6 Giants http://www.genesis6giants.com/index.php?s=568 (last accessed April 11, 2016).
8. Ibid.
9. Brad and Mary Sutherland, "Smithsonian Institute Cover-Up on Giant Race Pre-existing Modern Man," Burlington UFO and Paranormal Research Center, http://www.burlingtonnews.net/smithsonian.html (last accessed March 7, 2016).
10. David Hatcher Childress, "Archaeological Cover-Ups," http://www.onelight.com/hollow/giant/canyon.html (last accessed March 7, 2016).
11. Rich La Monica, "Ohio Valley Bones: Reality? Or Imagination?" Ampelos Logos, http://www.ampeloslogos.com/the-days-of-noah.html (last accessed April 11, 2016).
12. Smithsonian home page, http://www.si.edu/ (last accessed March 7, 2016).
13. Brad and Mary Sutherland, "Smithsonian Institute Cover-Up on Giant Race Pre-existing Modern Man," Burlington UFO and Paranormal Research Center, http://www.burlingtonnews.net/smithsonian.html (last accessed March 7, 2016).
14. David Hatcher Childress, "Archaeological Cover-Ups," http://www.bibliotecapleyades.net/ciencia/supressed_inventions/suppressed_inventions19.htm (last accessed March 7, 2016). This information is also found on another website: http://www.onelight.com/hollow/giant/canyon.html.

15. Ibid.
16. Ibid. Elements of this research are also found in other places on the internet, such as the website Giants, http://www.genesis6giants.com/index.php?s=389 (last accessed March 7, 2016).
17. Museo Oro del Peru (The Gold Museum official home page) http://www.museoroperu.com.pe/museum.html (last accessed April 21, 2016).

Chapter 4: Antichrists of the Past

1. John C. Brunt, *How to Survive Armageddon* (Hagerstown, MD: Review and Harold Publishing Association, 2011).
2. Todd Strandberg, "The Antichrist: have you seen this man?" Rapture Ready, https://www.raptureready.com/rr-antichrist.html (last accessed April 11, 2016). This website provides a list of people who were, and some still are, speculated to be the Antichrist.
3. Finis Dake, *God's Plan for Man* (Lawrenceville, GA: Dake Publishing Inc., 1977). Areas mentioning the law of double reference can be found by looking in the extensive index in the back of the book.
4. David M. Howard Jr., PhD, and Gary Burge, PhD, *Fascination Bible Facts: People, Places, and Events* (Lincolnwood, IL: Publications International, Ltd., 1999), 132.
5. Ibid, 120.
6. "Mark of the Beast" Parowan Prophet http://www.parowanprophet.com/A_Trojan_Horse/mark_of_the_beast.htm (last accessed April 17, 2016). This website provides a lengthy list of histograms related to the number of the beast.
7. Joel Richardson, *The Islamic Antichrist: The Shocking Truth About the Real Nature of the Beast* (Los Angeles: WorldNetDaily Books, 2009), 115–116.
8. Terese Pencak Schwartz, "The Holocaust: Non-Jewish Victims," Jewish Virtual Library, http://www.jewishvirtuallibrary.org/jsource/Holocaust/NonJewishVictims.html (last accessed April 11, 2016). Provided statistical estimates on holocaust victims.
9. *Expelled: No Intelligence Allowed*, directed by Nathan Frankowski (US: Premise Media Corporation Rampant Films, 2008).
10. *Wikipedia,* s.v. "Expelled: No Intelligence Allowed," http://en.wikipedia.org/wiki/Expelled:_No_Intelligence_Allowed (last accessed April 11, 2016).
11. Noah Charney, "Hitler's Hunt for the Holy Grail and the Ghent Altarpiece," The Daily Beast, http://www.thedailybeast.com/articles/2013/12/21/hitler-s-hunt-for-the-holy-grail-and-the-ghent-altarpiece.html (last accessed April 11, 2016). Information about Hitler's obsession with the occult.

12. Terrence Aym, "Alien Saucer Crash in 1973 Nazi Germany," International UFO Museum Research Center http://www.roswellufomuseum.com/research/ufotopics/naziufocrash.html (last accessed March 16, 2016).
13. Len Kasten, *The Secret History of Extraterrestrials: Advanced Technology and the Coming* (Rochester, VT: Bear & Company Books, 2010), 261.
14. Richard K. Wilson and Sylvan Burns, "Secret Treaty," The Watcher Files http://www.thewatcherfiles.com/alien-treaty.htm (last accessed April 21, 2016).
15. "Abortions Worldwide This Year," Worldometers http://www.worldometers.info/abortions/ (last accessed March 18, 2016).
16. Readers Digest, ed., *The World's Last Mysteries* (Pleasantville, NY: The Reader's Digest Association Inc., 1979), 14.
17. "The Meaning and Significance of Swastika in Hinduism," HinduWebsite.com http://www.hinduwebsite.com/hinduism/concepts/meaning-and-significance-of-swastika-in-hinduism.asp (last accessed March 18, 2016).

Chapter 5: The Rise of Islam

1. "Stunning Video: Obama Supports Cannibals in Syria," Before It's News, http://beforeitsnews.com/obama/2013/06/stunning-video-obama-supports-cannibals-in-syria-warning-graphic-2452782.html (last accessed April 11, 2016).
2. Francis Martel, "ISIS Jihad 'Vampire': We Love Drinking Infidel Blood." Breitbart, http://www.breitbart.com/Big-Peace/2014/09/18/We-Love-Drinking-Blood-ISIS-Vampire-Declares (last accessed April 11, 2016).
3. Jerry Trousdale, *Miraculous Movements* (Nashville, TN: Thomas Nelson Publishing, 2012). Christian revival is happening all across the Middle East.
4. "Iraq & Syria: Special Field Report," *Voice of the Martyrs Newsletter*, October 2015, 5–6.
5. Ibid, 5.
6. Ibid, 6.
7. Sister Gulshan Esther and Thelma Sangster, *The Torn Veil* (Fort Washington, PA: CLC Publications, 2010). Awesome book!
8. Keila Ochoa, "The God Who Paints," Our Daily Bread, http://odb.org/2016/04/19/the-god-who-paints/ (last accessed April 20, 2016).
9. "Hymen: Obama's Kenyan Ghosts," commentary, *The Washington Times*, http://www.washingtontimes.com/news/2008/oct/12/obamas-kenya-ghosts/?page=all (last accessed on March 24, 2016). Obama supported radical Muslim Odinga for his election in Kenya in 2007. When Odinga lost the election, mass riots broke out and his supporters butchered many people as a result.

10. Paul Wood, “Face-to-face with Abu Sakkar, Syria’s ‘heart-eating cannibal’,” BBC News-Syria, http://www.bbc.com/news/magazine-23190533 (last accessed March 24, 2016). Obama was in favor of supporting Syrian rebels; their leader was a cannibal.
11. Paul Joseph Watson, “Heart Eating Cannibal Demands Obama Send Weapons,” Infowars, http://www.infowars.com/heart-eating-cannibal-demands-obama-send-weapons/ (last accessed March 24, 2016).
12. Ed O’Keefe and Anne Gearan, “In Congress, Path Clearing for Obama Plan to Aid Syrian Rebels Fighting Islamic State,” *The Washington Post*, http://www.washingtonpost.com/politics/in-congress-path-clearing-for-obama-plan-to-aid-syrian-rebels-fighting-islamic-state/2014/09/15/5a53b506-3d0a-11e4-b03f-de718edeb92f_story.html (last accessed March 24, 2016).
13. Lori Hinnant, “Kerry: US Open to Talks with Iran on Islamic State,” Associated Press, CNSNews, http://cnsnews.com/news/article/kerry-us-open-talks-iran-islamic-state (last accessed March 24, 2016). US politicians vote to fund jihad, arming one group of terrorists to fight another group of terrorists.
14. Mike Whitney, “Did Obama Know that ISIS Planned to Invade Iraq?” Counter Punch, June 24, 2014, http://www.counterpunch.org/2014/06/24/did-obama-know-that-isis-planned-to-invade-iraq/ (last accessed March 24, 2016).
15. Jay Seculow, “No American Weapons or Money for Syrian Jihad,” American Center for Law and Justice, http://aclj.org/radical-islam/no-american-weapons-or-money-for-syrian-jihad (last accessed March 24, 2016). Petition to stop US politicians from funding jihad—many in Congress were in favor of arming one group of terrorists to fight another group of terrorists.
16. Jay Seculow, “Defend Christians and Israel; Confront Jihad,” American Center for Law and Justice, https://aclj.org/radical-islam/defend-christians-israel-confront-jihad (last accessed March 24, 2016). Petition to confront jihad and defend Israel; United Nations sides with terrorists to investigate Israel for war crimes.
17. Patrick Poole, “New Details in PJM Exclusive on Alleged Homeland Security Leaker Mohamed Elibiary,” PJ Media, November 2, 2011, https://pjmedia.com/blog/new-details-in-pjm-exclusive-on-alleged-homeland-security-leaker-mohamed-elibiary (last accessed March 24, 2016). Shady business going on with Islamic radical in high-ranking government position.
18. Leon Puissegur, “Sharia Advisors—Barak Obama’s Muslim Appointees in High Security Positions,” Freedom Outpost, April 29, 2014, http://freedomoutpost.com/sharia-advisers-barack-obamas-muslim-appointees/ (last accessed June 15, 2016). At least six radical Muslims appointed to high-ranking government positions.

19. Amir Taheri, "Obama and Ahmadinejad," Forbes.com, October 26, 2008, http://www.forbes.com/2008/10/26/obama-iran-ahmadinejad-oped-cx_at_1026taheri.html (last accessed March 24, 2016). This websites moves around, and trying to go directly to it will sometimes forward to a welcome page. The best way to find it is to search the Forbes sites for something like "Obama Hadith Promised Warrior." Google will also produce results, but if the links go to the Forbes site, they might not work.
20. Jerome R. Corsi, "Egypt Eyes Obama's Brother for Terror List," World Net Daily, September 5, 2012, http://www.wnd.com/2013/09/egypt-eyes-obamas-brother-for-terror-list/ (last accessed March 24, 2016).
21. Walid Shoebat and Ben Barrack, "Confirmed: Obama's Brother in Bed with Terrorists," Shoebat.com, http://shoebat.com/2013/05/28/confirmed-barack-obamas-brother-in-bed-with-man-wanted-by-international-criminal-court-icc-for-crimes-against-humanity/ (last accessed on March 24, 2016).
22. "Hymen: Obama's Kenyan Ghosts," commentary, *The Washington Times,* http://www.washingtontimes.com/news/2008/oct/12/obamas-kenya-ghosts/?page=all (last accessed on March 24, 2016). Obama supported radical Muslim Odinga for his election in Kenya in 2007. When Odinga lost the election, mass riots broke out and his supporters butchered many people as a result.
23. Matthew Levitt, "30 Years of Terror Sponsored by Iran," *New York Daily News*, October 23, 2013, http://www.nydailynews.com/opinion/30-years-terror-sponsored-iran-article-1.1493410 (last accessed September 27, 2016).
24. "Saeed Abedini, Freed from an Iranian Prison," Be Heard Project, https://beheardproject.com/saeed (last accessed March 24, 2016).
25. Jay Solomon and Carol E. Lee, "U.S. Sent Cash to Iran as Americans Were Freed," *The Wall Street Journal*, August 3, 2016, http://www.wsj.com/articles/u-s-sent-cash-to-iran-as-americans-were-freed-1470181874 (last accessed September 27, 2016).
26. Guy Taylor, "Iran Is Banking Billions More than Expected Thanks to Obama's Deal," *The Washington Times*, February 3, 2016, http://www.washingtontimes.com/news/2016/feb/3/iran-claims-100-billion-windfall-from-sanctions-re/ (last accessed September 27, 2016).
27. Robin Wright, "Prisoner Swap: Obama's Secret Second Channel to Iran," *The New Yorker*, January 16, 2016, http://www.newyorker.com/news/news-desk/prisoner-swap-obamas-secret-second-channel-to-iran (last accessed September 27, 2016).
28. Andrew C. McCarthy, "Swapping Prisoners with Terrorists," *National Review*, January 29, 2015, http://www.nationalreview.com/article/412975/swapping-prisoners-terrorists-andrew-c-mccarthy (last accessed September 27, 2016).

29. Kosar, "Obama Administration Breaking Law by Releasing 5 Terrorists," The Political Insider, http://www.thepoliticalinsider.com/obama-administration-breaking-law-by-releasing-5-terrorists/ (last accessed March 24, 2016).
30. Jerome R. Corsi, "Dershowitz: Obama Support of Arab Spring 'Big Mistake'," World Net Daily, September 15, 2014, http://www.wnd.com/2014/09/dershowitz-obama-support-of-arab-spring-big-mistake/ (last accessed March 24, 2016).
31. Patrick Poole, "New Details in PJM Exclusive on Alleged Homeland Security Leaker Mohamed Elibiary," PJ Media, November 2, 2011, https://pjmedia.com/blog/new-details-in-pjm-exclusive-on-alleged-homeland-security-leaker-mohamed-elibiary (last accessed March 24, 2016). Shady business going on with Islamic radical in high-ranking government position.
32. Paul Wood, "Face-to-face with Abu Sakkar, Syria's 'heart-eating cannibal'" BBC News-Syria, http://www.bbc.com/news/magazine-23190533 (last accessed March 24, 2016).
33. "Hazard Pay," Snopes, May 21, 2013, http://www.snopes.com/politics/military/hasansalary.asp (last accessed March 29, 2016).
34. Rowan Scarborough, "Families Suspect SEAL Team 6 Crash Was Inside Job on Worst Day in Afghanistan," *The Washington Times*, October 20, 2013, http://www.washingtontimes.com/news/2013/oct/20/families-suspect-seal-team-6-crash-was-inside-job-/?page=all (last accessed March 25, 2016).
35. Kosar, "Obama Administration Breaking Law by Releasing 5 Terrorists," The Political Insider, http://www.thepoliticalinsider.com/obama-administration-breaking-law-by-releasing-5-terrorists/ (last accessed March 24, 2016).
36. Geoffrey Grider, "Obama Refuses to Allow Yazidi and Assyrian Christians Fleeing ISIS to Enter United States," Now The End Begins, August 12, 2015, http://www.nowtheendbegins.com/obama-refuses-to-allow-yazidi-christians-fleeing-isis-to-enter-united-states/ (last accessed March 24, 2016).
37. Valerie Richardson, "U.S. 'Discriminates' Against Christian Refugees, Accepts 96% Muslims, 3% Christians," *The Washington Times*, November 17, 2015, http://www.washingtontimes.com/news/2015/nov/17/us-unintentionally-discriminates-against-christian/ (last accessed March 24, 2016).
38. Nina Shea, "The State Department Turns its Back on Syrian Christians and Other Non-Muslim Refugees," *National Review*, November 2, 2015, http://www.nationalreview.com/article/426419/state-department-turns-its-back-syrian-christians-and-other-non-muslim-refugees-nina (last accessed March 24, 2016).
39. Abraham H. Miller, "No Room in America for Christian Refugees," The Hill, January 7, 2015, http://thehill.com/blogs/congress-blog/foreign-policy/228670-no-room-in-america-for-christian-refugees (last accessed March 24, 2016).

40. Jim Hoft, "They Lied! Obama Admin Tried to Tie Benghazi Attack to Pastor's Video Before They Settled on 2nd Video," Gateway Pundit, October 21, 2015, http://www.thegatewaypundit.com/2015/10/shameless-liars-obama-admin-tried-to-tie-benghazi-attack-to-this-video-before-they-settled-on-second-video/ (last accessed March 24, 2016).
41. Hayes Thomas, "Obama and Hillary Blame YouTube Video for Benghazi Terrorist Attack as Coffins Arrive," YouTube, May 9, 2013, https://www.youtube.com/watch?v=QSooz2wXpes (last accessed March 24, 2016).
42. Jake Tapper and Kim Berryman, "Green Beret Discharged for Beating Alleged Child Rapist Speaks Out," CNN, http://www.cnn.com/2015/09/28/politics/green-beret-discharged-for-beating-alleged-child-rapist-speaks-out/ (last accessed March 24, 2016).
43. Michelle Malkin, "'Bacha Bazi': Obama's Silence on Afghan Military's Child Rape," Creators, September 25, 2015, http://www.creators.com/conservative/michelle-malkin/bacha-bazi-obamas-silence-on-afghan-militarys-child-rape.html (last accessed April 4, 2016).
44. Cortney O'Brien, "Prisoner Who Was Likely Bin Laden's Bodyguard Is Released from Gitmo," Townhall, March 24, 2016, http://townhall.com/tipsheet/cortneyobrien/2015/09/23/prisoner-who-was-likely-bin-ladens-bodyguard-is-released-from-gitmo-n2055859 (last accessed March 24, 2016).
45. Tricia Cunningham, "Obama Quietly Releases 9-11 Hacker from Gitmo," Patriot Update, September 26, 2015, http://patriotupdate.com/obama-quietly-releases-9-11-hacker-from-gitmo/ (last accessed March 24, 2016).
46. Elise Labott, "John Kerry: Some Sanctions Relief Money for Iran Will Go to Terrorism," CNN Politics, January 21, 2016, http://www.cnn.com/2016/01/21/politics/john-kerry-money-iran-sanctions-terrorism/ (last accessed September 27, 2016).
47. Hal Lindsey, *Planet Earth—2000 A.D.* (Palos Verdes, CA: Western Front, Ltd., 1994), 235. Hal says to keep your eyes on Europe concerning the rise of the Antichrist, expecting a European leader with a New Age-type religion, rather than a Middle Eastern Muslim man.
48. John F. Walvoord, *Armageddon, Oil, and the Middle East Crisis: What the Bible Says About the Future of the Middle East and the End of Western Civilization* (Grand Rapids, MI: Zondervan Publishing House, 1990), 114. Walvoord also suspects more of a European-type dictator with a New Age religion, rather than a man of Middle Eastern Muslim.

Chapter 6: Characteristics of the Antichrist

1. Daily Hadith Online, http://dailyhadith.abuaminaelias.com (last accessed April 21, 2016).

2. "353 Prophecies Fulfilled in Jesus Christ," According to the Scriptures, January 20, 2015, http://www.accordingtothescriptures.org/prophecy/353prophecies.html (last accessed April 20, 2016). This website features an excellent list of Old Testament prophecies corresponding with New Testament fulfillments.
3. Jamie Conklin, "Chromosomes," The Tech Museum of Innovation, January 7, 2009, http://genetics.thetech.org/ask/ask295 (last accessed March 20, 2016).
4. Imam Kamil Mufti, "The Miracles of Jesus," The Religion of Islam, May 2, 2006, http://www.islamreligion.com/articles/352/miracles-of-jesus/ (last accessed March 20, 2016).
5. Jesus in the Flesh Ministry, "Jesus Visits Muslim in Prison," July 4, 2012, https://www.youtube.com/watch?v=NmHshbKTk-M (last accessed September 27, 2016). This is an incredibly powerful testimony; I love this guy!
6. Divine Revelations Spiritlessons, "Jesus Christ Visiting Muslims, Bringing Truth to Them," January 18, 2011, https://www.youtube.com/watch?v=GkH8_C_lgjk (last accessed September 27, 2016).
7. Sister Gulshan Esther and Thelma Sangster, *The Torn Veil* (Fort Washington, PA: CLC Publications, 2010).
8. Professor Sharma, "How Many Muslims Are Terrorists?" Daniel Pipes: Middle East Forum, November 8, 2006, http://www.danielpipes.org/comments/65537 (last accessed March 20, 2016).
9. Ibid.
10. "Muslim Opinion Polls: A Tiny Minority of Extremists?" Religion of Peace website, http://www.thereligionofpeace.com/pages/articles/opinion-polls.aspx (last accessed March 20, 2016). The pages on this website are continually updated; statistics keep growing.
11. "Muslim Statistics," Wordpress.com, https://muslimstatistics.wordpress.com/ (last accessed March 20, 2016). This website is constantly updated and contains a continually growing list of compiled articles.
12. Abdullah Abbas, "Adolph Hitler on Islam and the Muslims," Islamic Awakenings, http://forums.islamicawakening.com/f20/adolf-hitler-on-islam-and-the-muslims-16502/ (last accessed March 20, 2016). This pro-Islamic website praises Hitler and describes him as a "great statesman." Note that these Islamic references to Hitler are transient in nature; as I was reverifying the above website to save as a PDF on my computer for future reference, the website disappeared (as of April 30, 2016). However, information about Hitler being a "great statesman" keeps showing up on the internet; here are two other websites that say the same thing, from an Islamic perspective: http://ibloga.blogspot.com/2013/06/hitler-on-islam-and-muslims.html and https://vnnforum.com/showthread.php?t=137316. If these sites disappear as well, simply conduct a Google search for "Adolf Hitler Great Statesman Islam," and new websites will most likely appear.

13. Mike Corder, "Dutch Holocaust Museum Exhibits Jeroen Krabbe Paintings," The Big Story, May 15, 2016, http://bigstory.ap.org/article/dbccb40333f04ed7ab47b197a74a61f7/dutch-holocaust-museum-exhibits-jeroen-krabbe-paintings (last accessed September 27, 2016).
14. Omar Alnatour, "Muslims Are Not Terrorists: A Factual Look at Terrorism and Islam," The World Post, December 9, 2015, http://www.huffingtonpost.com/omar-alnatour/muslims-are-not-terrorist_b_8718000.html (last accessed March 22, 2016).
15. Tara Culp-Ressler, "Why Abortion Clinics Need Buffer Zones," Think Progress, January 15, 2014, http://thinkprogress.org/health/2014/01/15/3163761/abortion-clinics-need-buffer-zones/ (last accessed March 22, 2016).
16. Dean Obeidallah, "Are All Terrorists Muslims? It's Not Even Close," The Daily Beast, January 14, 2015, http://www.thedailybeast.com/articles/2015/01/14/are-all-terrorists-muslims-it-s-not-even-close.html (last accessed March 22, 2016).
17. "Country Reports on Terrorism 2013," US Department of State, Bureau of Counterterrorism, http://www.state.gov/j/ct/rls/crt/2013/224823.htm (last accessed March 22, 2016).
18. Jeff Dunetz, "Nothing To Do with Islam? 450 of 452 Suicide Attacks in 2015 Were Conducted by Muslim Terrorists," MRCTV, January 10, 2016, http://www.mrctv.org/blog/450-452-suicide-attacks-2015-were-made-muslim-terrorists#.beyhzze:KUg1 (last accessed March 20, 2016).
19. Helier Cheung, "Global Terror Attack Deaths Rose Sharply in 2013, Says Report," BBC News, November 18, 2014, http://www.bbc.com/news/world-30086435 (last accessed March 20, 2015).
20. Ali Sina, "Aisha the Child Wife of Muhammad, FaithFreedom.org, http://www.faithfreedom.org/Articles/sina/ayesha.htm (last accessed March 31, 2016).
21. Stephen Robertson, "Age of Consent Laws," Children & Youth in History, item_#230, https://chnm.gmu.edu/cyh/case-studies/230 (last accessed April 1, 2016).
22. Don Boys, PhD, "Should Dr. Jerry Vines Be Tarred and Feathered?" Islam and the Facts, http://www.muslimfact.com/bm/who-was-muhammad-mohammed-mohamet/should-dr-jerry-vines-be-tarred-and-feathered~print.shtml (last accessed March 31, 2016).
23. Don Boys, PhD, "Was Mohammed a Pedophile or Jerry Vines a Hater?" CTSNews.com, http://www.cstnews.com/bm/religions-common-sense-for-today/the-threat-that-islam-poses-to-christians/was-mohammed-a-pedophile-or-jerry-vines-a-hater.shtml (last accessed March 31, 2016).
24. Ibid.

25. Anne Graham Lotz, "The Bible Is Crystal Clear on Gender Equality," On Faith, January 17, 2007, http://www.faithstreet.com/onfaith/2007/01/17/biblical-record-is-clear-godc/737 (last accessed April 1, 2016).
26. Naomi Chambers, "Houri The Islamic Sex Slave In Paradise," Europe News, May 20, 2010, http://en.europenews.dk/Houri-The-Islamic-Sex-Slave-In-Paradise-78423.html (last accessed March 30, 2016).
27. "72 Virgins and Boys," Albatrus.org, http://www.albatrus.org/english/religions/islam/72virgins_and_boys.htm (last accessed March 31, 2016).
28. Dallas M. Roark, PhD, "What is so bad about child brides?" Answering Islam, http://www.answering-islam.org/authors/roark/child brides.html (last accessed April 1, 2016).
29. Jare Llelaboye, "Nigeria: 800,000 Women Suffer from VVF," allAfrica, February 23, 2005, http://allafrica.com/stories/201508100521.html (last accessed June 10, 2016).
30. Dickson Salami Adama, "Vasico Vaginal Fistula: 80,000 Nigerian Women Suffer Annually," Borgen Magazine, February 1, 2014, http://www.borgenmagazine.com/vesico-vaginal-fistula-80000-nigerian-women-suffer-annually (last accessed April 1, 2016).
31. Daniel Fincke, "Khomeini, Iran, and More Islamic Clerics on Sex With Children," Pathos: Hosting the Conversation on Faith, July 21, 2014, http://www.patheos.com/blogs/camelswithhammers/2014/07/khomeini-iran-and-more-islamic-clerics-on-sex-with-children/ (last accessed April 1, 2016).
32. "Islam Unveiled: The Horrific Muslim Practice of Female Genital Mutilation," Before It's News, January 27, 2015, http://beforeitsnews.com/global-unrest/2015/01/islam-unveiled-the-horrific-muslim-practice-of-female-genital-mutilation-2-2462046.html (last accessed April 1, 2016).
33. WikiIslam, s.v. "Qur'an, Hadith and Scholars: Female Genital Mutilation," https://wikiislam.net/wiki/Qur'an,_Hadith_and_Scholars:Female_Genital_Mutilation (last accessed April 1, 2016)
34. Wikipedia, s.v. "Religious views on female genital mutilation," https://en.wikipedia.org/wiki/Religious_views_on_female_genital_mutilation (last accessed April 1, 2016)
35. Ayatollah Mosavi Khomeini, *The Little Green Book: The Astonishing Beliefs of the Man Who Has Shaken the Western World,* trans. Harold Salemson (Bantam Books, 1985), 56. I couldn't find out where this was published; I downloaded the PDF from the internet. The ISBN is 0553140329.
36. "Islamic Law on Female Circumcision," Answering Islam, http://answering-islam.org/Sharia/fem_circumcision.html (last accessed April 1, 2016)
37. "What is FGM?" End FGM European Network, http://www.endfgm.eu/female-genital-mutilation/what-is-fgm/ (last accessed April 1, 2016). This article is a summary of research compiled by the World Health Organization (WHO), in a seven-page report titled "Female Genital Mutilation and

Obstetric Outcome: WHO Collaborative Prospective Study in Six African Countries," which is found here: http://www.who.int/reproductivehealth/publications/fgm/fgm-obstetric-outcome-study/en/.

38. Katie Sanders, "Fact-Checking Reza Aslan on Bill Maher's 'Not Very Sophisticated' Rant on Islam," PunditFact, October 2, 2014, http://www.politifact.com/punditfact/statements/2014/oct/02/reza-aslan/fact-checking-reza-aslans-retort-bill-maher/ (last accessed April 1, 2016).
39. "One in every 20 Muslim women in Logon borough have been a victim of female genital mutilation," Muslim Statistics, July 22, 2015, https://muslimstatistics.wordpress.com/2015/07/22/one-in-every-20-muslim-women-in-london-borough-have-been-a-victim-of-female-genital-mutilation/ (last accessed April 1, 2016).
40. B. A. Robinson, "Female Genital Mutilation: In Africa, The Middle East & Far East," Sacramento State University, November 13, 2001, http://www.csus.edu/indiv/m/merlinos/femgenmut.html (last accessed April 1, 2016).
41. "Female Genital Mutilation," Edna Adan University Hospital, http://www.ednahospital.org/hospital-mission/female-genital-mutilation/ (last accessed April 1, 2016).
42. Abigail R. Esman, "ISIS Rapes Women toward Allah," The Investigative Project on Terrorism, October 23, 2015, http://www.investigativeproject.org/5013/isis-rapes-women-toward-allah (last accessed March 22, 2016).
43. "Does Islam Allow Muslims to Rape Female Captives and Slave Girls?" Answering Islam, February 2, 2014, http://www.answeringmuslims.com/2014/02/does-islam-allow-muslims-to-rape-female.html (last accessed April 2, 2016).
44. WikiIslam s.v. "Rape in Islam," https://wikiislam.net/wiki/Rape_in_Islam (last accessed April 2, 2016).
45. "Does Islam Allow Muslims to Rape Female Captives and Slave Girls?" Answering Islam, February 2, 2014, http://www.answeringmuslims.com/2014/02/does-islam-allow-muslims-to-rape-female.html (last accessed April 2, 2016).
46. "Slavery," The Religion of Peace, http://www.thereligionofpeace.com/pages/quran/slavery.aspx (last accessed April 2, 2016).
47. WikiIslam s.v. "Rape in Islam," https://wikiislam.net/wiki/Rape_in_Islam (last accessed April 2, 2016).
48. "Slavery," The Religion of Peace, http://www.thereligionofpeace.com/pages/quran/slavery.aspx (last accessed April 2, 2016).
49. "Beautiful Woman Who Was Horribly Raped Exposes 1 Vital Truth About Islam," Conservative Tribune, http://conservativetribune.com/woman-horribly-raped-exposes/ (last accessed April 2, 2016).
50. Ibid.

51. Pascale Harter, "Libya Rape Victims 'Face Honor Killings,'" BBC News, June 14, 2011, http://www.bbc.co.uk/news/world-africa-13760895 (last accessed April 2, 2016).
52. "Sydney Cleric Sheik Feiz Mohammed Stirs the Hatred," *The Herald Sun*, September 18, 2012, http://www.heraldsun.com.au/news/national/sydney-sheik-stirs-the-hatred/story-fndo317g-1226476066456 (last accessed April 2, 2016).
53. Belma Z. Golge, Faith M. Yavuz, Selin Muderrisoglu, and Sunay M. Yavuz, "Turkish University Students' Attitudes Toward Rape," Highbeam, December 1, 2003, https://business.highbeam.com/435388/article-1G1-111635867/turkish-university-students-attitudes-toward-rape (last accessed April 2, 2016).
54. "Saudi Arabia: 87% of Males Blame Women for Sexual Assault—Survey," Muslim Statistics, March 19, 2015, https://muslimstatistics.wordpress.com/2015/03/19/87-percent-of-saudi-males-blame-women-for-sexual-assault-survey/ (last accessed April 1, 2016).
55. "Asylum Reality: One in Three African Men Admit to Rape, Survey Fines," Muslim Statistics, August 15, 2015, https://muslimstatistics.wordpresscom/2015/08/15/asylum-reality-one-in-three-african-men-admit-to-rape-survey-finds/ (last accessed April 1, 2016).
56. "87% Female Students of Imam Muhammad Bin Saud University 'Abused by Faculty Staff,'" Muslim Statistics, July 7, 2014, https://muslimstatistics.wordpress.com/2014/06/07/87-female-students-of-imam-muhammad-bin-saud-university-abused-b (last accessed April 1, 2016).
57. Olivia Lang, "Maldives Girl To Get 100 Lashes for Pre-marital Sex," BBC News, February 26, 2013, http://www.bbc.com/news/world-asia-21595814 (last accessed April 2, 2016).
58. International Campaign for Human Rights in Iran, https://www.iranhumanrights.org/category/issues/womens-rights/ (last accessed April 1, 2016).
59. Donna Hughes, "Women's Activism for Freedom in Iran, Ladan Pardeshenas," Making the Harm Visible, http://www.uri.edu/artsci/wms/hughes/mhvact.htm (last accessed January 3, 2016). Note: This website keeps appearing and disappearing in different locations on the internet. This may be due to its controversial nature, pressure from organizations like CAIR, or even Iranian hackers. I downloaded it to my computer, so anyone who wants to see the original article can simply e-mail me at jmilor@yahoo.com. Also, it may pop back up on the internet from time to time. I found pieces of this original article on a blog, searching for the words "Ladan Pardeshenas sister Nassrin," http://terror-watch.blogspot.com/2005/06/ladan-pardeshenas-terrorist-activist.html, though I can't say for how long it will be there.

60. Salah Uddin Shoaib Choudhury, "Dirty Mullahs in Iran," Gatestone Institute, International Policy Council, September 28, 2009, http://www.gatestoneinstitute.org/826/dirty-mullahs-in-iran (last accessed April 1, 2016). This is the main website referenced for this section, and the two following references provide additional supporting information.
61. Saeed Kamali Dehghan, "Iran Giving Out Condoms for Criminals to Rape Us, Say Jailed Activists," *The Guardian*, June 24, 2011, http://www.theguardian.com/world/2011/jun/24/jailed-iran-opposition-activists-rape (last accessed April 1, 2016). This is additional supporting information about state-sanctioned rape in Iranian prisons.
62. Robert Mackey, "Iranians Say Prison Rape Is Not New," The Lede, Blogging the News with Robert Mackey, August 28, 2009, http://thelede.blogs.nytimes.com/2009/08/28/iranians-say-prison-rape-not-new/?_r=2 (last accessed April 1, 2016). This is additional supporting information about state-sanctioned rape in Iranian prisons.
63. Donna Hughes, "Women's Activism for Freedom in Iran, Ladan Pardeshenas," Making the Harm Visible, http://www.uri.edu/artsci/wms/hughes/mhvact.htm (last accessed January 3, 2016). This article might appear again if searching for the title or Ladan's full name.
64. Dictionary.com s.v. "Ayatollah," www.Dictionary.com (last accessed April 21, 2016).
65. Ayatollah Mosavi Khomeini, *The Little Green Book: The Astonishing Beliefs of the Man Who Has Shaken the Western World*, trans. Harold Salemson (Bantam Books, 1985), 56. I couldn't find out where this was published; I downloaded the PDF from the internet. The ISBN is 0553140329.
66. Ibid.
67. Ibid, 57.
68. Ibid, 63.
69. Imam Khomeini home page, http://en.imam-khomeini.ir (last accessed April 21, 2016). On this website, the PDF link with a list of Khomeini's publications is here: http://en.imam-khomeini.ir/en/pdf_issues/englishbooks.pdf. If this listing is removed, try Google searches such as "Khomeini's publications" or "Khomeini englishbooks.pdf." In the PDF, number 141 in the list is the *Tahrir Al-Wasilah*, vols. 1–4.
70. "Muhammad and the Thighing of Aisha," Answering Muslims, March 25, 2014, http://www.answeringmuslims.com/2014/03/muhammad-and-thighing-of-aisha.html (last accessed April 3, 2016).
71. "Fatwa Number 41409: Thighing—Muslim Scholars," Bharata Bharati, August 8, 2000, https://bharatabharati.wordpress.com/2011/10/11/fatwa-number-41409-thighing-muslim-scholars/ (last accessed April 2, 2016).

72. Ayatollah Mosavi Khomeini, *The Little Green Book: The Astonishing Beliefs of the Man Who Has Shaken the Western World*, tran. Harold Salemson (Bantam Books, 1985), 25.
73. "For Allah Then for History (Unveiling of Shiism)," SifatuSafwa, http://www.sifatusafwa.com/en/manhaj-and-groups/1295-for-allah-then-for-history-unveiling-of-shiism.html (last accessed April 3, 2016).
74. "When Imam Ayatollah Khomeini Raped a 4 Year Old Girl," The Muslim Issue, February 3, 2013, https://themuslimissue.wordpress.com/2013/02/03/when-imam-ayatollah-khomeini-raped-a-4-year-old-girl/ (last accessed April 3, 2016).
75. "72 Virgins and Boys," Albatrus.org, http://www.albatrus.org/english/religions/islam/72virgins_and_boys.htm (last accessed April 3, 2016).
76. "UK Islamic Child Sex Grooming up by 32% in a Year and Spread to Every Town and City," Muslim Statistics, January 21, 2015, https://muslimstatistics.wordpress.com/2015/01/21/uk-islamic-child-sex-grooming-up-by-32-in-a-year-and-spread-to-every-town-and-city/ (last accessed April 3, 2016).
77. Wikipedia s.v. "LGBT in Islam," https://en.wikipedia.org/wiki/LGBT_in_Islam (last accessed April 3, 2016).
78. Christopher Allard, "Report from Christopher Allard on Syrian Muslims," Exposing Modern Mugwumps, November 25, 2015, http://exposingmodernmugwumps.com/2015/11/25/report-from-christopher-allard-on-syrian-muslims/ (last accessed April 3, 2016).
79. Robert Long, "Routine Child Rape by Afghan Police," The American Conservative, July 10, 2013, http://www.theamericanconservative.com/2013/07/10/routine-child-rape-by-afghan-police/ (last accessed April 3, 2016).
80. Ibid.
81. Robert Long, "Routine Child Rape by Afghan Police," The American Conservative, July 10, 2013, http://www.theamericanconservative.com/2013/07/10/routine-child-rape-by-afghan-police/ (last accessed April 4, 2016).
82. Jake Tapper and Kim Berryman, "Green Beret Discharged for Beating Alleged Child Rapist Speaks Out," CNN Politics, September 28, 2015, http://www.cnn.com/2015/09/28/politics/green-beret-discharged-for-beating-alleged-child-rapist-speaks-out/ (last accessed April 4, 2016).
83. James Arlandson, "Insulting Muhammad: Free Speech, and Death in Islam," American Thinker, July 16, 2005, http://www.americanthinker.com/articles/2005/07/insulting_muhammad_free_speech.html (last accessed April 4, 2016).
84. Ibid.
85. Ibid.
86. Harry Richardson, "14 The Battle of Trench," The Story of Muhammad: Understand Islam Through the Story of Its Founder, Muhammad, September

29, 2013, http://thestoryofmohammed.blogspot.com/2013/09/chapter-fourteen-battle-of-trench.html (last accessed April 4, 2016).

87. James M. Arlandson, "Muhammad's Dead Poet Society: The Assassinations of Satirical Poets in Early Islam," Answering Islam, http://answeringislam.org/Authors/Arlandson/dead_poets.htm (last accessed April 4, 2016).
88. "Muslim Opinion Polls: A Tiny Minority of Extremists?" The Religion of Peace website, http://www.thereligionofpeace.com/pages/articles/opinion-polls.aspx (last accessed April 4, 2016).
89. "Killing Critics," The Religion of Peace website, http://www.thereligionofpeace.com/pages/quran/insulters-islam.aspx (last accessed April 4, 2016).
90. B. Christopher Agee, "The Outspoken Conservative Behind This Viral Video Has Gotten Thousands of Death Threats," Western Journalism, January 15, 2015, http://www.westernjournalism.com/outspoken-conservative-behind-viral-video-gotten-thousands-death-threats/ (last accessed April 4, 2016).
91. John W. Milor, *Aliens and the Antichrist: Unveiling the End Times Deception* (New York: iUniverse Inc., 2006), chapter 5.
92. Jared Malsin, "Christians Mourn Their Relatives Beheaded by ISIS," *Time*, February 23, 2015, http://time.com/3718470/isis-copts-egypt/ (last accessed April 4, 2016).
93. Paul Wood, "Face-to-face with Abu Sakkar, Syria's 'heart-eating cannibal'," BBC News-Syria, http://www.bbc.com/news/magazine-23190533 (last accessed March 24, 2016). Obama was in favor of supporting Syrian rebels; their leader was a cannibal.
94. Paul Joseph Watson, "Heart Eating Cannibal Demands Obama Send Weapons" Infowars, http://www.infowars.com/heart-eating-cannibal-demands-obama-send-weapons/ (last accessed March 24, 2016).

Chapter 7: Comparing Christian and Islamic Eschatology

1. *The Epic of Gilgamesh*, trans. Robert Temple, Biblioteca Pleyades website, http://www.bibliotecapleyades.net/serpents_dragons/gilgamesh.htm (last accessed April 8, 2016).
2. J. Pritchard, *Ancient Near Eastern Texts and the Old Testament*, 3rd edition (Princeton: University Press, 1969), quoted in Christian Answers Network Bible Encyclopedia, s.v. "Nimrod: Who was he? Was he godly or evil?" by Dr. David P. Livingston, http://www.christiananswers.net/dictionary/nimrod.html (last accessed April 11, 2016).
3. Scott Alan Roberts, *The Rise and Fall of the Nephilim* (Pompton Plains, NJ: New Page Books, 2012), 76.
4. Lisa Haven, "The Most Shocking Truth About the End of the Age and the Antichrist. A Major Revelation of End Time Prophecy Unfolds …" Before

It's News, May 30, 2014, http://beforeitsnews.com/prophecy/2014/05/the-most-shocking-truth-about-the-end-of-the-age-and-the-antichrist-a-major-revelation-of-end-time-prophecy-unfolds-and-it-will-scare-you-2461660-.html (last accessed April 5, 2016).

5. "Chapter Four, The Mahdi: Islam's Awaited Messiah," Answering Islam, http://www.answering-islam.org/Authors/JR/Future/ch04_the_mahdi.htm (last accessed April 5, 2016). This is all of chapter 4 of Joel Richardson's book *The Islamic Antichrist.*
6. Dr. Muhammad al-'Areefi, "The End of the World: Signs of the Hour, Major and Minor" (Darussalam Publishers and Distributors, 2008).
7. Lisa Haven, "The Most Shocking Truth About the End of the Age and the Antichrist. A Major Revelation of End Time Prophecy Unfolds ..." Before It's News, May 30, 2014, http://beforeitsnews.com/prophecy/2014/05/the-most-shocking-truth-about-the-end-of-the-age-and-the-antichrist-a-major-revelation-of-end-time-prophecy-unfolds-and-it-will-scare-you-2461660-.html (last accessed April 5, 2016). The entire table comparing the biblical Antichrist with the Muslim Mahdi is found on this website. Internal notes within this table are also found in Joel Richardson's book *The Islamic Antichrist.*
8. Joel Richardson, *The Islamic Antichrist: The Shocking Truth About the Real Nature of the Beast* (Los Angeles: WorldNetDaily Books, 2009), 37.
9. Ibid, 29.
10. Ibid, 37.
11. Ibid, 48.
12. Ibid, 29–30, 50.
13. Ibid, 32.
14. Ibid, 123–135.
15. Ibid, 39.
16. Ibid, 45.
17. Ibid, 28.
18. Ibid, 27.
19. Ibid, 27.
20. Ibid, 30.
21. Theodore Shoebat, "The Oldest Reference to Allah," Shoebat.com, Awareness and Action, September 12, 2012, http://shoebat.com/2012/09/13/the-oldest-reference-to-allah/ (last accessed April 5, 2016).
22. Joseph Farah, "IslamicTerror.com?" WorldNetDaily, November 13, 2001, http://www.wnd.com/2001/11/11651/ (last accessed April 5, 2016).
23. Joel Richardson, *The Islamic Antichrist: The Shocking Truth About the Real Nature of the Beast* (Los Angeles: WorldNetDaily Books, 2009), 103–104.
24. Ibid, 105–106.
25. Ibid, 105.

26. Ibid, 108–109.
27. Ibid, 23.
28. Ibid, 53
29. Ibid.
30. Ibid.
31. Ibid.
32. Ibid, 55.
33. Ibid, 53.
34. Ibid, 54.
35. Ibid, 56.
36. Ibid, 67.
37. Ibid.
38. Ibid.
39. Ibid, 54.
40. Ibid.
41. Ibid, 55.
42. Ibid, 56.
43. "Bukhari :: Muslim :: Malik :: Dawud Hadith Collection," Qur'an Explorer, http://www.quranexplorer.com/Hadith/English/Index.html (last accessed April 7, 2016). This is the main website I used for my Hadith research.
44. "Who Are the Two Witnesses in the Book of Revelation?" Got Questions, http://www.gotquestions.org/two-witnesses.html (last accessed April 7, 2016).
45. Owen Jarus, "Petra: Ancient City of Rock," Live Science, September 13, 2012, http://www.livescience.com/23168-petra.html (last accessed September 27, 2016)
46. Rick Meyers, Equipping Ministries Foundation, e-Sword Bible software, "Matthew Henry's Commentary on the Whole Bible," http://www.e-sword.net/downloads.html (downloaded April 7, 2000).
47. Ibid, "John Gill's Exposition on the Whole Bible," http://www.e-sword.net/downloads.html (downloaded April 7, 2000).
48. Lawrence O. Richards, *Bible Reader's Companion: Home Bible Study Library* (Colorado Springs, CO: Cook Communications Ministries, 2004), 580–581.
49. Kenneth Barker et al., *The NIV Study Bible* (Grand Rapids, MI: Zondervan Bible Publishers, 1985), 1,419.
50. Ben Hartman, "City of Ludd Running Fast Towards Its Destiny," Harbinger Blog, October 8, 2010, https://harbingerblog.wordpress.com/2010/10/08/city-of-ludd-running-fast-to-its-destiny/ (last accessed April 8, 2016).
51. "Tribes of the 12 Disciples," Sword Searcher, November 3, 2008, http://forums.swordsearcher.com/threads/tribes-of-the-12-disciples.953/ (last accessed April 8, 2016).

Chapter 8: Otherworldly Influences through the Ages

1. Zecharia Sitchin, "Chapter 5: The Gods Who Came to Planet Earth," Biblioteca Pleyades website, http://www.bibliotecapleyades.net/sitchin/sitchinbooks02_02.htm (last accessed April 8, 2016).
2. *The Epic of Gilgamesh,* trans. Robert Temple, Biblioteca Pleyades website, http://www.bibliotecapleyades.net/serpents_dragons/gilgamesh.htm (last accessed April 8, 2016).
3. James B. Jordan, "Five Cities and Isaiah 19," Biblical Horizons Newsletter, number 16, April 1999, http://www.biblicalhorizons.com/biblical-horizons/no-116-five-cities-and-isaiah-19/ (last accessed April 8, 2016).
4. Shianee Mamanglu-Regala, "Archaeologists Uncover Ruins of Sodom, the Lost Ancient Biblical City Destroyed by God," Christian Today website, October 4, 2015, http://www.christiantoday.com/article/archaeologists.uncover.ruins.of.sodom.the.ancient.biblical.city.destroyed.by.god/66471.htm (last accessed April 9, 2016).
5. "Sodom & Gomorrah: The Lost Cities Destroyed by Fire and Brimstone," Discovery News, http://discoverynews.us/DISCOVERIES/BibleLandsDisplay/Sodom_and_Gomorrah/sodom_and_gomorrah_1.html (last accessed April 9, 2016).
6. "How Tall Was Goliath?" Apologetics, WordPress, https://bibleapologetics.wordpress.com/2011/01/30/how-tall-was-goliath/ (last accessed April 9, 2016).
7. Michael S. Heiser, "Clash of the Manuscripts," *Bible Study Magazine*, October 31, 2014, http://www.biblestudymagazine.com/extras-1/2014/10/31/clash-of-the-manuscripts-goliath-the-hebrew-text-of-the-old-testament (last accessed April 9, 2016).
8. Richard D. Barnett, "Polydactylism in the Ancient World," Michael Heiser website, http://www.michaelsheiser.com/PaleoBabble/PolydactylismAncientWorld.pdf (last accessed April 8, 2016). This is a PDF linked on Michael Heiser's website.
9. "The Six Digits Phenomenon," House of the Sun, www.soul-guidance.com/houseofthesun/dp08.htm (last accessed April 8, 2016).
10. "Giants," 6000 Years.org: Amazing Bible Discoveries, http://www.6000years.org/frame.php?page=giants (last accessed April 9, 2016).
11. "13 Giant Human Skeletons, Are They Real or Fake?" Blank Exit, August 25, 2014, http://www.blankexit.com/13-giant-human-skeletons-real-fake/ (last accessed April 9, 2016).
12. David Mikkelson, "They Might Be Giants," Snopes, March 11, 2015, http://www.snopes.com/photos/odd/giantman.asp (last accessed April 9, 2016).
13. Bjorn Carey, "Gigantic Apes Coexisted With Early Humans, Study Finds," LiveScience, November 7, 2005, http://www.livescience.

com/467-gigantic-apes-coexisted-early-humans-study-finds.html (last accessed April 9, 2016).

14. Eliezer Segal, "King Solomon's Genie," From the Sources, http://people.ucalgary.ca/~elsegal/Shokel/940602_Genie.html (last accessed April 9, 2016).
15. Sam Shamoun, "Fables And Legends of the Qur'an: Solomon's Flying Carpet," Answering Islam, http://www.answering-islam.org/Quran/Sources/Legends/flying_carpet.htm (last accessed April 9, 2016).
16. "The Five Types of Jinn," Alif the Unseen, http://aliftheunseen.com/the-five-types-of-jinn/ (last accessed April 9, 2016).
17. Bob Utley, "Introduction to 1 John," Bible.org, https://bible.org/seriespage/introduction-1-john (last accessed April 9, 2016).
18. Peter Applebome, "Mystery Man's Death Can't End the Mystery; Fighting Over Carlos Castaneda's Legacy," *New York Times*, August 19, 1998, http://www.nytimes.com/1998/08/19/arts/mystery-man-s-death-can-t-end-mystery-fighting-over-carlos-castaneda-s-legacy.html?pagewanted=all (last accessed April 9, 2016).
19. John Foxe, *Foxe's Book of Martyrs, Updated and Abridged* (Uhrichsville, OH: Barbour Publishing, Inc., 2001).
20. Dan Graves, ed., "#107: Constantine's Vision," from *The Life of the Blessed Emperor Constantine*, by Eusebius Pamphilus, modernized by Stephen Tomkins, Christian History Institute, https://www.christianhistoryinstitute.org/study/module/constantine/ (last accessed April 8, 2016).
21. Ibid.
22. Ibid.
23. Toby McKeehan and Mark Heimermann, *Jesus Freaks: dc Talk and the Voice of the Martyrs* (Bloomington, MN: Bethany House Publishers, 1999).
24. Carolyn Trickey-Bapty, *Martyrs & Miracles: The Inspiring Lives of Saints and Martyrs* (Owing Mills, MD: Ottenheimer Publishers, Inc. 1995).
25. John D. Keyser, "The Trumpets of Revelation and the Scourge of Islam!" Hope of Israel Ministries, http://www.hope-of-israel.org/scourge.html (last accessed April 8, 2016).
26. "Revelation 9 Commentary," Amazing Discoveries, http://amazingdiscoveries.org/S-deception-angels-abyss-Revelation-9-commentary (last accessed April 8, 2016).
27. "The Fifth Trumpet of Revelation," Islam in Bible Prophecy, http://christianitybeliefs.org/islam-in-bible-prophecy/the-fifth-trumpet-of-revelation-islam-muslims (last accessed April 8, 2016).
28. Wikipedia s.v. "Beelzebub," https://en.wikipedia.org/wiki/Beelzebub (last accessed April 8, 2016).
29. "The Jinn," Mission Islam, http://www.missionislam.com/knowledge/Jinn.htm (last accessed April 9, 2016).

30. James M. Arlandson, "How Jesus and Muhammad Confronted Satan," Answering Islam, http://www.answering-islam.org/Authors/Arlandson/confronting_satan.htm (last accessed April 9, 2016).
31. "The Quranic Arabic Corpus," Qur'an, http://corpus.quran.com/translation.jsp (last accessed April 9, 2016). This is the main source I use for all my Qur'an quotes; multiple translations into English are available.
32. "Bukhari :: Muslim :: Malik :: Dawud Hadith Collection," Qur'an Explorer, http://www.quranexplorer.com/Hadith/English/Index.html (last accessed April 7, 2016). This is the main website I used for my Hadith research.
33. "The Jinn," Mission Islam, http://www.missionislam.com/knowledge/Jinn.htm (last accessed April 9, 2016).
34. "Bigfoot Exists: NSA Evidence Found," Before It's News, August 4, 2014, http://beforeitsnews.com/paranormal/2015/08/bigfoot-exists-dna-evidence-found-2-2493766.html (last accessed April 9, 2016). Interdimensional being theory has been proposed by paranormal investigator Jon-Erik Beckjord, but "many Bigfoot advocates distance themselves from the paranormal position and regard it as an embarrassment."
35. James Owen, "Study Reveals Biological Identities of Bigfoot, Yeti, Bolstering Case Against Them," *National Geographic*, July 1, 2014, http://voices.nationalgeographic.com/2014/07/01/yeti-bigfoot-dna-hair-study-science-animals-himalaya/ (last accessed April 9, 2016). This website focuses on skeptical elements of the DNA findings.
36. "Ketchum Bigfoot DNA Study 2011-2013 Timeline of Bigfoot DNA Events," Oregon Bigfoot website, February 13, 2013, http://www.oregonbigfoot.com/melba-ketchum-Bigfoot-DNA-study_2011.php (last accessed April 9, 2016).
37. Lee Spiegel, "Bigfoot DNA Tests Prove Hairy Creature Exists, Genetic Researcher Says," Huffington Post, November 20, 2012, http://www.huffingtonpost.com/2012/11/27/bigfoot-dna-proves-creature-exists-genetic_n_2199984.html (last accessed April 9, 2016).
38. Nina Golgowski, "Bigfoot Lives!? Existence Backed by DNA, Video, Claim Sasquatch Genome Project Researchers," *New York Daily News*, October 2, 2013, http://www.nydailynews.com/news/national/bigfoot-existence-backed-dna-video-report-article-1.1473883 (last accessed April 9, 2016).
39. "Who Were the Inhabitants of the Earth Before Humans?" Questions on Islam, April 16, 2004, http://www.questionsonislam.com/article/who-were-inhabitants-earth-humans (last accessed April 9, 2016).
40. "The Jinn," Mission Islam, http://www.missionislam.com/knowledge/Jinn.htm (last accessed April 9, 2016).
41. Guy Malone, "Modern Nephilim Hybrids Can Be Saved in Jesus Christ," Nephilim Hybrids, http://www.nephilimhybrids.com/home/ (last accessed April 9, 2016).

42. "Muhammad's Night Journey to Jerusalem," Jerusalem.com, July 23, 2013, http://jerusalem.com/articles/islam/muhammads_night_journey_to_jerusalem-a6295 (last accessed April 10, 2016).
43. Aisha Stacey, "The Night Journey and the Ascension (1 of 6): The Night Journey," The Religion of Islam, June 2, 2008, http://www.islamreligion.com/articles/1511/night-journey-and-ascension-part-1/ (last accessed April 10, 2016).
44. "The Prophet's Night Journey," Education & Dawah, November 25, 2009, http://www.iman.co.nz/ed/night.php (last accessed April 10, 2016).
45. Wikipedia s.v. "Buraq," https://en.wikipedia.org/wiki/Buraq (last accessed April 10, 2016).
46. Aisha Stacey, "The Night Journey and the Ascension (6 of 6): The Night Journey," The Religion of Islam, June 2, 2008, http://www.islamreligion.com/articles/1511/night-journey-and-ascension-part-6/ (last accessed April 10, 2016).
47. "The Prophet's Night Journey," Education & Dawah, November 25, 2009, http://www.iman.co.nz/ed/night.php (last accessed April 10, 2016).
48. Stephan Van Nattan, "Appendix Nine—Idris: The Prophet of Islam?" http://www.balaams-ass.com/alhaj/append-9.htm (last accessed April 10, 2016). This website is part of an extensive e-book.

Chapter 9: The Grand Conclusion

1. Janet Fang, "Pig Heart Transplants for Humans Could Be on Their Way," IFL Science! April 30, 2014, http://www.iflscience.com/health-and-medicine/pig-heart-transplants-humans-could-be-their-way (last accessed April 11, 2016).
2. Sarah Zhang, "The 8 Weirdest Mice in Research Labs," *Mother Jones*, August 22, 2012, http://www.motherjones.com/blue-marble/2012/08/weirdest-lab-mice (last accessed April 11, 2016).
3. Michio Kaku, *Hyperspace: A Scientific Odyssey Through Parallel Universes, Time Warps, and the 10th Dimension* (New York: Bantam Doubleday Dell Publishing Group, 1994).
4. John W. Milor, *Aliens and the Antichrist: Unveiling the End Times Deception* (New York: iUniverse Inc., 2006), 6.
5. Walid Shoebat, "Erdogan Is Emerging as the Best Candidate for Antichrist as He Is Now Demanding to Change Set Times and Set Laws (Daniel 8)," Shoebat.com, November 5, 2015, http://shoebat.com/2015/11/05/erdogan-is-emerging-as-the-best-candidate-for-antichrist-as-he-is-now-demanding-to-change-set-times-and-set-laws-daniel-8/ (last accessed April 11, 2016).
6. Eretz Zen, "Turkish PM Erdogan Tries to Ride an Arabian Horse and Falls Off," YouTube, June 1, 2013, https://www.youtube.com/watch?v=DbahxJuPPHw (last accessed April 11, 2016).

7. John W. Milor, *Aliens and the Antichrist: Unveiling the End Times Deception* (New York: iUniverse Inc., 2006), 223.
8. Ibid, 53.
9. Joel Richardson, *The Islamic Antichrist: The Shocking Truth About the Real Nature of the Beast* (Los Angeles: WorldNetDaily Books, 2009), 30–31.
10. Ibid.
11. John W. Milor, *Aliens and the Antichrist: Unveiling the End Times Deception* (New York: iUniverse Inc., 2006), 197–198.

ABOUT THE AUTHOR

John Milor, an author and speaker who explores paranormal phenomena from a biblical perspective, has written several books, including The Eaglestar Prophecy, Aliens in the Bible, Aliens and the Antichrist, and X-Phenomenon, as well as articles in a variety of publications. He has made guest appearances on radio talk shows and holds several academic degrees.

Printed in the United States
By Bookmasters